Learn T-SQL Querying

A guide to developing efficient and elegant T-SQL code

Pedro Lopes and Pam Lahoud

Learn T-SQL Querying

Second Edition

Copyright © 2024 Packt Publishing

Group Product Manager: Kaustubh Manglurkar
Publishing Product Manager: Heramb Bhavsar
Book Project Manager: Hemangi Lotlikar
Content Development Editor: Joseph Sunil
Technical Editor: Rahul Limbachiya
Copy Editor: Safis Editing
Proofreader: Safis Editing
Indexer: Tejal Daruwale Soni
Production Designer: Prafulla Nikalje
DevRel Marketing Executive: Nivedita Singh

First published: May 2019
Second edition: February 2024

Production reference: 2010324

Published by Packt Publishing Ltd.
Grosvenor House
11 St Paul's Square
Birmingham
B3 1RB, UK

ISBN 978-1-83763-899-4
www.packtpub.com

To my wife and life partner, Sandra, and to my esteemed friends, mentors, and former colleagues in Azure Data who develop the SQL Database Engine and keep pushing the boundaries of excellence – sorry, I can't list you all here! To the unique people I had the privilege of working with – Amit Banerjee, Bob Ward, Conor Cunningham, Hanuma Kodavalla, and Slava Oks – for inspiring me to always move forward and do better, and to everyone who keeps developing and supporting applications on this most-scalable RDBMS.

– Pedro Lopes

To Andrew and Linus, for spending countless nights and weekends without me. To the entire #SQLFamily, who continue to inspire me, support me (and each other), and drive me to be better every day. To my computer-illiterate friends, Jodie, Liza, and Erin, who I know will proudly display this book on their shelves despite having no idea what any of this means. And to my mom, who bought me my first computer when I was 8 years old and said "Sure!" when I decided that adding computer science as a second major in my junior year of college seemed like a good idea.

– Pam Lahoud

Foreword

When I first met Pedro Lopes and Pam Lahoud, I already knew that they had both achieved recognition as experts in SQL Server, especially in areas such as query processing and performance. As I started working with them, I quickly realized that not only was the reputation warranted but I also came to see their characteristics of professionalism, thoroughness, and presentation skills.

All these traits come out in this book, and you gain all the benefits. I love how this book is organized. If I want to read the entire book end to end, I will first learn the fundamentals and mechanics of the optimizer from the perspective of writing T-SQL queries. Then, I will get practical advice on how to write effective queries for maximum performance on topics such as indexing. And then, I'm able to dive deep into detailed query troubleshooting techniques using the full capabilities of SQL Server. This organization of the book also allows me to jump to any section aligning with my skills and knowledge. This powerful story is now brought to life in the second edition of this book, bringing in enhancements from SQL Server 2019, SQL Server 2022, and Azure SQL designed to make your applications faster with no code changes.

Even if you believe that you understand query processing with SQL Server, you will benefit from this book. Using visual flows and examples, the first part of the book gives you a great perspective on how queries in SQL Server are compiled, executed, and cached. This part also includes key details of query processing such as cardinality estimation, optimization phases, and methods to control query optimization.

The second part is the crown jewel of the book. Pedro and Pam pour in their years of experience to give you the advice you need on topics such as analyzing query plans, proper indexing, best practices for crafting T-SQL queries, and the often-overlooked area of anti-pattern queries. These chapters are full of rich advice and examples for you to try out yourself.

Finish off the book by learning how to get faster to tune and troubleshoot query performance using powerful tools such as Query Profiling, Query Store, and Extended Events. The power of the T-SQL language comes to life as you learn how to write queries to debug the queries from your application. As readers, you get the benefit of unique information throughout the book because the authors have directly worked on these parts of the product.

SQL Server and Azure SQL have evolved over the years to provide more automation and simplify the requirements to build and manage successful database applications. However, understanding how to use the power of T-SQL is critical to achieving maximum performance and efficiency. Furthermore, to take your game to the next level, you need to understand the nuances and mechanics of the query optimizer and query execution with T-SQL in the engine. This book provides it all in a manner that you can easily understand, with all the latest updates, and in a format that you can use as a reference for years to come.

– Bob Ward

Principal architect, Microsoft

Contributors

About the authors

Pedro Lopes is a senior director of engineering at Salesforce, based in WA, USA, leading the organization responsible for the Marketing Cloud's DB Management Plane. Previously, he was a principal architect in Microsoft Azure Data, leading the SQL Server 2022 release until its public preview. He has 20+ years of industry experience and was with Microsoft for 12+ years. He has extensive experience with query performance troubleshooting and has been a speaker at numerous conferences, such as SQLBits, PASS Summit, SQLIntersection, Microsoft Ignite, and Microsoft Build. He has written multiple technical articles about SQL that are currently in the product documentation, including several on Engine internals at `https://aka.ms/sqlserverguides`.

I want to thank the people who have been close to me and supported me throughout, especially my wife, Sandra. And special thanks to my writing partner and good friend Pam Lahoud, who is both a technical powerhouse and an outstanding human being, without whom this project would not have been nearly as rewarding to complete.

Pam Lahoud is a principal PM manager in Microsoft Azure Data, based in Seattle, WA, USA. She has been with Microsoft since 2006 and currently leads the SQL Server in Azure Virtual Machines product manager team. She is passionate about SQL Server performance and has focused on performance tuning and optimization, particularly from the developers' perspective, throughout her career. She is a SQL 2008 Microsoft Certified Master with over 20 years of experience working with SQL Server and has been a speaker at several global events such as the PASS Summit, SQLBits, Microsoft Build, and Microsoft Ignite.

A big thank you to my partner, Andrew, and our son, Linus, for putting up with countless Sundays at home with Mama locked up in the office. Thank you to my writing partner, Pedro; we are the classic example of better together, and this is a life achievement I never would have reached without you! Forever your work-spouse, no matter which companies we're at :-)

About the reviewer

Sergey Ten has been working in the database space for over 20 years, primarily on the Microsoft SQL Server and Oracle database servers. His main areas of expertise are data processing, programming language design, and high availability.

Sergey currently works at Microsoft as a principal software engineer, working in the SQL Server team in the areas of query processing and high availability. Prior to that, he worked at Quest Software developing various Oracle management solutions, and at Guidance Software working on computer forensics and eDiscovery products.

Table of Contents

Preface   xv

Part 1: Query Processing Fundamentals

1

Understanding Query Processing   3

Technical requirements	4	Prepared statements	19
Logical statement processing flow	4	How query processing impacts plan reuse	19
Query compilation essentials	6	The importance of parameters	21
Query optimization essentials	8	Security	22
Query execution essentials	12	Performance	22
Plan caching and reuse	14	Parameter sniffing	23
Stored procedures	14	To cache or not to cache	24
Ad hoc plan caching	15		
Parameterization	16	Summary	25
The sp_executesql procedure	18		

2

Mechanics of the Query Optimizer   27

Technical requirements	27	The Transaction Processing phase	38
Introducing the Cardinality Estimator	28	The Quick Plan phase	39
		The Full Optimization phase	39
Understanding the query optimization workflow	35	Knobs for query optimization	41
The Trivial Plan stage	36	Summary	43
The Exploration stage	38		

Part 2: Dos and Don'ts of T-SQL

3

Exploring Query Execution Plans   47

Technical requirements	47	Joins	68
What is a query plan?	48	Spools	78
Accessing a query plan	49	Sort and aggregation operators	81
Navigating a query plan	54	Query plan properties of interest	85
Query plan operators of interest	57	Plan-level properties	85
Blocking versus non-blocking operators	58	Operator-level properties	107
Data access operators	58	Summary	117

4

Indexing for T-SQL Performance   119

Technical requirements	119	Indexing strategy using rowstore indexes	129
Understanding predicate SARGability	120	Best practices for clustered indexes	130
Data access using indexes	124	Best practices for non-clustered indexes	132
Structure of a rowstore index	125	Index maintenance	146
Data access using rowstore indexes	126	Summary	147
Inserting and updating data in a rowstore index	128		

5

Writing Elegant T-SQL Queries   149

Technical requirements	150	The perils of SELECT *	154
Best practices for T-SQL querying	150	Functions in our predicate	158
Referencing objects	150	Deconstructing table-valued functions	161
Joining tables	151	Complex expressions	166
Using NOLOCK	152		
Using cursors	153		

Optimizing OR logic	169	EXECUTE versus sp_executesql	179
NULL means unknown	172	Composable logic	182
Fuzzy string matching	176	Summary	188
Inequality logic	178		

6

Discovering T-SQL Anti-Patterns in Depth   189

Technical requirements	189	Pitfalls of complex views	213
Implicit conversions	190	Pitfalls of correlated sub-queries	218
Avoiding unnecessary sort operations	196	Properly storing intermediate results	219
UNION ALL versus UNION	197	Using table variables and temporary tables	220
SELECT DISTINCT	200	Using Common Table Expressions (CTEs)	225
Avoiding UDF pitfalls	205	Summary	229
Avoiding unnecessary overhead with stored procedures	211		

Part 3: Assembling Our Query Troubleshooting Toolbox

7

Building Diagnostic Queries Using DMVs and DMFs   233

Technical requirements	233	sys.dm_exec_procedure_stats	243
Introducing DMVs	234	sys.dm_exec_query_plan	244
Exploring query execution DMVs	234	sys.dm_exec_cached_plans	246
sys.dm_exec_sessions	234	Troubleshooting common scenarios with DMV queries	247
sys.dm_exec_requests	236		
sys.dm_exec_sql_text	237	Investigating blocking	247
sys.dm_os_waiting_tasks	238	Cached query plan issues	250
Exploring query plan cache DMVs	241	Single-use plans (query fingerprints)	250
sys.dm_exec_query_stats	241	Finding resource-intensive queries	251

Queries with excessive memory grants   253

Mining XML query plans   255

Plans with missing indexes   255

Plans with warnings   258
Plans with implicit conversions   260
Plans with lookups   261

Summary   262

8

Building XEvent Profiler Traces   263

Technical requirements   263
Introducing XEvents   264
Getting up and running with XEvent Profiler   277
Remote collection with SQL LogScout   280

Analyzing traces with RML Utilities   285
Summary   291

9

Comparative Analysis of Query Plans   293

Technical requirements   293
Query plan analyzer   317

Summary   327

10

Tracking Performance History with Query Store   329

Technical requirements   329
Introducing the Query Store   330
Inner workings of the Query Store   330
Configuring the Query Store   332

Tracking expensive queries   339
Fixing regressed queries   348
Features that rely on the Query Store   353
Query Store for readable secondary replicas   353

Query Store hinting   354
Parameter Sensitive Plan Optimization   355
Automatic Plan Correction   355
Degree of parallelism feedback   356
Optimized plan forcing   358

Summary   359

11

Troubleshooting Live Queries   361

Technical requirements   362
Using Live Query Statistics   362
Understanding the need for
lightweight profiling   366

Diagnostics available with Lightweight
Profiling   369
Activity Monitor gets new life   387
Summary   397

12

Managing Optimizer Changes   399

Technical requirements   399
Understanding where QTA and
CE Feedback are needed   400
Understanding QTA fundamentals   404

Exploring the QTA workflow   406
Summary   419

Index   421

Other Books You May Enjoy   432

Preface

Experienced and novice users have always faced choices and trade-offs to achieve the very best performance when writing T-SQL code for their applications. This book is for all data professionals who want to master the art of writing efficient T-SQL code in modern SQL Server versions, as well as Azure SQL Database.

This book will start with query processing fundamentals to help you write solid, performant T-SQL queries. You will be introduced to query execution plans and how to leverage them for query troubleshooting. Later, you will learn how to identify various T-SQL patterns and anti-patterns. This will help you analyze execution plans to gain insights into current performance, as well as determine whether a query is scalable. You will learn how to build diagnostic queries using **dynamic management views** (**DMVs**) and **dynamic management functions** (**DMFs**) to unlock the secrets of T-SQL execution. Furthermore, you will learn how to leverage SQL Server's built-in tools to shorten the time to address query performance and scalability issues. You will learn how to implement various features such as Extended Events, Query Store, Query Tuning Assistant, and more, using hands-on examples.

By the end of the book, you will be able to determine where query performance bottlenecks are and understand what anti-patterns may be in use and what you need to do to avoid such pitfalls going forward. It's essentially all you need to know to squeeze every last bit of performance out of your T-SQL queries.

Who this book is for

This book is for database administrators, database developers, data analysts, data scientists, and T-SQL practitioners who want to master the art of writing efficient T-SQL code and troubleshooting query performance issues using practical examples. A basic understanding of T-SQL syntax, writing queries in SQL Server, and using the SQL Server Management Studio tool is helpful to get started.

What this book covers

Chapter 1, Understanding Query Processing, introduces T-SQL query optimization and execution essentials: how does SQL Server optimize and execute T-SQL? How does SQL Server use parameters? Are parameters an advantage? When and why does SQL Server cache execution plans for certain T-SQL statements but not for others? When is that an advantage and when is it a problem? This is information that any T-SQL practitioner needs to keep as a reference for proactive T-SQL query writing, as well as reactive troubleshooting and optimization purposes. This chapter will be referenced throughout the Execution Plan-related chapters, as we link architectural topics to real-world uses.

Chapter 2, Mechanics of the Query Optimizer, introduces T-SQL query optimization internals and architecture, starting with the infamous Cardinality Estimation process and its building blocks. From there, you will understand how the Query Optimizer uses that information to produce a just-in-time, good-enough execution plan. This chapter will be referenced throughout the Execution Plan-related chapters, as we bridge architectural topics to real-world uses.

Chapter 3, Exploring Query Execution Plans, shows you how to read and analyze a graphical query execution plan, where to look for relevant performance information in the plan, and how to use the plan to troubleshoot query performance issues.

Chapter 4, Indexing for T-SQL Performance, introduces guidelines to keep in mind for writing T-SQL queries that perform and scale well. Some basics of database physical design structure such as indexes will be covered, as well as how the optimizer estimates cost and chooses access methods based on how the query is written.

Chapter 5, Writing Elegant T-SQL Queries, reveals various common T-SQL patterns and anti-patterns, specifically those that should be easily identifiable just by looking at the T-SQL construct. This chapter will have more of a cookbook structure. For each of the patterns, we will show a T-SQL example that contains the pattern, learn how to rewrite the query to avoid the pattern, and examine query execution plans before and after the change to show improved performance.

Chapter 6, Discovering T-SQL Anti-Patterns in Depth, reveals various common T-SQL patterns and anti-patterns that require some more in-depth analysis to be identified – the proverbial elephant in the room. This chapter will also follow the cookbook structure introduced in *Chapter 5, Writing Elegant T-SQL Queries*.

Chapter 7, Building Diagnostic Queries Using DMVs and DMFs, introduces dynamic management views and functions that expose relevant just-in-time information to unlock the secrets of T-SQL execution. It includes real-world examples of how to use these artifacts to troubleshoot different poor performance scenarios, either leveraging snippets provided in this book or in GitHub, and how to build customized scripts.

Chapter 8, Building XEvent Profiler Traces, introduces **Extended Events** (**XEvents**), the lightweight infrastructure that exposes relevant just-in-time information from every component of the SQL Database Engine, focused on those related to T-SQL execution. You will get real-world examples of how to use these XEvents to troubleshoot different poor performance scenarios, leveraging collection and analysis tools such as the XEvent Profiler, LogScout, and Replay Markup Language for event analysis, and dropping a note on the infamously deprecated SQL Server Profiler.

Chapter 9, Comparative Analysis of Query Plans, introduces rich-UI tools that ship with SQL Server Management Studio to enable standalone query plan analysis or compare plans from different points in time. It then moves on to visually pinpoint the interesting parts that may provide the key to improving T-SQL query performance and scalability.

Chapter 10, Tracking Performance History with Query Store, introduces a flagship feature: Query Store. This is a practical approach to leveraging what is effectively a flight recorder for your SQL Database Engine T-SQL execution, for the purpose of trend analysis or T-SQL performance troubleshooting and analysis, through rich UI reports that ship with SQL Server Management Studio. Then, you will see how Query Store integrates with the Query Plan Comparison and Query Plan Analysis functionalities for a complete, UI-driven workflow for query performance insights. Lastly, we'll review some of the SQL Database Engine features that rely on the data collected by Query Store.

Chapter 11, Troubleshooting Live Queries, introduces the profiling infrastructure that exposes real-time query execution plans, which enable scenarios such as production system troubleshooting. You will see a real-world example of how to leverage rich UI tools: Live Query Statistics as a standalone case or as part of the Activity Monitor functionality of SQL Server Management Studio.

Chapter 12, Managing Optimizer Changes, discusses two features – QTA (client-side) and CE Feedback (server-side) – which aim to address some of the most common causes of **cardinality estimation** (**CE**)-related performance regressions that may affect our T-SQL queries after an upgrade from an older version of the SQL Database Engine to a newer version.

To get the most out of this book

A basic understanding of using the SQL Database Engine and writing T-SQL queries will help get you started with this book. Some familiarity with SQL Server Management Studio or Azure Data Studio is also helpful for running the sample queries and viewing query execution plans.

Software/hardware covered in the book	Operating system requirements
SQL Server (version 2012 or later) and Azure SQL Database	Windows or Linux
SQL Server Management Studio	Windows
Azure Data Studio	Windows, macOS, or Linux

The examples used in this book are designed for use on SQL Server 2022 and Azure SQL Database, but they should work on any version of SQL Server 2012 or later. The Developer Edition of SQL Server is free for development environments and can be used to run all the code samples. There is also a free tier of Azure SQL Database that you can use for testing at `https://aka.ms/freedb`.

You will need the `AdventureWorks2016_EXT` (referred to as `AdventureWorks`) and `AdventureWorksDW2016_EXT` (referred to as `AdventureWorksDW`) sample databases, which can be found on GitHub at `https://github.com/Microsoft/sql-server-samples/releases/tag/adventureworks`.

If you are using the digital version of this book, we advise you to type the code yourself or access the code from the book's GitHub repository (a link is available in the next section). Doing so will help you avoid any potential errors related to the copying and pasting of code.

> **Note**
> *This book contains many horizontally long screenshots. These have been captured to provide readers with an overview of the execution plans for various SQL queries. As a result, the text in these images may appear small at 100% zoom. Additionally, you will be able to see these plans in more depth in the output in SQL Server as you code along.*

Download the example code files

You can download the example code files for this book from GitHub at `https://github.com/PacktPublishing/Learn-T-SQL-Querying-Second-Edition`. If there's an update to the code, it will be updated in the GitHub repository.

We also have other code bundles from our rich catalog of books and videos available at `https://github.com/PacktPublishing/`. Check them out!

Conventions used

There are a number of text conventions used throughout this book.

`Code in text`: Indicates code words in text, database table names, folder names, filenames, file extensions, pathnames, dummy URLs, user input, and Twitter handles. Here is an example: "Mount the downloaded `WebStorm-10*.dmg` disk image file as another disk in your system."

A block of code is set as follows:

```
SELECT LastName, FirstName
FROM Person.Person
WHERE FirstName = N'Andrew';
```

Bold: Indicates a new term, an important word, or words that you see onscreen. For instance, words in menus or dialog boxes appear in **bold**. Here is an example: "Select **System info** from the **Administration** panel."

> **Tips or important notes**
> Appear like this.

Get in touch

Feedback from our readers is always welcome.

General feedback: If you have questions about any aspect of this book, email us at `customercare@packtpub.com` and mention the book title in the subject of your message.

Errata: Although we have taken every care to ensure the accuracy of our content, mistakes do happen. If you have found a mistake in this book, we would be grateful if you would report this to us. Please visit `www.packtpub.com/support/errata` and fill in the form.

Piracy: If you come across any illegal copies of our works in any form on the internet, we would be grateful if you would provide us with the location address or website name. Please contact us at `copyright@packt.com` with a link to the material.

If you are interested in becoming an author: If there is a topic that you have expertise in and you are interested in either writing or contributing to a book, please visit `authors.packtpub.com`.

Share Your Thoughts

Once you've read *Learn T-SQL Querying, Second Edition*, we'd love to hear your thoughts! Scan the QR code below to go straight to the Amazon review page for this book and share your feedback.

`https://packt.link/r/1-837-63899-3`

Your review is important to us and the tech community and will help us make sure we're delivering excellent quality content.

Download a free PDF copy of this book

Thanks for purchasing this book!

Do you like to read on the go but are unable to carry your print books everywhere?

Is your e-book purchase not compatible with the device of your choice?

Don't worry!, Now with every Packt book, you get a DRM-free PDF version of that book at no cost.

Read anywhere, any place, on any device. Search, copy, and paste code from your favorite technical books directly into your application.

The perks don't stop there, you can get exclusive access to discounts, newsletters, and great free content in your inbox daily

Follow these simple steps to get the benefits:

1. Scan the QR code or visit the following link:

https://packt.link/free-ebook/9781837638994

2. Submit your proof of purchase.
3. That's it! We'll send your free PDF and other benefits to your email directly.

Part 1:
Query Processing
Fundamentals

To understand how to write solid, performant T-SQL queries, users should know how SQL Server runs the T-SQL syntax to deliver the intended result sets in a scalable fashion. This part introduces you to concepts that are used throughout the remaining parts of the book to explain most patterns and anti-patterns, as well as mitigation strategies.

This part has the following chapters:

- *Chapter 1, Understanding Query Processing*
- *Chapter 2, Mechanics of the Query Optimizer*

1

Understanding Query Processing

Transact-SQL, or T-SQL as it has become commonly known, is the language used to communicate with Microsoft SQL Server and Azure SQL Database. Any actions a user wishes to perform in a server, such as retrieving or modifying data in a database, creating objects, or changing server configurations, are all done via T-SQL commands.

The first step in learning to write efficient T-SQL queries is understanding how the SQL Database Engine processes and executes the query. The Query Processor is a component, therefore a noun, should not be all lowercased includes query compilation, query optimization, and query execution essentials: how does the SQL Database Engine compile an incoming T-SQL statement? How does the SQL Database Engine optimize and execute a T-SQL statement? How does the SQL Database Engine use parameters? Are parameters an advantage? When and why does the SQL Database Engine cache execution plans for certain T-SQL statements but not for others? When is that an advantage and when is it a problem? This is information that any T-SQL practitioner needs to keep as a reference for proactive T-SQL query writing, as well as reactive troubleshooting and optimization purposes. This chapter will be referenced throughout all following chapters, as we bridge the gap between architectural topics and real-world usage.

In this chapter, we're going to cover the following main topics:

- Logical statement processing flow
- Query compilation essentials
- Query optimization essentials
- Query execution essentials
- Plan caching and reuse
- The importance of parameters

Technical requirements

The examples used in this chapter are designed for use on SQL Server 2022 and Azure SQL Database, but they should work on SQL Server version 2012 or later. The Developer Edition of SQL Server is free for development environments and can be used to run all the code samples. There is also a free tier of Azure SQL Database you can use for testing at `https://aka.ms/freedb`.

You will need the sample database `AdventureWorks2016_EXT` (referred to as `AdventureWorks`), which can be found on GitHub at `https://github.com/Microsoft/sql-server-samples/releases/tag/adventureworks`. The code samples for this chapter can also be found on GitHub at `https://github.com/PacktPublishing/Learn-T-SQL-Querying-Second-Edition/tree/main/ch1`.

Logical statement processing flow

When writing T-SQL, it is important to be familiar with the order in which the SQL Database Engine interprets queries, to later create an execution plan. This helps anticipate possible performance issues arising from poorly written queries, as well as helping you understand cases of unintended results. The following steps outline a summarized view of the method that the Database Engine follows to process a T-SQL statement:

1. Process all the source and target objects stated in the `FROM` clause (tables, views, and TVFs), together with the intended logical operation (`JOIN` and `APPLY`) to perform on those objects.

2. Apply whatever pre-filters are defined in the `WHERE` clause to reduce the number of incoming rows from those objects.

3. Apply any aggregation defined in the `GROUP BY` or aggregate functions (for example, a `MIN` or `MAX` function).

4. Apply filters that can only be applied on the aggregations as defined in the `HAVING` clause.

5. Compute the logic for windowing functions such as `ROW_NUMBER`, `RANK`, `NTILE`, `LAG`, and `LEAD`.

6. Keep only the required columns for the output as specified in the `SELECT` clause, and if a `UNION` clause is present, combine the row sets.

7. Remove duplicates from the row set if a `DISTINCT` clause exists.

8. Order the resulting row set as specified by the `ORDER BY` clause.

9. Account for any limits stated in the `TOP` clause.

It becomes clearer now that properly defining how tables are joined (the logical join type) is important to any scalable T-SQL query, namely by carefully planning on which columns the tables are joined. For example, in an inner join, these join arguments are the first level of data filtering that can be enforced, because only the rows that represent the intersection of two tables are eligible for subsequent operations.

Then it also makes sense to filter out rows from the result set using a WHERE clause, rather than applying any post-filtering conditions that apply to sub-groupings using a HAVING clause. Consider these two example queries:

```
SELECT p.ProductNumber, AVG(sod.UnitPrice)
FROM Production.Product AS p
INNER JOIN Sales.SalesOrderDetail AS sod ON p.ProductID = sod.
ProductID
GROUP BY p.ProductNumber
HAVING p.ProductNumber LIKE 'L%';
SELECT p.ProductNumber, AVG(sod.UnitPrice)
FROM Production.Product AS p
INNER JOIN Sales.SalesOrderDetail AS sod ON p.ProductID = sod.
ProductID
WHERE p.ProductNumber LIKE 'L%'
GROUP BY p.ProductNumber;
```

While these two queries are logically equivalent, the second one is more efficient because the rows that do not have a ProductNumber starting with L will be filtered out of the results before the aggregation is calculated. This is because the SQL Database Engine evaluates a WHERE clause before a HAVING clause and can limit the row count earlier in the execution phase, translating into reduced I/O and memory requirements, and also reduced CPU usage when applying the post-filter to the group.

The following diagram summarizes the logical statement-processing flow for the building blocks discussed previously in this chapter:

Figure 1.1: Flow chart summarizing the logical statement-processing flow of a query

Now that we understand the order in which the SQL Database Engine processes queries, let's explore the essentials of query compilation.

Query compilation essentials

The main stages of query processing can be seen in the following overview diagram, which we will expand on throughout this chapter:

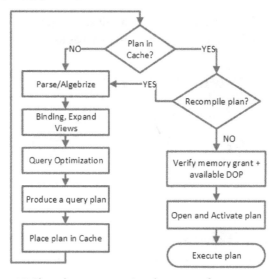

Figure 1.2: Flow chart representing the states of query processing

The Query Processor is the component inside the SQL Database Engine that is responsible for compiling a query. In this section, we will focus on the highlighted steps of the following diagram that handle query compilation:

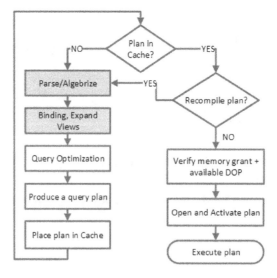

Figure 1.3: States of query processing related to query compilation

The first stage of query processing is generally known as query compilation and includes a series of tasks that will eventually lead to the creation of a query plan. When an incoming T-SQL statement is `parsed` to perform syntax validations and ensure that it is correct T-SQL, a query hash value is generated that represents the statement text exactly as it was written. If that query hash is already mapped to a cached query plan, then it can just attempt to reuse that plan. However, if a query plan for the incoming query is not already found in the cache, query compilation proceeds with the following tasks:

1. Perform **binding**, which is the process of verifying that the referenced tables and columns exist in the database schema.

2. References to a view are replaced with the definition of that view (this is called **expanding the view**).

3. **Load metadata** for the referenced tables and columns. This metadata is as follows:

    A. The definition of tables, indexes, views, constraints, and so on, that apply to the query.

    B. Data distribution statistics on the applicable schema object.

4. Verify whether **data conversions** are required for the query.

> **Note**
>
> When the query compilation process is complete, a structure that can be used by the Query Optimizer is produced, known as the algebrizer tree or query tree.

The following diagram further details these compilation tasks:

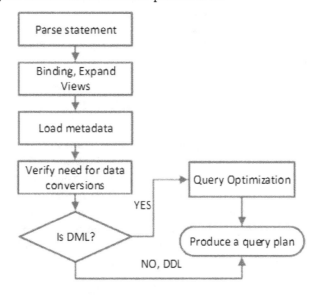

Figure 1.4: Flow of compilation tasks for T-SQL statements

If the T-SQL statement is a **Data Definition Language** (DDL) statement, there's no possible optimization, and so a plan is produced immediately. However, if the T-SQL statement is a **Data Manipulation Language** (DML) statement, the SQL Database Engine will move to an exploratory process known as query optimization, which we will explore in the next section.

Query optimization essentials

The Query Processor is also the component inside the SQL Database Engine that is responsible for query optimization. This is the second stage of query processing and its goal is to produce a query plan that can then be cached for all subsequent uses of the same query. In this section, we will focus on the highlighted sections of the following diagram that handle query optimization:

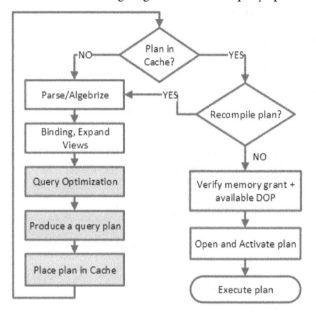

Figure 1.5: States of query processing related to query optimization

The SQL Database Engine uses cost-based optimization, which means that the Query Optimizer is driven mostly by estimations of the required cost to access and transform data (such as joins and aggregations) that will produce the intended result set. The purpose of the optimization process is to reasonably minimize the I/O, memory, and compute resources needed to execute a query in the fastest way possible. But it is also a time-bound process and can time out. This means that the Query Optimizer may not iterate through all the possible optimization permutations of a given T-SQL statement, but rather stops itself after finding an estimated "good enough" compromise between low resource usage and faster execution times.

For this, the Query Optimizer takes several inputs to later produce what is called a query execution plan. These inputs are the following:

- The incoming T-SQL statement, including any input parameters

- The loaded metadata, such as statistics histograms, available indexes and indexed views, partitioning, and the number of available schedulers

> **Note**
>
> We will further discuss the role of statistics in *Chapter 2, Mechanics of the Query Optimizer*, and dive deeper into execution plans in *Chapter 3, Exploring Query Execution Plans*, later in this book.

As part of the optimization process, the SQL Database Engine also uses internal transformation rules and some heuristics to narrow the optimization space – in other words, to narrow the number of transformation rules that can be applied to the incoming T-SQL statement. The SQL Database Engine has over 400 such transformation rules that are applicable depending on the incoming T-SQL statement. For reference, these rules are exposed in the undocumented dynamic management view `sys.dm_exec_query_transformation_stats`. The name column in this DMV contains the internal name for the transformation rule. An example is `LOJNtoNL`: an implementation rule to transform a logical LEFT OUTER JOIN to a physical nested loops join operator.

And so, the Query Optimizer may transform the T-SQL statement as written by a developer before it is allowed to execute. This is because T-SQL is a declarative language: the developer declares what is intended, but the SQL Database Engine determines how to carry out the declared intent. When evaluating transformations, the Query Optimizer must adhere to the rules of logical operator precedence. When a complex expression has multiple operators, operator precedence determines the sequence in which the operations are performed. For example, in a query that uses comparison and arithmetic operators, the arithmetic operators are handled before the comparison operators. This determines whether a Compute Scalar operator can be placed before or after a Filter operator.

The Query Optimizer will consider numerous strategies to search for an efficient execution plan, including the following:

- **Index selection**

  Are there indexes to cover the whole or parts of the query? This is done based on which search and join predicates (conditions) are used, and which columns are required for the query output.

- **Logical join reordering**

  The order in which tables are actually joined may not be the same order as they are written in the T-SQL statement itself. The SQL Database Engine uses heuristics as well as statistics to narrow the number of possible join permutations to test, and then estimate which join order results in early filtering of rows and less resource usage. For example, depending on how a query that joins 6 tables is written, possible join reordering permutations range from roughly 700 to over 30,000.

- **Partitioning**

  Is data partitioned? If so, and depending on the predicate, can the SQL Database Engine avoid accessing some partitions that are not relevant for the query?

- **Parallelism**

  Is it estimated that execution will be more efficient if multiple CPUs are used?

- **Whether to expand views**

  Is it better to use an indexed view, or conversely expand and inline the view definition to account for the base tables?

- **Join elimination**

  Are two tables being joined in a way that the number of rows resulting from that join is zero? If so, the join may not even be executed.

- **Sub-query elimination**

  This relies on the same principle as join elimination. Was it estimated that the correlated or non-correlated sub-query will produce zero rows? If so, the sub-query may not even be executed.

- **Constraint simplification**

  Is there an active constraint that prevents any rows from being generated? For example, does a column have a non-nullable constraint, but the query predicate searches for null values in that column? If so, then that part of the query may not even be executed.

- **Eligibility for parameter sensitivity optimization**

  Is the database where the query is executing subject to Database Compatibility Level 160? If so, are there parameterized predicates considered at risk of being impacted by parameter sniffing?

- **Halloween protection**

  Is this an update plan? If so, is there a need to add a blocking operator?

> **Note**
>
> An update plan has two parts: a read part that identifies the rows to be updated and a write part that performs the updates, which must be executed in two separate steps. In other words, the actual update of rows must not affect the selection of which rows to update. This problem of ensuring that the write cursor of an update plan does not affect the read cursor is known as "Halloween protection" as it was discovered by IBM researchers more than 40 years ago, precisely on Halloween.

For the Query Optimizer to do its job efficiently in the shortest amount of time possible, data professionals need to do their part, which can be distilled into three main principles:

- **Design for performance**

  Ensure that our tables are designed with purposeful use of the appropriate data types and lengths, that our most used predicates are covered by indexes, and that the engine is allowed to identify and create the required statistical information.

- **Write simple T-SQL queries**

  Be purposeful with the number of joined tables, how the joins are expressed, the number of columns needed for the result set, how parameters and variables are declared, and which data transformations are used. Complexity comes at a cost and it may be a wise strategy to break down long T-SQL statements into smaller parts that create intermediate result sets.

- **Maintain our database health**

  From a performance standpoint alone, ensure that index maintenance and statistics updates are done regularly.

At this point, it starts to become clear that how we write a query is fundamental to achieving good performance. But it is equally important to make sure the Query Optimizer is given a chance to do its job to produce an efficient query plan. That job is dependent on having metadata available that accurately portrays the data distribution in base tables and indexes. Later in this book, in *Chapter 5, Writing Elegant T-SQL Queries*, we will further distill what data professionals need to know to write efficient T-SQL that performs well.

Also, in the *Mechanics of the Query Optimizer* chapter, we will cover the Query Optimizer and the estimation process in greater detail. Understanding how the SQL Database Engine optimizes a query and what the process looks like is a fundamental step toward troubleshooting query performance – a task that every data professional will do at some point in their career.

Now that we have reviewed query compilation and optimization, the next step is query execution, which we will explore in the following section.

Query execution essentials

Query execution is driven by the Relational Engine in the SQL Database Engine. This means executing the plan that resulted from the optimization process. In this section, we will focus on the highlighted parts of the following diagram that handle query execution:

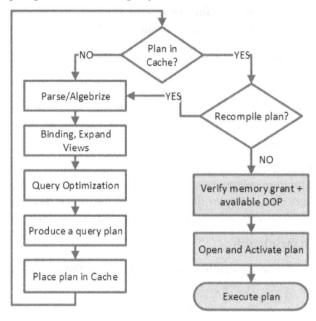

Figure 1.6: States of query processing related to query execution

Before execution starts, the Relational Engine needs to initialize the estimated amount of memory needed to run the query, known as a **memory grant**. Along with the actual execution, the Relational Engine schedules the worker threads (also known as *threads* or *workers*) for the processes to run on and provides inter-thread communication. The number of worker threads spawned depends on two key aspects:

- Whether the plan is eligible for parallelism as determined by the Query Optimizer.

- What the actual **available degree of parallelism (DOP)** is in the system based on the current load. This may differ from the estimated DOP, which is based on the server configuration **max degree of parallelism (MaxDOP)**. For example, the MaxDOP may be 8 but the available DOP at runtime can be only 2, which impacts query performance.

During execution, as parts of the plan that require data from the base tables are processed, the Relational Engine requests that the Storage Engine provide data from the relevant rowsets. The data returned from the Storage Engine is processed into the format defined by the T-SQL statement, and returns the result set to the client.

This doesn't change even on highly concurrent systems. However, as the SQL Database Engine needs to handle many requests with limited resources, waiting and queuing are how this is achieved.

To understand waits and queues in the SQL Database Engine, it is important to introduce other query execution-related concepts. From an execution standpoint, this is what happens when a client application needs to execute a query:

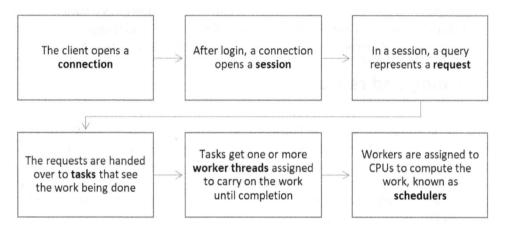

Figure 1.7: Timeline of events when a client application executes a query

Tasks and workers can naturally accumulate waits until a request completes – we will see how to monitor these in *Building diagnostic queries using DMVs and DMFs*. These waits are surfaced in each request, which can be in one of three different statuses during its execution:

Figure 1.8: States of task execution in the Database Engine

- `Running`: When a task is actively running within a scheduler.

- `Suspended`: When a task that is running in a scheduler finds out that a required resource is not available at the moment, such as a data page, it voluntarily yields its allotted processor time so that another request can proceed instead of allowing for idle processor time. But a task can be in this state before it even gets on a scheduler. For example, if there isn't enough memory to grant to a new incoming query, that query must wait for memory to become available before starting actual execution.

- `Runnable`: When a task is waiting on a first-in first-out queue for scheduler time, but otherwise has access to the required resources such as data pages.

All these concepts and terms play a fundamental role in understanding query execution and are also important to keep in mind when troubleshooting query performance. We will further explore how to detect some of these execution conditions in *Chapter 3, Exploring Query Execution Plans*.

Plan caching and reuse

As we have now established, the process of optimizing a query can consume a large amount of resources and take a significant amount of time, so it makes sense to avoid that effort if possible whenever a query is executed. The SQL Database Engine caches nearly every plan that is created so that it can be reused when the same query is executed again. But not all execution plans are eligible for caching; for example, no DDL statements are cached, such as `CREATE TABLE`. As for DML statements, most simple forms that only have one possible execution plan are also not cached, such as `INSERT INTO ... VALUES`.

There are several different methods for plan caching. The method that is used is typically based on how the query is called from the client. The different methods of plan caching that will be covered in this section are the following:

- Stored procedures
- Ad hoc plan caching
- Parameterization (simple and forced)
- The `sp_executesql` procedure
- Prepared statements

Stored procedures

A stored procedure is a group of one or more T-SQL statements that is stored as an object in a SQL database. Stored procedures are like procedures in other programming languages in that they can accept input parameters and return output parameters, they can contain control flow logic such as conditional statements (`IF ... ELSE`), loops (`WHILE`), and error handling (`TRY ... CATCH`), and they can return a status value to the caller indicating success or failure. They can even contain calls to other stored procedures. There are many benefits to using stored procedures, but in this section, we will focus mainly on their benefit of reducing the overhead of the compilation process through caching.

The first time a stored procedure is executed, the SQL Database Engine compiles and optimizes the T-SQL within the procedure, and the resulting execution plan is cached for future use. Every subsequent call to the procedure reuses the cached plan, until such a time as the plan is removed from the cache due to reasons such as the following:

- Memory pressure
- Server restart
- Plan invalidation – when the underlying objects are changed in some way or a significant amount of data is changed

Stored procedures are the preferred method for plan caching as they provide the most effective mechanism of caching and reusing query plans in the SQL Database Engine.

Ad hoc plan caching

An ad hoc query is a T-SQL query that is sent to the server as a block of text with no parameter markers or other constructs. They are typically built on the fly as needed, such as a query that is typed into a query window in **SQL Server Management Studio** (**SSMS**) and executed, or one that is sent to the server using the EXECUTE command as in the following code example, which can be executed in the AdventureWorks sample database:

```
EXECUTE (N'SELECT LastName, FirstName, MiddleName
FROM Person.Person
WHERE PersonType = N''EM'';')
```

> **Note**
> The letter N preceding a string in a T-SQL script indicates that the string should be interpreted as Unicode with UTF-16 encoding. In order to avoid implicit data-type conversions, be sure to specify N for all Unicode string literals when writing T-SQL scripts that involve the *NCHAR* and *NVARCHAR* data types. We discuss implicit conversions and their impact on performance in *Chapter 6, Discovering T-SQL Anti-Patterns in Depth*.

The process of parsing and optimizing an ad hoc query is like that of a stored procedure, and will be just as costly, so it is worth the SQL Database Engine storing the resulting plan in the cache in case the exact same query is ever executed again. The problem with ad hoc caching is that it is extremely difficult to ensure that the resulting plan is reused.

For the SQL Database Engine to reuse an ad hoc plan, the incoming query must match the cached query exactly. Every character must be the same, including spaces, line breaks, and capitalization. The reason for this is that the SQL Database Engine uses a hash function across the entire string to match the T-SQL statement. If even one character is off, the hash values will not match, and the SQL Database Engine will again compile, optimize, and cache the incoming ad hoc statement. For this reason, ad hoc caching cannot be relied upon as an effective caching mechanism.

> **Note**
>
> Even if the database is configured to use case-insensitive collation, this does not apply to query parsing. The ad hoc plan matching is still case sensitive because of the algorithm used to generate the hash value for the query string.

If there are many ad hoc queries being sent to an instance of the SQL Database Engine, the plan cache can become bloated with single-use plans. This can cause performance issues on the system as the plan cache will be unnecessarily large, taking up memory that could be better used elsewhere in the system. In this case, turning on the **optimize for ad hoc workloads** server configuration option is recommended. When this option is turned on, the SQL Database Engine will cache a small plan stub object the first time an ad hoc query is executed. This object takes up much less space than a full plan object and will minimize the size of the ad hoc cache. If the query is ever executed a second time, the full plan will be cached.

> **Tip**
>
> See the chapter *Building Diagnostic Queries using DMVs and DMFs* later in this book for a query that will help identify single-use plans in the cache.

Parameterization

Parameterization is the practice of replacing a literal value in a T-SQL statement with a parameter marker. Building on the example from the *Ad hoc plan caching* section, the following code block shows an example of a parameterized query executed in the AdventureWorks sample database:

```
DECLARE @PersonType AS nchar(2) = N'EM';
SELECT LastName, FirstName, MiddleName
FROM Person.Person
WHERE PersonType = @PersonType;
```

In this case, the literal value 'EM' is moved from the T-SQL statement itself into a DECLARE statement, and the variable is used in the query instead. This allows the query plan to be reused for different @PersonType values, whereas sending different values directly in the query string would result in a separate cached ad hoc plan.

Simple parameterization

In order to minimize the impact of ad hoc queries, the SQL Database Engine will automatically parameterize some simple queries by default. This is called *simple* parameterization and is the default setting of the **Parameterization** database option. With parameterization set to **Simple**, the SQL Database Engine will automatically replace literal values in an ad hoc query with parameter markers in order to make the resulting query plan reusable. This works for some queries, but there is a very small class of queries that can be parameterized this way.

As an example, the query we introduced previously in the *Parameterization* section would not be automatically parameterized in simple mode because it is considered unsafe. This is because different `PersonType` values may yield a different number of rows, and thus require a different execution plan. However, the following query executed in the `AdventureWorks` sample database would qualify for simple automatic parameterization:

```
SELECT LastName, FirstName, MiddleName
FROM Person.Person
WHERE BusinessEntityID = 5;
```

This query would not be cached as-is. The SQL Database Engine would convert the literal value of 5 to a parameter marker, and it would look something like this in the cache:

```
(@1 tinyint) SELECT LastName, FirstName, MiddleName
FROM Person.Person
WHERE BusinessEntityID = @1;
```

Forced parameterization

If an application tends to generate many ad hoc queries, and there is no way to modify the application to parameterize the queries, the **Parameterization** database option can be changed to **Forced**. When forced parameterization is turned on, the SQL Database Engine will replace *all* literal values in *all* ad hoc queries with parameter markers for the majority of use cases. However, note that there are documented exceptions that are either of the following:

- Edge cases that most developers will not face, such as statements that contain more than 2,097 literals

- Non-starters because statements will not be parameterized irrespective of whether forced parameterization is enabled or not, such as when statements contain the RECOMPILE query hint, statements inside the bodies of stored procedures, triggers, user-defined functions, or prepared statements that have already been parameterized on the client-side application

Take the example of the following query executed in the `AdventureWorks` sample database:

```
SELECT LastName, FirstName, MiddleName
FROM Person.Person
WHERE PersonType = N'EM' AND BusinessEntityID IN (5, 7, 13, 17, 19);
```

This query would be automatically parameterized under forced parameterization as follows:

```
(@1 nchar(2), @2 int, @3 int, @4 int, @5 int, @6 int) SELECT LastName,
FirstName, MiddleName
FROM Person.Person
WHERE PersonType = @1 AND BusinessEntityID IN (@2, @3, @4, @5, @6);
```

This has the benefit of increasing the reusability of all ad hoc queries, but there are some risks to parameterizing all literal values in all queries, which will be discussed later in the *The importance of parameters* section.

The sp_executesql procedure

The `sp_executesql` procedure is the recommended method for sending an ad hoc T-SQL statement to the SQL Database Engine. If stored procedures cannot be leveraged for some reason, such as when T-SQL statements must be constructed dynamically by the application, `sp_executesql` allows the user to send an ad hoc T-SQL statement as a parameterized query, which uses a similar caching mechanism to stored procedures. This ensures that the plan can be reused whenever the same query is executed again. Building on our example from the *Ad hoc plan caching* section, we can re-write the query using `sp_executesql` as in the following example, which can be executed in the `AdventureWorks` sample database:

```
EXECUTE sp_executesql @stmt = N'SELECT LastName,
        FirstName, MiddleName
        FROM Person.Person
        WHERE PersonType = @PersonType;',
@params = N'@PersonType nchar(2)',
@PersonType = N'EM';
```

This ensures that any time the same query is sent with the same parameter markers, the plan will be reused, even if the statement is dynamically generated by the application.

Prepared statements

Another method for sending parameterized T-SQL statements to the SQL Database Engine is by using prepared statements. Leveraging prepared statements involves three different system procedures:

1. `sp_prepare`: Defines the statement and parameters that are to be executed, creates an execution plan for the query, and sends a statement handle back to the caller that can be used for subsequent execution.

2. `sp_execute`: Executes the statement defined by `sp_prepare` by sending the statement handle along with any parameters to the SQL Database Engin.

3. `sp_unprepare`: Discards the execution plan created by `sp_prepare` for the query specified by the statement handle

Steps 1 and *2* can optionally be combined into a single `sp_prepexec` statement to save a round-trip to the server.

This method is not generally recommended for plan reuse as it is a legacy construct and may not take advantage of some of the benefits of parameterized statements that `sp_executesql` and stored procedures can leverage. It is worth mentioning, however, because it is used by some cross-platform database connectivity libraries such as **Open Database Connectivity** (**ODBC**) and **Java Database Connectivity** (**JDBC**) as the default mechanism for sending queries to the SQL Database Engine.

Now that we've learned the different ways that plans may be cached, let's explore how plans may be reused during query processing.

How query processing impacts plan reuse

It's important to contextualize what happens in terms of query processing that can result in plan caching and reuse. In this section, we will focus on the highlighted section of the following diagram that determines whether a query plan can be reused from the cache or needs to be recompiled:

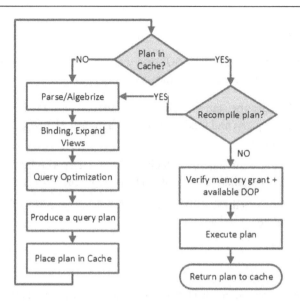

Figure 1.9: States of query processing related to query compilation/recompilation

As mentioned before, when an incoming T-SQL statement is parsed, a query hash value representing that statement is generated, and if that query hash is already mapped to a cached query plan, then it can just attempt to reuse that plan – unless special circumstances exist that don't even allow plan caching, such as when the RECOMPILE hint is present in the T-SQL statement.

Assuming no such pre-existing conditions exist, after matching the query hash with a plan hash, the currently cached plan is tested for correctness, meaning that the SQL Database Engine will check whether anything has changed in the underlying referenced objects that would require the plan to be recompiled. For example, if a new index was created or an existing index referenced in the plan was dropped, the plan must be recompiled.

If the cached plan is found to be correct, then the SQL Database Engine also checks whether enough data has changed to warrant a new plan. This refers to the statistics objects associated with tables and indexes used in the T-SQL statement, and if any are deemed outdated – meaning its modification counter is high enough as it relates to the overall cardinality of the table to consider it stale.

> **Note**
>
> In SQL Server 2022 and Azure SQL Database, if the new **Parameter Sensitive Plan** (PSP) Optimization feature is used, one query hash can map to multiple query plan hashes. Each different plan hash is a standalone query plan called a variant, and maps to a single query hash that was deemed eligible for PSP Optimization. Each plan variant can be recompiled independently. PSP Optimization will be discussed later in the *The importance of parameters* section.
>
> We will further discuss the role of statistics in the chapter *Mechanics of the Query Optimizer*, and query hashes and query plan hashes in the chapter *Exploring Query Execution Plans*, in the *Operator-level properties* section.

If nothing has significantly changed, then the query plan can be executed, as we discussed in this chapter in the *Query execution essentials* section.

The following picture depicts the high-level process for an already cached plan that can be executed as-is:

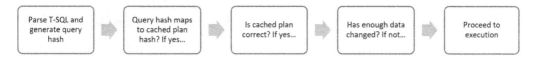

Figure 1.10: Process for executing a cached plan as-is

However, if any of the preceding checks fail, then the SQL Database Engine invalidates the cached plan and a new query plan needs to be compiled, as the available optimization space may be different from the last time the plan was compiled and cached. In this case, the T-SQL statement needs to undergo recompilation and go through the optimization process driven by the Query Optimizer so that a new query execution plan is generated (we will describe this process in greater detail in the chapter *Mechanics of the Query Optimizer*). If eligible, this newly generated query plan is cached.

> **Note**
>
> The same process is followed for new incoming queries where no query plan is yet cached.

Now that we understand how the SQL Database Engine caches and reuses query plans, let's explore one of the most important factors that determines whether a plan may be reused – parameters.

The importance of parameters

As we discussed in the previous section on caching methods, the primary reason to parameterize queries is to ensure that query execution plans get reused – but why is this important and what other reasons might there be to use parameters?

Security

One reason for using parameterized queries is for security. Using a properly formatted parameterized query can protect against SQL injection attacks. A SQL injection attack is one where a malicious user can execute database code (in this case, T-SQL) on a server by appending it to a data entry field in the application. As an example, assume we have an application that contains a form that asks the user to enter their name into a text box. If the application were to use an ad hoc statement to insert this data into the database, it would generally concatenate a T-SQL string with the user input, as in the following code:

```
DECLARE @sql nvarchar(MAX);
SET @sql = N'INSERT Users (Name) VALUES (''' + <user input> + ''');';
EXECUTE (@sql);
```

A malicious user might enter the following value into the text box:

```
Bob'); DROP TABLE Users; --
```

If this is the case, the actual code that gets sent to the SQL Database Engine would look like the following:

```
INSERT Users (Name) VALUES ('Bob'); DROP TABLE Users; --');
```

This is a valid T-SQL syntax that would successfully execute. It would first insert a row into the **Users** table with the **Name** column set to 'Bob', then it would drop the **Users** table. This would of course break the application, and unless there was some sort of auditing in place, we would never know what happened.

Let's look at this example again using a parameterized query. The code might look like the following:

```
EXECUTE sp_executesql @stmt = N'INSERT Users (Name) VALUES (@name)', @
params = N'@name nvarchar(100)', @name = <user input>
```

This time, if the user were to send the same input, rather than executing the query that the user embedded in the string, the Database Engine would insert a row into the **Users** table with the **Name** column set to 'Bob'); DROP TABLE Users; --'. This would obviously look a bit strange, but it wouldn't break the application nor breach security.

Performance

Another reason to leverage parameters is performance. In a busy SQL system, particularly one that has a primarily **Online Transaction Processing** (**OLTP**) workload, we may have hundreds or even thousands of queries executing per second.

Assume that each one of these queries takes about 100 ms to compile and consumes about the same amount of CPU. This would mean that each second on the system, the server could be consuming hundreds of seconds of CPU time just compiling queries. That's a lot of resources to consume just for preparing the queries for execution, and it doesn't leave a lot of overhead for actually executing them.

Also recall that when plans are not reused, the procedure cache can become very large and consume memory that in turn won't be available for storing data and executing queries. In short, a system that spends too much time compiling queries may become CPU and/or memory bound and may perform poorly.

Parameter sniffing

Given that query plan reuse is so important, why wouldn't the SQL Database Engine parameterize every query that comes in by default? One of the reasons for this is to avoid query performance issues that may result from parameter sniffing. Parameter sniffing is something the SQL Database Engine does in order to optimize a parameterized query. The first time a stored procedure or other parameterized query executes, the input parameter values are used to drive the optimization process and produce the execution plan, as discussed in the *Query optimization essentials* section.

That execution plan will then be cached and reused by subsequent executions of the procedure or query. For most queries, this is a good thing because using a specific value will result in a more accurate cost estimation. In some situations, however, particularly where the data distribution is skewed in some way, the parameters that are sent the first time the query is executed may not represent the typical use case of the query, and the plan that is generated may perform poorly when other parameter values are sent. This is a case where reusing a plan might not be a good thing, because the plan is highly sensitive to user-defined runtime parameters that have widely different data distributions for the same column.

Parameter sniffing, or parameter sensitivity, is a very common cause of plan variability and performance issues in the SQL Database Engine.

Parameter Sensitive Plan Optimization

SQL Server 2022 introduces the *Parameter Sensitive Plan Optimization* feature (commonly referred to as PSP Optimization), which allows the Database Engine to simultaneously cache multiple plans for a single parameterized query that uses equality predicates.

With PSP Optimization, during the initial compilation of a parameterized query, the Query Optimizer will evaluate up to three parameters that are likely sensitive to non-uniform (skewed) data distributions. The feature uses the statistics histograms to search for where the cardinality difference between the least-occurring value and the most-occurring value for a given column is orders of magnitude off. The result is the creation of what is called a dispatcher plan, which contains the logic (dispatcher expression) that bucketizes the predicates' values, upon which different plan variants can be compiled independently.

For each cardinality bucket, a query plan variant will only be compiled if needed, based on actual runtime parameters. If the parameter values that would result in a given plan variant are never used at runtime, then that variant of the plan defined in the dispatcher plan will never actually get compiled. This behavior prevents plan-cache bloating by compiling a plan only if and when its predicate value demands it.

The following diagram shows the possible plan variants found for a parameterized query with a `WHERE person.ID = @param` search predicate:

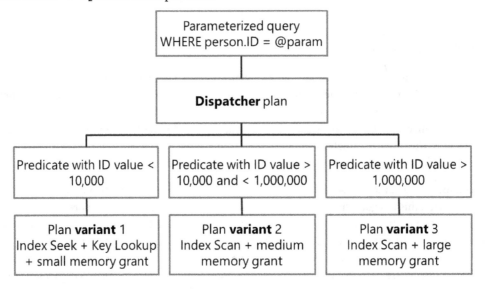

Figure 1.11: Example of a dispatcher plan defining three query plan variants

We will discuss parameter sensitivity behavior in more detail later in this book, in *Chapter 5, Writing Elegant T-SQL Queries*, and *Chapter 6, Discovering T-SQL Anti-Patterns in Depth*.

To cache or not to cache

In general, caching and reusing query plans is a good thing, and writing T-SQL code that encourages plan reuse is recommended.

In some cases, such as with a reporting or OLAP workload, caching queries might make less sense. These types of systems tend to have a heavy ad hoc workload. The queries that run are typically long-running and, while they may consume a large amount of resources in a single execution, they typically run with less frequency than OLTP systems. Since these queries tend to be long-running, saving a few hundred milliseconds by reusing a cached plan doesn't make as much sense as creating a new plan that is designed specifically for that execution of the query. Spending that time compiling a new plan may even result in saving more time in the long run, since a fresh plan will likely perform better than a plan that was generated based on a different set of parameter values.

In summary, for most workloads in the SQL Database Engine, leveraging stored procedures and/ or parameterized queries is recommended to encourage plan reuse. For workloads that have heavy ad hoc queries and/or long-running reporting-style queries, consider enabling the **optimize for ad hoc workloads** server setting and leveraging the RECOMPILE hint to guarantee a new plan for each execution (provided that the queries are run with a low frequency), or use forced parameterization to improve plan reuse opportunities. Also, be sure to review *Chapter 8, Building Diagnostic Queries Using DMVs and DMFs*, for techniques to identify single-use plans, monitor for excessive recompilation, and identify plan variability and potential parameter sniffing issues.

Summary

As this chapter has shown, the way a T-SQL query is written and submitted to the server influences how it is interpreted and executed by the SQL Database Engine. Even before a single T-SQL query is written, the choice of development style (for example, using stored procedures versus ad hoc statements) can have a direct impact on the performance of the application. As we continue our exploration of the internals of SQL Database Engine query processing and optimization, we will find more and more opportunities to write T-SQL queries in a way that encourages optimal query performance, starting with the next chapter.

2

Mechanics of the Query Optimizer

The next step in our journey to writing efficient T-SQL queries is understanding how the SQL Database Engine optimizes a query by exploring T-SQL query optimization internals and architecture, starting with the infamous cardinality estimation process and its building blocks. From there, understand how the Query Optimizer uses that information to produce a just-in-time good-enough execution plan. This chapter will be referenced throughout all chapters, as we bridge architectural topics to real-world uses.

In this chapter, we're going to cover the following main topics:

- Introducing the **Cardinality Estimator** (**CE**)
- Understanding the query optimization workflow

Technical requirements

The examples that will be used in this chapter are designed for use on SQL Server 2022 and Azure SQL Database, but they should work on any version of SQL Server, 2012 or later. The Developer Edition of SQL Server is free for development environments and can be used to run all the code samples. There is also a free tier of Azure SQL Database you can use for testing at `https://aka.ms/freedb`.

You will need the sample `AdventureWorks2016_EXT` database (referred to as `AdventureWorks`), which can be found on GitHub at `https://github.com/Microsoft/sql-server-samples/releases/tag/adventureworks`.

The code samples for this chapter can also be found on GitHub at `https://github.com/PacktPublishing/Learn-T-SQL-Querying-Second-Edition/tree/main/ch2`.

Introducing the Cardinality Estimator

Before we get started, it's important to have a common frame of reference for a few terms that will be referenced throughout this book:

- **Cardinality**: Cardinality in a database is defined as the number of records, also called **tuples**, in each table or view.

- **Density**: This term represents the average number of duplicate values in each column or column set – in other words, the average distribution of unique values in the data. It's defined as 1 divided by the number of distinct values.

- **Frequency**: This term represents the average number of occurrences of a given value in a column or column set. It's defined as the number of rows times the density.

- **Selectivity**: This term represents the fraction of the row count that satisfies a given predicate, between zero and one. This is calculated as the **predicate cardinality (Pc)** divided by the **table cardinality (Tc)** multiplied by 100: $(Pc \div Tc) \times 100$. As the average number of duplicates decreases (the density), the selectivity of a value increases. For example, in a table representing streets and cities in a country, many streets and cities have the same name, but each street and city combination has a unique ZIP code. An index on the ZIP code is more selective than an index on the street or city because the ZIP code has a much lower density than streets or cities alone.

- **Statistics**: Statistics are the metadata objects that we referred to in *Chapter 1, Understanding Query Processing*, and maintain information on the distribution of data in a table or indexed view, over a specific column or column set. We'll discuss the role of statistics in more detail later in this section.

- **Histogram**: This is a bucketized representation of the distribution of data in a specific column that is kept in a statistic object. These histograms hold aggregate information on the number of rows (cardinality) and distinct values (density) for up to 200 ranges of data values, named histogram steps. For any statistics object, the histogram is always created for the first column only.

In *Chapter 1, Understanding Query Processing*, we discussed how the Query Optimizer is a fundamental piece of the overall Query Processor. In this chapter, we will dig deeper into the core component of cost-based query optimization – the **Cardinality Estimator (CE)**.

As the name suggests, the role of the CE is to provide fundamental estimation inputs to the query optimization process. For example, at the time of writing, the cardinality of a table containing the names of every living human on Earth is about 8,000,000,000. But if a predicate is applied to this table to only find inhabitants in the US, the cardinality after the predicate is applied is only 333,000,000. Reading through 8,000,000,000 or 333,000,000 records may result in different data-access operations, such as a full scan or a range scan in this case. As such, early knowledge of the estimated number of rows is fundamental for creating an accurate query execution plan. It would be very inefficient if the SQL Database Engine had to incur the high cost of accessing actual data to make this estimation – that would be like executing the query to figure out how to execute the query. Instead, it uses metadata kept in statistics.

Statistics are the building blocks for the process of cardinality estimation: if statistics don't accurately portray underlying data distributions, then the Query Optimizer will work with inaccurate data and estimate cardinalities that don't adhere to the reality of the data.

To ensure statistics are kept updated, the SQL Database Engine keeps a modification counter on each table referenced by the statistic; when enough changes have been made to the table or indexed view columns tracked by a statistic, an update to that statistic is needed. When a query is compiled or recompiled, the SQL Database Engine loads all required statistics based on which columns are being used and determines whether statistics need to be updated.

If the database option for automatic statistics update is enabled (which is the default), the SQL Database Engine will update the outdated statistic before proceeding with query execution of any execution plan that referenced that statistic – this is known as a synchronous update. If asynchronous automatic statistics update is enabled, the SQL Database Engine will proceed with query execution based on the existing statistic as-is and update the outdated statistic as a background process. Once any statistics object has been updated, the next time any cached query plan that references that statistic is loaded for use, it is recompiled.

Up to SQL Server 2014, unless trace flag 2371 is used, the SQL Database Engine uses a threshold based on the percent of rows changed. This is irrespective of the number of rows in the table. The threshold is as follows:

- If the table cardinality was 500 or less at the time statistics were evaluated, update every 500 modifications
- If the table cardinality was above 500 at the time statistics were evaluated, update every 500 + 20% of modifications

Starting with SQL Server 2016 and Azure SQL Database, under database compatibility level 130, the SQL Database Engine uses a dynamic threshold that had been introduced in earlier versions under trace flag 2371, which keeps adjusting to the number of rows in the table or indexed view. This is the result of comparing the SQL Server 2014 threshold with the square root of the product of 1,000 and the current table cardinality. The smallest number resulting from this comparison is used. For example, if our table contains 1 million rows, then the calculation is SQRT(1,000 * 1,000,000) = 31,622. However, when the table grows to 2 million rows, the threshold is only 44,721 rows, whereas the SQL Server 2014 threshold would be 400,500 rows. With this change, statistics on large tables are updated more often, which decreases the chances of producing an inefficient query execution plan and the likely consequence is poor query performance.

> **Note**
>
> Database compatibility level is a setting that signals the SQL Database Engine to execute T-SQL statements in that database using the same functional and query optimization behaviors that were defaulted for a given Database Engine version. For example, SQL Server 2016 introduced database compatibility level 130 and a set of new default behaviors, but setting database compatibility level 120 forces functional and query optimization behaviors that were default in SQL Server 2014, which maps to the version when database compatibility level 120 was introduced.

The CE operates with mathematical models based on certain assumptions about the T-SQL statements that will be executed. These assumptions are considered during computations to find reasonable predictions about how many rows are expected to flow through each plan operator. These predictions are used in the query optimization process to estimate the cost of each query plan.

CE 70, which was introduced back in SQL Server 7.0, used four basic assumptions about how users queried their data:

- **Independence assumption**: Data distributions on different columns of the same table are assumed to be independent of each other, and predicates on different columns of the same table are therefore also independent of each other. This is known as the independence assumption.

  For example, in a fictitious database for a large retail store chain where customer data is stored, a report shows which customers exist per store location using a query such as `SELECT * FROM Customers WHERE FirstName = 'James' AND City = 'San Francisco'`. We can assume there are many Jameses not only in San Francisco but in other cities as well, so these two columns are independent.

- **Uniformity assumption**: Distinct values are evenly distributed in each histogram, and all have the same frequency. This is known as the uniformity assumption.

- **Simple containment**: Join predicates are assumed to be dependent on filter predicates. When users query data joining different tables and set a filter predicate on these tables, it's assumed that the filters apply to the joined data and are considered when estimating the number of rows returned by the join.

  Using the example of a fictitious database for the same large retail store chain, different tables record items sold and items returned, and a report shows the number of returns per sold item type and date, using a query such as `SELECT * FROM Sales INNER JOIN Returns ON Sales. ReceiptID = Returns.ReceiptID WHERE Sales.Type = 'Toys' AND Returns.Date = '2019-04-18'`. Throughout the year, a fairly steady number of returns per item are sold, and the estimation shouldn't change for any given day. However, when the query predicate changes to `WHERE Sales.Type = 'Toys' AND Returns. Date = '2018-12-27'`, and the SQL Database Engine is compiling a plan for this new query, accounting for the filters can greatly impact the join cardinality estimations because in the days after Christmas, it's expected that many toys are returned.

Whenever we know the filter predicates and the join predicates are highly dependent, as is the case here, with sales and returns of toys for specific dates greatly dictating the cardinality, simple containment can yield better estimations and therefore potentially a better plan.

- **Inclusion assumption**: For filter predicates where a column equals a constant (for example, `WHERE col1 = 10`), it is assumed the constant always exists in that column. This is called the **inclusion** assumption.

However, application workloads don't always follow these model assumptions, which can result in inefficiently optimized query execution plans.

> **Note**
> We will discuss more about some out-of-model T-SQL constructs in *Chapter 5, Writing Elegant T-SQL Queries*, and *Chapter 6, Discovering T-SQL Anti-Patterns in Depth*.

The observation and experience of query performance that's been accrued over the years led to a major redesign of the cardinality estimator with the release of SQL Server 2014 and CE 120.

The main objectives of this new CE were to improve the quality of cardinality estimation for a broad range of queries and modern workloads, such as **online transaction processing (OLTP)**, **data warehousing (DW)**, and **decision support systems (DSS)**, as well as to generate more efficient and predictable query execution plans for most use cases, especially complex queries.

With that new release, some model assumptions about how users queried their data were changed:

- **Independence** became partial **Correlation**, where the combination of the different column values is not necessarily independent, and it's assumed this resembles more real-life data querying patterns. For the example of a fictitious database for a large retail store chain where customer data is stored, a report lists the names of all customers using a query such as `SELECT * FROM Customers WHERE FirstName = 'James' AND LastName = 'Kirk'`. We can assume a tight correlation between a customer's first and last names, meaning that while there are many Jameses, there are not many James Kirks.

- **Simple Containment** Becomes **Base Containment**, meaning that filter predicates and join predicates are independent. The previous example for simple containment uses a set of join and filter predicates that are very much dependent. Therefore, the base containment default would yield less accurate cardinality estimations.

  However, consider the same fictitious database for the same large retail store chain, where the HR department runs a report that shows the base salary for full-time employees, using a query such as `SELECT * FROM Payroll INNER JOIN Employee ON Payroll.EmployeeID = Employee.EmployeeID WHERE Payroll.CompType = 'Base' AND Employee.Type = 'FTE'`.

In this example, all employees have a base salary, and because this company's workforce has one-third FTEs, one-third part-time employees, and one-third contractors, for any employee type that is queried, the join cardinality estimation wouldn't change much whether the filter predicates (the WHERE clause) is there or not. Base containment works best here because we know that the filter predicates and the join predicates are not necessarily dependent, and filter values wouldn't **necessarily** affect cardinality estimations. Therefore, base containment can yield better estimations and potentially a better plan for most use cases.

It's common to see these CE models referred to as **Legacy CE** and **New CE**. These are side-by-side implementations and are more accurately referred to as CE 70, and CE 120 or higher. Being side-by-side means that developers can opt-in for either CE version as new changes and enhancements are gated by the database compatibility level.

CE versions are tied to the **Database Compatibility Level** setting of the SQL Server version when it was first introduced. These are also available in Azure SQL Database, where the default compatibility level is the same as the latest version of SQL Server, after the general availability of that version. The following table contains a mapping reference between database compatibility levels and CE versions:

Introduced in SQL Server Version	Database Compatibility Level	CE Version
2008 and 2008 R2	100	70
2012	110	70
2014	120	120
2016	130	130
2017	140	140
2019	150	150
2022	160	160

Table 2.1: Database compatibility levels and their corresponding versions and CE versions

This mapping between database compatibility levels and CE versions is especially useful when the topic is application certification. For example, if a given application was written and optimized for SQL Server 2012 (CE 70) and later upgraded as-is to SQL Server 2017 (CE 140), then there's a chance that a part of that application's workload may be susceptible to the model changes of a higher CE version, and as a result, perform worse than it did in SQL Server 2012. These types of performance regressions can be handled easily, and the SQL Database Engine includes several features designed to assist in overcoming a number of these regressions.

SQL Server 2022 introduced a new feature named **CE Feedback**. As the name suggests, the SQL Database Engine has a feedback loop that allows it to detect whether a given query has encountered a performance regression that aligns with the changes in CE assumptions we already mentioned: **Independence** versus **Correlation**, **Simple Containment** versus **Base Containment**, and another scenario we'll discuss later in this book, which is **Row Goal**.

When a regression is detected, the SQL Database Engine uses a test-and-verify principle. It will automatically enforce the use of a contrary (CE70) assumption and in the next execution of that same query, determine whether the newly compiled plan has improved cardinality estimations. If the plan has improved, it remains as the cached plan for that query. If not, the SQL Database Engine recompiles that plan with default CE 160 assumptions. This feature automatically removes much of the risk in upgrading CE versions for application workloads that may be susceptible to the model changes of a higher CE version.

> **Note**
>
> At the time this book is written, **CE Feedback** is not yet generally available in Azure SQL Database. Also, in this first release, **CE Feedback** only handles SELECT queries..

If you are not using SQL Server 2022, we will discuss these later in this book, where we'll discuss how to assemble our query troubleshooting toolbox.

> **Note**
>
> CE 120+ changes mainly target non-leaf-level operators that support logical operations such as JOIN, UNION, GROUP BY, and DISTINCT. Other T-SQL constructs that only exist at runtime still behave the same, such as **Multi-Statement Table-Valued Functions (MSTVFs)**, table variables, local variables, and table-valued parameters. We will discuss these out-of-model constructs in *Chapter 6, Discovering T-SQL Anti-Patterns in Depth*.

The inverse is the more common case, though, where without refactoring a query, CE 120+ can do a better job of optimizing a query plan than CE 70. For example, the AdventureWorks sample database has several tables the contain employee data. To write a query that returns the employee name and details such as contacts, address, and job title, a series of inner joins are used. The query would look like this:

```
SELECT e.[BusinessEntityID], p.[Title], p.[FirstName],
p.[MiddleName], p.[LastName],p.[Suffix], e.[JobTitle],          pp.
[PhoneNumber], pnt.[Name] AS [PhoneNumberType],     ea.[EmailAddress],
p.[EmailPromotion], a.[AddressLine1], a.[AddressLine2], a.[City],
sp.[Name] AS [StateProvinceName], a.[PostalCode], cr.[Name] AS
[CountryRegionName], p.[AdditionalContactInfo]
FROM [HumanResources].[Employee] AS e
INNER JOIN [Person].[Person] AS p  ON RTRIM(LTRIM(p.
[BusinessEntityID])) = RTRIM(LTRIM(e.[BusinessEntityID]))
INNER JOIN [Person].[BusinessEntityAddress] AS bea   ON
RTRIM(LTRIM(bea.[BusinessEntityID])) = RTRIM(LTRIM(e.
```

```
[BusinessEntityID]))
INNER JOIN [Person].[Address] AS a ON RTRIM(LTRIM(a.[AddressID])) =
RTRIM(LTRIM(bea.[AddressID]))
INNER JOIN [Person].[StateProvince] AS sp ON RTRIM(LTRIM(sp.
[StateProvinceID])) = RTRIM(LTRIM(a.[StateProvinceID]))
INNER JOIN [Person].[CountryRegion] AS cr ON RTRIM(LTRIM(cr.
[CountryRegionCode])) = RTRIM(LTRIM(sp.[CountryRegionCode]))
LEFT OUTER JOIN [Person].[PersonPhone] AS pp ON RTRIM(LTRIM(pp.
BusinessEntityID)) = RTRIM(LTRIM(p.[BusinessEntityID]))
LEFT OUTER JOIN [Person].[PhoneNumberType] AS pnt ON RTRIM(LTRIM(pp.
[PhoneNumberTypeID])) = RTRIM(LTRIM(pnt.[PhoneNumberTypeID]))
LEFT OUTER JOIN [Person].[EmailAddress] AS ea ON RTRIM(LTRIM(p.
[BusinessEntityID])) = RTRIM(LTRIM(ea.[BusinessEntityID]));
```

> **Note**
>
> We are using RTRIM(LTRIM()) functions around the join columns here to prevent the SQL
> Database Engine from being able to use indexes effectively and force a more complex cardinality
> estimation. Using functions like this is a T-SQL anti-pattern that we will cover in more detail
> in *Chapter 5, Writing Elegant T-SQL Queries.*

With CE 70, the elapsed execution time for this query is 101,975 ms. But with the same query on the
same database on CE 140, the elapsed execution time is only 103 ms.

As shown in the following figure, the query execution plans are radically different in shape and, given
the observed execution times, better optimized using newer versions of the cardinality estimator.

The following figure shows the query plan shape for CE 70:

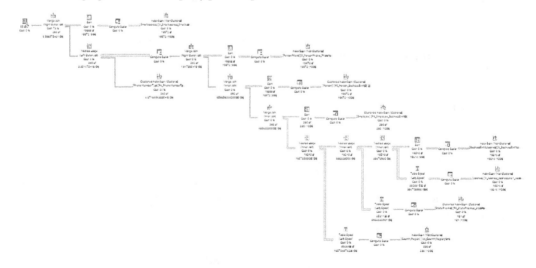

Figure 2.1: Query plan shape for the example query under CE 70

The query plan shape for CE 140 is as follows:

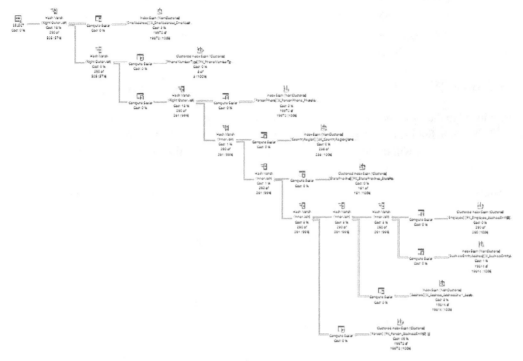

Figure 2.2 Query plan shape for the example query under CE 140

We will revisit the preceding query example in greater depth in *Exploring Query Execution Plans*, and *Troubleshooting Live Queries*.

Understanding the query optimization workflow

Now, it's time to take a deeper look at how the SQL Database Engine creates optimized query execution plans. As referenced in *Chapter 1, Understanding Query Processing*, this is the second phase of query processing and for the most part, only **Data Manipulation Language** (DML) statements undergo query optimization. The query optimization process is defined by the following cumulative stages:

- **Trivial Plan**
- **Exploration**, which, in turn, includes three phases:
  - Transaction Processing
  - Quick Plan
  - Full Optimization

In the Exploration stage, what differentiates between the several phases is the increasing sets of rules that apply to each one as the search for a good-enough query plan progresses. Users can learn about the optimization level of a given query execution plan by looking at the properties of that plan. The following sections include sample execution plans to illustrate the concepts covered here. Query execution plans will be discussed in much further detail in *Chapter 3, Exploring Query Execution Plans*.

The Trivial Plan stage

As mentioned in the *Query optimization essentials* section of *Chapter 1, Understanding Query Processing*, the SQL Database Engine does cost-based optimization. But this has an expensive startup cost, so the SQL Database Engine will try to avoid this cost for simple queries that may only have one possible query execution plan.

The Trivial Plan stage generates plans for which there are no alternatives that require a cost-based decision. The following examples can be executed in the `AdventureWorks` sample database:

- Using a `SELECT ... INTO` or `INSERT INTO` statement over a single table with no conditions:

  ```
  SELECT NationalIDNumber, JobTitle, MaritalStatus
  INTO HumanResources.Employee2
  FROM HumanResources.Employee;
  ```

  This produces the following execution plan:

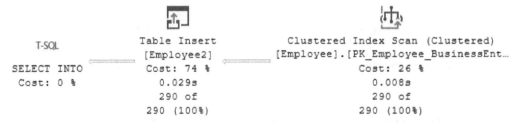

Figure 2.3: Execution plan for the SELECT … INTO query example

- Using an `INSERT INTO` statement over a single table with a simple condition covered by an index:

  ```
  INSERT INTO HumanResources.Employee2
  SELECT NationalIDNumber, JobTitle, MaritalStatus
  FROM HumanResources.Employee
  WHERE BusinessEntityID < 10;
  ```

  This produces the following execution plan:

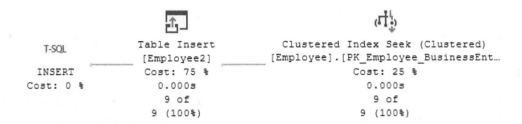

Figure 2.4: Execution plan for the INSERT ... INTO query example

- Using an INSERT statement with a VALUES clause:

```
INSERT INTO HumanResources.Employee2
VALUES (87656896, 'CIO', 'M');
```

This produces the following execution plan:

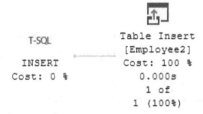

Figure 2.5: Execution plan for the INSERT ... VALUES query example

The information on the optimization level is stored in the execution plan under the **Optimization Level** property, with a value of **TRIVIAL**:

Properties	
INSERT	
⊟ **Misc**	
Cached plan size	24 KB
CardinalityEstimationModelVersion	130
CompileCPU	1
CompileMemory	120
CompileTime	1
DatabaseContextSettingsId	3
Degree of Parallelism	1
Estimated Number of Rows	1
Estimated Operator Cost	0 (0%)
Estimated Subtree Cost	0.0100022
⊞ MemoryGrantInfo	
Optimization Level	TRIVIAL

Figure 2.6: The Properties window of an execution plan showing an Optimization Level value of TRIVIAL

The Trivial Plan stage typically finds very inexpensive query plans that are not affected by cardinality estimations.

The Exploration stage

If the Trivial Plan stage doesn't find a suitable plan, then it's time to enter the cost-based optimization stage known as Exploration, whose goal is to find a good enough query execution plan based on the minimum estimated cost to access and join data. If this stage is used, the information on the optimization level is still stored in the execution plan under the same **Optimization Level** property, with a value of **FULL**.

> **Note**
>
> A good-enough plan refers to the search optimization space and how the SQL Database Engine may not iterate through all possible plan combinations, but rather look for a plan that meets its internal thresholds for a good-enough balance of estimated resource usage and execution times.

The Exploration stage is where the CE comes into play. The SQL Database Engine loads statistics and performs some tasks in preparation for cost-based optimization. These tasks are as follows:

- **Simplification**, which transforms some sub-queries into semi-joins and even detects if parts of the query can skip execution, such as avoiding empty tables or searching a table column for a NULL predicate when that table column has a trusted NOT NULL constraint

- **Normalization**, which uses the query's filter predicates and some heuristics to reorder join operations, and predicates are pushed down to the algebrizer tree to eliminate non-qualifying rows as early as possible, making later joins more efficient

The cost-based optimization process itself is composed of three phases that we'll discuss in the next sections: *Transaction Processing*, *Quick Plan*, and *Full Optimization*.

The Transaction Processing phase

This is phase zero and is suitable for OLTP-centric queries that are simple yet may have more than one possible query plan. When this phase is completed, the SQL Database Engine compares the estimated cost of the plan that was found with an internal cost threshold. If the cost of the plan that was found is cheaper than this internal threshold, the SQL Database Engine will stop further optimizations and use the plan found by the Transaction Processing phase.

The Quick Plan phase

This is phase one and is used if the plan found by the Transaction Processing phase is still more expensive than the internal threshold. This phase expands the search for a good-enough plan to cover rule-based join reordering and spools that may benefit moderately complex queries. To determine if a good-enough plan has been found, since the Query Optimizer generates each potential query plan, it compares the cost of the plan that was just evaluated with the estimated cost of continuing to search for better plan alternatives. This effectively establishes a timeout so that we don't spend more time optimizing the query than we would spend executing the current plan. If a plan has been found with a cost lower than the cost threshold for the Quick Plan phase and lower than the timeout, optimization is stopped, and that good-enough plan is used. This avoids incurring additional compilation costs.

> **Note**
>
> This timeout is not a fixed number, but rather a non-linear value that is related to the complexity of the incoming T-SQL statement. Complexity is translated into cost, so the higher the cost of the query plan, the higher the threshold will be for that plan.

If the plan cost that the Quick Plan phase found is greater than the server configuration for **Cost Threshold for Parallelism** and the server is a multi-processor machine, then parallelism is considered. However, if the plan cost from the Quick Plan phase is less than the configured **Cost Threshold for Parallelism**, only serial plans are considered going forward.

> **Note**
>
> Even if a parallel plan is produced, this doesn't mean the query plan will be executed on multiple processors. If existing processors are too busy to withstand running a query on multiple CPUs – technically meaning that there aren't enough available schedulers – then the plan will be executed on a single processor. If the **Max Degree of Parallelism** server configuration is set to 1, parallelism is not considered at all in the optimization process.

The Full Optimization phase

This is phase two and is used for complex queries, where the plan produced by phase one is still considered more expensive than the cost of searching for more alternative plans – the timeout defined previously. All internal transformation rules are available for use at this point but scoped to the search space defined in the preparation tasks, and parallelism is also considered.

The Full Optimization phase can go through a comprehensive set of optimization alternatives, which can make it time-consuming, especially if a query plan was not found in any preceding phase – because phase two must produce a plan.

The timeout defined in the Quick Plan section is the only condition that limits searching for a good-enough plan during Full Optimization. If a query plan was found before the timeout is hit, the execution plan will store information under the **Reason For Early Termination Of Statement Optimization** property about the outcome of the optimization stage, in this case showing a value of **Good Enough Plan Found**.

If the timeout is hit, the Query Optimizer will fall back on the lowest cost plan found so far. The execution plan will still store information under the **Reason For Early Termination Of Statement Optimization** property, in this case showing a value of **Time Out**.

This property can be seen in the following example of a query executed in the `AdventureWorks` sample database:

```
SELECT pp.FirstName, pp.LastName, pa.AddressLine1, pa.City,
pa.PostalCode
FROM Person.Address AS pa
INNER JOIN Person.BusinessEntityAddress AS pbea ON pa.AddressID =
pbea.AddressID
INNER JOIN Person.Person AS pp ON pbea.BusinessEntityID =
pp.BusinessEntityID
WHERE pa.AddressID = 100;
```

See the following screenshot of the **Reason For Early Termination Of Statement Optimization** property:

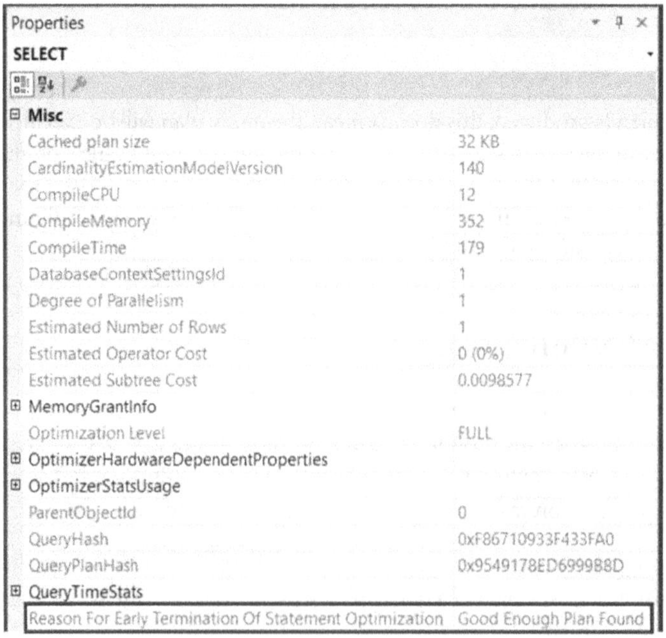

Figure 2.7: The Properties window for the example query showing the Reason For Early Termination of Statement Optimization property

The following figure shows the query optimization workflow that has been described in this chapter:

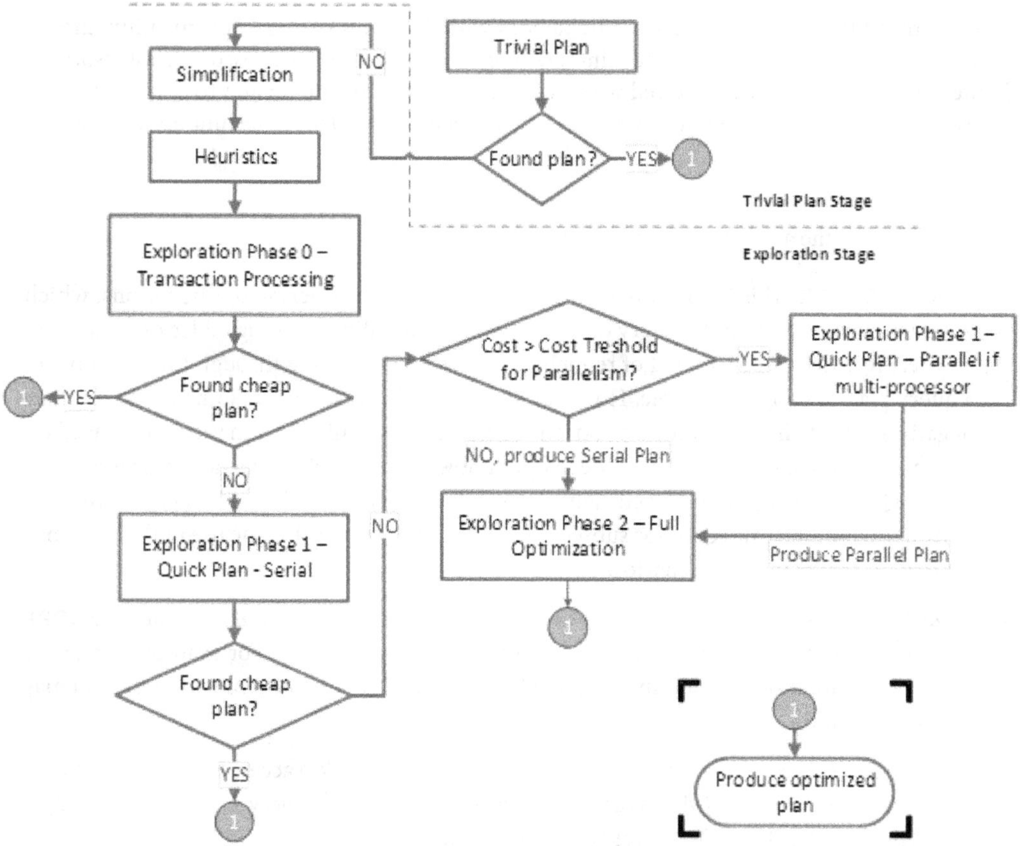

Figure 2.8: Flowchart illustrating the query optimization workflow

For reference, the undocumented dynamic management view, **sys.dm_exec_query_optimizer_info**, exposes some interesting statistics gathered by Query Optimizer, such as the number of optimizations that have been evaluated, as well as the drill-down of optimizations per stage, or the number of optimization-affecting hints have been used.

Knobs for query optimization

As advanced as the query optimization process is, inefficient plans are still a possibility, which is why a database developer can use hints in the T-SQL statement and guide the Query Optimizer toward producing an intended plan. There are several classes of thoroughly documented query hints that affect query optimization, and it is important to call out a few that can be useful when troubleshooting a query performance issue, some of which we will use in upcoming chapters.

> **Note**
>
> Keep in mind that hints force certain behaviors with T-SQL statement optimization and execution. Microsoft recommends that hints are thoroughly tested and only used as a last resort. Hinted statements must be reviewed with every upgrade to a major version to determine if they are still needed since new versions may change behavior, rendering the hint unnecessary or even harmful.

Let's look at some of the available hints for the Query Optimizer:

- FORCE ORDER: This is a hint that will prevent any join reordering optimizations, which has a tangible impact on the query optimization process. When joining tables or views, join reordering is driven by the goal of reducing the row count flowing through the operators in a query plan as early as possible. However, there are edge cases where join reordering may negatively affect the search for a good-enough plan, especially if estimations are based on skewed or outdated statistics. If the developer knows that the join order, as it was written in the T-SQL statement, should be efficient enough, because the smaller tables are already used upfront to limit the row count for subsequent table joins, then testing the use of this hint may yield good results in such scenarios.

- MAXDOP: This is the hint for overriding system-wide **Max Degree of Parallelism** (MAXDOP). Depending on its setting, this hint can affect parallel plan eligibility. For example, if a query has excessive waits on parallelism, using the MAXDOP hint to lower or remove parallelism may be a valid option.

- NOEXPAND: This is a hint that directs the Query Optimizer to skip access to underlying tables when evaluating an indexed view as a possible substitute for part of a query. When the NOEXPAND hint is present, the Query Optimizer will use the view as if it were a table with a clustered index, including automatically creating statistics if needed. For example, if a query uses an indexed view that is being expanded by the Query Optimizer and results in an inefficient query plan, a developer can include the NOEXPAND hint to make the Query Optimizer forcibly evaluate the use of an index on a view. Note that Azure SQL Database, while sharing the same Database Engine code, doesn't require this hint to automatically use indexed views.

- USE HINT: This hint is not a single hint like the other query hints, but rather a new class of hints introduced in SQL Server 2016. Its goal is to provide knobs to purposefully guide the Query Optimizer and query execution toward an intended outcome set by the developer. Every version of SQL Server since 2016 has introduced new USE HINT hints, and the list of supported hints can be accessed using the **sys.dm_exec_valid_use_hints** dynamic management view. Hints that are included here can change some of the Query Optimizer model assumptions, disable certain default behaviors, or even force the entire Query Optimizer to behave as it would under a given database compatibility level. There are many uses for these hints, depending on the query performance troubleshooting scenario that database professionals may face; we will look into some of these in upcoming chapters. In *Chapter 12, Managing optimizer changes*, we will also cover another feature which uses such hints.

Now, let's summarize this chapter.

Summary

In this chapter, we explored the internals of the SQL Database Engine's query optimization process and defined many important concepts that any database professional writing T-SQL queries will keep coming back to, especially when troubleshooting query performance issues. The CE is a fundamental part of the SQL Database Engine's Query Optimizer: knowing how it uses statistics and the importance of keeping updated and relevant statistics for the overall query optimization process empowers database professionals to write good queries – queries that both drive and leverage good database schema designs. But also, understanding the main estimation model assumptions allows us to account for these when writing queries and avoid pitfalls that hurt query performance. We will see these pitfalls in much more detail in *Chapter 5, Writing Elegant T-SQL Queries*, and *Chapter 6, Discovering T-SQL Anti-Patterns in Depth*.

If, at the end of the optimization process, we still have a perceived inefficient plan, then some avenues of investigation are possible to determine what were the potential reasons for this inefficiency:

- Is it bad cardinality estimation? Analyze the execution plan to find the ratio between estimated and actual rows in costly operators. Perhaps statistics are stalled and need to be updated.

- Is it a parameter-sensitive plan? Is it a dynamic un-parameterized T-SQL statement? Or perhaps parameter-sniffing has caused a skewed query plan? The importance of parameters was discussed in *Chapter 1, Understanding Query Processing*, in the *The importance of parameters* section.

- Is it an inadequate physical database design? Are there missing indexes? Are data types for keys not adequate and leading to unwarranted conversions that affect estimations? Is referential integrity enforced by triggers instead of indexed foreign keys?

These are some of the aspects we must investigate regarding the potential source of plan inefficiency. In the next chapter, *Chapter 3, Exploring Query Execution Plans*, we will learn how to identify these inefficiencies by investigating the various aspects of query execution plans.

Part 2:
Dos and Don'ts of T-SQL

This part serves as an introduction to query execution plans and how to leverage them for query troubleshooting. It also covers basic guidelines for writing efficient queries, and common T-SQL query patterns and anti-patterns.

This part has the following chapters:

- *Chapter 3, Exploring Query Execution Plans*
- *Chapter 4, Indexing for T-SQL Performance*
- *Chapter 5, Writing Elegant T-SQL Queries*
- *Chapter 6, Discovering T-SQL Anti-Patterns in Depth*

3

Exploring Query Execution Plans

In the previous chapters, we learned how to construct a **Transact-SQL (T-SQL)** query, how the SQL Database Engine processes a query, and how the query is optimized, which results in an execution plan that can be cached and reused by subsequent query executions. Now that we understand the steps the SQL Database Engine follows to produce a plan and execute a query, we can investigate an execution plan to examine the results of this process and begin analyzing how we can improve the performance of our queries.

In this chapter, we're going to cover the following main topics:

- What is a query plan?
- Accessing a query plan
- Navigating a query plan
- Query plan operators of interest
- Query plan properties of interest

Technical requirements

The examples used in this chapter are designed for use on SQL Server 2022 and Azure SQL Database, but they should work on any version of SQL Server, 2012 or later. The Developer Edition of SQL Server is free for development environments and can be used to run all the code samples. There is also a free tier of Azure SQL Database that you can use for testing at `https://aka.ms/freedb`.

You will need the `AdventureWorks2016_EXT` (referred to as `AdventureWorks`) and `AdventureWorksDW2016_EXT` (referred to as `AdventureWorksDW`) sample databases, which can be found on GitHub at `https://github.com/Microsoft/sql-server-samples/releases/tag/adventureworks`. Code samples for this chapter can also be found on GitHub at `https://github.com/PacktPublishing/Learn-T-SQL-Querying-Second-Edition/tree/main/ch3`.

What is a query plan?

Think of a query execution plan as a map that provides information on the physical operators that implement the logical operations discussed in the *Understanding Query Processing* chapter, as well as the execution context for that query that provides information about the system on which the query was executed. Each physical operator is identified in the plan with a unique node ID.

> **Note**
> Query execution plans are often referred to as a showplan, which is a textual, XML, or graphical representation of the plan.

So far, we've used the terms *query plan* and *query execution plan* interchangeably. However, in the SQL Database Engine, there is the notion of an "actual plan" and an "estimated plan." These differ only in the fact that an "actual plan" has runtime data collected during actual execution (hence, query execution plan), whereas an "estimated plan" is the output of the Query Optimizer that is put in the plan cache (hence, query plan, without the *execution* moniker).

> **Note**
> Going forward, we will refer to plans in a more precise fashion, depending on whether these have runtime data or not.

The "estimated plan," known simply as a query plan, includes the following:

- Methods used to retrieve data from a table or indexed view
- Sequence of data retrieval operations
- Order in which tables or indexed views are joined: refer to the *Mechanics of the Query Optimizer* chapter, where we discussed join reordering
- Use of temporary structures in `tempdb` (worktables and workfiles)
- Estimated row counts, iterations, and costs from each step
- How data is aggregated

Additionally, an "actual plan," also known as a query execution plan, includes the following:

- Use of parallelism

- Actual row counts and iterations

- Query execution warnings

- Query execution metrics such as elapsed time, CPU time, presence of trace flags, memory usage, version of the **Cardinality Estimator** (**CE**), top waits, and more

> **Note**
> Whether all this information is available or just a subset depends on the version of the SQL Database Engine on which the query execution plan was captured.

So, analyzing a query execution plan is a skill that allows database professionals to identify the following:

- High-cost operations in a single query or batch

- Indexing needs, for example, identifying when a scan is better than a seek or vice versa

- Outdated statistics that no longer accurately portray underlying data distributions

- Unexpected large row counts being passed from operator to operator

- Query or schema modification needs, for example, when a query references multiple levels of nested views: views that reference views that reference views that reference common tables at all levels

With this skill, developers and query writers in general can visually analyze how the queries they write actually perform beyond simply looking at elapsed time. For **database administrators** (**DBAs**) and database reliability engineers, this skill allows them to identify heavy hitters running in the SQL Database Engine that perhaps weren't a problem during development time, analyze queries, and provide mitigations based on query execution plan analysis.

Accessing a query plan

To access estimated plans, which are a direct result of the optimization process, we can use either T-SQL commands or graphical tools. For the examples shown in this chapter, we use **SQL Server Management Studio** (**SSMS**).

> **Note**
>
> For most users, query plans in text format are harder to read and analyze; therefore, we will use graphical query plan examples throughout the book.
>
> The SET command options SHOWPLAN_TEXT, SHOWPLAN_ALL, and SHOWPLAN_XML provide text-based information on query plans with different degrees of detail. Using any of these commands means the SQL Database Engine will not execute the T-SQL statements but show the query plan as produced by the Query Optimizer.

Take an example of a query that can be executed in the scope of the AdventureWorks sample database:

```
SELECT pp.FirstName, pp.LastName, pa.AddressLine1, pa.City,
pa.PostalCode
FROM Person.Address AS pa
INNER JOIN Person.BusinessEntityAddress AS pbea ON pa.AddressID =
pbea.AddressID
INNER JOIN Person.Person AS pp ON pbea.BusinessEntityID =
pp.BusinessEntityID
WHERE pa.AddressID = 100;
```

Let's see what each of the following options provides in terms of the query plan view:

- SHOWPLAN_TEXT: This option shows all the steps involved in processing the query, including the type of join that was used, the order in which tables are accessed, and the indexes used for each table:

Stmt Text
|--Nested Loops(Inner Join)
   |--Clustered Index Seek(OBJECT:([AdventureWorks2016_EXT].[Person].[Address].[PK_Address_AddressID] AS [pa]), SEEK:([pa].[AddressID]=(100)) ORDERED FORW...
   |--Nested Loops(Inner Join, OUTER REFERENCES:([pbea].[BusinessEntityID]))
      |--Index Seek(OBJECT:([AdventureWorks2016_EXT].[Person].[BusinessEntityAddress].[IX_BusinessEntityAddress_AddressID] AS [pbea]), SEEK:([pbea].[AddressID]=...
      |--Clustered Index Seek(OBJECT:([AdventureWorks2016_EXT].[Person].[Person].[PK_Person_BusinessEntityID] AS [pp]), SEEK:([pp].[BusinessEntityID]=[Adventure...

Figure 3.1: Showplan in text format with all the plan operators

- SHOWPLAN_ALL: This option shows the same estimated plan as SHOWPLAN_TEXT – a text output tree – but adds details on each of the physical operations that would be executed, such as the estimated size of the result rows, the estimated CPU time, and the total cost estimations. Notice the amount of information produced here:

Stmt Text	Stmt Id	Node Id	Parent	PhysicalOp	LogicalOp
SELECT pp.FirstName, pp.LastName, pa.AddressLine...	1	1	0	NULL	NULL
I--Nested Loops(Inner Join)	1	2	1	Nested Loops	Inner Join
I--Clustered Index Seek(OBJECT:([AdventureWor...	1	3	2	Clustered Index Seek	Clustered Index Seek
I--Nested Loops(Inner Join, OUTER REFERENCE...	1	4	2	Nested Loops	Inner Join
I--Index Seek(OBJECT:([AdventureWorks2016...	1	5	4	Index Seek	Index Seek
I--Clustered Index Seek(OBJECT:([Adventure...	1	6	4	Clustered Index Seek	Clustered Index Seek

Argument	DefinedValues	EstimateRows	EstimateIO
1	NULL	1	NULL
NULL	NULL	1	0
OBJECT:([AdventureWorks2016CTP3].[Person].[Address].....	[pa].[AddressLine1], [pa].[City], [pa].[PostalCo...	1	0.003125
OUTER REFERENCES:([pbea].[BusinessEntityID])	NULL	1	0
OBJECT:([AdventureWorks2016CTP3].[Person].[Business...	[pbea].[BusinessEntityID]	1	0.003125
OBJECT:([AdventureWorks2016CTP3].[Person].[Person].[...	[pp].[FirstName], [pp].[LastName]	1	0.003125

EstimateCPU	AvgRowSize	TotalSubtreeCost	Output List	Warnings	Type	Parallel	EstimateExecutions
NULL	NULL	0.00985766	NULL	NULL	SELECT	0	NULL
4.18E-06	224	0.00985766	[pa].[AddressLine1], [pa].[City], [pa].[PostalCo...	NULL	PLAN_ROW	0	1
0.0001581	120	0.0032831	[pa].[AddressLine1], [pa].[City], [pa].[PostalCo...	NULL	PLAN_ROW	0	1
4.18E-06	113	0.00657038	[pp].[FirstName], [pp].[LastName]	NULL	PLAN_ROW	0	1
0.0001581	11	0.0032831	[pbea].[BusinessEntityID]	NULL	PLAN_ROW	0	1
0.0001581	113	0.0032831	[pp].[FirstName], [pp].[LastName]	NULL	PLAN_ROW	0	1

Figure 3.2: Showplan in tabular format with all the plan operators

- SHOWPLAN_XML: This option produces the same estimated plan but as an XML output tree:

Microsoft SQL Server 2005 XML Showplan

`<ShowPlanXML xmlns="http://schemas.microsoft.com/sqlserver/2004/07/showplan" Version="1.481" Build="14.0.3045.14"><BatchSequence><Batch><Statemen...`

Figure 3.3: Showplan as clickable XML link

Because it is generated as a link when used in SSMS, it can be interpreted by SSMS as a graphical "estimated plan," and clicking the link will display this graphical plan:

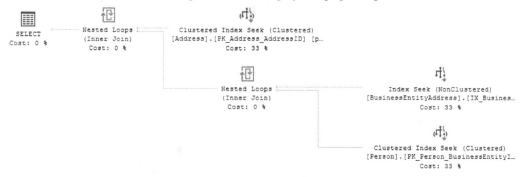

Figure 3.4: Graphical showplan rendered by SSMS

Notice that because it is an estimated plan, the arrows are all the same width. This is because there's no actual data movement between operators given that this plan was not executed. To access all the properties returned by SHOWPLAN_ALL, plus many more, right-click the SELECT operator and click on **Properties**. We will see these properties in greater detail in the *Query plan properties of interest* section.

SHOWPLAN_XML is the option used by SSMS when the **Display Estimated Execution Plan (Ctrl+L)** button is clicked:

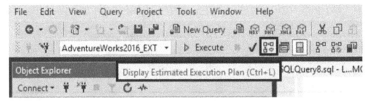

Figure 3.5: SSMS button to enable SHOWPLAN_XML

To access actual plans, which are optimized plans after being executed, we can again use either T-SQL commands or graphical tools. The STATISTICS PROFILE and STATISTICS XML commands provide text-based information on query plans with different degrees of detail. Using either of these commands means the SQL Database Engine will execute the T-SQL statements and generate an actual plan or a query execution plan.

- STATISTICS PROFILE shows the same plan as SHOWPLAN_ALL, incremented with actual rows, and executes to display an actual plan or a query execution plan:

Rows	Executes	Stmt Text	Stmt Id	Node Id	Parent	PhysicalOp	LogicalOp
1	1	SELECT pp.FirstName, pp.LastName, pa.AddressLine...	1	1	0	NULL	NULL
1	1	|--Nested Loops(Inner Join)	1	2	1	Nested Loops	Inner Join
1	1	|--Clustered Index Seek(OBJECT:([AdventureWor...	1	3	2	Clustered Index Seek	Clustered Index Seek
1	1	|--Nested Loops(Inner Join, OUTER REFERENC...	1	4	2	Nested Loops	Inner Join
1	1	|--Index Seek(OBJECT:([AdventureWorks2016...	1	5	4	Index Seek	Index Seek
1	1	|--Clustered Index Seek(OBJECT:([Adventure...	1	6	4	Clustered Index Seek	Clustered Index Seek

Argument	DefinedValues	EstimateRows	EstimateIO
NULL	NULL	1	NULL
NULL	NULL	1	0
OBJECT:([AdventureWorks2016CTP3].[Person].[Addre...	[pa].[AddressLine1], [pa].[City], [pa].[PostalCo...	1	0.003125
OUTER REFERENCES:([pbea].[BusinessEntityID])	NULL	1	0
OBJECT:([AdventureWorks2016CTP3].[Person].[Busin...	[pbea].[BusinessEntityID]	1	0.003125
OBJECT:([AdventureWorks2016CTP3].[Person].[Perso...	[pp].[FirstName], [pp].[LastName]	1	0.003125

EstimateCPU	AvgRowSize	TotalSubtreeCost	OutputList	Warnings	Type	Parallel	EstimateExecutions
NULL	NULL	0.00985766	NULL	NULL	SELECT	0	NULL
4.18E-06	224	0.00985766	[pa].[AddressLine1], [pa].[City], [pa].[PostalCo...	NULL	PLAN_ROW	0	1
0.0001581	120	0.0032831	[pa].[AddressLine1], [pa].[City], [pa].[PostalCo...	NULL	PLAN_ROW	0	1
4.18E-06	113	0.00657038	[pp].[FirstName], [pp].[LastName]	NULL	PLAN_ROW	0	1
0.0001581	11	0.0032831	[pbea].[BusinessEntityID]	NULL	PLAN_ROW	0	1
0.0001581	113	0.0032831	[pp].[FirstName], [pp].[LastName]	NULL	PLAN_ROW	0	1

Figure 3.6: STATISTICS PROFILE enables SHOWPLAN_ALL

- **STATISTICS XML**: This option is the "actual plan" counterpart of SHOWPLAN_XML. Next, we see what appears to be the same output as SHOWPLAN_XML:

Microsoft SQL Server 2005 XML Showplan

`<ShowPlanXML xmlns="http://schemas.microsoft.com/sqlserver/2004/07/showplan" Version="1.481" Build="14.0.3045.14"><BatchSequence><Batch><Statemen...`

Figure 3.7: Showplan as a clickable XML link

However, by expanding the XML (or if using SSMS, by clicking on the link), we see we have the "actual plan" or the query execution plan:

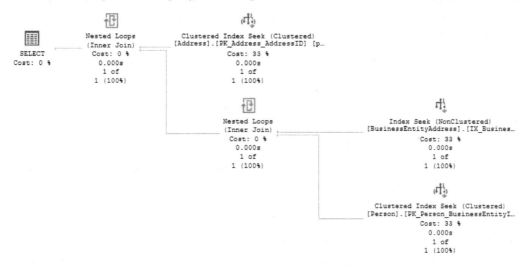

Figure 3.8: Graphical showplan rendered by SSMS

STATISTICS XML is the option used by SSMS when the **Include Actual Execution Plan (Ctrl+M)** button is clicked:

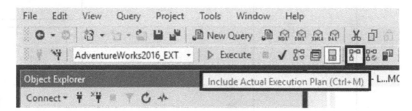

Figure 3.9: SSMS button to enable STATISTICS XML

To access all the properties already seen with SHOWPLAN_XML incremented with runtime statistics and warnings (if any), right-click the SELECT operator and click on **Properties**. Again, we will see these properties in greater detail in the *Query plan properties of interest* section.

Navigating a query plan

Up until this point, we have mentioned query execution plans, and even shown simple examples to illustrate some points during the *Mechanics of the Query Optimizer* chapter. However, it is important for any database professional to understand how to read and analyze a query execution plan as a way to visually identify positive changes in a plan shape. The remaining chapters in the book will show query execution plans in more detail for different scenarios of T-SQL patterns and anti-patterns.

Query plans are like trees, where each join branch can represent an entirely separate query. To understand how to navigate a showplan or query plan, let's use a practical example of a query executed in the AdventureWorks sample database:

```
SELECT p.Title + ' ' + p.FirstName + ' ' + p.LastName AS FullName,
c.AccountNumber, s.Name AS StoreName
FROM Person.Person p
INNER JOIN Sales.Customer c ON c.PersonID = p.BusinessEntityID
INNER JOIN Sales.Store s ON s.BusinessEntityID = c.StoreID
WHERE p.LastName = 'Koski';
```

This query generates the execution plan seen in the following screenshot. For any graphical query execution plan, the flow of data is read from right to left and top to bottom:

- Result sets 1 and 2 are joined using a Nested Loops join, creating result set 3

- Then, result sets 3 and 4 are joined using a Hash Match join, creating result set 5

- Finally, result sets 5 and 6 are joined using a Nested Loops join, creating a result set for the SELECT clause:

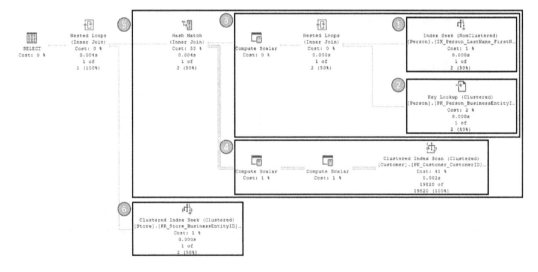

Figure 3.10: Graphical showplan with several result sets

In an actual plan, the width of the arrows provides an indication of the number of rows flowing through each operator, such as the thicker arrow seen coming from `Clustered Index Scan` on the `Customer` table (as seen in the following region of the preceding plan). This can often be a clue to high resource usage and a potential hotspot in the plan:

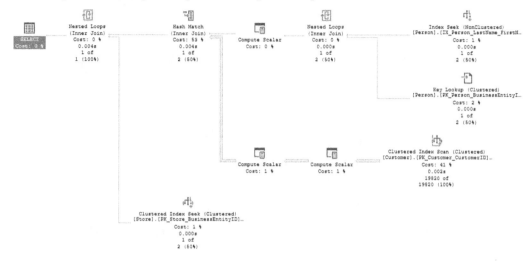

Figure 3.11: Detail of the actual plan

Also, notice how in the latest versions of SSMS, it becomes easier to distinguish an actual plan from an estimated plan. In an actual plan or query execution plan, each operator has information about the elapsed execution time and a comparison of the estimated and actual number of rows flowing through the operator. In the previous `Clustered Index Scan` instance, we see this operator read 19,820 rows of 19,820 estimated rows, with a 100 percent match and a perfect estimation.

> **Tip**
> Recent versions of SSMS have greatly improved the navigation experience of a graphical query plan: Click + hold the mouse button anywhere inside the **Execution Plan** tab, and then drag the mouse to quickly navigate the query plan. Or, use *Ctrl* + the mouse wheel to zoom in and out easily.

For joins, how the showplan is read depends on the type of physical join: the top represents the outer table for `Nested Loops` and the build table for a Hash; the bottom represents the inner table for `Nested Loops` and the probe table for the Hash. Result sets are created from each join pair, which are then passed to the next join. We will further discuss join types, seeks, lookups, and other operators later in this chapter under the *Query plan operators of interest* section.

The following screenshot shows a Nested Loops join with an Index Seek operator on the Person table as the outer table, and a Key Lookup operator on the Person table as the inner table:

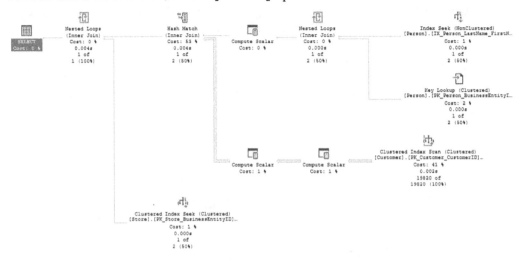

Figure 3.12: Nested Loops join with different operators as the inner and outer sides of the join

In the preceding Index Seek operator, we see this operator read 1 row of 2 estimated rows, with a 50 percent match and a skewed estimation.

> **Tip**
>
> If the difference between estimated rows and actual rows is large, one or several orders of magnitude, for example, this means that the Query Optimizer may not have had good statistics on the table's data distribution during query optimization. Usually, the first reaction to such a scenario is to update the relevant statistics on the table and verify whether estimations improved to be a near 100 percent match.

For any plan captured as text (actual or estimated), note that these are read top to bottom, with the "| --" characters indicating the nesting levels of the tree. For the same query we used to generate the graphical plan, STATISTICS PROFILE shows the following query tree:

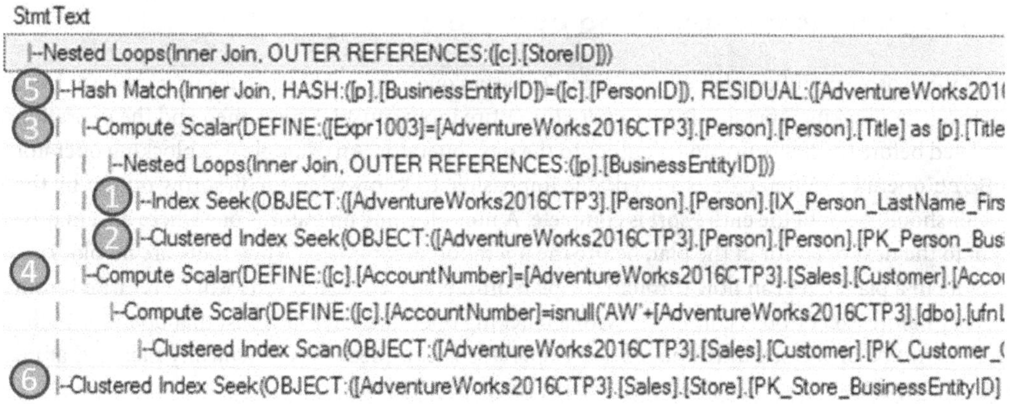

Stmt Text

```
|--Nested Loops(Inner Join, OUTER REFERENCES:([c].[StoreID]))
 ⑤ |--Hash Match(Inner Join, HASH:([p].[BusinessEntityID])=([c].[PersonID]), RESIDUAL:([AdventureWorks201(
 ③ |   |--Compute Scalar(DEFINE:([Expr1003]=[AdventureWorks2016CTP3].[Person].[Person].[Title] as [p].[Title
   |   |   |--Nested Loops(Inner Join, OUTER REFERENCES:([p].[BusinessEntityID]))
   |   ① |--Index Seek(OBJECT:([AdventureWorks2016CTP3].[Person].[Person].[IX_Person_LastName_Firs
   |   ② |--Clustered Index Seek(OBJECT:([AdventureWorks2016CTP3].[Person].[Person].[PK_Person_Bus
 ④ |   |--Compute Scalar(DEFINE:([c].[AccountNumber]=[AdventureWorks2016CTP3].[Sales].[Customer].[Acco(
   |       |--Compute Scalar(DEFINE:([c].[AccountNumber]=isnull('AW'+[AdventureWorks2016CTP3].[dbo].[ufn(
   |           |--Clustered Index Scan(OBJECT:([AdventureWorks2016CTP3].[Sales].[Customer].[PK_Customer_(
 ⑥ |--Clustered Index Seek(OBJECT:([AdventureWorks2016CTP3].[Sales].[Store].[PK_Store_BusinessEntityID]
```

Figure 3.13: Reading order for showplan in text format

For this query's plan, we apply the same approach to read the plan:

- Result sets 1 and 2 are joined using a Nested Loops join, creating result set 3

- Then, result sets 3 and 4 are joined using a Hash Match join, creating result set 5

- Finally, result sets 5 and 6 are joined using a Nested Loops join

Next, we will cover some query plan operators that are important to understand to write scalable T-SQL queries.

Query plan operators of interest

The different icons that are visible in a query execution plan are called operators. Logical operators describe a relational operation – for example, an INNER JOIN operation. Physical operators implement the logical operation with a specific algorithm. So, when we examine a query plan, we are looking at physical operators.

Each physical operator represents a task that needs to be performed to complete the query such as accessing data with a seek or a scan, joining data with a Hash Match join or a Nested Loops join, and sorting data. Some operators are especially relevant to understand while writing T-SQL that scales well. We will look at these operators, understand what they do and how they implement the physical operation behind the logical operation in T-SQL statements, and become familiar with aspects that will be important in the upcoming chapters where we explore T-SQL patterns and anti-patterns.

Blocking versus non-blocking operators

We can think of an execution plan as a pipeline. Data from one operator flows to the next operator from right to left. A blocking operator is one where the entire input must be consumed and the operation completed before the first row can be output to the next operator. An example of a blocking operator is a `Sort` operator. When data is sorted, it is impossible to know what the first row output by the operator should be until the entire sort is complete. A non-blocking operator is one where data may be output to the next operator in the plan before the operation is complete. When there are no blocking operators in a plan, data can flow through the plan uninterrupted, and results will be returned from the query before execution is complete. With a blocking operator, anything past that operator in the query cannot be processed until the blocking operator is complete, which typically means that no results will be returned to the client until the entire query is complete.

Data access operators

Data access operators are used to retrieve data from tables and indexes in the SQL Database Engine. A rowstore is the traditional storage mechanism for most **relational database management systems (RDBMSs)**. In a rowstore index, each page of data contains all the columns for one or more rows of data in the table, and so the entire row is stored contiguously across all columns. There are two types of rowstore indexes in the SQL Database Engine – clustered and non-clustered. Both index types are stored as a **B+ tree** data structure, but clustered indexes contain the entire data row at the leaf level while non-clustered indexes contain only the index columns and a pointer to the data row.

> **Note**
>
> Instead of treating all nodes equally like a B-Tree, the B+Tree structure has two types of nodes. The lowest-level nodes, also called leaf nodes, hold the actual data. All other nodes, including the root node, only hold key values and pointers to the next nodes. B+Trees are self-balancing tree data structures that tend to be wide rather than tall, although the specific structure depends on the definition of the index. We will discuss index structures in more detail later in this section.

There are two different ways to access data in an index – a seek or a scan. A seek is used when a predicate present in the query matches the key(s) of an index. In this case, SQL Database Engine can use the values of the predicate to limit the amount of data that must be searched by following the pointers within the index from the root to the leaf page to locate matching rows.

As mentioned previously, this applies to both clustered and non-clustered indexes; the only difference is that with a clustered index, the leaf level contains the actual data pages, while a non-clustered index contains index pages with pointers to the data pages. We will explore this data access operator in greater detail in *Chapter 4, Indexing for T-SQL Performance*.

During optimization, the SQL Database Engine will decide how to access the data required to satisfy the query based on the columns referenced in the query, the available indexes, and the cost of the different operations using the estimated cardinality as a cost basis. On the surface, it may seem like a scan is more expensive than a seek, but depending on how many rows are returned, it may be more efficient to scan.

As we discussed earlier in the *Mechanics of the Query Optimizer* chapter, the SQL Database Engine uses statistics along with some basic assumptions to estimate cardinality. If the estimation is off by a large amount, the SQL Database Engine may choose an inefficient operator to access the data. If creating appropriate indexes and updating statistics does not correct the issue, it's possible that an incorrect assumption is causing the cardinality estimate to be off. In this case, employing a hint may be the easiest way to improve the query. The following hints are helpful in influencing the Query Optimizer to choose a more efficient data access operator:

- `INDEX (index name)`: This hint forces the SQL Database Engine to use an index that we specify.

- `FORCESEEK (index name (column name))`: This hint forces the SQL Database Engine to perform a seek operation. Optionally, we can specify the index and columns to be used in the seek. It can also be combined with the `INDEX` hint in order to supply an index for the seek without specifying columns.

- `FORCESCAN`: This hint forces the SQL Database Engine to perform a scan operation. It can also be combined with the `INDEX` hint to force a scan of a specific index.

Table Scan

The `Table Scan` operator represents a scan operation on a heap. We will explore heaps in greater detail in *Chapter 4, Indexing for T-SQL Performance*.

`Table Scan` is a non-blocking operator that reads every page of the object and scans them for the desired rows. A heap does not have any order or structure, so the rows will be output in random order. Here is an example of a query executed in the `AdventureWorks` sample database with a `Table Scan` operator:

```
SELECT * FROM DatabaseLog;
```

The query generates the following execution plan:

Figure 3.14: Execution plan for the SELECT * query

While a table scan may generate a large amount of I/O depending on the size of the table, the operator itself does not require a large amount of additional memory or CPU, and the cost is generally based on the cost of the I/O.

Clustered Index Scan

The Clustered Index Scan operator is non-blocking and represents a scan operation on a clustered index. We will explore this index type in greater detail in *Chapter 4, Indexing for T-SQL Performance*.

A clustered index contains the data pages of the table, so this is effectively a table scan. Because the clustered index is organized into a tree structure, the data is logically ordered by the keys of the index. This doesn't necessarily mean the data will be returned in order; if no ORDER BY clause is specified in the query, the data may be returned in random order. If there is an ORDER BY clause in the query that matches the clustered index key or there is some other benefit to outputting the data in order, the SQL Database Engine may choose to do an ordered scan of the clustered index. This is helpful because it may prevent the SQL Database Engine from having to sort the data later, which can be an expensive operation. As with a table scan, the cost of a clustered index scan is generally based on the cost of the I/O generated; there is no additional memory or CPU required. Here is an example of a query executed in the AdventureWorks sample database with a Clustered Index Scan operator:

```
SELECT * FROM Person.Person;
```

The query generates the following execution plan:

```
                              Clustered Index Scan (Clustered)
                              [Person].[PK_Person_BusinessEntityI…
   SELECT                            Cost: 100 %
   Cost: 0 %                            0.284s
                                     19972 of
                                    19972 (100%)
```

Figure 3.15: Execution plan for the SELECT * query

In this case, there was no ORDER BY clause in the query, so the SQL Database Engine performed an unordered scan. We can confirm this by looking at the properties of the operator, either by hovering over the icon with our mouse or by right-clicking it and choosing **Properties** from the pop-up menu, as in the next screenshot:

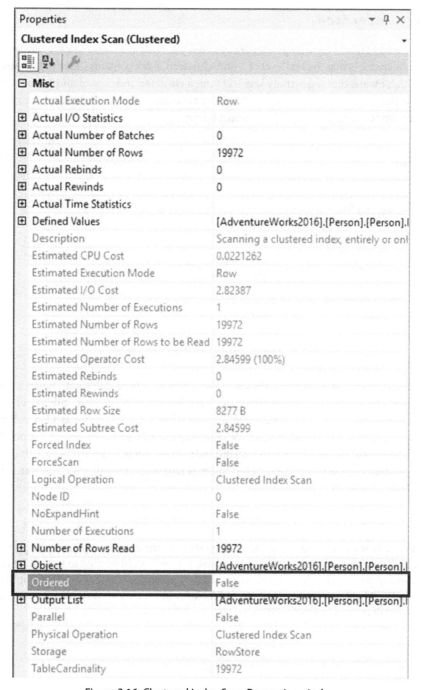

Figure 3.16: Clustered Index Scan Properties window

NonClustered Index Scan

A NonClustered Index Scan operator is effectively the same as a Clustered Index Scan operator. The difference is that the leaf level of a non-clustered index contains index pages rather than data pages, which means this is generally less I/O than a clustered index scan and is not analogous to a table scan. The following is an example of a query executed in the AdventureWorks sample database with a NonClustered Index Scan operator:

```
SELECT LastName, FirstName
FROM Person.Person
WHERE FirstName = N'Andrew';
```

The query generates the following execution plan:

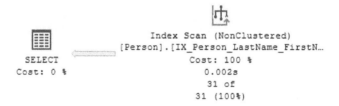

Figure 3.17: Execution plan for the SELECT query

The SQL Database Engine will generally choose to do a non-clustered index scan when an index is present that contains all the columns in the query (also known as a covering index) but does not support the predicate. In this case, the index contains the FirstName column as a key column, but it is the second column in the index, so if we are searching for FirstName only, it cannot be used as a seek predicate in the index. This non-clustered index scan will be slightly cheaper than doing a clustered index scan because the non-clustered index is narrower (meaning it has fewer columns) and will take less I/O to scan.

> **Note**
>
> We may notice that there is a missing index suggestion in the execution plan in the previous example. This is generated when the SQL Database Engine would be able to benefit from an index that is not present. Looking for missing index suggestions is one way to help optimize our queries. We'll be discussing more things to look for in execution plans later in the *Query plan properties of interest* section of this chapter.

NonClustered Index Seek

A NonClustered Index Seek operator represents a seek operation against a non-clustered index. This is also a non-blocking operator, and again is based mainly on the cost of I/O, requiring no additional memory or CPU. An index seek is a quick way to locate rows that match a predicate in the WHERE clause of a query, if the keys of the index match the predicate. The following example shows a query executed in the AdventureWorks sample database with a NonClustered Index Seek operator:

```
SELECT LastName, FirstName
FROM Person.Person
WHERE LastName = N'Maxwell';
```

The query generates the following execution plan:

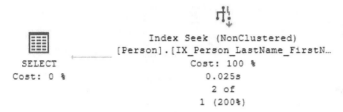

Figure 3.18: Execution plan for the SELECT query

A NonClustered Index Seek operator may also be used to return a contiguous range of rows based on the keys of the index. This is referred to as a range scan. This is different from a non-clustered index scan in that not every row of the index is scanned; the SQL Database Engine uses the values in the predicate to search only the range of matching keys in the index. The only way to know whether an index seek is a singleton seek or a range scan is to look at the properties of the index, as seen in the following screenshot. If the seek predicate is a single value, it's a seek; if the seek predicate is a range of values, it's a range scan:

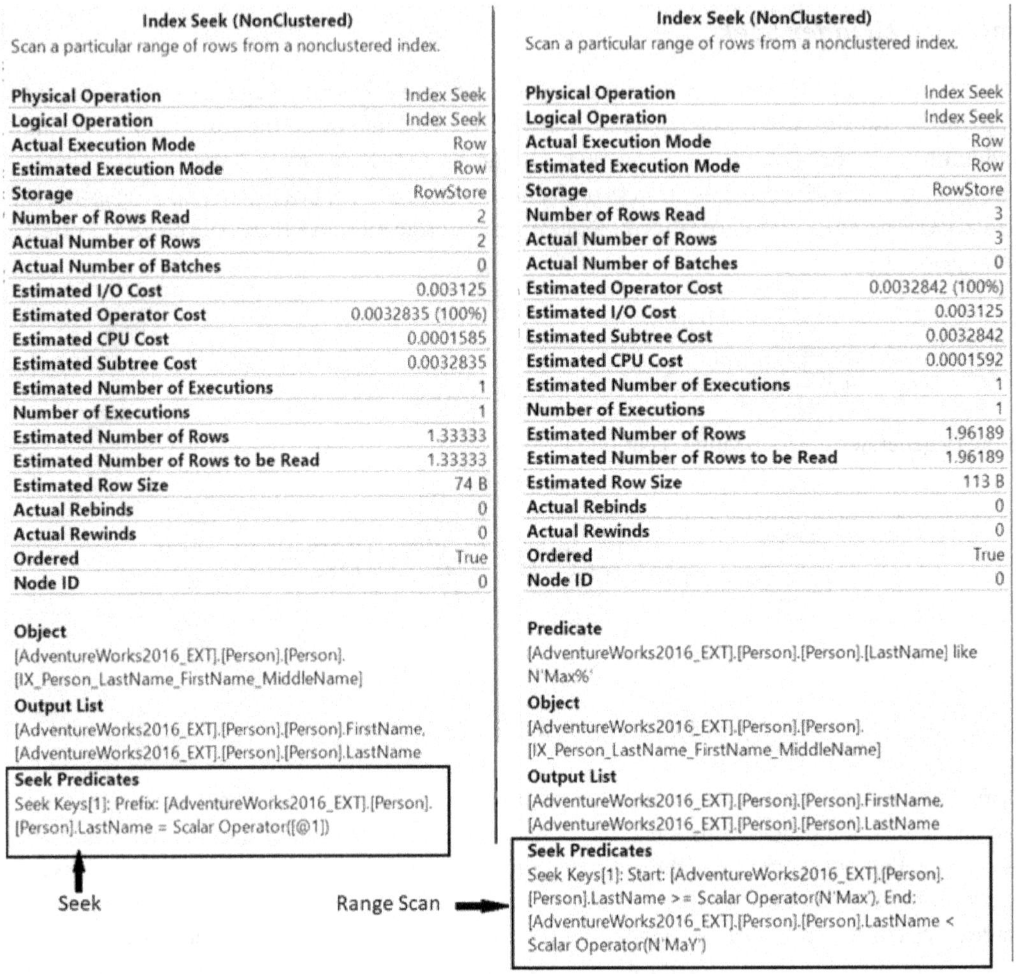

Index Seek (NonClustered)
Scan a particular range of rows from a nonclustered index.

Physical Operation	Index Seek
Logical Operation	Index Seek
Actual Execution Mode	Row
Estimated Execution Mode	Row
Storage	RowStore
Number of Rows Read	2
Actual Number of Rows	2
Actual Number of Batches	0
Estimated I/O Cost	0.003125
Estimated Operator Cost	0.0032835 (100%)
Estimated CPU Cost	0.0001585
Estimated Subtree Cost	0.0032835
Estimated Number of Executions	1
Number of Executions	1
Estimated Number of Rows	1.33333
Estimated Number of Rows to be Read	1.33333
Estimated Row Size	74 B
Actual Rebinds	0
Actual Rewinds	0
Ordered	True
Node ID	0

Object
[AdventureWorks2016_EXT].[Person].[Person].
[IX_Person_LastName_FirstName_MiddleName]

Output List
[AdventureWorks2016_EXT].[Person].[Person].FirstName,
[AdventureWorks2016_EXT].[Person].[Person].LastName

Seek Predicates
Seek Keys[1]: Prefix: [AdventureWorks2016_EXT].[Person].
[Person].LastName = Scalar Operator([@1])

↑
Seek

Index Seek (NonClustered)
Scan a particular range of rows from a nonclustered index.

Physical Operation	Index Seek
Logical Operation	Index Seek
Actual Execution Mode	Row
Estimated Execution Mode	Row
Storage	RowStore
Number of Rows Read	3
Actual Number of Rows	3
Actual Number of Batches	0
Estimated Operator Cost	0.0032842 (100%)
Estimated I/O Cost	0.003125
Estimated Subtree Cost	0.0032842
Estimated CPU Cost	0.0001592
Estimated Number of Executions	1
Number of Executions	1
Estimated Number of Rows	1.96189
Estimated Number of Rows to be Read	1.96189
Estimated Row Size	113 B
Actual Rebinds	0
Actual Rewinds	0
Ordered	True
Node ID	0

Predicate
[AdventureWorks2016_EXT].[Person].[Person].[LastName] like
N'Max%'

Object
[AdventureWorks2016_EXT].[Person].[Person].
[IX_Person_LastName_FirstName_MiddleName]

Output List
[AdventureWorks2016_EXT].[Person].[Person].FirstName,
[AdventureWorks2016_EXT].[Person].[Person].LastName

Seek Predicates
Seek Keys[1]: Start: [AdventureWorks2016_EXT].[Person].
[Person].LastName >= Scalar Operator(N'Max'), End:
[AdventureWorks2016_EXT].[Person].[Person].LastName <
Scalar Operator(N'MaY')

Range Scan ━▶

Figure 3.19: NonClustered Index Seek properties' detail for lookup versus range scan operations

Clustered Index Seek

A `Clustered Index Seek` operator represents a seek operation against a clustered index. This is essentially the same as a `NonClustered Index Seek` operator, except that the leaf level contains data pages, so the entire row can be output in addition to the index columns. The following example shows a query executed in the `AdventureWorks` sample database with a `Clustered Index Seek` operator:

```
SELECT LastName, FirstName
FROM Person.Person
WHERE BusinessEntityID = 5;
```

The query generates the following execution plan:

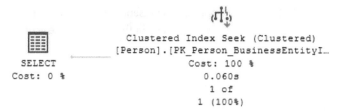

Clustered Index Seek (Clustered)
[Person].[PK_Person_BusinessEntityI...
Cost: 100 %
0.060s
1 of
1 (100%)

SELECT
Cost: 0 %

Figure 3.20: Execution plan for the SELECT query

Lookups

When a non-clustered index is used to locate rows, only the index columns are present at the leaf level of the index. If there are additional columns required from the underlying data pages because they are referenced in the SELECT list or elsewhere in the query, an additional step is required to retrieve this data. The leaf level of the non-clustered index contains a pointer to the data row that must be followed in order to retrieve the rest of the data in the row. This operation is called a lookup.

The format of the pointer in the non-clustered index depends on the underlying table storage. For heaps, we store a row ID, which is made up of the file ID, page ID, and slot ID (a slot is where the row is stored on the page) of the row. For clustered indexes, we can leverage the B+ Tree structure of the index to find the row instead, so the key of the clustered index is stored in the non-clustered indexes. Because of this difference, there are two different types of lookup operations: key lookups and **row ID (RID)** lookups. If the underlying table is stored as a heap, a RID lookup is used. If the underlying table is stored as a clustered index, a key lookup is used (note that a key lookup is simply a clustered index seek under the covers).

> **Note**
>
> If you've been working with the SQL Database Engine for a while, you may remember lookups being referred to as "bookmark lookups". This is what they were called in SQL Server 2000. A bookmark lookup refers to lookups in general but doesn't distinguish between a key lookup and an RID lookup. This distinction wasn't made in the execution plan until SQL Server 2005.

The presence of a lookup operator in a query plan indicates that the query is not covered. A covered query means that all columns required to satisfy the query are present in a single index. Similarly, a covering index is an index that contains all the columns necessary to satisfy the query without accessing the base table. We will talk more about covering indexes in *Chapter 5, Writing Elegant T-SQL Queries.*

RID Lookup

As mentioned previously, a RID Lookup operator represents a lookup from a non-clustered index into a heap. The following example shows a query executed in the AdventureWorks sample database with a RID Lookup operator:

```
SELECT *
FROM DatabaseLog
WHERE DatabaseLogID = 5;
```

The query generates the following execution plan:

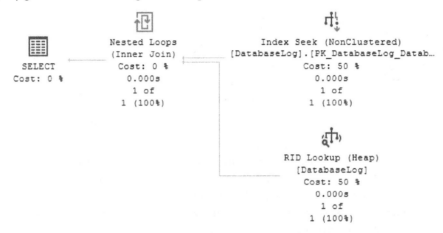

Figure 3.21: Execution plan for the SELECT * query

Notice that the results of the RID Lookup operator are being joined to the non-clustered index seek via a Nested Loops join operator (we will discuss join operators later in this section).

Key Lookup

A Key Lookup operator represents a lookup from a non-clustered index into a clustered index. It is effectively a clustered index seek. The following example shows a query executed in the AdventureWorks sample database with a Key Lookup operator:

```
SELECT *
FROM Person.Person
WHERE LastName = N'Maxwell';
```

The query generates the following execution plan:

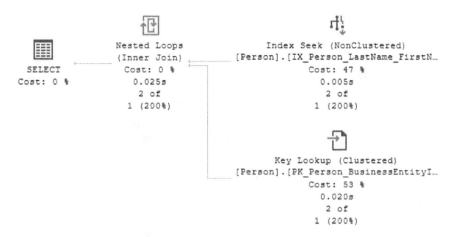

Figure 3.22: Execution plan for the SELECT * query

Notice how the key lookup is joined to the non-clustered index seek in the same manner as the RID lookup.

Columnstore Index Scan

The indexes we've discussed so far are what are referred to as rowstore indexes. These perform well for **online transaction processing (OLTP)** workloads, but **data warehousing (DW)** or **online analytical processing (OLAP)** workloads often benefit from a different type of data storage called columnstore. In a columnstore index, a page of data contains a single column for one or more rows of data in the table. Columnstore indexes were introduced in SQL Server 2012 and provide a way to store large amounts of read-only or read-mostly data in a heavily compressed format with specialized operators that can process large amounts of data quickly. The only way to access data in a columnstore index is with the Columnstore Index Scan operator. The following example shows a query executed in the AdventureWorksDW sample database with a Columnstore Index Scan operator:

```
SELECT *
FROM FactResellerSalesXL_CCI
WHERE SalesAmount > 10000;
```

The query generates the following execution plan:

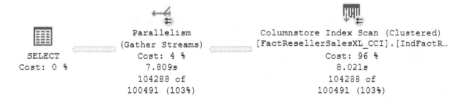

Figure 3.23: Execution plan for the SELECT * query

Joins

Join operators are used to join the results of two previous operators in the query plan. They may be joining entire tables or indexes, or they may be joining the results of previous operators in the plan. When we think about joins, we may think of INNER, OUTER, and CROSS joins. These are logical joins that we would write in our T-SQL statement that tell the SQL Database Engine how to combine the rows of multiple tables and views. The join operators in a query plan define the algorithm that the SQL Database Engine will use to perform the join. The choice of which join algorithm to use is based on a cost estimate, not on the type of join being performed.

The physical join operators that the SQL Database Engine may choose from are Nested Loops, Adaptive, Merge, and Hash joins. The choice of which operation to perform is generally based on how many rows will be joined and whether there are appropriate indexes to support the join. As with data access operators, if the SQL Database Engine estimates this cost incorrectly, it may choose an inefficient join operation. If updating statistics and creating appropriate indexes does not solve the problem, hints can be used to force the SQL Database Engine to use the join operation that we specify. The following join hints are available:

- LOOP: Specifies that the SQL Database Engine should perform a Nested Loops join

- HASH: Specifies that the SQL Database Engine should perform a Hash join

- MERGE: Specifies that the SQL Database Engine should perform a Merge join

- REMOTE: Specifies that when joining with a table on a remote SQL Database Engine instance via a Linked Server connection, the SQL Database Engine should perform the join on the remote instance

There are two inputs to each join operator in an execution plan. While these inputs may be tables, indexes, or even the results of a previous join, they are generally referred to as the **outer table** and **inner table**. The outer table is the first input accessed in the join algorithm and will appear on the top of the join. The inner table is accessed second and appears at the bottom of the join. The choice of which input should be the inner table and which should be the outer table is relevant in the join because, depending on the algorithm, it may influence the cost of the overall join and the order in which rows are output.

Nested Loops joins

A Nested Loops join is a non-blocking operator. In a Nested Loops join, a row is fetched from the outer table, and the inner table is searched for a matching row. The SQL Database Engine loops on the inner table until no more rows are found, then it loops on the outer table. Because the number of iterations of the inner loop is determined by the number of rows in the outer table, the SQL Database Engine will generally choose the smaller of the two inputs to be the outer table in order to minimize the cost of the join. Also, since the outer table is the driver of the algorithm, the rows will be output from the Nested Loops join in the same order as they are input from the outer table.

The following diagram depicts the operation of a Nested Loops join:

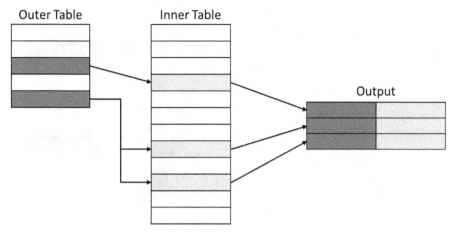

Figure 3.24: Representation of a Nested Loops join

If used correctly, the Nested Loops join is generally the most efficient join algorithm for joining a small number of rows with supporting indexes as it requires a small amount of memory and CPU.

> **Note**
>
> Two additional concepts are applicable to Nested Loops joins during execution:
>
> Rewind: This concept is defined as an execution using the same value as the immediately preceding execution. In other words, while an inner table is being scanned for matches with the outer table, if a previously scanned value is found again, then it is said that the value is rewound.
>
> Rebind: This concept is defined as an execution using a different value. In other words, when a new value is picked from the outer table to be scanned in the inner table, it is said that the value is rebound.

The following example shows a query executed in the AdventureWorks sample database with a Nested Loops operator:

```
SELECT p.LastName, p.FirstName, e.JobTitle
FROM Person.Person AS p
LEFT JOIN HumanResources.Employee AS e ON p.BusinessEntityID =
e.BusinessEntityID
WHERE p.LastName = N'Maxwell';
```

The query generates the following execution plan:

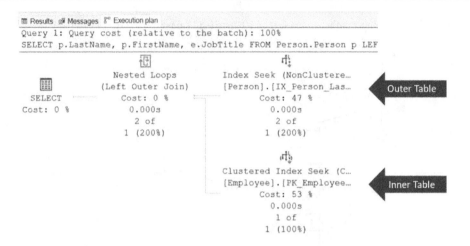

Figure 3.25: Execution plan for the SELECT query

Merge joins

A Merge Join operator represents a merge join in the execution plan. Merge joins are typically used to join two large input tables that have ordered indexes to support the join. In a Merge join, the size of the outer table and the inner table doesn't affect the cost of the join, but both input tables must be sorted by the same keys in the same order for the join to work. A row is retrieved from the outer table, then matched with rows from the inner table and the results output. Once all matches have been exhausted on the inner table, the SQL Database Engine moves to the next row in the outer table. Since both the inner and outer tables are sorted in the same order going into the Merge join operation, the output is returned in the same order.

The following diagram depicts the operation of a Merge join:

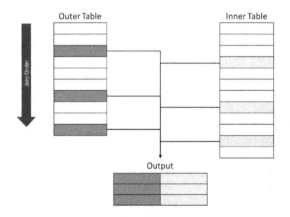

Figure 3.26: Representation of a Merge join

If there are indexes to support the join and the inputs are already sorted in the proper order, a merge operation is a very efficient way to join two large tables as it requires very little additional memory or CPU. This is often the method of choice when joining two tables on a primary key/foreign key relationship without a WHERE clause to limit the rows returned. The following example shows a query executed in the AdventureWorks sample database with a Merge Join operator:

```
SELECT h.AccountNumber, d.ProductID, d.OrderQty
FROM Sales.SalesOrderHeader AS h
INNER JOIN Sales.SalesOrderDetail AS d ON h.SalesOrderID =
d.SalesOrderID;
```

The query generates the following execution plan:

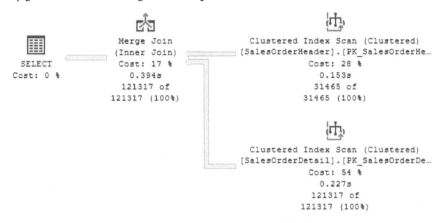

Figure 3.27: Execution plan for the SELECT query

Hash Match joins

A Hash Match operator is a blocking operator that represents a Hash join operation in an execution plan. Hash joins are the most efficient way to join two large inputs that are not sorted and/or do not have any indexes that support the join. A Hash Match operation is expensive in that it consumes a significant amount of memory and CPU and may generate additional I/O if it does not fit in memory, but it is generally faster than both Nested Loops and Merge joins when joining a large number of unsorted rows.

With a Hash Match operator, the outer table is also referred to as the **build table**, and the inner table is referred to as the **probe table**. The smaller of the two inputs will be chosen as the build table, which will be used to build a hash table in memory. The SQL Database Engine will then apply a hash function to the join key of each row of the probe table, look it up in the hash table, and output the results if a match is found.

The following diagram depicts the operation of a Hash Match join:

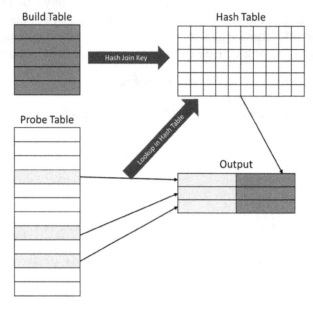

Figure 3.28: Representation of a Hash Match join

If the build table is too large for the entire hash table to fit in memory, intermediate results will be saved in a workfile in tempdb, and the operation will have to be done recursively. This is called hash recursion and will generate a **hash warning** in the execution plan. We can see this as a yellow caution symbol in the following screenshot, and viewing the properties will tell us that a spill has occurred. In extreme cases, a hash bailout may occur. This happens when the maximum recursion level is reached but the hash table still does not fit in memory. A hash bailout will also show up as a hash warning; we'll need to look at the spill level specified in the properties of the plan to determine whether a hash bailout has occurred. There are two different spill levels:

- **Spill level 1**: This indicates hash recursion. This occurs when the build input does not fit into available memory, resulting in the split of input into multiple partitions that are processed separately. If any of these partitions still do not fit into available memory, they are split into sub-partitions, which are also processed separately. This splitting process continues until each partition fits into the available memory or until the maximum recursion level is reached.

- **Spill level 2 or higher**: This indicates a hash bailout. This occurs when a hashing operation reaches its maximum recursion level and shifts to an alternate plan to process the remaining partitioned data.

The following query executed in the AdventureWorksDW database includes a Hash Match operator with a hash warning. For this example, the query memory is purposefully limited using the MAX_GRANT_PERCENT query hint to produce a spill:

```
SELECT s.*, c.AverageRate
FROM FactResellerSales AS s
INNER JOIN FactCurrencyRate AS c ON c.CurrencyKey = s.CurrencyKey AND
c.DateKey = s.OrderDateKey
OPTION (MAX_GRANT_PERCENT = 0.01);
```

The query generates the following execution plan:

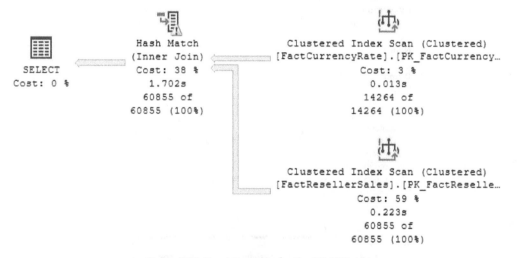

Figure 3.29: Execution plan for the SELECT query

Hovering over the Hash Match operator reveals the properties of the operator with details on the warning:

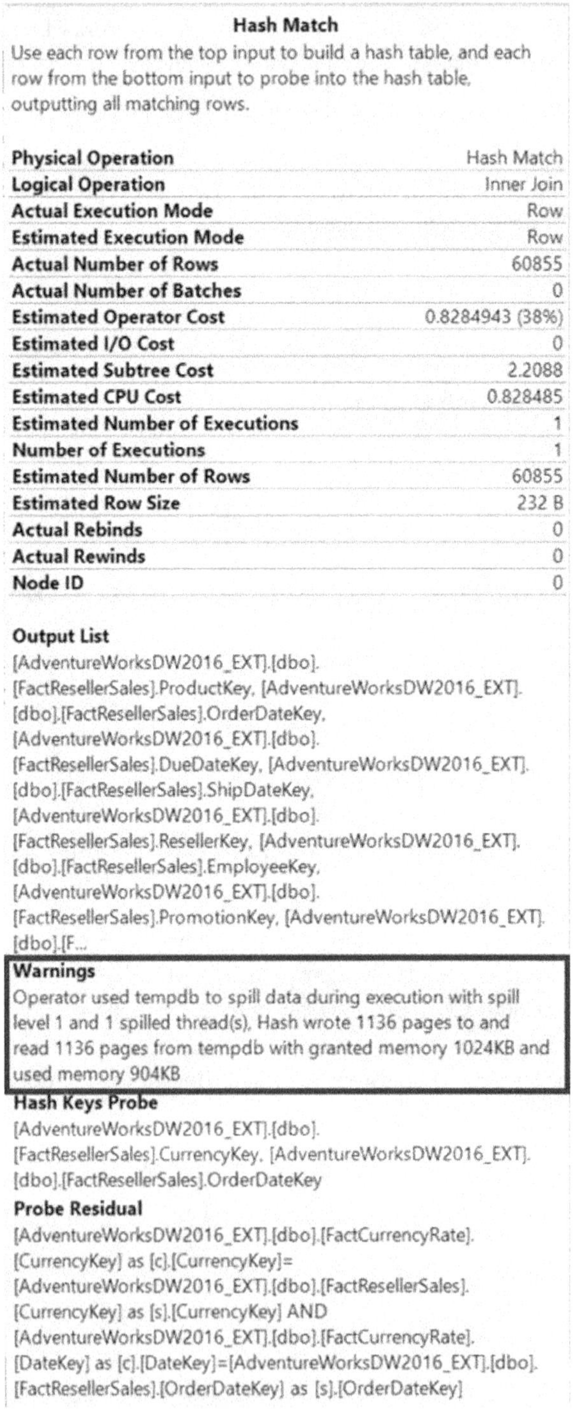

Hash Match

Use each row from the top input to build a hash table, and each row from the bottom input to probe into the hash table, outputting all matching rows.

Physical Operation	Hash Match
Logical Operation	Inner Join
Actual Execution Mode	Row
Estimated Execution Mode	Row
Actual Number of Rows	60855
Actual Number of Batches	0
Estimated Operator Cost	0.8284943 (38%)
Estimated I/O Cost	0
Estimated Subtree Cost	2.2088
Estimated CPU Cost	0.828485
Estimated Number of Executions	1
Number of Executions	1
Estimated Number of Rows	60855
Estimated Row Size	232 B
Actual Rebinds	0
Actual Rewinds	0
Node ID	0

Output List

[AdventureWorksDW2016_EXT].[dbo].
[FactResellerSales].ProductKey, [AdventureWorksDW2016_EXT].
[dbo].[FactResellerSales].OrderDateKey,
[AdventureWorksDW2016_EXT].[dbo].
[FactResellerSales].DueDateKey, [AdventureWorksDW2016_EXT].
[dbo].[FactResellerSales].ShipDateKey,
[AdventureWorksDW2016_EXT].[dbo].
[FactResellerSales].ResellerKey, [AdventureWorksDW2016_EXT].
[dbo].[FactResellerSales].EmployeeKey,
[AdventureWorksDW2016_EXT].[dbo].
[FactResellerSales].PromotionKey, [AdventureWorksDW2016_EXT].
[dbo].[F...

Warnings

Operator used tempdb to spill data during execution with spill level 1 and 1 spilled thread(s), Hash wrote 1136 pages to and read 1136 pages from tempdb with granted memory 1024KB and used memory 904KB

Hash Keys Probe

[AdventureWorksDW2016_EXT].[dbo].
[FactResellerSales].CurrencyKey, [AdventureWorksDW2016_EXT].
[dbo].[FactResellerSales].OrderDateKey

Probe Residual

[AdventureWorksDW2016_EXT].[dbo].[FactCurrencyRate].
[CurrencyKey] as [c].[CurrencyKey]=
[AdventureWorksDW2016_EXT].[dbo].[FactResellerSales].
[CurrencyKey] as [s].[CurrencyKey] AND
[AdventureWorksDW2016_EXT].[dbo].[FactCurrencyRate].
[DateKey] as [c].[DateKey]=[AdventureWorksDW2016_EXT].[dbo].
[FactResellerSales].[OrderDateKey] as [s].[OrderDateKey]

Figure 3.30: Properties window of the Hash Match operator with a spill warning

We will further describe warnings in this chapter, under the *Query plan properties of interest* section.

Adaptive joins

SQL Server 2017 introduced adaptive query processing, which includes, among other enhancements, `Batch Mode Adaptive` joins. Batch mode refers to the query processing method used to process many rows in bulk or batches. When first introduced, batch mode execution was closely integrated with the columnstore storage format. Starting with SQL Server 2019, traditional rowstore objects can also benefit from batch-mode processing. Whether used for columnstore or rowstore objects, batch-mode processing is best suited for analytical workloads because of its better parallelism and faster performance.

> **Note**
> `Adaptive` joins are only used if the outer side of a join can run in batch mode. Depending on the type of physical join selected later, this outer side becomes either the outer table of a `Nested Loops` join or the build table for a `Hash Match` join.

Normally, if cardinality estimations are skewed, the SQL Database Engine may choose an inadequate physical join based on wrong data, which results in performance degradation. To avoid this, `Adaptive` joins will defer the choice of using a `Hash Match` join or a `Nested Loops` join until after the first join input has been scanned.

This means that the `Adaptive` join implements both join types and then adapts to runtime conditions by only continuing to execute the appropriate join type on the fly. As discussed in the previous sections, `Nested Loop` joins are suitable for small inputs, and `Hash Match` joins for large inputs.

The SQL Database Engine starts the `Adaptive` join process by providing rows to a spool-like structure called the **Adaptive Buffer** and defines a dynamic threshold that is used to decide when to use a `Hash Match` or a `Nested Loops` plan:

- If the threshold is hit, the SQL Database Engine will use a `Hash Match` join and the **Adaptive Buffer** becomes the build table

- If the actual row count doesn't exceed the threshold, then the SQL Database Engine uses a `Nested Loops` join and the **Adaptive Buffer** becomes the outer table

The following diagram illustrates the `Adaptive` join processing flow:

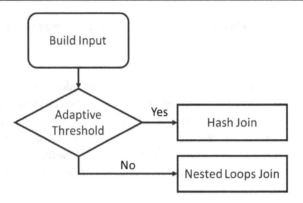

Figure 3.31: Representation of an Adaptive join

The following query executed in the `AdventureWorksDW` database includes an `Adaptive Join` operator. Because adaptive joins are only available when the database compatibility level is mapped to SQL Server 2017 or higher, we need to set it to at least compatibility level 140 with the following command:

```
USE [master];
GO
ALTER DATABASE [AdventureWorksDW] SET COMPATIBILITY_LEVEL = 140;
GO
```

For this example, because the outer table of a join must run in batch mode for `Adaptive Join` to be eligible, we are forcing a table with a `Clustered Columnstore Index` operator to be on the outer side of the join using the FORCE ORDER query hint:

```
SELECT s.ProductKey,
SUM(s.OrderQuantity) AS SumOrderQuantity,
     AVG(s.UnitPrice) AS AvgUnitPrice,
AVG(s.DiscountAmount) AS AvgDiscountAmount,        c.AverageRate
FROM FactResellerSalesXL_CCI AS s
INNER JOIN FactCurrencyRate AS c ON c.CurrencyKey = s.CurrencyKey AND
c.DateKey = s.OrderDateKey
GROUP BY s.ProductKey, c.AverageRate
OPTION (FORCE ORDER);
```

The query generates the following execution plan:

Figure 3.32: Execution plan for the SELECT query

Hovering over the `Adaptive Join` operator reveals the properties of the operator with details on the adaptive threshold for this specific query, as well as the estimated and actual join type:

Adaptive Join

Chooses dynamically between hash join and nested loops.

Physical Operation	Adaptive Join
Logical Operation	Inner Join
Actual Join Type	HashMatch
Actual Execution Mode	Batch
Estimated Join Type	HashMatch
Is Adaptive	True
Estimated Execution Mode	Batch
Adaptive Threshold Rows	306.817
Actual Number of Rows	434626
Actual Number of Batches	2073
Estimated I/O Cost	0
Estimated Operator Cost	0 (0%)
Estimated Subtree Cost	7.04138
Estimated CPU Cost	0.0014646
Estimated Number of Executions	1
Number of Executions	8
Estimated Number of Rows	439383
Estimated Row Size	37 B
Actual Rebinds	0
Actual Rewinds	0
Node ID	3

Figure 3.33: Adaptive Join Properties window

In this query execution plan, we can see that because the actual number of rows was 434,626, which exceeds the 307 rows in the *adaptive threshold*, the SQL Database Engine uses a Hash join for this query. The second branch in the plan represents the probe phase of a standard Hash join. The third branch is the Clustered Index Seek operator that would be used by the Nested Loops join if the threshold had not been exceeded: notice the 0 of 11669631 (0%) row, which means the branch was unused.

Spools

Spools are expensive operators, but they are introduced in a query plan as an optimization, typically to compensate for inadequate indexes, or to optimize otherwise complex queries by significantly speeding up the overall runtime of a query. A spool operator reads data and saves it in a worktable in tempdb. This process is used whenever the Query Optimizer knows that the density of a column is high (therefore, having low selectivity) and the intermediate result is very complex to calculate. If this is the case, the SQL Database Engine computes the result once and stores it in a spool so that it can be searched later in the execution. Spools only exist while the query is being executed.

Conceptually, all physical spool operators function in the same way:

- Read all rows from an input operator downstream
- Store them in a worktable in tempdb
- Allow upstream operators to read from this cache

There are three types of physical spool operators:

- Table Spool: This spool opeator scans the input and places a copy of each row in a worktable. This is also called a Performance Spool operator, and it can be introduced to support a Nested Loops join upstream.
- Index Spool: A non-clustered index spool contains a seek predicate. The Index Spool operator scans the input rows, places a copy of each row in a worktable, and builds a non-clustered index on the rows. This allows the SQL Database Engine to use the seeking capability of indexes to output only those rows that satisfy the seek predicate and is usually introduced when a proper index doesn't exist for the required predicates.
- Row Count Spool: This spool operator scans the input, counts how many rows are present, and then returns the row count without any data attached to it. This allows the SQL Database Engine to check for the existence of rows when the data contained in the rows is not required and can be introduced by certain T-SQL constructs such as an EXISTS clause dependent on a COUNT clause.

All the preceding spool operators can implement one of the following two logical operations:

- `Eager Spool`: This spool operation causes the physical spool to become a non-blocking operator that will read *all* rows from the input operator at one time. It populates its worktable in an "eager" way. In other words, when the spool's upstream operator asks for the first row, the spool operator consumes all rows from its input operator and stores them in the worktable.

- `Lazy Spool`: This spool operation causes the physical spool to become a blocking operator that reads and stores data only when individual rows are required. It populates the worktable in a "lazy" fashion. In other words, each time the spool's upstream operator asks for a row, the spool operator gets a row from its input operator and stores it in the worktable, rather than consuming all rows at once. Because of this behavior, memory consumption for a `Lazy Spool` operation is smaller than the memory needed for an `Eager Spool` operation.

For both logical spools, if the operator is rewound (for example, by a `Nested Loops` operator) but no rebinding is needed, the spooled data is used instead of rescanning the input. If rebinding is needed, the spooled data is discarded, and the spool object is rebuilt by re-scanning the input.

> **Tip**
>
> If a spool is causing a bottleneck in a query, refactor it to try to eliminate the spool. Creating and populating a temp table can sometimes perform better than a spool, and it can be indexed. If the same spool is used several times, this method can yield better results.

The SQL Database Engine can introduce a `Spool` or `Sort` operation to enforce Halloween protection during a T-SQL statement that updates rows. We introduced Halloween protection in the *Query optimization essentials* section of *Chapter 1, Understanding Query Processing*.

Here is an example of a query executed in the `AdventureWorks` sample database with a `Table Spool` operator:

```
SELECT WO.WorkOrderID, WO.ProductID, WO.OrderQty, WO.StockedQty,
WO.ScrappedQty, WO.StartDate, WO.EndDate, WO.DueDate,
WO.ScrapReasonID, WO.ModifiedDate, WOR.WorkOrderID, WOR.ProductID,
WOR.LocationID
FROM Production.WorkOrder AS WO
LEFT JOIN Production.WorkOrderRouting AS WOR ON WO.WorkOrderID = WOR.
WorkOrderID AND WOR.WorkOrderID = 12345;
```

The query generates the following execution plan:

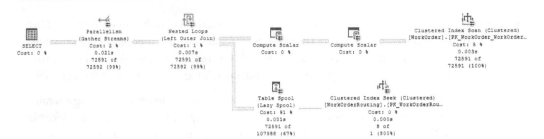

Figure 3.34: Execution plan for the SELECT query

In the following screenshot, notice the difference between actual and estimated rows for the spool (72,591 of 107,588). The SQL Database Engine doesn't hold statistics on worktables, so estimations are based on the estimated number of rows (1.48211) multiplied by the estimated number of executions (72,591). In turn, notice the number of rewinds and rebinds; these match the number of executions because executing a spool is the action of rewinding and rebinding values as the Nested Loops operator requires rows to process:

Table Spool	
Stores the data from the input into a temporary table in order to optimize rewinds.	
Physical Operation	Table Spool
Logical Operation	Lazy Spool
Actual Execution Mode	Row
Estimated Execution Mode	Row
Actual Number of Rows	72591
Actual Number of Batches	0
Estimated I/O Cost	0.01
Estimated Operator Cost	7.2884664 (91%)
Estimated Subtree Cost	7.29175
Estimated CPU Cost	0.0001006
Number of Executions	72591
Estimated Number of Executions	72591
Estimated Number of Rows	1.48211
Estimated Row Size	17 B
Actual Rebinds	8
Actual Rewinds	72583
Node ID	5

Output List
[AdventureWorks2016CTP3].[Production].
[WorkOrderRouting].WorkOrderID,
[AdventureWorks2016CTP3].[Production].
[WorkOrderRouting].ProductID,
[AdventureWorks2016CTP3].[Production].
[WorkOrderRouting].LocationID

Figure 3.35: Table Spool Properties window

In *Chapter 6, Discovering T-SQL Anti-Patterns in Depth*, we will discuss some methods for avoiding Spool operators in our queries.

The spool was included for performance reasons, to cache the result set from the inner side of the `Nested Loops` join. The idea is that if the next iteration of the `Nested Loops` join uses the same correlated parameters, the spool can "rewind" – replay the results from the prior execution. This saves the cost of evaluating the inner side subtree, at the cost of caching the result in a worktable. As such, the `NO_PERFORMANCE_SPOOL` hint can apply to these scenarios to remove this type of spool. As always, hints should be used only as a last resort, as they limit the Query Optimizer search space and may preclude a query from leveraging future query optimization enhancements.

To prove that the spool was beneficial, we can add the hint to the query, like so:

```
SELECT WO.WorkOrderID, WO.ProductID, WO.OrderQty, WO.StockedQty,
WO.ScrappedQty, WO.StartDate,        WO.EndDate, WO.DueDate,
WO.ScrapReasonID, WO.ModifiedDate, WOR.WorkOrderID, WOR.ProductID,
WOR.LocationID
FROM Production.WorkOrder AS WO
LEFT JOIN Production.WorkOrderRouting AS WOR ON WO.WorkOrderID = WOR.
WorkOrderID AND WOR.WorkOrderID = 12345
OPTION (NO_PERFORMANCE_SPOOL);
```

The query generates the following execution plan:

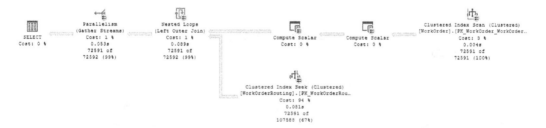

Figure 3.36: Execution plan for the SELECT query

Instead of a spool, the SQL Database Engine now accesses the clustered index for every single search on the inner table. We started this section by saying spools are expensive operators, but that they are also an optimization. That is proven here, whereby eliminating the spool degrades query performance by using much more CPU.

Sort and aggregation operators

Sort and aggregation operators are present in an execution plan when a query contains an ORDER BY and/or a GROUP BY clause. In some cases, the SQL Database Engine will introduce a Sort operator in order to optimize the execution of a query, such as to enable a Merge join or to improve the performance of a Nested Loops join. We may also see a Sort operator in an execution plan that contains a SELECT DISTINCT clause. DISTINCT is effectively an aggregation as it requires grouping the rows and only returning one row per distinct set of values. A Sort operation is a simple way to perform this type of aggregation. As discussed in the *Query optimization essentials* section of *Chapter 1, Understanding Query Processing*, the SQL Database Engine may also add a Sort operator to an UPDATE plan in order to enforce Halloween protection.

Sort

Sort is a blocking operator that is used to order the input based on one or more columns. Sort operations can be expensive operations since they require additional memory to store intermediate results and CPU to perform the sort. If the intermediate results do not fit in memory, Sort operations may also generate I/O as the results will be saved in a worktable in tempdb.

If any of these happens, a **sort warning** will be visible in the execution plan. As with a hash warning, it will appear as a yellow caution symbol in the plan, and the properties will give more details on how much data was spilled. There are two spill levels:

- **Spill level 1**: This means one pass over the data was enough to complete the sort
- **Spill level 2**: This means multiple passes over the data are required to sort the data

The following query executed in the AdventureWorksDW database includes a Sort operation with a sort warning:

```
SELECT *
FROM FactResellerSalesXL_PageCompressed s
ORDER BY ProductKey;
```

The query generates the following execution plan:

Figure 3.37: Execution plan for the SELECT * query

Hovering over the **Sort** icon will pop up the **Properties** window, where we can see the **sort warning** details, as shown here:

Sort	
Sort the input.	
Physical Operation	Sort
Logical Operation	Sort
Actual Execution Mode	Row
Estimated Execution Mode	Row
Actual Number of Rows	11669638
Actual Number of Batches	0
Estimated Operator Cost	2265.6196 (88%)
Estimated I/O Cost	2053.36
Estimated CPU Cost	212.26
Estimated Subtree Cost	2336.45
Number of Executions	2
Estimated Number of Executions	1
Estimated Number of Rows	11669600
Estimated Row Size	224 B
Actual Rebinds	2
Actual Rewinds	0
Node ID	1

Output List
[AdventureWorksDW2016_EXT].[dbo].
[FactResellerSalesXL_PageCompressed].ProductKey,
[AdventureWorksDW2016_EXT].[dbo].
[FactResellerSalesXL_PageCompressed].OrderDateKey,
[AdventureWorksDW2016_EXT].[dbo].
[FactResellerSalesXL_PageCompressed].DueDateKey,
[AdventureWorksDW2016_EXT].[dbo].
[FactResellerSalesXL_PageCompressed].ShipDateKey,
[AdventureWorksDW2016_EXT].[dbo].
[FactResellerSalesXL_PageCompressed].ResellerKey,
[AdventureWorksDW2016_EXT].[dbo].
[FactResellerSalesXL_PageCompressed].EmployeeKey,
...

Warnings
Operator used tempdb to spill data during execution
with spill level 1 and 2 spilled thread(s), Sort wrote
315397 pages to and read 315397 pages from
tempdb with granted memory 1571264KB and used
memory 1571264KB

Order By
[AdventureWorksDW2016_EXT].[dbo].
[FactResellerSalesXL_PageCompressed].ProductKey
Ascending

Figure 3.38: Properties window of the Clustered Index Scan operator with a spill warning

We will further describe warnings in this chapter, under the *Query plan properties of interest* section.

Stream aggregation

As mentioned previously, aggregation is used to group rows together when a query contains a GROUP BY clause. With a GROUP BY clause, the SELECT list typically has one or more aggregate functions such as SUM, MIN, or MAX. If the input to the aggregation operation is already sorted by the GROUP BY columns, a Stream Aggregate operator can be used. Stream aggregation is the more efficient of the two aggregation operators in that it does not require much additional CPU or memory; the rows are processed as they pass through the operator. The following example shows a query executed in the AdventureWorks sample database with a Stream Aggregate operator:

```
SELECT SalesOrderID, COUNT(*) AS ItemCount
FROM Sales.SalesOrderDetail
GROUP BY SalesOrderID;
```

The query generates the following execution plan:

Figure 3.39: Execution plan for the SELECT query

Hash aggregation

The Hash Match (Aggregate) operator also performs aggregation to support a GROUP BY clause, but while stream aggregation requires the input to be sorted, hash aggregation does not. Hash aggregation is effectively the same as a Hash join; the difference is that there is only a single input to process. As with a Hash join, hash aggregation consumes additional CPU and memory to store the hash table and may be subject to hash recursion and additional I/O in the form of spills to tempdb. The following example shows a query executed in the AdventureWorks sample database with a Hash Match (Aggregate) operator:

```
SELECT p.Name AS ProductName, SUM(OrderQty) AS TotalProductSales
FROM Sales.SalesOrderDetail sod
INNER JOIN Production.Product p on p.ProductID = sod.ProductID
GROUP BY p.Name;
```

The query generates the following execution plan:

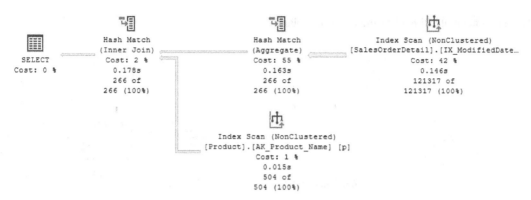

Figure 3.40: Execution plan for the SELECT query

Query plan properties of interest

Each operator in a query execution plan has several properties that provide context and metrics around its compilation, optimization, and execution. The plans also have global properties to provide overall context. Examining some key properties for the overall plan and some operators is especially relevant to writing T-SQL that scales well. We will look at these properties, understand their meaning, and become familiar with their significance, which will be important in the chapters where we explore T-SQL patterns and anti-patterns.

Plan-level properties

The root node of a plan has a few properties that are important for understanding the context of execution. Different trace flags or SET options change execution context and may drive query optimization choices, so having this information persisted in the showplan is a valuable tool.

The following example shows a query executed in the AdventureWorks sample database that allows us to examine most of these properties:

```
SELECT *
FROM Sales.SalesOrderDetail AS sod
INNER JOIN Production.Product AS p ON sod.ProductID = p.ProductID
ORDER BY Style DESC
OPTION (MAXDOP 1);
```

The query generates the following execution plan:

Figure 3.41: Execution plan for the SELECT * query

Right-click on the root node (SELECT) of the plan, open the context menu, and click on **Properties**:

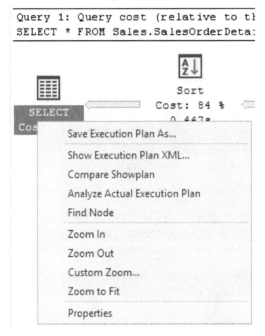

Figure 3.42: Context menu on the plan's root node

This opens the **Properties** window, as seen next:

Figure 3.43: Plan's Properties window

For each property selected, the lower part of the **Properties** window displays some informational text such as the size of the plan in the plan cache, as highlighted in *Figure 3.43*.

> **Note**
>
> The properties available depend on the version and build of the SQL Database Engine on which the plan was captured. As of the time this book was written, all the plan-level properties described here exist in SQL Server 2016 **Service Pack 2 (SP2)**, SQL Server 2017 **Cumulative Update 3 (CU3)**, SQL Server 2019, SQL Server 2022, and Azure SQL Database. A subset of these properties will also be available in SQL Server 2016 SP1 and higher builds, SQL Server 2014 SP3, and SQL Server 2012 SP4.

Not all properties are available with an estimated plan because this refers to a compiled plan that has not yet been executed. Some properties exist at runtime only and, therefore, are only available for an actual plan; however, all properties in an estimated plan are also available in an actual plan. In order to distinguish between compile-time and runtime properties in this book, if a property only exists at runtime, we will use one asterisk after the property name – for example, `Degree of Parallelism`*, as seen in the previous screenshot.

With this, let's look at some of the most important properties as seen in the preceding **Properties** window screenshot.

CardinalityEstimationModelVersion

`CardinalityEstimationModelVersion` indicates the CE version with which the plan was compiled. In this case, we see **130**, mapping to the CE released with SQL Server 2016. While this query is being executed in a SQL Server 2017 Database Engine, the compatibility level of the `AdventureWorks` database is set to **130**, because it hasn't been upgraded since being restored from a SQL Server 2016 system where it was first created. Because the CE version is a main driver for the query optimization process, it represents vital information when database professionals analyze query plans. For more information on CE and database compatibility, see the *Mechanics of the Query Optimizer* chapter.

Degree of Parallelism

`Degree of Parallelism`* indicates the number of CPUs actually used to process a query that was eligible to execute in parallel. In this case, we see the value is zero because the query was not executed in parallel. We have discussed how the query optimization process evaluates parallelism in the *Mechanics of the Query Optimizer* chapter. If the query had a cost that was high enough to go parallel but didn't, an extra property named `NonParallelPlanReason`* is also shown. In this case, we can see the reason was `MaxDOPSetToOne`, and indeed notice the query used the `MAXDOP 1` hint, forcing the Query Optimizer to not evaluate a parallel plan. Compare this with the `EstimatedAvailableDegreeOfParalellism` property: for example, if the actual parallelism was smaller than the estimated parallelism, this may indicate a CPU contention problem.

Memory Grant

`Memory Grant`* indicates the amount of memory in **kilobytes** (**KB**) that the SQL Database Engine had to acquire to even start executing this query. In this case, we see 57,544 KB, roughly 56 **megabytes** (**MB**). Being limited, memory is one of the most important resources for the SQL Database Engine. Even when our SQL Database Engine has **terabytes** (**TB**) of memory at its disposal, it is most likely still less than the overall storage taken by all our databases. This means that making sure the SQL Database Engine can properly estimate the amount of memory to use for a given query to execute and then use it without waste is a measure of scalability and enhanced concurrency in our database system. We will discuss this in more detail later in this chapter as we look at possible warnings output by the SQL Database Engine during execution.

MemoryGrantInfo

`MemoryGrantInfo` can expand to show additional information on memory usage in KB, to report on all memory calculations accounted for during query optimization. Next is the detail for this property for the example query:

Memory Grant	57544
⊟ MemoryGrantInfo	
DesiredMemory	57544
GrantedMemory	57544
GrantWaitTime	0
MaxQueryMemory	1908928
MaxUsedMemory	40648
RequestedMemory	57544
RequiredMemory	1536
SerialDesiredMemory	57544
SerialRequiredMemory	1536

Figure 3.44: Memory grant information in the Properties window

The detailed elements of `MemoryGrantInfo` are the following:

- `GrantedMemory`* indicates the memory acquired by the Database Engine at runtime.

- `GrantWaitTime`* indicates the time in seconds the query had to wait for a successful memory grant. This translates into `RESOURCE_SEMAPHORE` waits. If no waits occur, the wait time will be zero.

- `MaxQueryMemory`* indicates the maximum memory allowed for a single query under the applicable Resource Governor pool's `MAX_MEMORY_PERCENT` configuration. If there are operators spilling and estimations are mostly correct, the query may be running into memory starvation.

- `MaxUsedMemory`* indicates the maximum memory used by the query during execution. If there is a large skew between the granted memory and the used memory, the SQL Database Engine will generate warnings, which will be discussed later in this section.

- `RequiredMemory`* indicates the required memory for the chosen degree of parallelism when a query runs in parallel. If the query runs in serial mode, this is the same as `SerialRequiredMemory`. The query will not start without at least this much memory being available.

- `SerialRequiredMemory` indicates the required memory for a serial query plan to execute. The query will not start without at least this much memory being available.

OptimizationLevel

`OptimizationLevel` refers to the Query Optimizer phase and can be either `TRIVIAL` or `FULL`. For more information on the Query Optimizer workflow, see the *Mechanics of the Query Optimizer* chapter.

OptimizerHardwareDependentProperties

`OptimizerHardwareDependentProperties` can expand to show additional information on system-reported conditions that are accounted for during query optimization. Next is the detail for this property for the example query:

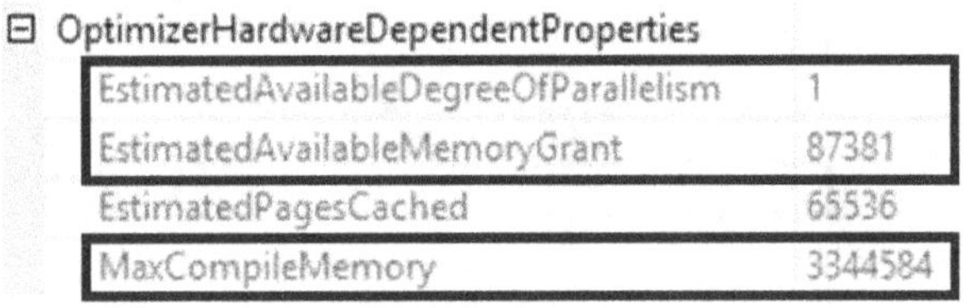

Figure 3.45: Hardware-dependent optimizer information in the Properties window

The detailed elements of `OptimizerHardwareDependentProperties` are the following:

- `EstimatedAvailableDegreeOfParallelism`: This indicates the expected number of schedulers available for query processing. One means that no parallelism will be available; a number greater than one allows a parallel plan to be evaluated during query optimization. Compare this with the `Degree of Parallelism`* property: for example, if the actual parallelism was smaller than the estimated parallelism, this may indicate a CPU contention problem.

- `EstimatedAvailableMemoryGrant`: This indicates the expected amount of memory (in KB) available for a single query under the applicable Resource Governor pool's `MAX_MEMORY_PERCENT` configuration.

- `MaxCompileMemory`: This indicates the maximum Query Optimizer memory available (in KB) during compilation under the applicable Resource Governor pool's `MAX_MEMORY_PERCENT` configuration. If the system is accumulating `RESOURCE_SEMAPHORE_QUERY_COMPILE` waits, then queries are waiting to be compiled long before they can execute. This then surfaces as a high compilation or recompilation scenario. We will further detail this scenario in *Chapter 6, Discovering T-SQL Anti-Patterns in Depth*.

OptimizerStatsUsage

`OptimizerStatsUsage` can expand to show additional information on which statistics objects were used by the Query Optimizer for a given compilation. When analyzing a query plan that has performance problems, a database professional can use this information to see which statistics were loaded for use during query optimization, and also, whether statistics need to be updated, which may be a root cause of performance problems grounded on CE issues. Next is the detail for this property for the example query:

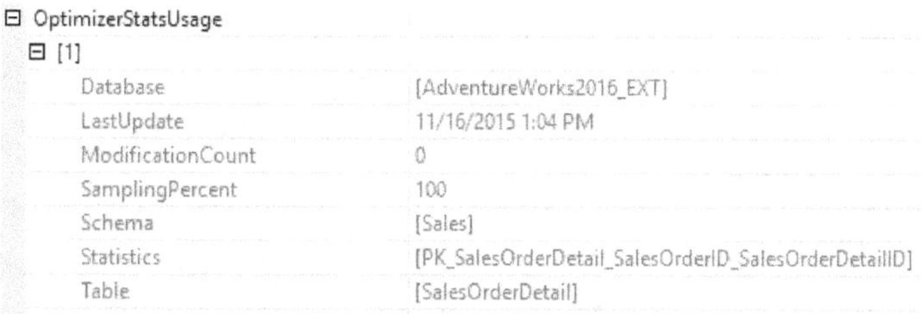

```
☐ OptimizerStatsUsage
  ☐ [1]
      Database                    [AdventureWorks2016_EXT]
      LastUpdate                  11/16/2015 1:04 PM
      ModificationCount           0
      SamplingPercent             100
      Schema                      [Sales]
      Statistics                  [PK_SalesOrderDetail_SalesOrderID_SalesOrderDetailID]
      Table                       [SalesOrderDetail]
```

Figure 3.46: Statistics used by the optimizer in the Properties window

The detailed elements of `OptimizerStatsUsage` are the following, and are repeated for every statistic object loaded for this plan:

- `Database`, `Schema`, `Table`, and `Statistics` refer to the respective four-part name of the statistic object.

- `LastUpdate` refers to the date and time the statistic object was last updated.

- `ModificationCount` refers to the internal modification counter for each statistic that drives automatic updates. For more information on statistics, see the *Mechanics of the Query Optimizer* chapter.

- `SamplingPercent` refers to the sampling rate with which a statistic was last updated. It can reach 100 percent, meaning the statistic was updated as part of a full scan of the underlying table or indexed view.

QueryPlanHash

`QueryPlanHash` is a binary hash value calculated on the query plan and used to uniquely identify a query execution plan. In other words, this is a query plan fingerprint.

QueryHash

`QueryHash` is a binary hash value calculated on the query text and used to uniquely identify a query. In other words, this is a query fingerprint. We will see several examples of using the query hash in the *Building diagnostic queries using DMVs and DMFs* chapter.

Set Options

`Set Options` lists the SET options that were current as of compile time. These options determine the handling of specific information and may be different at runtime because they are based on the current session. The options tracked are `ANSI_NULLS`, `ANSI_PADDING`, `ANSI_WARNINGS`, `ARITHABORT`, `CONCAT_NULL_YIELDS_NULL`, `NUMERIC_ROUNDABORT`, and `QUOTED_IDENTIFIER`. These SET options affect estimations and query results, which means that if one option is changed inside of a batch, a recompilation must happen. Keep these options in mind when analyzing a query that may meet the expected performance in a development or pre-production system but performs poorly in a production system.

For example, `ANSI_NULLS` specifies the ISO-compliant behavior for `NULL` equality and inequality comparison, which dramatically changes the resulting query plan. The following examples executed in the `AdventureWorks` sample database differ only in the `ANSI_NULLS` setting. First, set `ANSI_NULLS` to ON as recommended:

```
SET ANSI_NULLS ON
GO
SELECT *
FROM Sales.SalesOrderDetail AS sod
INNER JOIN Production.Product AS p ON sod.ProductID = p.ProductID
WHERE SellEndDate = NULL
ORDER BY Style DESC
OPTION (MAXDOP 1);
```

The query generates the following execution plan:

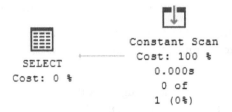

Figure 3.47: Execution plan for the SELECT * query

Then, set `ANSI_NULLS` to OFF:

```
SET ANSI_NULLS OFF
GO
SELECT *
FROM Sales.SalesOrderDetail AS sod
INNER JOIN Production.Product AS p ON sod.ProductID = p.ProductID
WHERE SellEndDate = NULL
ORDER BY Style DESC
OPTION (MAXDOP 1);
```

The query generates the following execution plan:

Figure 3.48: Execution plan for the SELECT * query

The first query returns zero rows and the second returns 99,469 rows, which has an obvious impact on resource usage. The ISO-compliant statement for NULL equality should instead be the following:

```
SET ANSI_NULLS ON
GO
SELECT *
FROM Sales.SalesOrderDetail AS sod
INNER JOIN Production.Product AS p ON sod.ProductID = p.ProductID
WHERE SellEndDate IS NULL
ORDER BY Style DESC
OPTION (MAXDOP 1);
```

The query generates the same execution plan as the preceding ANSI_NULLS OFF example. This is because when ANSI_NULLS is on, a comparison to NULL must use the ISO convention that a NULL value evaluates to an unknown value, and as such is not equal to another NULL value. If SET ANSI_NULLS is not specified for the session or statement, then the ANSI_NULLS database option stands.

Statement

Statement is the actual T-SQL statement that was executed. The statement captured in the plan is limited to the first 4,000 characters.

TraceFlags

TraceFlags can expand to show additional information on trace flags present during compilation and execution. Trace flags may change the behavior of the SQL Database Engine during query compilation and optimization, during query execution, or both. Therefore, during any query performance troubleshooting exercise, it's important to know which trace flags were influencing a given query at any stage. Under the TraceFlags property, two lists can be expanded:

- [1] IsCompileTime | True: This returns a list of all trace flags active in the system when the query was undergoing the process of compilation and optimization

- [2] IsCompileTime | False*: This returns a list of all trace flags active in the system when the query was being executed

In *Figure 3.49*, on the left side, we see two trace flags present at both compile and execution time: 7412 and 4199.

> **Tip**
> These are documented trace flags. For more information, refer to the SQL Database Engine documentation page at http://aka.ms/traceflags.

On the right side of *Figure 3.49*, we see the same two trace flags present at compile time, but only one at execution time (7412). This means that between the time the query was compiled and the current query execution plan was captured, trace flag 4199 was disabled at the system level using the DBCC TRACEOFF (4199, -1) T-SQL command:

Figure 3.49: Trace flags information in the Properties window

Because trace flag 4199 enables Query Optimizer hotfixes, we immediately know that the plan to which the left side of *Figure 3.49* belongs was compiled using a non-default set of query optimization options. Because trace flag 4199 was since disabled using the **Database Console Command (DBCC)** TRACEOFF, such options are not available for new incoming T-SQL queries that have not been compiled yet. This provides important context for the query performance troubleshooting exercise.

WaitStats

WaitStats* can expand to show additional information about the top 10 waits accrued while the query was executing in the scope of the current session, in ascending order of wait time in SQL Server 2019, and descending order up to SQL Server 2017. For each wait, three properties are available:

- `WaitCount*` refers to the number of times that tasks associated with this request had to wait for a required resource to become available

- `WaitTimeMs*` refers to the overall wait time in milliseconds for the number of times a query had to wait during query execution

- `WaitType*` refers to the wait type as documented in the SQL Database Engine documentation under the `sys.dm_os_wait_stats` **dynamic management view (DMV)**

Next is the detail for this property for the example query:

⊟ WaitStats		
⊟ [1]		
	WaitCount	1493
	WaitTimeMs	1
	WaitType	MEMORY_ALLOCATION_EXT
⊟ [2]		
	WaitCount	5081
	WaitTimeMs	7
	WaitType	RESERVED_MEMORY_ALLOCATION_EXT
⊟ [3]		
	WaitCount	21
	WaitTimeMs	231
	WaitType	PAGEIOLATCH_SH
⊟ [4]		
	WaitCount	289
	WaitTimeMs	2198
	WaitType	SOS_SCHEDULER_YIELD
⊟ [5]		
	WaitCount	53
	WaitTimeMs	4102
	WaitType	ASYNC_NETWORK_IO

Figure 3.50: Wait information in the Properties window

QueryTimeStats

QueryTimeStats* can expand to show additional information on time metrics for a given execution. The detailed elements in **QueryTimeStats** include **CpuTime*** and **ElapsedTime*** for the overall query and are available starting with SQL Server 2012 SP4, SQL Server 2014 SP3, SQL Server 2016 SP1, SQL Server 2017, and in Azure SQL Database. Both are measured in milliseconds and can replace the need to execute the query with `SET STATISTICS TIME` separately.

Next is the detail for this property for the example query:

⊟ QueryTimeStats		
	CpuTime	557
	ElapsedTime	3251

Figure 3.51: Query time statistics information in the Properties window

For queries that call **User-Defined Functions** (**UDFs**), the **UdfCpuTime*** and **UdfElapsedTime*** elements are also included under **QueryTimeStats**. These are available starting with SQL Server 2014 SP3, SQL Server 2016 SP2, SQL Server 2017 CU3, and Azure SQL Database. Both are also measured in milliseconds and provide insight into the cost of executing a UDF, which can otherwise go unnoticed by simply looking at a plan. The following example creates a scalar UDF in the `AdventureWorks` sample database:

```
CREATE FUNCTION ufn_CategorizePrice (@Price money)
RETURNS NVARCHAR(50)
AS
BEGIN
      DECLARE @PriceCategory NVARCHAR(50)
IF @Price < 100 SELECT @PriceCategory = 'Cheap'
IF @Price BETWEEN 101 and 500 SELECT @PriceCategory = 'Mid Price'
IF @Price BETWEEN 501 and 1000 SELECT @PriceCategory = 'Expensive'
IF @Price > 1001 SELECT @PriceCategory = 'Unaffordable'
RETURN @PriceCategory
END;
```

And now for a query executed in the `AdventureWorks` sample database that uses the newly created UDF:

```
SELECT dbo.ufn_CategorizePrice(UnitPrice),  SalesOrderID,
SalesOrderDetailID, CarrierTrackingNumber, OrderQty, ProductID,
SpecialOfferID, UnitPrice, UnitPriceDiscount,  LineTotal, rowguid,
ModifiedDate
FROM Sales.SalesOrderDetail;
```

In the generated execution plan, we can see the two additional properties under **QueryTimeStats**:

Figure 3.52: Query time statistics information in the Properties window

MissingIndexes

`MissingIndexes` refers to potentially missing indexes that may benefit the query's performance, as identified by the Query Optimizer during query compilation. During the compilation process, which we discussed in the *Query compilation essentials* section of *Chapter 1, Understanding Query Processing*, the SQL Database Engine matches existing indexes where any of the columns required for the query predicates, aggregates, and output are present. Then, it chooses to access the existing index or set of indexes that minimize the cost of access to the required columns; in other words, the index or set of indexes that are the cheapest to read data from.

As this matching process occurs, the SQL Database Engine can identify whether the current set of indexes already covers the query, partially or as a whole, or if a more optimized index could be created to lower the cost of accessing the required columns. For each table mentioned in the query, if the SQL Database Engine can find an index that might provide cheaper access to data, then it will store that missing index recommendation in the cached plan.

The missing index recommendation builds a recommendation based on the following criteria:

- Columns present in join or search equality predicates such as `WHERE column = value`, `WHERE column IS NULL` for a nullable column, or an `ON column = column` join

- Columns present in join or search inequality predicates such as `WHERE column <> value`, `WHERE column > value`, or `WHERE column IS NOT NULL` for a nullable column

- Columns present in the output such as those in the `SELECT` clause or an `UPDATE … FROM`

For all these conditions, the columns will be listed in the order that they appear in the underlying tables.

The query execution plan for which we have been examining all the previous properties doesn't have missing index recommendations, so we need to use a different query. The following example is a query that executes in the `AdventureWorks` sample database with an existing `NonClustered Index Scan` operator and a `Clustered Index Scan` operator:

```
SELECT p.FirstName, p.LastName, c.AccountNumber
FROM Person.Person p
INNER JOIN Sales.Customer c ON c.PersonID = p.BusinessEntityID
WHERE p.FirstName = 'Robert';
```

The query generates the following execution plan:

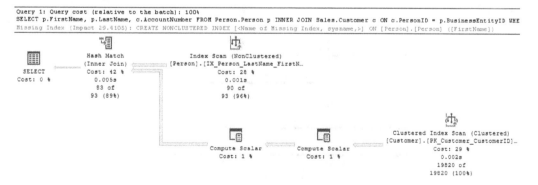

Figure 3.53: Execution plan for the SELECT query

Recall what we discussed in the previous section, *Query plan operators of interest*, under *NonClustered Index Scan*. In this case, the SQL Database Engine uses the following:

- An existing non-clustered index of the `Person` table that doesn't contain the `FirstName` column as a leading key column, but it is the second column in the index. Because the query is searching for `FirstName` only, the SQL Database Engine cannot seek the index.

- The clustered index of the `Customer` table because none of the existing non-clustered indexes contains the `PersonID` as a key column. Because the query is joining on `PersonID` only, the SQL Database Engine cannot seek the index.

Note that in the graphical query plan, we can only see one index recommendation with an estimated impact of 29.4 percent. However, the query plan may have more than one index recommendation because the query uses several tables. To see all index recommendations, we need to look at the XML of the plan or open the **Properties** window by right-clicking the root node (SELECT), which we can see in the following screenshot:

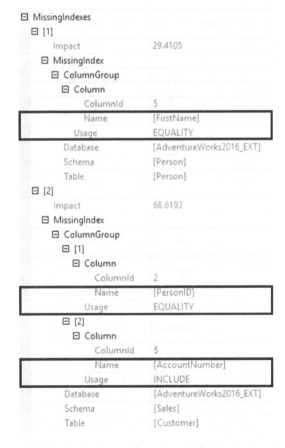

Figure 3.54: Missing indexes information in the Properties window

Now, we can see that two index recommendations exist in the screenshot. Based on the order in which the SQL Database Engine builds index recommendations, we need to look at EQUALITY columns, then INEQUALITY columns (if any), and finally, at any output columns (identified as INCLUDE). I can derive index creation statements from this information – in fact, that is what SSMS did in the graphical query plan:

- One index recommendation for the Person table, with the following index creation statement: CREATE INDEX IX_FirstName ON [Person].[Person] ([FirstName])

- One index recommendation for the Customer table, with the following index creation statement: CREATE INDEX IX_PersonID ON [Sales].[Customer] ([PersonID]) INCLUDE ([AccountNumber])

Because there aren't any existing indexes that even closely match these definitions, we can create the indexes. Then, we can execute the query again, which generates the following execution plan without missing index recommendations:

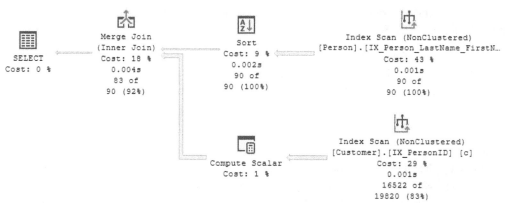

Figure 3.55: Execution plan for the same SELECT query using the same indexes

However, notice the new index on the Person table was not used. We created the new index with the key on the FirstName column as recommended, so why was the previous index used? The answer is that the new index doesn't include the other required column in the Person table – LastName. It was still cheaper to use the previous index than to use the new non-clustered index, which requires a lookup in the clustered index. Also, notice the SQL Database Engine changed the join type due to improved statistical information that became available after the index creation was executed. Recreating the index to include the LastName column should allow the new index to be used. The following index creation statement does this: CREATE INDEX IX_FirstName ON [Person]. [Person] ([FirstName]) INCLUDE ([LastName]).

Then, we can execute the query again, which generates the following execution plan:

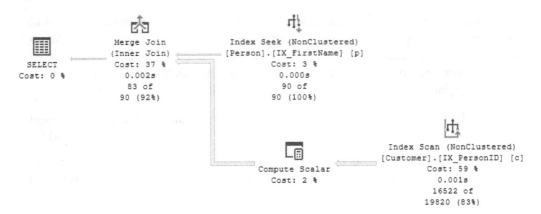

Figure 3.56: Execution plan for the same SELECT query using a new index

As expected, the revised index on the `Person` table is used. Look for missing index suggestions as one way to help optimize our queries. All index types and options mentioned will be discussed in *Chapter 4, Indexing for T-SQL Performance*.

In the *Troubleshooting Common Scenarios with DMV Queries* section of *Chapter 7, Building Diagnostic Queries Using DMVs and DMFs,* we will see examples of how to leverage DMVs to programmatically access missing index information that our the SQL Database Engine may be storing.

Parameter List

`Parameter List` can expand to show additional information on which parameters the current plan was compiled with and is available for parameterized queries only. This can be useful to troubleshoot issues such as parameter sniffing and data type conversion issues from within a showplan, without the need to access the database. That is very useful in case the user who's analyzing the plan is working remotely or lacks permission to access the database schema. For each parameter, four elements are available:

- `Column` identifies the parameter name in the current plan

- `Parameter Compiled Value` refers to the first incoming value for the parameter that drove the process of query optimization

- `Parameter Data Type` refers to the data type of the first incoming value for the parameter

- `Parameter Runtime Value`* refers to the last used value for the parameter, for a plan that had been previously compiled and cached

> **Note**
>
> We will further detail implicit conversion issues in *Chapter 6, Discovering T-SQL Anti-Patterns in Depth.*

Take the following example of a stored procedure created and executed in the `AdventureWorks` sample database:

```
CREATE OR ALTER PROCEDURE usp_SalesProds (@P1 NVARCHAR(10))
AS
SELECT *
FROM Sales.SalesOrderDetail AS sod
INNER JOIN Production.Product AS p ON sod.ProductID = p.ProductID
WHERE SalesOrderID = @P1
ORDER BY Style DESC;
GO
EXEC usp_SalesProds @P1 = 49879;
GO
EXEC usp_SalesProds @P1 = 48766;
GO
```

In the generated execution plan, we can see the information under `Parameter List`:

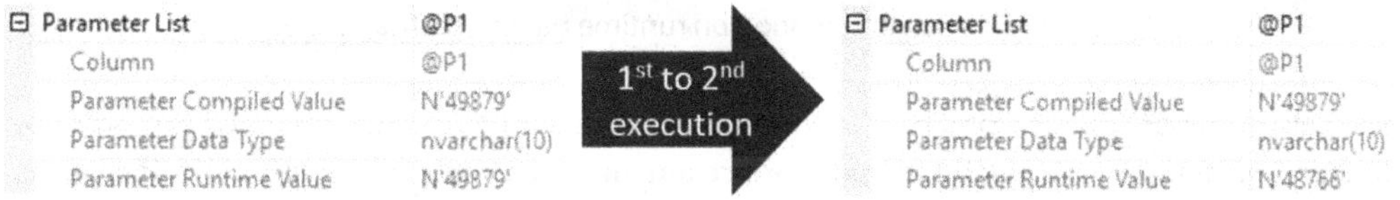

Figure 3.57: Plan information on compile-time and runtime parameter usage

On the first execution of the stored procedure, the SQL Database Engine reads the incoming parameters and uses that information plus statistics to generate a plan that's optimized to retrieve the required set of data. This is the reason we see `Parameter Compiled Value` equal to `Parameter Runtime Value`.

On the second execution, notice how `Parameter Runtime Value` changed but `Parameter Compiled Value` remained the same. This indicates that the query plan was reused from the cache.

Now, let's see an example of a query using `sp_prepare` in the `AdventureWorks` sample database:

```
DECLARE @P1 int;
EXEC sp_prepare @P1 output, N'@P1 int',
N'SELECT *
FROM Sales.SalesOrderDetail AS sod
INNER JOIN Production.Product AS p ON sod.ProductID = p.ProductID
WHERE SalesOrderID = @P1
ORDER BY Style DESC
OPTION (MAXDOP 1);';
SELECT @P1;
GO
```

This returns a handle with value 1, which applications can use by executing `sp_execute`, before evicting the plan from the cache with `sp_unprepare`:

```
EXEC sp_execute 1, N'49879';
GO
EXEC sp_execute 1, N'48766';
GO
EXEC sp_unprepare 1;
GO
```

In the generated execution plan, we can see the information under `Parameter List`:

Figure 3.58: Plan information on runtime parameter usage

Notice that `Parameter Compiled Value` is absent. This is because the prepared plan was not parameterized, and so the cached plan does not retain any parameter information. Furthermore, unlike a stored procedure where a DBA can ultimately see the parameter data type by opening the T-SQL definition, a prepared query is not an object inside a database. So, having the information on the parameter data type becomes valuable to troubleshoot conversion issues that could otherwise only be found by tracing workload activity to detect the `sp_prepare` statement.

Warnings

`Warnings*` can expand to show the type of warning and additional information that helps the troubleshooting process. Plan-level warnings will show as a yellow triangle sign in the graphical query execution plan at the root-node level (`SELECT`). Hovering over the operators that display such a triangle will also show details on the warning. As of the time this book was written, the existing plan-level warning types were the following.

PlanAffectingConvert

`PlanAffectingConvert*` happens when the Query Optimizer encounters the need to convert data types and the conversion operation affects the cardinality estimation process or the ability to seek an existing index. Because conversions occur at runtime and query optimization happens before execution, the Query Optimizer cannot account for such information during compilation. This is a direct result of the developers' choices, either at the query or database schema level, but can usually be remediated. The following example shows a query executed in the `AdventureWorks` sample database with a conversion warning about cardinality estimates:

```
CREATE TABLE #tmpSales (SalesOrderID CHAR(10) PRIMARY KEY CLUSTERED);
INSERT INTO #tmpSales
SELECT TOP 1000 SalesOrderID FROM Sales.SalesOrderHeader;
GO
SELECT * FROM #tmpSales WHERE SalesOrderID = 44360;
```

Next is the warning detail for the example query, where the two cardinality estimation warning types are present:

Warnings	Type conversion in expression (CONVERT_IMPLICIT(int,[tempdb].[dbo].[#tmpSa
PlanAffectingConvert	
ConvertIssue	CardinalityEstimate
Expression	CONVERT_IMPLICIT(int,[tempdb].[dbo].[#tmpSales].[SalesOrderID],0)
PlanAffectingConvert	
ConvertIssue	SeekPlan
Expression	CONVERT_IMPLICIT(int,[tempdb].[dbo].[#tmpSales].[SalesOrderID],0)=(44360)

Figure 3.59: Plan warning on type conversion affecting estimations

Looking at the query predicate and the table schema, we see the converted expression happens because of a mismatch between data types: the query predicate is passed as an integer, while the table's data type is a string. This affects the ability to do accurate estimations but also prevents seeking the clustered index for the same reason. All warnings can also be seen in the generated execution plan by hovering over the `SELECT` icon:

Figure 3.60: All applicable warnings for the execution plan

To remediate this case, simply change either the base table data type to integer or the predicate to string. This eliminates both warnings because there will be no conversion, and therefore an index seek can be used rather than a scan.

WaitForMemoryGrant*

WaitForMemoryGrant* happens when a query waits more than 1 second to acquire a memory grant or when the initial attempt to get the memory fails. RESOURCE_SEMAPHORE waits may indicate an excessive number of concurrent queries or an excessive amount of memory grant requests that the current resources cannot handle. The warning reports the number of seconds the query had to wait for MemoryGrant during execution:

⊟ Warnings	The query had to wait 127 seconds for MemoryGrant during execution
⊟ Wait	
WaitTime	127
WaitType	MemoryGrant

Figure 3.61: Plan warning on memory grant waits

MemoryGrantWarning*

MemoryGrantWarning* happens when the SQL Database Engine detects that memory grants were not estimated properly, as it relates to the comparison between the initial memory grant and the memory used throughout execution. This warning happens when one of three conditions occur:

- ExcessiveGrant is fired when the max used memory is too small when compared to the granted memory. This scenario can cause blocking and severely affect the SQL Database Engine's ability to run concurrent workloads efficiently. For example, if the SQL Database Engine has 10 GB of memory, and each request is granted 1 GB of memory but only uses a small fraction of that, then, at most, only 10 queries can be active simultaneously, but looking at the actual used memory, this number could be far greater. Next is the warning detail where the ExcessiveGrant condition is present:

⊟ Warnings	The query memory grant detected "ExcessiveGrant", which may impact the reliability.
— ⊟ MemoryGrantWarning	—
GrantedMemory	67808
GrantWarningKind	ExcessiveGrant
MaxUsedMemory	984
RequestedMemory	67808

Figure 3.62: Plan warning on excessive memory grant size

Memory estimations are directly related to the query optimization process and the estimated plan. There are several ways to attempt remediation, and updating statistics can usually help improve estimations. Recent versions of the SQL Database Engine can administratively address these with the use of the `MIN_PERCENT_GRANT` and the `MAX_PERCENT_GRANT` query hints.

- `GrantIncrease` is fired when the grant starts to increase too much, based on the ratio between the max used memory and the initial requested memory grant. Unlike row mode, where the initial memory grant is not dynamic, batch mode allows for the initial grant to be exceeded to a point before a spill occurs. This is done because spilling in batch mode has a greater cost than spilling in row mode. For example, consider the SQL Database Engine with 10 GB of memory, where each request is running in batch mode and granted 512 MB of memory. If around 20 requests are executing simultaneously and can exceed that initial amount of memory, this can cause server instability and unpredictable workload performance.

- `UsedMoreThanGranted` is fired when the max used memory exceeds the initially granted memory. Much as with the `GrantIncrease` scenario, this can cause **out-of-memory (OOM)** conditions on the server.

SpatialGuess*

`SpatialGuess*` happens when the SQL Database Engine must use a fixed selectivity estimation (also called guess) when optimizing a query that uses spatial data types and indexes. Next is the warning detail where the `SpatialGuess*` condition is present:

Figure 3.63: Plan warning on a guess being used for cardinality estimation in a spatial query

UnmatchedIndexes*

`UnmatchedIndexes*` happens when the Query Optimizer cannot match an existing filtered index with a query predicate due to parameterization.

> **Note**
> The SQL Database Engine can use optimized non-clustered indexes that are defined using a `WHERE` clause. These are called filtered indexes and are especially suitable for narrow query coverage. Being defined on a subset of data, these indexes can significantly improve query performance.

The following example creates a filtered index in the `AdventureWorks` sample database and then executes a query with an unmatched index warning:

```
CREATE NONCLUSTERED INDEX FIProductAccessories ON Production.
Product (ProductSubcategoryID, ListPrice) INCLUDE (Name) WHERE
ProductSubcategoryID >= 27 AND ProductSubcategoryID <= 36;
GO
DECLARE @i int = 33
SELECT Name, ProductSubcategoryID, ListPrice
FROM Production.Product
WHERE ProductSubcategoryID = @i AND ListPrice > 25.00;
```

Next is the `UnmatchedIndexes` warning detail for the example query. Also, notice the extra element, `UnmatchedIndexes`:

⊟ UnmatchedIndexes	
⊟ Parameterization	[AdventureWorks2016].[Production].[Product].[FIProductAccessories]
Database	[AdventureWorks2016]
Index	[FIProductAccessories]
Schema	[Production]
Table	[Product]
⊟ Warnings	
UnmatchedIndexes	True

Figure 3.64: Plan warning on a filtered index that could not be used due to an out-of-range predicate

It's clear that the SQL Database Engine was able to identify an eligible filtered index but was unable to use it because, if a query is parameterized, that means that an incoming parameter with a value outside the defined filter would not produce a result. In the following example, the SQL Database Engine can leverage the filtered index:

```
SELECT Name, ProductSubcategoryID, ListPrice
FROM Production.Product
WHERE ProductSubcategoryID = 33 AND ListPrice > 25.00;
```

This is because the query is not parameterized, which means the SQL Database Engine can match the incoming predicate with an existing filtered index and use it to read only the relevant subset of data.

One other alternative to make the SQL Database Engine leverage the filtered index is to build the variable into the string and then execute it, like so:

```
DECLARE @i int = 33, @sqlcmd NVARCHAR(500)
SELECT @sqlcmd = 'SELECT Name, ProductSubcategoryID, ListPrice
FROM Production.Product WHERE ProductSubcategoryID = ' + CAST(@i AS
NVARCHAR(5)) + ' AND ListPrice > 25.00;'
EXECUTE sp_executesql @sqlcmd;
```

This way, the SQL Database Engine executes a query that matches the non-parameterized version, and the filtered index predicate can be matched.

FullUpdateForOnlineIndexBuild*

FullUpdateForOnlineIndexBuild* happens when converting a partial index update to a full index update during an online index create or rebuild operation.

Operator-level properties

Analyzing plan-level properties provides context for the overall plan and the system in which the query plan is executed. After that step, it's very important to keep in mind some of the key properties that can be found in the query plan operators of interest that we discussed earlier in this chapter.

The following example shows a query executed in the AdventureWorks sample database that allows us to examine most of these properties:

```
SELECT *
FROM Sales.SalesOrderDetail AS sod
INNER JOIN Production.Product AS p ON sod.ProductID = p.ProductID
WHERE p.ProductID BETWEEN 850 AND 860
ORDER BY Style DESC
OPTION (USE HINT('ENABLE_PARALLEL_PLAN_PREFERENCE'));
```

The query generates the following execution plan:

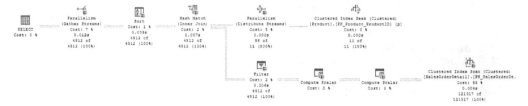

Figure 3.65: Execution plan for the SELECT * query

Right-click on the most expensive operator in the plan, open the context menu, and click on **Properties**:

Figure 3.66: Opening the operator Properties window

Tip

To identify the most expensive operators, follow the thickest arrows from left to right, top to bottom. Note that the **Cost** label in every operator refers to the estimated cost, not the actual execution cost. Therefore, do *not* use this label as a method of finding the most expensive operators in an actual execution plan.

This opens the **Properties** window:

Figure 3.67: Clustered Index Scan Properties window

RunTimeCountersPerThread*

When troubleshooting query performance problems, having the right metrics available in the query plan avoids unnecessary roundtrips and delays that can be critical. The SQL Database Engine stores several runtime statistics per operator and per thread under `RunTimeCountersPerThread*`, providing great insights into the performance metrics of various data access operators.

Actual I/O Statistics

Optimizing I/O is usually the best tuning approach because with higher I/O comes higher memory consumption, as the SQL Database Engine needs to store more data pages in the buffer pool, and higher CPU, as cycles are spent processing I/O requests and data movement.

`Actual I/O Statistics*` provides information on **Large Object** (**LOB**), Physical, and Logical reads, allowing for immediate insight into the cost of an operator without the need to collect or interpret the information from `SET STATISTICS IO`.

If the query was executed in parallel, then we can see how many data pages were read by each thread. Next is the detail for the most expensive operator in the aforementioned plan, a clustered index scan:

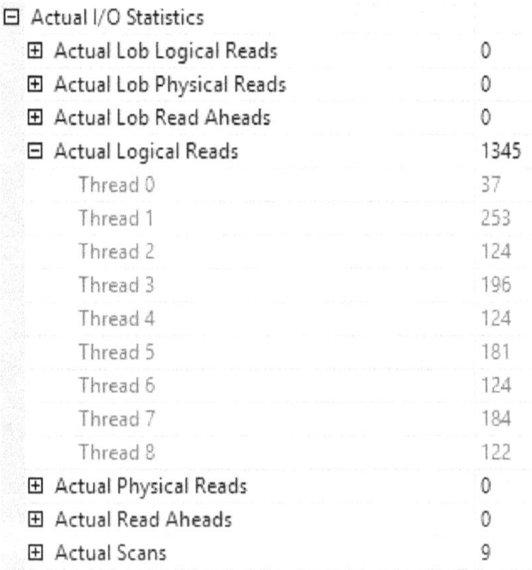

⊟ Actual I/O Statistics	
⊞ Actual Lob Logical Reads	0
⊞ Actual Lob Physical Reads	0
⊞ Actual Lob Read Aheads	0
⊟ Actual Logical Reads	1345
Thread 0	37
Thread 1	253
Thread 2	124
Thread 3	196
Thread 4	124
Thread 5	181
Thread 6	124
Thread 7	184
Thread 8	122
⊞ Actual Physical Reads	0
⊞ Actual Read Aheads	0
⊞ Actual Scans	9

Figure 3.68: Logical reads per thread in the Properties window

Actual Number of Rows

Similarly, having information on the actual number of rows that flowed through the operators allows database professionals to track the most expensive areas of a plan. Actual Number of Rows (ActualRows* in the showplan XML) shows the number of rows output by an operator after any predicates were applied. Number of Rows Read (ActualRowsRead* in the showplan XML) shows the number of rows read before predicates were applied. Next is the detail for both properties in the same clustered index scan:

Actual Number of Rows	121317	Number of Rows Read	121317
Thread 0	0	Thread 1	23109
Thread 1	23109	Thread 2	11174
Thread 2	11174	Thread 3	18209
Thread 3	18209	Thread 4	11421
Thread 4	11421	Thread 5	17864
Thread 5	17864	Thread 6	11469
Thread 6	11469	Thread 7	16792
Thread 7	16792	Thread 8	11279
Thread 8	11279		

Figure 3.69: Rows per thread in the Properties window

> **Note**
>
> Thread zero is the coordinating thread and does not accumulate I/O, which is handled by all the other threads for the request.

Actual time statistics

Time is an important measurement, not only by itself but because these properties track the time in milliseconds an operator spent during execution. As such, comparing these with waits accrued during execution and the overall query elapsed execution time allows database professionals to pinpoint expensive areas of the plan with great accuracy.

Actual Elapsed CPU Time (ActualCPUms* in the showplan XML) shows the CPU time accumulated over all threads, with details on each thread for parallel queries. Actual Elapsed Time (ActualElapsedms* in the showplan XML) shows the elapsed time the operator took to execute. Although there is detail on each thread for parallel queries, the overall elapsed time is the same as the slowest thread time. Having this information in the showplan removes the need to collect or interpret information from SET STATISTICS TIME.

Next is the detail for both properties in the same clustered index scan:

⊟ Actual Time Statistics	
⊟ Actual Elapsed CPU Time (ms)	20
Thread 0	0
Thread 1	2
Thread 2	2
Thread 3	4
Thread 4	2
Thread 5	4
Thread 6	2
Thread 7	2
Thread 8	2
⊟ Actual Elapsed Time (ms)	4
Thread 0	0
Thread 1	3
Thread 2	3
Thread 3	4
Thread 4	2
Thread 5	4
Thread 6	3
Thread 7	2
Thread 8	3

Figure 3.70: Time elapsed per thread in the Properties window

Estimated rows

When analyzing a plan retrieved from the plan cache, which is an estimated plan or query plan, only the estimations are available. In an actual plan or query execution plan, this information is present, and it becomes useful to compare it with the actual rows we just discussed. This is because significant differences between estimated and actual rows usually expose cardinality estimation issues and whether queries are using underlying indexes efficiently.

> **Note**
>
> We will further discuss remediation techniques for cardinality estimation issues in *Chapters 9* through *11* of the book.

Estimated Number of Rows (EstimateRows in the showplan XML) shows the estimated number of rows output by an operator after any predicates are applied. Estimated Number of Rows to be Read (EstimatedRowsRead in the showplan XML) shows the estimated number of rows read before predicates are applied. Next is the detail for both properties in the same clustered index scan:

Estimated Number of Rows	121317
Estimated Number of Rows to be Read	121317

Figure 3.71: Estimated rows information in the Properties window

EstimateRowsWithoutRowGoal

The `EstimateRowsWithoutRowGoal` property is available starting with SQL Server 2016 SP2 and SQL Server 2017 CU3 when the Query Optimizer uses an optimization technique called a **Row Goal**. If the Query Optimizer used a row goal, this property expresses the estimated number of rows that would be processed if the row goal hadn't been used.

Normally, when the Query Optimizer estimates the cost of a query plan, it usually assumes that all qualifying rows from all tables must be processed. However, when a query uses a TOP, IN, or EXISTS clause, a FAST query hint, or a SET ROWCOUNT statement, this causes the Query Optimizer to search for a query plan that will quickly return a smaller number of rows. This makes a row goal a very useful optimization strategy for certain query patterns.

The following example shows a query executed in the `AdventureWorks` sample database that allows us to examine this property:

```
SELECT TOP (100) *
FROM Sales.SalesOrderHeader AS s
INNER JOIN Sales.SalesOrderDetail AS d ON s.SalesOrderID =
d.SalesOrderID
WHERE s.TotalDue > 1000;
```

In the generated execution plan, we can see the `EstimateRowsWithoutRowGoal` property of the `Clustered Index Scan` operator on the `SalesOrderDetail` table:

EstimateRowsWithoutRowGoal   121317

Figure 3.72: Estimated row information in the Properties window, if a row goal was not used

These can be compared with the estimated rows we discussed in the previous section to determine whether the row goal is being used to the query's advantage or not. If `Estimated Number of Rows` is significantly lower than `Estimated Number of Rows to be Read` and the row goal is used, it may be the case that the row goal is not improving the plan quality. We will see more of this property and how to use it for troubleshooting in the *Query plan comparison* section of *Chapter 9, Comparative Analysis of Query Plans*.

In *Chapter 2, Mechanics of the Query Optimizer*, we discussed the new SQL Server 2022 feature named CE Feedback, and how it can automatically remove much of the risk in upgrading CE versions for application workloads that may be susceptible to the model changes of a higher CE version. We mentioned that Row Goal is also a scenario handled by CE Feedback. The same test-and-verify principle is used: CE Feedback can detect whether a row goal is being used to the query's advantage or not, and if not, disable the row goal for that query.

> **Note**
>
> At the time this book is written, CE Feedback is not yet generally available in Azure SQL Database.

Warnings

`Warnings*` also surface on specific operators. These contain information that helps the troubleshooting process when drilling through a plan. As with plan-level warnings, operator-level warnings show as a yellow triangle sign in the graphical query execution plan. Again, hovering over the operators that display such a triangle will also show details on the warning. As of the time this book was written, the existing operator-level warning types were the following.

Columns With No Statistics

`Columns With No Statistics*` happens when the Query Optimizer needs to load statistics on any given column that's relevant for the query, but none exist. If **Auto-Create Statistics** is disabled in the database, the SQL Database Engine cannot automatically create missing statistics, and this warning persists between executions. The following example shows a query executed in the `AdventureWorks` sample database with a `Columns With No Statistics*` warning:

```
USE [master]
GO
ALTER DATABASE [AdventureWorks]
SET AUTO_CREATE_STATISTICS OFF
GO
SELECT [CarrierTrackingNumber]
FROM Sales.SalesOrderDetail
WHERE [OrderQty] > 10
ORDER BY OrderQty;
GO
ALTER DATABASE [AdventureWorks]
SET AUTO_CREATE_STATISTICS ON
GO
```

In the generated execution plan, we can see the warning under the properties of the `Clustered Index Scan` operator that generated it:

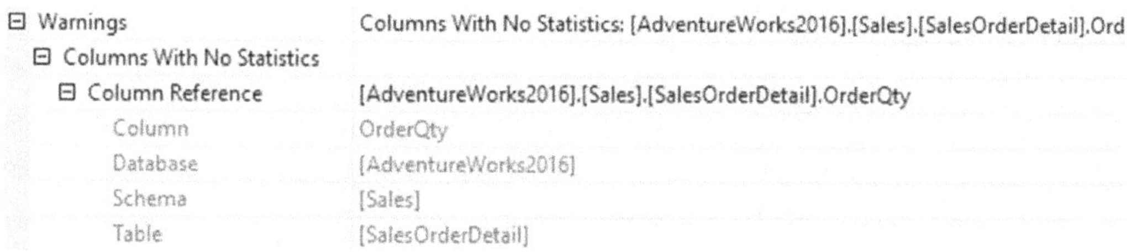

⊟ Warnings	Columns With No Statistics: [AdventureWorks2016].[Sales].[SalesOrderDetail].Ord
⊟ Columns With No Statistics	
⊟ Column Reference	[AdventureWorks2016].[Sales].[SalesOrderDetail].OrderQty
Column	OrderQty
Database	[AdventureWorks2016]
Schema	[Sales]
Table	[SalesOrderDetail]

Figure 3.73: Plan warning on columns without statistics in the Properties window

If **Auto-Create Statistics** is enabled, as it is by default and as a best practice, then the SQL Database Engine will create a single-column statistic on the column that triggered the warning condition if the column is eligible.

> **Note**
>
> This warning is always present for the inner side of a Nested Loops join involving a spatial index. This is a by-design behavior.

> **Tip**
>
> Because statistics cannot be created on a non-persisted computed column, **Auto-Create Statistics** cannot automatically create a statistic object on these column types. Mark the computed column as *persisted* to allow **Auto-Create Statistics**.

Starting with SQL Server 2019 and in Azure SQL Database, the time spent creating the statistic triggered by this warning will also be visible as an accumulated wait with the WAIT_ON_SYNC_STATISTICS_REFRESH type.

Spill To Tempdb*

Spill To Tempdb* happens when the available query memory (known as the memory grant) is not enough to run the required operation in memory and, rather than halting execution, the operation instead runs with the support of tempdb workfiles or worktables, depending on the type of spill. By resorting to I/O rather than being executed solely in memory, spills usually must be remediated as they can severely slow down query performance. We covered common Sort and Hash spills in the *Query plan operators of interest* section of this chapter; they include the following:

- Sort Spill*
- Hash Spill*
- Exchange Spill*

No Join Predicate

No Join Predicate happens when the SQL Database Engine cannot identify a join predicate to apply to a join between two or more tables, and none has been specified in the T-SQL statement text. The following example shows a query executed in the AdventureWorks sample database with a No Join Predicate warning:

```
SELECT *
FROM Sales.SalesOrderHeader AS h,
     Sales.SalesOrderDetail AS d,
     Production.Product AS p
WHERE h.SalesOrderID = 49879;
```

Unlike all other warnings, the No Join Predicate warning is shown as a red circle with a white X in the graphical query execution plan:

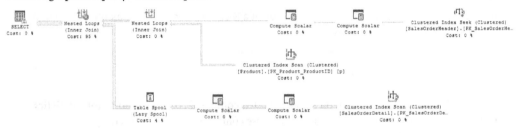

Figure 3.74: Execution plan for the SELECT * query with a No Join Predicate warning

In the generated plan, we can see the warning under the properties of the Nested Loops operator that generated it:

| ⊟ Warnings | No Join Predicate |
| No Join Predicate | True |

Figure 3.75: No Join Predicate warning information in the Properties window

To remediate this case, rewrite the query to state the intended join operation and join predicates:

```
SELECT *
FROM Sales.SalesOrderHeader AS h
INNER JOIN Sales.SalesOrderDetail AS d ON h.SalesOrderID =
d.SalesOrderID
INNER JOIN Production.Product AS p ON d.ProductId = p.ProductID
WHERE h.SalesOrderID = 49879;
```

The query then generates the following execution plan:

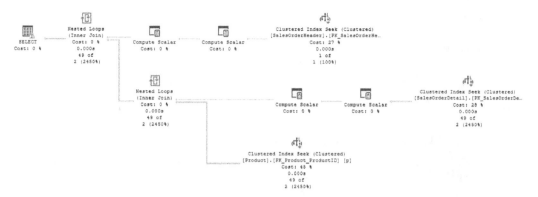

Figure 3.76: Execution plan for the SELECT * query without the No Join Predicate warning

Summary

Hopefully, after reading this chapter, you have a good understanding of the various elements that make up a query execution plan in the SQL Database Engine. Nearly everything we need to understand and troubleshoot the performance of our T-SQL queries can be found somewhere in the plan, either in the visible part of the plan or in the **Properties** windows, which we can access by right-clicking the operators. In the next chapter and throughout the rest of this book, we will use query execution plans to illustrate various T-SQL patterns and anti-patterns so that we can identify and remediate them in our own code.

Indexing for T-SQL Performance

In the previous chapter, we explored execution plans and the various operators that the SQL Database Engine uses to retrieve the data requested by a query. While the Query Optimizer does most of the heavy lifting when choosing the best way to retrieve the data required to satisfy the query, it can only do so efficiently if the proper indexes are in place.

An index is a structure in the database that speeds up access to data by organizing it in a specific way based on the type of index. The data structure that works best for your application will depend on many factors, including the type of data being stored, the volatility of the data, and the data access patterns that will be used to retrieve the data. The SQL Database Engine offers a few different index types, such as rowstore, columnstore, XML, and others. Rowstore indexes are the most common indexes in the SQL Database Engine and are what most people think of when considering indexes for query tuning, so these are what we will be focusing on for this discussion.

In this chapter, we will dive deeper into how the SQL Database Engine uses rowstore indexes to access data more efficiently, and how you can develop an indexing strategy that will set you up for better query performance.

In this chapter, we're going to cover the following main topics:

- Understanding predicate SARGability
- Data access using rowstore indexes
- Indexing strategy using rowstore indexes
- Index maintenance

Technical requirements

The examples used in this chapter are designed for use on SQL Server 2022 and Azure SQL Database, but they should work on any version of SQL Server, 2012 or later. The Developer Edition of SQL Server is free for development environments and can be used to run all the code samples. There is also a free tier of Azure SQL Database you can use for testing at https://aka.ms/freedb.

You will need the `AdventureWorks2016_EXT` (referred to as `AdventureWorks`) and `AdventureWorksDW2016_EXT` (referred to as `AdventureWorksDW`) sample databases, which can be found on GitHub at `https://github.com/Microsoft/sql-server-samples/releases/tag/adventureworks`. The code samples for this chapter can also be found on GitHub at `https://github.com/PacktPublishing/Learn-T-SQL-Querying-Second-Edition/tree/main/ch4`.

Understanding predicate SARGability

A **predicate** is a filter that can be used to determine the set of conditions to apply to a query to trim the result set. As we have discussed in previous chapters, these are typically applicable to the following clauses:

- `JOIN` clauses, which filter the rows matching the type of join
- `WHERE` clauses, which filter source rows from a table or an index
- `HAVING` clauses, which filter the results

Most queries will make use of predicates, usually through a `WHERE` clause. When a predicate is serviceable by an index, it is said the predicate is **SARGable**, which is an acronym for **S**earch **ARG**ument-**able**. Having SARGable predicates should be a goal for our T-SQL queries because it can reduce the number of rows that need to be processed by a plan earlier in the execution – that is, when the data is being read by the SQL Database Engine. The implementation of this early row count reduction is called *predicate pushdown*; it is the action of using the predicate directly in the seek or scan operation and reading only the rows that match the given predicate. When predicate pushdown is not used, the cost implications are high: the SQL Database Engine needs to read a larger number of rows from the source table or index and then filter down to the number of rows that match the predicate.

> **Note**
> The SQL Database Engine always optimizes for predicate pushdown, sometimes even when part of the predicate cannot be serviced by an index, meaning when part of the predicate is non-SARGable. Even when it results in a higher number of rows being read, this optimization can eliminate the need for filter operators in a query plan.

Let's see how to identify whether predicate pushdown is used efficiently with two examples of queries executing in the scope of the `AdventureWorks` sample database:

```
SELECT FirstName, LastName
FROM Person.Person
WHERE LastName like 'S%'
AND FirstName = 'John';
SELECT FirstName, LastName
```

```
FROM Person.Person
WHERE LastName = 'Smith'
AND FirstName like 'J%';
```

The queries generate the following result sets:

Results | Messages | Execution plan

	FirstName	LastName
1	John	Sandstone
2	John	Smith

	FirstName	LastName
1	Jacob	Smith
2	James	Smith
3	Jasmine	Smith
4	Jeff	Smith
5	Jennifer	Smith
6	Jeremiah	Smith
7	Jessica	Smith
8	John	Smith
9	Jonathan	Smith
10	Jose	Smith
11	Joseph	Smith
12	Joshua	Smith
13	Julia	Smith
14	Justin	Smith

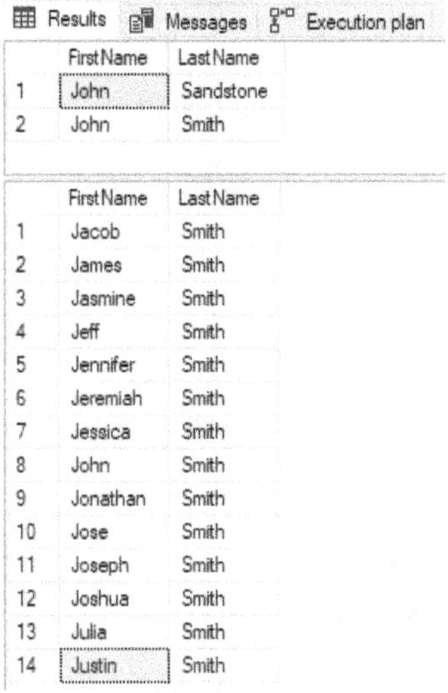

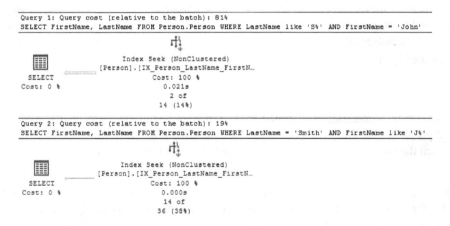

Figure 4.1: Result sets for the predicate pushdown example queries

Here are the respective execution plans:

Figure 4.2: Execution plans for the predicate pushdown example queries

Observe how the plans look the same. However, the estimated cost for *Query 1* is much higher than *Query 2* as it relates to the entire batch: 81% and 19%, respectively. This also translates into the time stats shown in the preceding plans – 64 ms and 1 ms, respectively.

Why such a big difference? By looking at the `OptimizerStatsUsage` plan property, we know the plans loaded the same statistics objects:

```
⊟ OptimizerStatsUsage
   ⊟ [1]
         Database                    [AdventureWorks2016_EXT]
         LastUpdate                  2/17/2019 11:21 AM
         ModificationCount           0
         SamplingPercent             41.5782
         Schema                      [Person]
         Statistics                  [_WA_Sys_00000005_7C4F7684]
         Table                       [Person]
   ⊟ [2]
         Database                    [AdventureWorks2016_EXT]
         LastUpdate                  11/16/2015 1:04 PM
         ModificationCount           0
         SamplingPercent             100
         Schema                      [Person]
         Statistics                  [IX_Person_LastName_FirstName_MiddleName]
         Table                       [Person]
```

Figure 4.3: The Properties window for the execution plans for the example queries showing the OptimizerStatsUsage property

The `IX_Person_LastName_FirstName_MiddleName` statistic has its histogram on the `LastName` column, and the `_WA_Sys_00000005_7C4F7684` statistics has its histogram on the `FirstName` column. This makes sense because both queries have their predicates on those two columns, and the Query Optimizer requires this information to be able to produce an optimized query plan. Looking at the actual rows and estimated rows, we can see that *Query 1* returned two rows out of 15 estimated rows, and *Query 2* returned 14 rows out of 35 estimated rows. This is a low number of rows, and the absolute difference is not significant, so it does not appear that the cost difference can be explained by an incorrect estimation of the number of rows.

> **Tip**
> Statistics that are automatically generated by the Database Engine are always named with the `_WA_Sys` prefix. The Database Engine will automatically generate single-column statistics only when the auto-create statistics option is enabled, which is the default.

As we discussed in *Chapter 3, Exploring Query Execution Plans*, the `Actual Number of Rows` and `Estimated Number of Rows` properties refer to the number of rows output by an operator after any predicates were applied. While this can give us an indication of whether the Query Optimizer has accurately estimated the cost of the query, it is not an accurate measure of whether predicate pushdown was effective. Instead, comparing the `Actual Number of Rows` and `Number of Rows Read` properties for an actual plan, or the `Estimated Number of Rows` and `Estimated Number of Rows to be Read` properties for an estimated plan, is the correct approach.

Those properties are available for the `IX_Person_LastName_FirstName_MiddleName` index in the seek operator:

Query 1

Index Seek (NonClustered)
Scan a particular range of rows from a nonclustered index.

Physical Operation	Index Seek
Logical Operation	Index Seek
Actual Execution Mode	Row
Estimated Execution Mode	Row
Storage	RowStore
Number of Rows Read	2130
Actual Number of Rows	2
Actual Number of Batches	0
Estimated Operator Cost	0.0145016 (100%)
Estimated I/O Cost	0.0120139
Estimated Subtree Cost	0.0145016
Estimated CPU Cost	0.0024877
Estimated Number of Executions	1
Number of Executions	1
Estimated Number of Rows	14.8156
Estimated Number of Rows to be Read	2118.84
Estimated Row Size	74 B
Actual Rebinds	0
Actual Rewinds	0
Ordered	True
Node ID	0

Predicate
[AdventureWorks2016_EXT].[Person].[Person].[FirstName]
=N'John' AND [AdventureWorks2016_EXT].[Person].[Person].
[LastName] like N'S%'
Object
[AdventureWorks2016_EXT].[Person].[Person].
[IX_Person_LastName_FirstName_MiddleName]
Output List
[AdventureWorks2016_EXT].[Person].[Person].FirstName,
[AdventureWorks2016_EXT].[Person].[Person].LastName
Seek Predicates
Seek Keys[1]: Start: [AdventureWorks2016_EXT].[Person].
[Person].LastName, [AdventureWorks2016_EXT].[Person].
[Person].FirstName >= Scalar Operator(N'S'), Scalar Operator
(N'John'), End: [AdventureWorks2016_EXT].[Person].
[Person].LastName < Scalar Operator(N'T')

Query 2

Index Seek (NonClustered)
Scan a particular range of rows from a nonclustered index.

Physical Operation	Index Seek
Logical Operation	Index Seek
Actual Execution Mode	Row
Estimated Execution Mode	Row
Storage	RowStore
Number of Rows Read	14
Actual Number of Rows	14
Actual Number of Batches	0
Estimated Operator Cost	0.0033209 (100%)
Estimated I/O Cost	0.003125
Estimated Subtree Cost	0.0033209
Estimated CPU Cost	0.0001959
Estimated Number of Executions	1
Number of Executions	1
Estimated Number of Rows	35.3287
Estimated Number of Rows to be Read	35.3287
Estimated Row Size	74 B
Actual Rebinds	0
Actual Rewinds	0
Ordered	True
Node ID	0

Predicate
[AdventureWorks2016_EXT].[Person].[Person].[FirstName] like
N'J%'
Object
[AdventureWorks2016_EXT].[Person].[Person].
[IX_Person_LastName_FirstName_MiddleName]
Output List
[AdventureWorks2016_EXT].[Person].[Person].FirstName,
[AdventureWorks2016_EXT].[Person].[Person].LastName
Seek Predicates
Seek Keys[1]: Prefix: [AdventureWorks2016_EXT].[Person].
[Person].LastName = Scalar Operator(N'Smith'), Start:
[AdventureWorks2016_EXT].[Person].[Person].FirstName >=
Scalar Operator(N'J'), End: [AdventureWorks2016_EXT].[Person].
[Person].FirstName < Scalar Operator(N'K')

Figure 4.4: Properties of the index seek operator from each of the example queries

For **Query 1**, we can see that 2,130 rows were read to return two rows after the seek predicate (also in Figure 4.4) was applied, so there is a significant difference. The predicate that was used for this query translates a seek condition where the `LastName` column values are greater than or equal to S, and `LastName` is smaller than T. We can also see that that the SQL Database Engine estimated that 2,118 rows would have to be read to return 14 rows, which is a similar ratio. This indicates that the SQL Database Engine worked with accurate statistics and came up with good estimates; it just so happens that the index is not optimal for the query.

> **Note**
>
> The non-SARGable predicate on the `FirstName` column was also pushed down, for the condition when values equal `John`. Although no I/O was saved, this engine optimization avoided a filter operator to be applied after the seek, saving CPU cycles.

If this query is executed often, then creating a better index for this query may be required, namely making `FirstName` the first key column: a full name such as "John" is more selective than one character followed by a wildcard.

For **Query 2**, only 14 rows were read to return 14 rows, meaning predicate pushdown read only the required number of rows for our query, which is also visible in the estimations: both `Estimated Number of Rows` and `Estimated Number of Rows to be Read` match at 35.3287 rows.

The predicates used by queries determine the database index design and vice versa. Predicate pushdown, namely SQL Server's ability to push down both SARGable and non-SARGable predicates to the Storage Engine, is an important performance feature that database professionals must be aware of when writing T-SQL queries that are expected to perform and scale well.

To summarize, the next time you see a query that returns only a few rows but comparatively takes a long time to execute and has relatively disproportionate CPU and I/O usage, investigate whether the query is making efficient use of our indexes. The next section discusses how data access using indexes works and how we can build more efficient indexes that allow our T-SQL queries to perform well from an I/O standpoint.

Data access using indexes

Now that we have discussed how the Query Optimizer uses indexes to facilitate predicate pushdown and make queries more efficient, let's explore how indexes are structured and why they are so important for query performance.

Before we begin discussing the structure of indexes, it's worth understanding how data is stored and accessed in the SQL Database Engine. Data is stored on 8 KB pages. An object such as a table or an index is essentially a collection of pages, along with metadata that maps out the structure of the object. The SQL Database Engine uses a special metadata page called an **Index Allocation Map (IAM)** page to locate the pages in an object. IAM pages contain a list of all the pages in a database file that belong to an object. Each object will have at least one IAM page but depending on the size of the object and the file structure of the database, there may be more than one IAM page, forming a chain.

Tables that do not have a clustered index are stored as *heaps*. Heaps do not have any sort of order or structure; they are simply a collection of pages. *Figure 4.5* illustrates a heap in the SQL Database Engine:

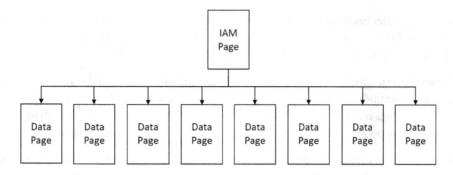

Figure 4.5: Illustration of a heap in the SQL Database Engine

The only way to locate all the pages that belong to a heap is to use the IAM page(s), so the SQL Database Engine stores a pointer to the first IAM page in the metadata for each object. If there is a chain of IAM pages, the first page will contain a pointer to the next IAM page, and so on. As you can imagine, using these IAM pages to return lists of random pages scattered throughout a database file is not the most efficient way to access data. This is where indexes come in.

Structure of a rowstore index

Rowstore indexes are stored as a special version of a B-tree known as a *B+ tree*. A B+ tree consists of a root node, one or more levels of intermediate nodes, and a leaf level. *Figure 4.6* illustrates the structure of B+ trees in the SQL Database Engine:

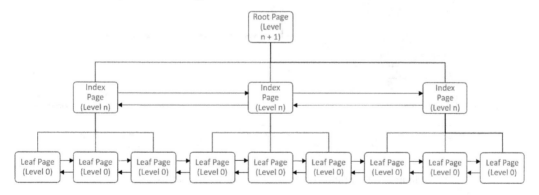

Figure 4.6: Illustration of the B+ tree data structure that is used
for rowstore indexes in the SQL Database Engine

Each node of the tree is a single page. The root and intermediate level pages contain rows that include ranges of index keys, along with a pointer to the page on the next level down that contains that range. Each page also includes a pointer to the previous page and the next page in the same level to allow for ordered scanning of any level of the index.

The leaf level pages differ based on whether the index is clustered or non-clustered. In clustered indexes, the leaf level contains the actual data pages. When you create a clustered index on a table, the table is converted from a heap to a B+ tree and the table becomes a clustered index.

In non-clustered indexes, the leaf level contains index pages that store rows of index keys with pointers to the data rows. If the underlying table is a heap, the pointer is a **row ID (RID)** that is a physical pointer to the file number, page number, and row number where the row is located. If the underlying table is a clustered index, the pointer is the clustered index key, which provides a logical pointer to the data.

The B+ tree structure is designed to minimize I/O when accessing data, particularly when accessing a small number of rows in a large table. Each row on an index page contains only index keys and pointers to child pages, which means that a single index page can hold many rows (the exact number depends on the size of the index key). Each of these rows points to a child page, so indexes in the SQL Database Engine tend to fan out wide but do not typically get very deep. This is what leads to efficient data access.

Data access using rowstore indexes

There are two ways to access data in a rowstore index: a seek or a scan. A seek involves using the keys of the index to traverse from the root to the leaf to find the rows that match a given predicate. *Figure 4.7* shows an illustration of an index seek:

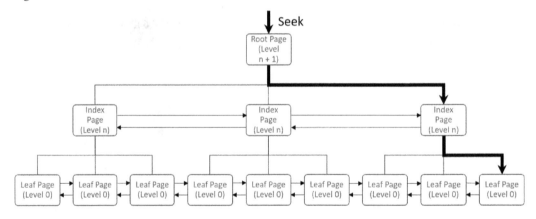

Figure 4.7: Illustration of an index seek on a rowstore index

Assuming that the index is three levels deep, as *Figure 4.7* shows, this index seek would require only three page reads. An index seek is generally the most efficient way to access data using a rowstore index, but it requires the predicate to be SARGable. If, for some reason, the index keys can't be used to locate rows in the index, a scan may be required.

Scanning an index is usually slightly more efficient than scanning a heap. As we described at the beginning of this chapter, scanning a heap involves using the IAM pages to locate all the pages of the table, which may be scattered throughout the data file(s). This leads to inefficient random I/O. While random I/O may not be an issue for modern storage systems, the SQL Database Engine has optimizations built around sequential I/O that may not be used when data is accessed randomly throughout the file.

Since rowstore indexes are stored in a B+ tree structure with pointers to the pages contained within the index itself, the IAM pages are not required. The metadata for the index contains a pointer to the root page, which serves as the entry point to the index. The Database Engine starts a scan operation at the root page, follows the pointers contained in the index pages to traverse from the root to the first leaf page, and then scans across the leaf level following the next page pointers in the leaf pages. *Figure 4.8* shows an illustration of an index scan:

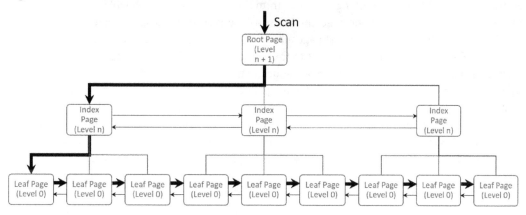

Figure 4.8: Illustration of an index scan on a rowstore index

Assuming we have the same three-level structure that's illustrated in *Figure 4.7*, this index scan would require three page reads to get from the root to the first leaf level page, plus however many additional pages are contained at the leaf level. Since index pages are ordered, this generally lends itself to more efficient sequential I/O. The Query Optimizer also has the option of returning the rows in the order of the index keys, known as an ordered scan, which may help make the rest of the query more efficient, especially if there is an ORDER BY clause that matches the index keys, or if it can facilitate the use of a MERGE join downstream in the plan.

When accessing data using a non-clustered index, whether by a seek or a scan, one additional operation might be required – a *lookup*. A lookup is needed when the columns required to satisfy the query are not contained in the non-clustered index and must be retrieved from the data rows. To perform the lookup, the SQL Database Engine follows the pointer at the leaf level of the non-clustered index to find the underlying data row. If the underlying table is a heap, this results in a **RID lookup** since the pointer is a RID. If the underlying table is a clustered index, this results in a **key lookup** (which is effectively a seek on the clustered index) since the pointer is the clustered index key. When seeking a clustered index, lookups are never needed because the clustered index contains the actual data rows at the leaf level.

Inserting and updating data in a rowstore index

B+ trees are not only efficient when returning data – they are also efficient when inserting and updating data as well. There is a common misconception that rowstore indexes need to be rebuilt periodically to rebalance the tree, but B+ trees are self-balancing. This means the path from the root to the leaf is always the same depth, no matter which leaf page you are accessing. So, the number of page reads required to perform an index seek can be predicted based on the depth of the index.

Building an upside-down tree

Self-balancing is achieved by building the index from the bottom up. When a table with a clustered index is small enough to fit on one page, the index will consist of only a single page that serves as both the root and the leaf. Once the first page fills up, a second page is added to the leaf level, which necessitates a third page be added to point to the original page and the new page. This third page becomes the new root page. As more pages are added to the leaf level, more rows will be added to the root page to point to these new pages until the root page eventually fills up and another page is added to this level, causing the SQL Database Engine to add a new root page to point to the original root page and the new page at this level. As the table grows, the SQL Database Engine continues pushing up new levels as needed, so when looking at the metadata for an index, you will notice that the leaf level is always level 0, the parent level (the level directly above the leaf) is always level 1, and so on until you reach the root. Thus, a B+ tree is upside down, with the leaves at the bottom and the root at the top, as illustrated in *Figure 4.6*.

Page splits

This practice of building the index from the bottom up ensures that the index structure remains balanced and the cost of an index seek operation remains consistent across the entire index. However, to avoid restructuring the tree every time a new page is added to the index, the new page must always be added to the end of the level.

The operation that adds a new page to an index is called a *page split*. If rows are inserted in the same order as the index key, new pages will naturally belong at the end of the level, so the SQL Database Engine simply adds an empty page and adds the new row to this empty page, along with the required pointers. This is sometimes referred to as an optimized page split. If rows are inserted out of order, or if updates to existing rows increase their size and cause them to be relocated to a new page, the SQL Database Engine must perform an out-of-order page split. In this case, a new empty page is added to the end of the level and half the rows from the original page are relocated to this new page, after which the pointers are adjusted so that the logical order of the index is maintained, even though the pages are now physically out of order. *Figure 4.9* shows an example of the leaf level after an out-of-order page split:

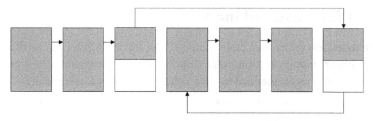

Figure 4.9: Illustration of the leaf level of an index after an out-of-order page split. Note that for simplicity, only the forward pointers are shown

As *Figure 4.9* shows, even though the pages are no longer physically ordered in the file, the pointers maintain the logical order of the index. This is what is known as *logical fragmentation*. Provided that the pages are in memory, logical fragmentation doesn't typically cause performance issues because the data is accessed via the pointers within the index. If the pages are not in memory, index seeks will generally remain unaffected by logical fragmentation, but index scan performance may be impacted because accessing the various fragments of the index will generate additional non-sequential I/O. We will discuss index fragmentation and how to address it later in this chapter.

As you can see, the B+ tree structure of rowstore indexes provides an efficient way to access data not only for reading but for inserting and updating as well. They are ideal for traditional OLTP application patterns that deal with a small number of rows at a time.

Indexing strategy using rowstore indexes

Now that we've covered the basics of how rowstore indexes are structured and how they are used to access data, let's move on to where and when they should be used, along with some best practices for efficient index design.

The goal of an indexing strategy is to minimize the amount of I/O required to satisfy the queries being generated against the database. This translates into a few simple guidelines:

- Keep indexes as small as possible. The more rows that fit on a page, the fewer page reads that are required to access the data.

- Avoid lookups – they add unnecessary I/O and can sometimes lead to suboptimal query plans.

- Choose index keys that support query predicates so that indexes can be used for seeks rather than scans.

- When creating indexes with multiple key columns, columns used for equality comparisons should be first, followed by columns used for inequality comparisons. The leading column should be the most selective column used for equality comparisons.

- Consider index overhead and index for database use. Do not over-index heavily updated tables.

Best practices for clustered indexes

Typically, the first index you create on a table should be the clustered index. As we discussed in the *Data access using rowstore indexes* section, retrieving data from a clustered index is generally more efficient than a heap, so it is recommended to have a clustered index on every table.

> **Note**
>
> One case where heaps may be more efficient than clustered indexes is as an interim step when bulk loading data as part of an ETL process. Reading data from a heap is less efficient than a clustered index, so the ultimate destination of the data should be a clustered index structure.

Remember that the data pages are stored within the clustered index structure, so there can only be one clustered index on a table. Also, since the clustered index key serves as the pointer to the data rows in non-clustered indexes, the structure of the clustered index can have an impact on all the non-clustered indexes on the table.

When choosing which column or columns to create a clustered index on, there are a few guidelines to consider:

- **Uniqueness**: The key should be unique
- **Size**: The key should be as narrow as possible
- **Volatility**: The key should not be frequently updated (preferably not at all)
- **Usability**: The key should be created on a column that is frequently used to access the table, particularly if it's used in wide queries (SELECT *)
- **Order**: The key should be on a column that is self-ordering

While these guidelines are not specifically required or enforced by the SQL Database Engine, following them will lead to more efficient data access.

Uniqueness

The SQL Database Engine needs to have a way to uniquely identify each of the rows in a table. When there is a clustered index on the table, the clustered index key serves as this unique identifier. If the key you choose for the clustered index is already unique, the SQL Database Engine can use the key as-is. If the key is not unique, the SQL Database Engine must make it unique by adding a *uniqueifier*. The uniqueifier is an integer stored in a hidden 4-byte column in the table and becomes part of the clustered index key, so it will increase the size of the key. By choosing an index key that is unique up front, you can avoid this overhead altogether and make the clustered index key smaller and more useful.

Size

The size of data has an impact on query performance, and this is equally – if not more – important when it comes to index keys, particularly clustered index keys. The pages of an index are made up of rows that contain index keys, so the smaller the index key, the smaller the row, and the more rows will fit on a page. The smaller the index, the fewer page reads required to access the index, both for seeks and for scans. With a clustered index, this is even more critical because the clustered index key serves as the pointer to the data in a non-clustered index. This means that the size of the clustered index key will influence not only the size of the clustered index but the size of all the non-clustered indexes as well.

Volatility

The keys of a rowstore index provide the order and structure of the index. If the key values change, the structure of the index must change to accommodate this. Rows may need to be relocated at the leaf level, which triggers changes up the tree. With clustered indexes, the key is also part of all the non-clustered indexes, so changes to key values impact not only the clustered index structure but all the non-clustered indexes on the table as well. It's important to choose index keys that are static to avoid unnecessary overhead.

Usability

Since the clustered index structures the entire table around the keys, it's a good idea to create the clustered index key from a column that is commonly used to access the table. This is particularly important if there are wide queries (queries that return a large number of columns) that can make use of the key. A clustered index seek is the most efficient way to return an entire row from a table, so think about how useful the column or columns may be to your application when choosing a clustered index key.

Order

As we discussed in the index structure section of this chapter, inserting data out of order causes unnecessary overhead in the form of out-of-order page splits. Using a column that is self-ordered, such as an identity column (which is integer-based), ensures that data is always inserted in order and keeps page split overhead at a minimum. This will also lead to less logical fragmentation and reduce the need for frequent index maintenance.

> **Tip**
>
> It's become common practice to use **globally unique identifiers (GUIDs)** as primary keys (and thus as clustered index keys) in many databases. By their nature, GUIDs are not necessarily sequential, so their use can lead to out-of-order page splits, as discussed earlier. If you must use a GUID as a clustered index key, consider generating new GUIDs using the NEWSEQUENTIALID() function rather than NEWID(). This will generate a sequential GUID and avoid the problem of out-of-order inserts and page splits.

Primary keys

If you've already been working with SQL Server or Azure SQL Database, you might have had a lightbulb go off after reading the best practices for clustered indexes. When you create a primary key on a table, by default, the SQL Database Engine creates a clustered index to support the key, also known as a *clustered primary key*. A primary key lends itself nicely to a clustered index – it's unique, it typically does not change, it's often an identity column that is small and self-ordering, and it's one of the most common ways to return data from a table, either directly or through a join with another table.

In most cases, the primary key should be the clustered index on a table. There are a few exceptions to this rule where it might make sense to create a non-clustered primary key and a clustered index on a different column or columns in the table:

- **Surrogate keys**: If the primary key is a surrogate key that only exists in the database and is not used for filtering rows either as a predicate or a join condition, choosing the natural key as the clustered index key might make more sense. An example of a natural key versus a surrogate key might be a product UPC stored as a string versus a database-assigned identity column called `ProductID`.

- **Dates**: If the table contains a date column and data access is always done by date range (for example, where the table contains archive data but the most recent data is accessed more frequently), it might make sense to have the date column be the leading column of the clustered index, although it's generally a good idea to keep the primary key column as a secondary column in the index to avoid the overhead of a unique identifier.

As with anything in the SQL Database Engine, there may be other exceptions to this rule, so use the guidelines discussed in this section to make the best choice for your application.

Best practices for non-clustered indexes

While the choice of columns for a clustered index is generally based on the structure and nature of the data, the choice of columns for non-clustered indexes depends on how the data is going to be accessed by the application. Generally, you want to create non-clustered indexes on any columns that will frequently be used to filter data, either as a predicate in a WHERE clause or as a join condition.

Foreign keys

Unlike with primary keys, the SQL Database Engine does not automatically create an index on foreign key columns. As foreign keys are used to establish relationships between columns in different tables and to enforce referential integrity, it is important to have indexes on those columns, not only because they are frequently used for joins, but because they are needed to make referential integrity checks more efficient.

> **Note**
>
> While referential integrity can be enforced at the application level using coding techniques, it's a best practice to use declarative referential integrity in the database (foreign keys).

Once you have your primary keys and clustered indexes in place, the next indexes to consider are non-clustered indexes on all your foreign key columns. After the indexes on foreign key columns are in place, you will need to begin analyzing the queries generated by your application to determine any further non-clustered index requirements. As you begin this analysis, it is usually preferable to add columns to an existing index that supports a foreign key rather than creating a whole new index, provided that the foreign key column remains the leading column of the index. If you need an index where the foreign key column is not the leading column of the index, it's best to create a new index. We will discuss best practices for multi-column indexes in the next section.

Key column order

The leading column of an index determines the sort order of the index and is where a statistics histogram will be created as discussed in *Chapter 1, Overview of Query Optimization*. For the SQL Database Engine to use a predicate as a seek predicate against an index, the column in the predicate must match the leading column of the index since this is the column for which the data distribution is known. For example, consider the following query:

```
SELECT LastName, FirstName, MiddleName, BusinessEntityID
FROM Person.Person
WHERE LastName = N'Smith';
```

In the AdventureWorks database, there is a non-clustered index on the Person.Person table called IX_Person_LastName_FirstName_MiddleName that contains LastName, FirstName, and MiddleName as key columns in that order. Since LastName is the leading column of the index, the LastName = N'Smith' predicate can be used as a seek predicate against this index. *Figure 4.10* shows the execution plan for this query:

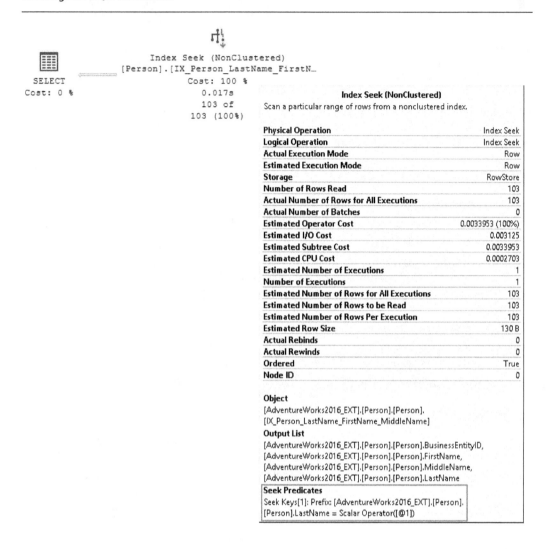

Figure 4.10: Screenshot of the execution plan for the example query showing the seek predicates

If we were to change the predicate of the query to FirstName, the index can still be used, but since FirstName is not the leading column, it can't be used as a seek predicate and the index will have to be scanned. Here's the example query using FirstName in the predicate:

```
SELECT LastName, FirstName, MiddleName, BusinessEntityID
FROM Person.Person
WHERE FirstName = N'John';
```

Figure 4.11 shows the execution plan:

```
Query 1: Query cost (relative to the batch): 100%
SELECT [LastName],[FirstName],[MiddleName],[BusinessEntityID] FROM [Person].[Person] WHERE [FirstName]=@1
Missing Index (Impact 96.7592): CREATE NONCLUSTERED INDEX [<Name of Missing Index, sysname,>] ON [Person].[Person] ([FirstName])
```

```
                              Index Scan (NonClustered)
                           [Person].[IX_Person_LastName_FirstN...
  SELECT                            Cost: 100 %
  Cost: 0 %                          0.006s
                                      58 of
                                    45 (128%)
```

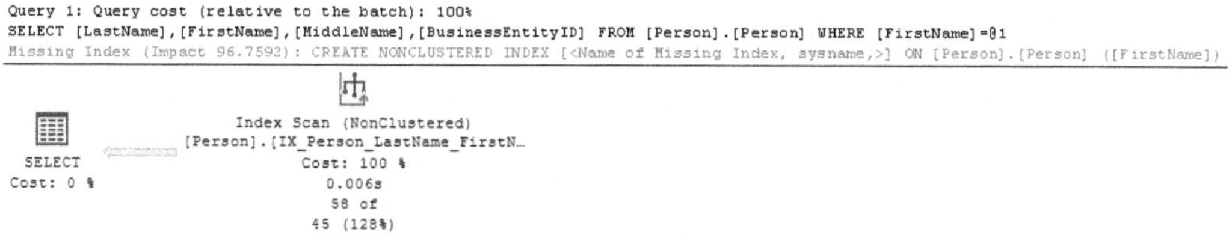

Figure 4.11: Screenshot of the execution plan for the example query
showing an index scan, as well as a missing index suggestion

As shown in *Figure 4.11*, not only did the index get scanned, but the Query Optimizer suggested creating a new index on the `FirstName` column since there are no indexes on the table with `FirstName` as the leading column.

While the leading column is the most important key column, if the predicate contains more than one condition, additional key columns will make the key more selective and therefore more efficient. Let's combine the two example queries into a single query:

```
SELECT LastName, FirstName, MiddleName, BusinessEntityID
FROM Person.Person
WHERE FirstName = N'John' and LastName = N'Smith';
```

Figure 4.12 shows the execution plan for this query:

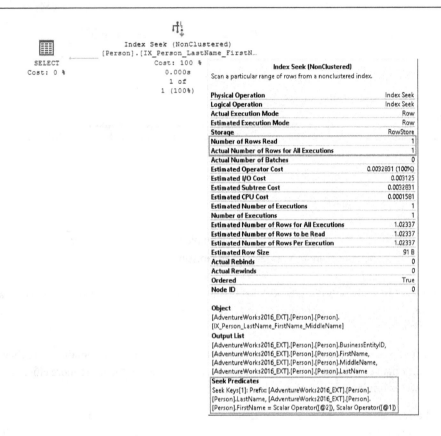

Figure 4.12: Screenshot of the execution plan for the example query showing the seek predicates,
along with the Number of Rows Read and Actual Number of Rows for All Executions properties

Notice that the execution plan looks very similar to the one in *Figure 4.10*, but both conditions are
being used in the seek predicate since both columns are in the index. This query now returns a single
row, and only this one row had to be read because of the structure of the index. But do you need
both columns in the index? Wouldn't having the LastName column alone in the index also yield an
index seek? Yes, it would, but it wouldn't be quite as efficient. Let's create a new index to test this out:

```
CREATE NONCLUSTERED INDEX IX_Person_LastName
ON Person.Person (LastName)
INCLUDE(FirstName, MiddleName);
```

> **Note**
>
> We're using an INCLUDE clause to avoid having to do a lookup so that we can compare the
> results evenly with earlier queries. We will discuss INCLUDE columns in more detail in the
> next section.

The Query Optimizer probably won't choose this index on its own, so we'll need to force it with a hint to see the execution plan:

```
SELECT LastName, FirstName, MiddleName, BusinessEntityID
FROM Person.Person
WITH (INDEX (IX_Person_LastName))
WHERE FirstName = N'John' AND LastName = N'Smith';
```

Figure 4.13 shows the execution plan for this query:

Figure 4.13: Screenshot of the execution plan for the example query showing the Predicate and Seek Predicates values, along with the Number of Rows Read and Actual Number of Rows for All Executions properties

As predicted, we still have an index seek, but if you look closer at the plan, you can see that this is not quite as efficient as the index that has both `LastName` and `FirstName` in the key columns. This query still returns one row, but 103 rows had to be read to find this one row. While the entire predicate was able to be evaluated within the index seek, only `LastName` was part of the seek predicate because it's the only key column in the index. `FirstName` does appear as a predicate, meaning that the rows were filtered within the index seek operation, but since `FirstName` isn't one of the key columns, all 103 rows with `LastName = N'Smith'` had to be read to find all the rows that also had `FirstName = N'John'`.

Now that we've determined having multiple columns in a non-clustered index key can be useful, how do you know the order in which the columns should appear? There's a simple rule for this that we mentioned at the beginning of this section: the most selective equality column should be first, followed by the rest of the equality columns, then the inequality columns.

As we discussed in *Chapter 2, Mechanics of the Query Optimizer*, selectivity refers to how distinct the data is. For example, the queries we've reviewed in this chapter so far have all been using an index on `LastName`, `FirstName`, and `MiddleName`. The order of this index isn't arbitrary; it's based on the selectivity of the columns. In Western cultures, `LastName` is more selective than `FirstName` because there are fewer duplicate last names than there are duplicate first names. In many Eastern cultures, the selectivity of last names and first names is reversed, with first names being more selective than last names. If your database contains names like these, it may make sense for an index on names to have a different column order. The most selective column needs to be listed first because it allows the Query Optimizer to make the most efficient use of predicate pushdown, narrowing down the set of rows it must read from the database and making the rest of the operations in the plan more efficient.

The rule also mentions equality versus inequality, which has to do with how the column is used in a query. An *equality column* is a column that is used in an equality predicate in a query. In our example query, both `LastName` and `FirstName` are being used as equality columns. An *inequality column* is a column that is used in an inequality comparison in a query. An example of an inequality comparison would be `FirstName LIKE N'J%'`, which returns a range of names that all start with the letter J. You can think of this as predicate selectivity, an equality comparison is typically more selective than an inequality comparison.

Let's look at a query example that shows the importance of column order:

```
SELECT LastName, FirstName, MiddleName, BusinessEntityID
FROM Person.Person
WHERE PersonType = N'SP'
AND LastName LIKE N'S%';
```

In this case, we're using the `PersonType` column for an equality comparison and the `LastName` column for an inequality comparison. There's no index on the `PersonType` column, so we'll need to create one for this query. There are only six distinct values for `PersonType` in the table, but there are over 1,000 distinct values for `LastName`, meaning that `LastName` is much more selective than `PersonType`. Let's see what happens if we only take selectivity into account and create an index with `LastName` first:

```
CREATE NONCLUSTERED INDEX IX_Person_LastName_PersonType
ON Person.Person (LastName , PersonType);
```

When you're doing index tuning in an isolated development environment with no other activity, it's sometimes difficult to tell how efficient an index is because the query may run fast, even if the index isn't efficient. Looking at the logical reads generated by a query is helpful when fine-tuning indexes. You can find this information by looking at the `Actual Logical Reads` property of an index operation in an execution plan, or you can use the following command before running the query:

```
SET STATISTICS IO ON;
```

This command turns on `STATISTICS IO` at the session level. Once this is on, every query run from the same session will report the I/O generated by the query on the **Messages** tab.

The plan for the example query is shown in *Figure 4.14*:

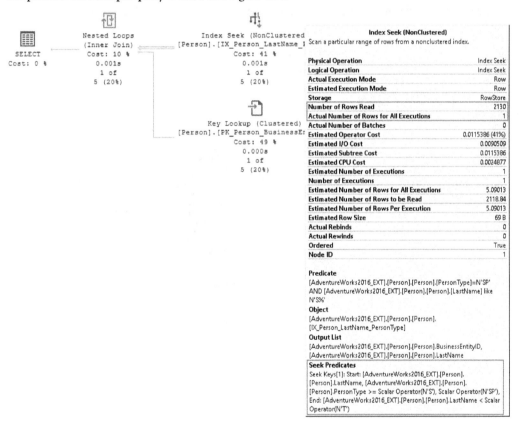

Figure 4.14: Screenshot of the execution plan from the example query showing the Seek
Predicates, Number of Rows Read, and Actual Number of Rows for All Executions properties

As you can see, the Query Optimizer was able to seek an index, and both `LastName` and `PersonType` were used in the seek predicate. However, if you look closer at the properties of the index seek, you may notice that it wasn't a particularly efficient seek. The query returns a single row, but it had to read

2,130 rows to find that one row. If you think back to how an index is structured, this makes sense. Since `LastName` is the leading column, the index is sorted first by `LastName`, then by `PersonType`. There are 2,130 rows in the `Person.Person` table that have a last name that begins with S, so the SQL Database Engine must traverse the index from the root to the leaf to find the first one, then scan across the leaf level until it finds the last one, ultimately keeping only the one row where `PersonType` is `SP`. The query generated 15 logical reads.

Let's try this query again with the index created the correct way:

```
CREATE NONCLUSTERED INDEX IX_Person_PersonType_LastName
ON Person.Person (PersonType, LastName);
```

Figure 4.15 shows the execution plan for the same query with this new index in place:

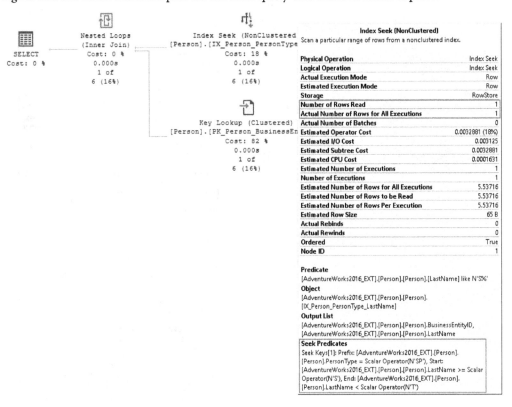

Figure 4.15: Screenshot of the execution plan from the example query showing the Seek Predicates, Number of Rows Read, and Actual Number of Rows for All Executions properties

At first glance, the execution plan in *Figure 4.15* might not look much different than the one in *Figure 4.14*, but if you look closely at the arrow between the Index Seek and Nested Loops join, you might notice that it's much thicker in the first plan than it is in the second plan. This is because the number of rows read in the first plan was higher than in the second plan. If you look at the index seek properties in *Figure 4.15*, you will see that Number of Rows Read was 1, the same as the number of rows returned by the query. Again, think back to the index structure. By changing the order of the columns, we change the way the index is accessed. Now, the SQL Database Engine can seek directly to the one row where PersonType is SP and LastName starts with S, there's no need to scan an entire range of rows that don't meet the predicate. For this run of the query, we can see that only five logical reads were generated rather than the 15 that were needed when the column order was reversed.

Covering indexes

One of the rules we highlighted at the beginning of this section is that you should avoid lookups when possible. The way you avoid lookups in your query plans is to use *covering indexes*. A covering index is a non-clustered index that contains all the columns required to satisfy the query without having to go to the base table. Similarly, a query that doesn't have any lookups may be called a covered query.

> **Note**
> A clustered index is always a covering index because the leaf level contains the data pages, so the entire row is available.

Columns that are used for filtering, either in the WHERE clause or in a JOIN condition, should be key columns in the index, but what about columns in the SELECT list? It doesn't make sense to have these as key columns because they would increase the size of the index unnecessarily, so the best way to add columns from the SELECT list to an index is by using an INCLUDE clause when creating the index. *Included columns* are columns that are included at the leaf level of the index, but are not part of the key, and therefore not used in the sorting and structuring of the index.

Let's look at our example from the previous section once more:

```
SELECT LastName, FirstName, MiddleName, BusinessEntityID
FROM Person.Person
WHERE PersonType = N'SP'
AND LastName LIKE N'S%';
```

We created an index on PersonType and LastName, but we didn't include any other columns from the SELECT list. BusinessEntityID is the clustered index key on the table, so this column is included by default (recall that the clustered index key is the pointer to the data row in a non-clustered index). This means that to avoid the lookup in the plan shown in *Figure 4.15*, we would need to add FirstName and MiddleName to the index. Let's modify that CREATE INDEX statement accordingly:

```
CREATE NONCLUSTERED INDEX IX_Person_PersonType_LastName
ON Person.Person (PersonType, LastName)
INCLUDE (FirstName, MiddleName)
WITH (DROP_EXISTING = ON);
```

Now, if we execute the query again, we'll see the plan shown in *Figure 4.16*:

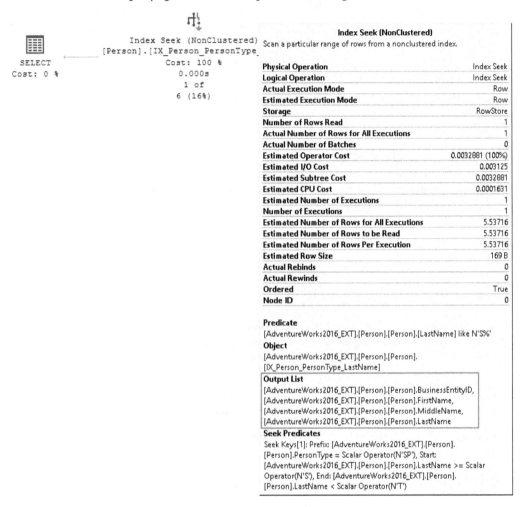

Figure 4.16: Screenshot of an execution plan for the example query showing the output list

As shown in *Figure 4.16*, the key lookup is gone, and the plan consists of only an index seek. Also, if you look at the properties of the index seek, you will see that the output list contains all the columns needed by the query, including the columns in the SELECT list. The index is now a covering index. You will also see that the number of logical reads has decreased from 5 to 2, simply by covering the query.

Creating covering indexes for your queries makes them efficient, but there is a tradeoff. While included columns don't increase the size of an index as much as key columns, they do increase the size, so you don't want to add every column in the table. This refers not only to the number of columns but also to the size of the columns and how much of the total row size is being duplicated in each index. Keep in mind that indexes are creating duplicate copies of your data, so you want to carefully balance the storage overhead with the performance benefit. Be sure to consider how often the query is being executed, and how important the performance of that query is to your application. Also, if you include columns that are frequently updated, this can cause even more overhead since the columns will need to be updated in the base table and in any indexes that contain those columns. Covering a query that is executed frequently, particularly one whose performance is critical, may be worth the added overhead. It's also worth mentioning that limiting the columns that are returned by a query can make it easier to cover the query. In other words, don't use SELECT * if you can avoid it; returning only the columns that are needed can help avoid lookups.

Filtered indexes

A *filtered index* is a non-clustered index that is created on a subset of the data in a table. Filtered indexes can be useful if there is a subset of the data that is queried frequently for which you want to create specialized indexes and/or statistics. When you create a filtered index on a table, the statistics that are created to support the index are also filtered.

One common use case for filtered indexes is in a system that uses soft deletes where rows are marked as deleted but kept in the table, either for a short period or indefinitely. In systems such as these, nearly every query in the application will likely need to filter out all the deleted rows. If the deleted rows never get cleaned up because they are needed for historical purposes, over time, this can create a significant skew in data distribution. Queries that only need non-deleted data can get less and less efficient as the number of deleted rows outnumbers the number of non-deleted rows. In this case, filtered indexes will not only be smaller and more efficient to query, but the statistics that are created for these indexes are likely to be more accurate as they represent the distribution of only the active data.

In the AdventureWorks database, there is one table that uses a concept like soft deletes – BillOfMaterials. This table stores a hierarchical list of all the components that make up each of the products that AdventureWorks sells. Each component has a start date that indicates when the component began to be used in the assembly, and if the component is discontinued, an end date is also recorded. Since most of the components are still in use, the components that have a NULL end date far outnumber the components that have a non-NULL end date. In this case, a filtered index can come in handy if you want to do any sort of reporting on discontinued components. Take the following query as an example:

```
SELECT ProductAssemblyID, p.Name AS ProductName,
    ComponentID, comp.Name AS DiscontinuedComponent,
    StartDate, EndDate
FROM Production.BillOfMaterials AS bom
LEFT JOIN Production.Product AS p
```

```
    ON bom.ProductAssemblyID = p.ProductID
LEFT JOIN Production.Product AS comp
    ON bom.ComponentID = comp.ProductID
WHERE EndDate IS NOT NULL
    AND StartDate BETWEEN '01/01/2010' AND '12/31/2010';
```

This query returns a list of 199 components that were introduced in 2010 that have been discontinued. *Figure 4.17* shows the plan for this query:

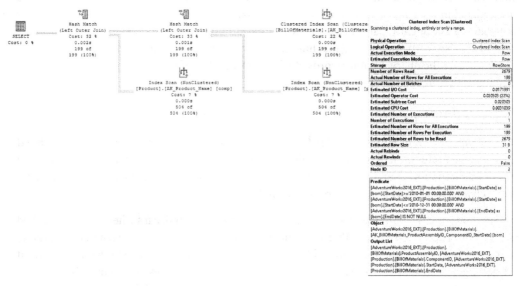

Figure 4.17: Screenshot of the execution plan for the example query showing the
Number of Rows Read, Actual Number of Rows for All Executions, and Predicate
for the Clustered Index Scan properties on the BillOfMaterials table

As shown in *Figure 4.17*, the `BillOfMaterials` table is being accessed by a clustered index scan, which means the predicate wasn't SARGable. The properties of the clustered index scan show that 2,679 rows had to be read to return only 199 rows, resulting in 22 logical reads against this index.

Based on what we've learned so far about non-clustered indexes, we can try to add a covering index for this query:

```
CREATE NONCLUSTERED INDEX IX_BillOfMaterials_StartDate_EndDate
ON Production.BillOfMaterials (StartDate, EndDate);
```

> **Tip**
>
> Since the clustered index on the `BillOfMaterials` table contains both `ProductAssemblyID` and `ComponentID` in the key, there's no need to explicitly add these columns to the non-clustered index as included columns – they will be part of the index by default.

With this new index in place, the query gets a bit more efficient. *Figure 4.18* shows the plan:

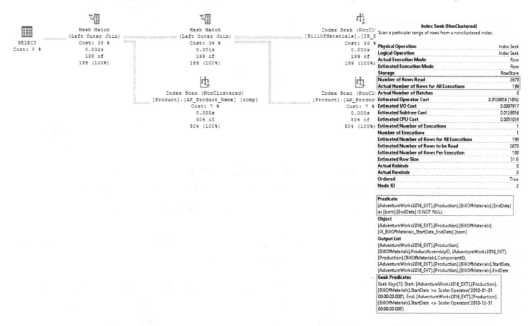

Figure 4.18: Screenshot of the execution plan for the example query with the properties
of the index seek on the new covering index showing the Number of Rows Read, Actual
Number of Rows for All Executions, Predicate, and Seek Predicates properties

Now, there is a seek predicate, and the number of logical reads on the `BillOfMaterials` table has been reduced from 22 to 12, but the query is still reading 2,679 rows. Let's try the filtered index instead:

```
CREATE NONCLUSTERED INDEX IX_BillOfMaterials_StartDate_Filtered
ON Production.BillOfMaterials (StartDate)
INCLUDE (EndDate)
WHERE (EndDate IS NOT NULL);
```

Figure 4.19 shows the execution plan for the query:

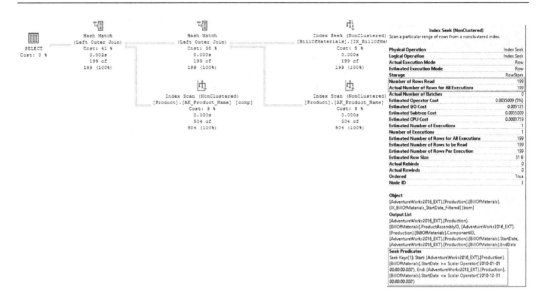

Figure 4.19: Screenshot of the execution plan for the example query with the properties of the index seek on the filtered index showing the Number of Rows Read, Actual Number of Rows for All Executions, and Seek Predicates properties

Now, the number of rows read matches the number of rows returned – 199. Also, the logical reads on the BillOfMaterials table are reduced even further from 12 to 2.

There are a few caveats to using filtered indexes. It should be obvious that the filter condition in the index must be present somewhere in the predicate of the query for the index to be used, but keep in mind that it must match exactly. If any literal values from the filter condition are parameterized in the query, the index cannot be used. Also, it generally makes more sense to have a single non-clustered index with the filter column as a key column rather than to create multiple filtered indexes for different values in the same column.

Index maintenance

While index maintenance is more of a database administration topic than a developer topic, it's worth discussing the importance of index maintenance. As we discussed in the section on index structure, over time, INSERT, UPDATE, and DELETE operations can cause an index to become fragmented. Once the data is in memory, fragmentation doesn't cause a noticeable performance issue, so the main concern is I/O. The SQL Database Engine has a few I/O optimizations, such as the readahead mechanism that's used when scanning an index, that rely on the data being stored contiguously. When the data is fragmented, I/O may not be as efficient.

Another side effect of fragmentation is lower page density. A page is the smallest unit of I/O in the SQL Database Engine, so an index that contains a lot of partially empty pages will generate a lot more I/O than necessary. If the pages are full, it will take fewer of them to store the same amount of data. This is a problem that can impact performance, even if the data is in memory, because it will increase the number of logical reads needed to complete each query, and it will waste precious memory that can be used for other things. In short, this is a problem that is much more likely to cause performance issues than logical fragmentation alone.

Reducing fragmentation and increasing page density can be accomplished by periodically rebuilding or reorganizing indexes. How often index maintenance should be performed for a given system depends on many factors and requires a much larger conversation than would be appropriate for this book. So, for more information on maintaining indexes, consider reviewing the newly updated index maintenance documentation for SQL Server and Azure SQL at `https://aka.ms/IndexMaintenance`.

Summary

This chapter covered a lot of ground, so let's review the overall indexing strategy guidance:

1. Clustered index data access is generally more efficient than heaps and every table in the database should have a clustered index, except for short-lived tables such as staging tables.

2. Create clustered indexes first based on the data structure. These should generally be primary keys unless there's a specific reason to cluster a different column or columns (for example, surrogate versus natural keys).

3. Create non-clustered indexes on all foreign key columns.

4. Once you begin writing queries, create additional non-clustered indexes to support the application queries, or add additional columns to existing foreign key indexes.

5. Create covering indexes where practical, balancing overhead with performance.

6. Do not over-index heavily updated tables; balance the cost of index maintenance with the benefit to queries. Just because the SQL Database Engine allows you to create 999 non-clustered indexes per table doesn't mean you should.

7. Keep indexes as small as possible – the more rows that fit on a page, the less I/O is required to read the data.

5

Writing Elegant T-SQL Queries

At this point, we should have a good understanding of how to build a T-SQL query, and the building blocks of writing T-SQL code such as query optimization fundamentals, reading and interpreting query plans, and some best practices around indexing and writing efficient T-SQL code. But how do we build an elegant T-SQL query? One that not only gets the job done but does so efficiently?

There are a few guidelines that are important to keep in mind when writing T-SQL queries to ensure that they perform and scale well while avoiding some common pitfalls that even experienced T-SQL developers can encounter that will make a query perform poorly.

In this chapter, we will examine some common T-SQL patterns and anti-patterns, specifically those that should be easily identified just by looking at the T-SQL code. We're going to cover the following main topics:

- Best practices for T-SQL querying
- The perils of SELECT *
- Functions in our predicate
- Deconstructing table-valued functions
- Complex expressions
- Optimizing OR logic
- NULL means unknown
- Fuzzy string matching
- Inequality logic
- EXECUTE versus sp_executesql
- Composable logic

Technical requirements

The examples used in this chapter are designed for use on SQL Server 2022 and Azure SQL Database, but they should work on any version of SQL Server, 2012 or later. The "Developer Edition" of SQL Server is free for development environments and can be used to run all the code samples. There is also a free tier of Azure SQL Database you can use for testing at `https://aka.ms/freedb`.

You will need the sample databases `AdventureWorks2016_EXT` (referred to as `AdventureWorks`) and `AdventureWorksDW2016_EXT` (referred to as `AdventureWorksDW`), which can be found on GitHub at `https://github.com/Microsoft/sql-server-samples/releases/tag/adventureworks`. Code samples for this chapter can also be found on GitHub at `https://github.com/PacktPublishing/Learn-T-SQL-Querying-Second-Edition/tree/main/ch5`.

Best practices for T-SQL querying

There are a number of best practices for writing good T-SQL that don't constitute a pattern or anti-pattern, which is something we will discuss next in this chapter, but are important enough to observe when we want to write good queries. This section covers those practices.

Referencing objects

Always reference objects by their two-part name (<schema>.<name>) in T-SQL code because not doing so has some performance implications.

Using two-part object names prevents name resolution delays during query compilation: if the default schema for a user connecting to the SQL Database Engine is `HumanResources`, and that user attempts to execute the stored procedure `dbo.uspGetEmployeeManagers` for which it also has permissions, but simply references `uspGetEmployeeManagers`, the SQL Database Engine first searches the `HumanResources` schema for that stored procedure before searching other schemas, thus delaying resolution and therefore execution. When that stored procedure is used at scale, it may introduce unwarranted overhead.

Two-part object names also provide more opportunities for plan reuse and reduce the likelihood of failed executions if multiple objects with the same name exist across schemas. For cached query plans to be reused, it is necessary that the objects referenced by the query don't require name resolutions. For example, referencing the `Sales.SalesOrderDetail` table does not require name resolution, but simply `SalesOrderDetail` does because there could be tables named `SalesOrderDetail` in other schemas.

Joining tables

When writing T-SQL queries, it's important to distinguish between proper join predicates and search predicates.

For inner joins, it is best to keep only join arguments in the ON clause, and move all search arguments to a WHERE clause. Performance-wise there is no difference if the generated query plan is the same, but the T-SQL is more readable. The following query examples can be executed in the scope of the AdventureWorks sample database, and yield the same query plans:

```
SELECT p.ProductID, p.Name, wo.StockedQty, wor.WorkOrderID
FROM Production.WorkOrder AS wo
INNER JOIN Production.Product AS p ON wo.ProductID = p.ProductID
INNER JOIN Production.WorkOrderRouting AS wor ON wo.WorkOrderID = wor.
WorkOrderID
WHERE p.ProductID = 771 AND wor.WorkOrderID = 852;


SELECT p.ProductID, p.Name, wo.StockedQty, wor.WorkOrderID
FROM Production.WorkOrder AS wo
INNER JOIN Production.Product AS p ON wo.ProductID = p.ProductID
    AND p.ProductID = 771
INNER JOIN Production.WorkOrderRouting AS wor ON wo.WorkOrderID = wor.
WorkOrderID
      AND wor.WorkOrderID = 852;
```

In the first query, it's immediately readable which conditions are join predicates and which are search predicates.

For LEFT JOIN, add any search predicates for the table on the right side of the join. This is because adding filters that eliminate the possibility of NULL values to the table on the right side of a join in the WHERE clause will convert the OUTER join to an INNER join." We also added a Note callout box after this sentence and before the next one that reads "Whenever possible we should optimize for INNER joins because they are inherently more selective than OUTER joins. The following query examples can be executed in the scope of the AdventureWorks sample database:

```
SELECT wo.StockedQty, wor.WorkOrderID
FROM Production.WorkOrder AS wo
LEFT JOIN Production.WorkOrderRouting AS wor ON wo.WorkOrderID = wor.
WorkOrderID
WHERE wor.WorkOrderID = 12345;
SELECT wo.StockedQty, wor.WorkOrderID
FROM Production.WorkOrder AS wo
LEFT JOIN Production.WorkOrderRouting AS wor ON wo.WorkOrderID = wor.
WorkOrderID
WHERE wo.WorkOrderID = 12345;
```

These queries yield different query plans but the same result sets. In the first query, a reference to the Production.WorkOrderRouting table was added as a predicate. Since that table is on the right side of the join, this resulted in the LEFT OUTER JOIN becoming an INNER JOIN, as seen in the Nested Loops operator in the query plans:

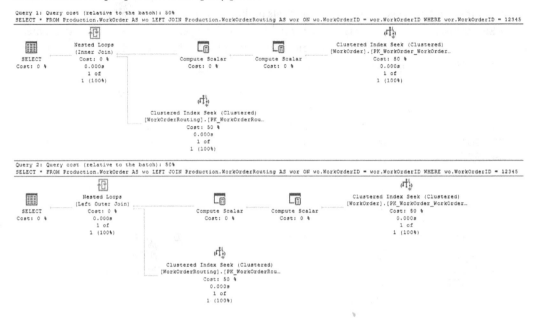

Figure 5.1 – Execution plan for the two queries on the Production schema

In some cases, this can result in different choices for physical joins, and so impact I/O, memory, and CPU resources. This also applies in the inverse case – adding a reference to the table on the left side of a RIGHT JOIN.

Using NOLOCK

The SQL Database Engine uses isolation levels to preserve the logical order of all transactions, and to protect transactions from the effects of updates performed by other concurrent transactions. The goal is to uphold the ACID properties of relational databases: Atomicity, Consistency, Isolation, and Durability.

> **Tip**
> Read more about ACID at http://en.wikipedia.org/wiki/ACID.

Different isolation levels have trade-offs between concurrency and isolation requirements: using more restrictive isolation means fewer concurrent transactions. In a nutshell, the SQL Database Engine complies with ANSI-99 standard isolation levels:

- In **Read Uncommitted** (lowest isolation level, maximum concurrency), statements can read rows that have been modified by other transactions but not yet committed

- In **Read Committed** (the default isolation level in the SQL Database Engine), statements cannot read data that has been modified but not committed by other transactions

- In **Repeatable Read**, statements cannot read data that has been modified but not yet committed by other transactions, and no other transactions can modify data that has been read by the current transaction

- In **Serializable** (highest isolation level, no concurrency), statements cannot read data that has been modified but not yet committed by other transactions, no other transactions can modify data that has been read by the current transaction, and other transactions cannot insert new rows with key values that would fall in the range of keys read by any statements in the current transaction

> **Note**
>
> The SQL Database Engine adds two isolation levels above the ANSI standard that are not discussed in this book: **Snapshot** and **Read Committed Snapshot Isolation (RCSI)**.

The NOLOCK hint implements the same behavior as Read Uncommitted at the statement level. When this hint is used, it's possible to read uncommitted modifications, which are called dirty reads. This means that by using NOLOCK, a developer is explicitly allowing uncommitted data to be used for other transactions. Allowing dirty reads allows higher concurrency at the cost of reading data that can still be rolled back by other transactions. In turn, this may generate application errors, present uncommitted data to users, or cause users to see duplicate records, or no records at all. This is the sort of hint that should not be used in queries that require operational precision such as banking or trade.

Using cursors

Cursor usage must be kept to a minimum. Depending on the cursor type, they may use tempdb worktables, which causes an I/O penalty. Because cursors operate in a row-by-row fashion, they force the SQL Database Engine to repeatedly fetch a new row, negotiate blocking, and manage locks, to then output each row result individually.

Consider whether set-based logic can be used. In some cases, cursors appear more straightforward, but using T-SQL constructs such as **common table expressions (CTEs)** or temporary tables may achieve the same results with less overhead. If a set-based approach is not possible, most cursors can be avoided by using a WHILE loop, namely if there is a Primary Key or Unique Key in the table. However, there are scenarios where cursors are not only unavoidable, but they are actually needed. If this is the case but tables don't need to be updated based on the cursor position, then the recommendation is to use *firehose* cursors, meaning forward-only and read-only cursors.

Now that we've covered some general T-SQL best practices, let's move on to some common anti-patterns, starting with SELECT *.

The perils of SELECT *

SELECT * should be avoided in stored procedures, views, and **Multi-Statement Table-Valued Functions** (**MSTVFs**) because our T-SQL code might break if there are any changes to the underlying schema. For example, applications that reference SELECT * may rely on the ordinal position rather than column names and may encounter errors if the underlying table definition is changed. Instead, fully qualify the names of columns that are relevant to our result set.

This also has important performance implications. Some application patterns may rely on reading an entire dataset and applying filters in the client layer only. For example, imagine a web application where a sales supervisor can see a report of orders registered for a given month, with details per product. The application connects to the AdventureWorks sample database and runs a query:

```
Dim myConnection As New SqlConnection("Our Connection String")
Dim cmd As New SqlCommand
Dim reader As SqlDataReader
cmd.CommandText = "SELECT *
    FROM Sales.SalesOrderHeader AS h
    INNER JOIN Sales.SalesOrderDetail AS d ON h.SalesOrderID =
d.SalesOrderID
    INNER JOIN Production.Product AS p ON d.ProductId = p.ProductID
    WHERE h.OrderDate BETWEEN '2013-02-28 00:00:00.000'
AND '2013-03-30 00:00:00.000';"
cmd.CommandType = CommandType.Text
cmd.Connection = myConnection
myConnection.Open()
reader = cmd.ExecuteReader()
while (reader.Read())
{
    return reader["ProductLine"] as string;
    return reader["Name"] as string;
    return reader["OrderDate"] as DateTime;
    return reader["SalesOrderID"] as Int32;
    return reader["OrderQty"] as Int32;
    return reader["LineTotal"] as double;
    return reader["TotalDue"] as double;
}
reader.Close()
myConnection.Close()
```

Let's observe the generated query execution plan:

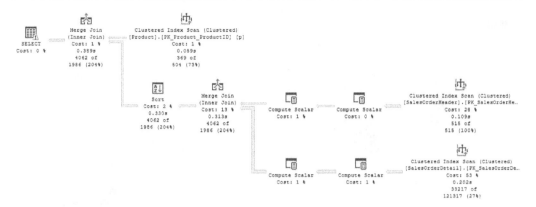

Figure 5.2 – Execution plan for the SELECT * query building the report of orders

Notice that the SQL Database Engine chose to scan all clustered indexes, even on the table where a predicate exists. Given that we are retrieving all columns, there is no missing index suggestion about creating non-clustered indexes because these would be similar in size to the clustered indexes.

Note the execution time statistics for the SELECT * query, and the amount of memory required to execute that query.

⊟ QueryTimeStats	
CpuTime	90
ElapsedTime	430

Figure 5.3 – QueryTimeStats for the query execution plan in Figure 5.2

⊟ MemoryGrantInfo	
DesiredMemory	2400
GrantedMemory	2400

Figure 5.4 – MemoryGrantInfo for the query execution plan in Figure 5.2

Also note in the application code that after getting the entire result set, only the relevant columns for our report are being used. So, instead of selecting all columns in the table to then trim the number of columns in the client layer, it is preferable to issue a query that only retrieves the required columns from the table:

```
SELECT p.ProductLine, p.[Name], h.OrderDate,
h.SalesOrderID, d.OrderQty, d.LineTotal, h.TotalDue
FROM Sales.SalesOrderHeader AS h
INNER JOIN Sales.SalesOrderDetail AS d ON h.SalesOrderID =
d.SalesOrderID
INNER JOIN Production.Product AS p ON d.ProductId = p.ProductID
WHERE h.OrderDate BETWEEN '2013-02-28 00:00:00.000' AND '2013-03-30
00:00:00.000';
```

Let's observe the new query execution plan:

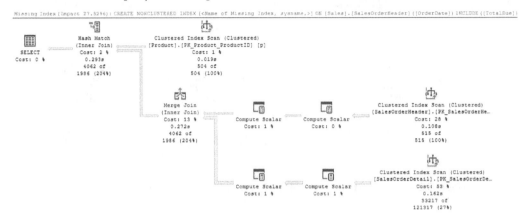

Figure 5.5 – Execution plan for the narrower SELECT query

Now compare the execution time statistics for the new SELECT query, and the amount of memory required to execute that query:

⊟ QueryTimeStats	
CpuTime	61
ElapsedTime	299

Figure 5.6 – QueryTimeStats for the query execution plan in Figure 5.5

⊟ MemoryGrantInfo	
DesiredMemory	1312
GrantedMemory	1312

Figure 5.7 – MemoryGrantInfo for the query execution plan in Figure 5.5

Even though the plan shape hasn't changed, we can clearly see a lower memory requirement (only 1.3 MB instead of 2.4 MB) and lower CPU use and execution time. Reading all columns from a table usually means accessing the underlying heap or clustered index directly, rather than using narrower non-clustered indexes. Conversely, reading only the relevant subset of columns unlocks better usage of our existing index design, or allows for new covering indexes to be created, which can significantly improve read performance.

Precisely because we need fewer columns, the SQL Database Engine was able to identify an index suggestion that may yield even better results. This was not possible before because all the columns were being selected. Because there is no current index that would be useful to change even marginally, we can create this index suggestion as follows:

```
CREATE NONCLUSTERED INDEX IX_OrderDate_TotalDue ON [Sales].
[SalesOrderHeader] (
```

```
        [OrderDate]
)
INCLUDE ([TotalDue]);
```

Although it was not suggested, keeping in mind the indexing guidelines we discussed in *Chapter 4, Indexing for T-SQL Performance*, we can create an additional covering index for the largest scan in the query execution plan:

```
CREATE NONCLUSTERED INDEX IX_SalesOrderID_ProductID_OrderQty_LineTotal
ON [Sales].[SalesOrderDetail] (
        [SalesOrderID],
        [ProductID]
)
INCLUDE (
        [OrderQty],
        [LineTotal]
);
```

The new query execution plan looks much better, leveraging the two new indexes:

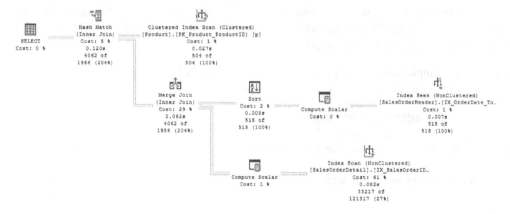

Figure 5.8 – Execution plan for the narrower SELECT query using new indexes

The **QueryTimeStats** for this query execution plan confirm this; CPU time dropped from 61 ms to 24 ms (61 percent less), and execution time dropped from 299 ms to 57 ms (81 percent less):

QueryTimeStats	
CpuTime	24
ElapsedTime	57

Figure 5.9 – QueryTimeStats for the query execution plan in Figure 5.8

If you use columnstore indexes, even without specifying any predicates, the same recommendation of not using `SELECT *` still applies. Selecting just the column names that are needed for the application can translate to significant I/O savings as well, because while you are still retrieving all the data in the columns without filters, being stored in columnar format means that only the columns required are read. Also, note that sending only the columns needed by the application to the client layer prevents unnecessary network I/O and reduces the memory footprint of the client. This can improve the overall performance and scalability of our application as well as the underlying T-SQL queries. Now that we've discussed the perils of `SELECT *`, let's move on to another common anti-pattern – functions in the `WHERE` clause.

Functions in our predicate

Search predicates should only use deterministic function calls. Calls to non-deterministic functions with columns for parameters cause the SQL Database Engine to be unable to reference the selectivity of those columns, as the result of the function is unknown at compile time. Because of this, they cause unnecessary scans.

Keep in mind what was discussed in previous chapters: that the Query Optimizer uses statistics and some internal transformation rules and heuristics at compile time to determine a good enough plan to execute a query; and how the `WHERE` clause is one of the first to be evaluated during logical query processing. The Query Optimizer depends on the estimated cost to resolve the search predicates to choose whether to do seeks or scans over indexes.

The following example shows a query executed in the `AdventureWorks` sample database that uses non-deterministic function calls in the search predicate:

```
SELECT SalesOrderID, OrderDate
FROM Sales.SalesOrderHeader
WHERE YEAR(OrderDate) = 2013 AND MONTH(OrderDate) = 7;
```

Let's observe the query execution plan:

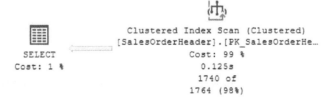

Figure 5.10 – Execution plan for the query

We have a scan of the clustered index. Notice that while we have a non-SARGable predicate, it was pushed down to be resolved during the Clustered Index Scan to return 1,740 rows, but the full 31,465 rows were still read.

Clustered Index Scan (Clustered)

Scanning a clustered index, entirely or only a range.

Physical Operation	Clustered Index Scan
Logical Operation	Clustered Index Scan
Actual Execution Mode	Row
Estimated Execution Mode	Row
Storage	RowStore
Number of Rows Read	31465
Actual Number of Rows	1740
Actual Number of Batches	0
Estimated I/O Cost	0.514977
Estimated Operator Cost	0.549745 (99%)
Estimated CPU Cost	0.0347685
Estimated Subtree Cost	0.549745
Number of Executions	1
Estimated Number of Executions	1
Estimated Number of Rows	1763.91
Estimated Number of Rows to be Read	31465
Estimated Row Size	19 B
Actual Rebinds	0
Actual Rewinds	0
Ordered	False
Node ID	1

Predicate
datepart(year,[AdventureWorks2016_EXT].[Sales].
[SalesOrderHeader].[OrderDate])=(2013) AND datepart(month,
[AdventureWorks2016_EXT].[Sales].[SalesOrderHeader].
[OrderDate])=(7)

Object
[AdventureWorks2016_EXT].[Sales].[SalesOrderHeader].
[PK_SalesOrderHeader_SalesOrderID]

Output List
[AdventureWorks2016_EXT].[Sales].
[SalesOrderHeader].SalesOrderID, [AdventureWorks2016_EXT].
[Sales].[SalesOrderHeader].OrderDate

Figure 5.11 – Clustered index scan properties

Recall what we discussed in the *chapter Indexing for T-SQL Performance*, in the *Understanding predicate SARGability* section. What we have seen calls for a better index, and knowing more about index tuning recommendations now, I can identify that the following index could be useful:

```
CREATE NONCLUSTERED INDEX IX_OrderDate ON Sales.SalesOrderHeader (
    OrderDate
);
```

Executing the same query results in the following query execution plan:

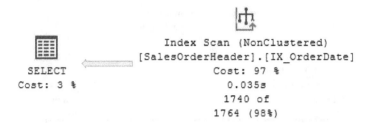

Figure 5.12 – Execution plan for the query using the new index

This is still an index scan, although on the newly created index. The new index is narrower, but the scan still reads 31,645 rows. This is because of the non-deterministic YEAR and DATE functions being used in the predicate. The same result set can be achieved by rewriting the query to avoid these function calls in the search predicate and enable the Query Optimizer to consider other options. The following is just a quick example of how to express the same condition without the use of functions:

```
DECLARE @start DATETIME = '07/01/2013', @end DATETIME = '07/31/2013'
SELECT SalesOrderID, OrderDate
FROM Sales.SalesOrderHeader
WHERE OrderDate BETWEEN @start AND @end;
```

Let's observe the new query execution plan:

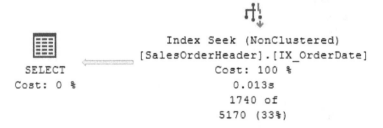

Figure 5.13 – Execution plan for the query using local variables

This is now a seek operation that only reads the 1,740 rows that match the search predicate because the query no longer needs to search based on non-deterministic functions. We could stop the rewrite here, but we are looking to write efficient T-SQL and one of the main goals is to ensure row estimations are always as close as possible to actual rows. Notice how the estimations are very skewed. The seek operation returned 1,740 rows of 5,170 estimated rows. The misestimation comes from the fact that the query uses local variables that prevent the Query Optimizer from using the statistics histogram to get accurate estimations.

This can be addressed by using the RECOMPILE hint, or better yet, using sp_executesql. The following examples show both options; first, here's the RECOMPILE hint:

```
DECLARE @start DATETIME = '07/01/2013', @end DATETIME = '07/31/2013'
SELECT SalesOrderID, OrderDate
FROM Sales.SalesOrderHeader
WHERE OrderDate BETWEEN @start AND @end
OPTION (RECOMPILE);
```

And here's the sp_executesql method:

```
EXECUTE sp_executesql @stmt = N'SELECT SalesOrderID, OrderDate FROM
Sales.SalesOrderHeader
WHERE OrderDate BETWEEN @start AND @end;'
                , @params = N'@start DATETIME, @end DATETIME'
                , @start = '07/01/2013', @end = '07/31/2013';
```

We can observe the new query execution plan:

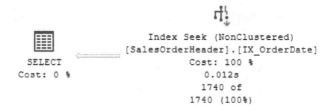

Figure 5.14 – Execution plan for the query using sp_executesql

Notice the estimation now matches the actual rows, denoting accurate estimations, and a perfect example of Predicate Pushdown, as we discussed in *Chapter 4, Indexing for T-SQL Performance*. Now that we've covered the issues with functions in our predicates, let's dig a little deeper into how table-valued functions can impact query performance.

Deconstructing table-valued functions

A **User-Defined Function (UDF)** is like a stored procedure in that it is a block of T-SQL statements saved as an object, but it differs in that it does not generate a result set; it returns a value of a specified type. A scalar UDF is a function that returns a single value; a **Table-Valued Function (TVF)** is a function that returns a table.

There are two types of TVFs in the SQL Database Engine:

- **Multi-statement TVFs (MSTVFs)**: MSTVFs declare a return table type, populate the table, then return the table at the end of the function

- **Inline TVFs**: You can think of an inline TVF as a view that takes a parameter, the body of the function is a single query, and the return value is the result of that query

The following is an example of an MSTVF that we can create in the AdventureWorks sample database:

```
CREATE OR ALTER FUNCTION dbo.ufn_FindReports (@InEmpID INTEGER)
RETURNS @retFindReports TABLE
(
    EmployeeID int primary key NOT NULL,
    FirstName nvarchar(255) NOT NULL,
    LastName nvarchar(255) NOT NULL,
    JobTitle nvarchar(50) NOT NULL,
    RecursionLevel int NOT NULL
)
/*Returns a result set that lists all the employees who report to the
specific employee directly or indirectly. */
AS
BEGIN
WITH EMP_cte(EmployeeID, OrganizationNode, FirstName, LastName,
JobTitle, RecursionLevel) -- CTE name and columns
    AS (
        -- Get the initial list of Employees for Manager n
        SELECT e.BusinessEntityID, e.OrganizationNode, p.FirstName,
p.LastName, e.JobTitle, 0
        FROM HumanResources.Employee e
INNER JOIN Person.Person p
ON p.BusinessEntityID = e.BusinessEntityID
        WHERE e.BusinessEntityID = @InEmpID
        UNION ALL
        -- Join recursive member to anchor
        SELECT e.BusinessEntityID, e.OrganizationNode, p.FirstName,
p.LastName, e.JobTitle, RecursionLevel + 1
        FROM HumanResources.Employee e
            INNER JOIN EMP_cte
            ON e.OrganizationNode.GetAncestor(1) = EMP_cte.
OrganizationNode
INNER JOIN Person.Person p
ON p.BusinessEntityID = e.BusinessEntityID)

-- copy the required columns to the result of the function
    INSERT @retFindReports
```

```
    SELECT EmployeeID, FirstName, LastName, JobTitle, RecursionLevel
    FROM EMP_cte
    RETURN
END;
```

Since this function returns a table, we can reference it in a T-SQL query just like we would a table. The following is a sample query that uses this function:

```
SELECT EmployeeID, FirstName, LastName, JobTitle, RecursionLevel
FROM dbo.ufn_FindReports(25);
```

The problem with MSTVFs is the cost of the function can't be determined at compile time, so a fixed estimation of rows is used to create the query plan. Let's look at the query execution plan for the previous example in the following screenshot:

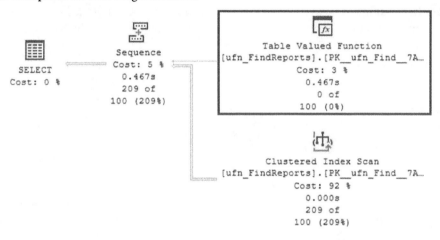

Figure 5.15 – Execution plan for the query using an MSTVF

Notice that the TVF appears as an input to the join as if it were a table with an estimate of 100 rows, but an actual row count of 0.

> **Note**
>
> Prior to SQL Server 2014, the fixed estimate for MSTVFs was 1. In this case, it would have been a better estimate, but most MSTVFs return more than 1 row, so 100 is generally a better fixed estimate.

This inaccurate cardinality estimate could cause the plan to be inefficient, but since the true cardinality can't be determined without executing the function, there is not much that can be done to improve this estimate.

<table>
<tbody>
<tr><td colspan="2">⊟ QueryTimeStats</td></tr>
<tr><td>CpuTime</td><td>261</td></tr>
<tr><td>ElapsedTime</td><td>468</td></tr>
<tr><td>UdfCpuTime</td><td>0</td></tr>
<tr><td>UdfElapsedTime</td><td>117</td></tr>
</tbody>
</table>

Figure 5.16 – QueryTimeStats for the query execution plan in Figure 5.15

The query took 468 ms to execute, with 261 ms of CPU time. Note the **UdfElapsedTime** is 117 ms and has to do with this query referencing the GetAncestor system function.

Starting with SQL Server 2017, a new feature called **Interleaved Execution** for MSTVFs was introduced. With interleaved execution, rather than using a fixed estimate, optimization is paused when an MSTVF is encountered, the function is materialized, and the actual row count is used to optimize the rest of the plan. The resulting plan is then cached, so this process will not be repeated when subsequent executions reuse the plan. Using the previous example, if we change the database compatibility to level 140, which maps to the SQL Server 2017 release, we get an accurate row count for our query, as in the following screenshot:

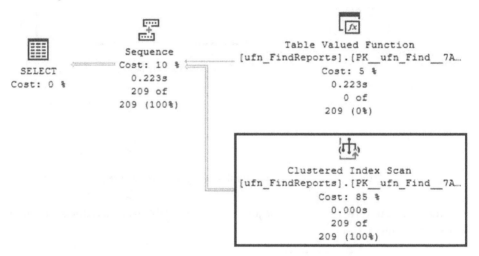

Figure 5.17 – Execution plan for the query using the Interleaved Execution feature

The **QueryTimeStats** for this query are improved from the non-interleaved version: CPU time dropped from 261 ms to 223 ms (~14 percent less), and execution time dropped from 468 ms to 224 ms (~51 percent less), as seen in the following screenshot:

QueryTimeStats	
CpuTime	223
ElapsedTime	224
UdfCpuTime	0
UdfElapsedTime	115

Figure 5.18 – QueryTimeStats for the query execution plan in Figure 5.17

An even better way to do this would be to write the function as an inline TVF. As we mentioned earlier in this section, inline TVFs behave like views – they can be folded into the query, allowing their cardinality to be known at compile time, thus generating a more efficient query plan. In the following example, let's look at how we can create an inline TVF that returns the same results as the MSTVF:

```
CREATE OR ALTER FUNCTION dbo.ufn_FindReports_inline (@InEmpID int)
RETURNS TABLE
AS
RETURN
WITH EMP_cte(EmployeeID, OrganizationNode, FirstName, LastName,
JobTitle, RecursionLevel) -- CTE name and columns
    AS (
        -- Get the initial list of Employees for Manager n
        SELECT e.BusinessEntityID AS EmployeeID, e.OrganizationNode,
p.FirstName, p.LastName, e.JobTitle, 0 AS RecursionLevel
        FROM HumanResources.Employee e
    INNER JOIN Person.Person p
    ON p.BusinessEntityID = e.BusinessEntityID
        WHERE e.BusinessEntityID = @InEmpID
        UNION ALL
        -- Join recursive member to anchor
        SELECT e.BusinessEntityID AS EmployeeID, e.OrganizationNode,
p.FirstName, p.LastName, e.JobTitle, RecursionLevel + 1 AS
RecursionLevel
        FROM HumanResources.Employee e
            INNER JOIN EMP_cte
            ON e.OrganizationNode.GetAncestor(1) = EMP_cte.
OrganizationNode
INNER JOIN Person.Person p
ON p.BusinessEntityID = e.BusinessEntityID)
SELECT EmployeeID, FirstName, LastName, JobTitle, RecursionLevel
FROM EMP_cte;
```

The plan shape for this query looks very different than the previous one:

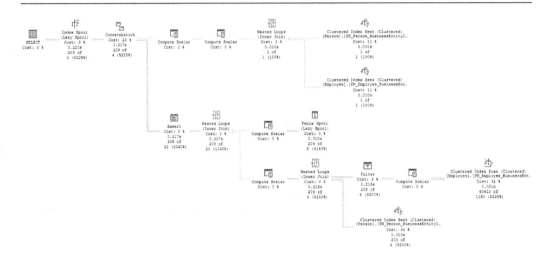

Figure 5.19 – Execution plan for the query using an inline TVF

This is because the function is not being referenced as an object in this plan. The inline TVF is folded into the query as a table or view would be, allowing for a better overall plan and opening new opportunities for adjusting the indexes for an even better result. In this case, the performance of the query is like the interleaved MSTVF – CPU time dropped from 261 ms to 220 ms (~16 percent less), and execution time dropped from 468 ms to 221 ms (~52 percent less), as seen in the following screenshot:

QueryTimeStats	
CpuTime	220
ElapsedTime	221
UdfCpuTime	0
UdfElapsedTime	115

Figure 5.20 – QueryTimeStats for the query execution plan in Figure 5.19

The takeaway here is to write TVFs as inline TVFs rather than MSTVFs where possible. If the logic is too complex to make an inline TVF feasible, upgrading to SQL Server 2017 or higher to be able to leverage interleaved execution might improve query performance when leveraging TVFs. Now that we understand how proper use of TVFs can improve performance, let's dig into another common anti-pattern – complex expressions in a WHERE clause.

Complex expressions

Search predicates should not use complex expressions. Much like the deterministic function calls we discussed in the *Functions in our predicate* section, complex expressions can also cause unnecessary scans.

As was discussed in previous chapters, the Query Optimizer uses statistics, internal transformation rules, and heuristics at compile time to determine a good enough plan to execute a query. This includes the ability to fold expressions, which is the process of simplifying constant expressions at compile time. For example, a predicate such as WHERE Column = 320 * 200 * 32 is computed at compile time to its arithmetic result and, internally, the predicate is evaluated as WHERE Column = 2048000. But unlike constants, calculations that involve column values, parameters, non-deterministic functions, or variables are only evaluated at runtime – this is another example of how the Query Optimizer can't accurately estimate row counts beforehand, resulting in an inefficient query plan.

The following example shows a query executed in the AdventureWorks sample database that uses a calculation with a table column in the search predicate. The query lists all ordered products where an additional 10 percent discount can be added if the final discount is less than or equal to 30 percent:

```
SELECT ProductID, [UnitPrice], [UnitPriceDiscount],
    [UnitPrice] * (1 - [UnitPriceDiscount]) AS FinalUnitPrice,
    [UnitPriceDiscount] + 0.10 AS NewUnitPriceDiscount,
    [UnitPrice] * (1 - 0.30) AS NewFinalUnitPrice
FROM Sales.SalesOrderDetail
WHERE [UnitPriceDiscount] + 0.10 <= 0.30
GROUP BY ProductID, [UnitPrice], [UnitPriceDiscount];
```

Let's observe the query execution plan:

Figure 5.21 – Execution plan for the query

Much as we discussed in the *Functions in our predicate* section, we see a scan of the clustered index. The requirement for the query is to find ordered products where the company can add an additional 10 percent and still not go above a 30 percent discount, and the predicate [UnitPriceDiscount] + 0.10 <= 0.30 accomplishes that.

But the same requirement can be expressed using a search predicate that does not use a complex expression, such as seen in the following query:

```
SELECT ProductID, [UnitPrice], [UnitPriceDiscount],
    [UnitPrice] * (1 - [UnitPriceDiscount]) AS FinalUnitPrice,
    [UnitPriceDiscount] + 0.10 AS NewUnitPriceDiscount,
    [UnitPrice] * (1 - 0.30) AS NewFinalUnitPrice
FROM Sales.SalesOrderDetail
WHERE [UnitPriceDiscount] <= 0.20
GROUP BY ProductID, [UnitPrice], [UnitPriceDiscount];
```

Let's observe the new query execution plan:

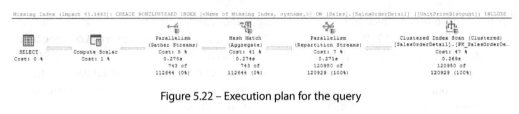

Figure 5.22 – Execution plan for the query

Figure 5.23 – QueryTimeStats for the query execution plan in Figure 5.22

There is no discernible change, but that's because there isn't a better index to use in the current schema. However, the SQL Database Engine found an index suggestion that may yield better results, and this was possible because the search predicate could now be evaluated at compile time. We can create the index suggestion as follows:

```
CREATE NONCLUSTERED INDEX IX_UnitePriceDiscount ON [Sales].
[SalesOrderDetail] (
        [UnitPriceDiscount]
)
INCLUDE (
        [ProductID],
        [UnitPrice]
);
```

> **Tip**
>
> It's a good idea to assess the current index design after getting an index suggestion to determine if an existing index is a subset of the suggested index. If such an index already exists, it is better to alter this index rather than create a new index that would be redundant and unnecessarily increase index overhead.

Executing the same query results in the following query execution plan:

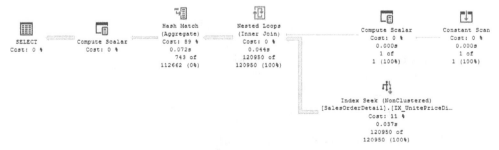

Figure 5.24 – Execution plan for the query using the new index

The new plan is much cheaper to execute, which is why it didn't even qualify for parallelism. And in fact, if we compare the **QueryTimeStats** from before and after the index was created, the improvements are also obvious: CPU time dropped from 140 ms to 67 ms (52 percent less), and execution time dropped from 276 ms to 74 ms (73 percent less):

⊟ QueryTimeStats

CpuTime	67
ElapsedTime	74

Figure 5.25 – QueryTimeStats for the query execution plan in Figure 5.24

Now that we understand the impact complex expressions can have on query performance, let's move on to another potential anti-pattern – OR logic.

Optimizing OR logic

A common query pattern involves the need to express several conditions of which at least one must be true to filter the result set, usually with OR logic. Expressing these OR conditions can have serious performance drawbacks and can often be replaced with other constructs that provide better scalability and performance.

The following example shows a query executed in the AdventureWorks sample database that uses an OR condition in the search predicate. The query lists all rows for a specific product, or where the price is set at a predetermined value:

```
SELECT ProductID, [UnitPrice], [UnitPriceDiscount],
    [UnitPrice] * (1 - [UnitPriceDiscount]) AS FinalUnitPrice,
    [UnitPriceDiscount] + 0.10 AS NewUnitPriceDiscount,
    [UnitPrice] * (1 - 0.30) AS NewFinalUnitPrice
FROM Sales.SalesOrderDetail
WHERE ProductID = 770
    OR UnitPrice = 3399.99
GROUP BY ProductID, [UnitPrice], [UnitPriceDiscount];
```

With the following query execution plan:

Figure 5.26 – Execution plan for the query

For reference, the **QueryTimeStats** for this query execution plan are as follows:

⊟ QueryTimeStats
   CpuTime   42
   ElapsedTime   287

Figure 5.27 – QueryTimeStats for the query execution plan in Figure 5.26

Looking at the search predicates, they are not necessarily mutually exclusive. Still, they can effectively be expressed as two separate queries that are joined by a UNION operator, as in the following example:

```
SELECT ProductID, [UnitPrice], [UnitPriceDiscount],
       [UnitPrice] * (1 - [UnitPriceDiscount]) AS FinalnitPrice,
       [UnitPriceDiscount] + 0.10 AS NewUnitPriceDiscount,
       [UnitPrice] * (1 - 0.30) AS NewFinalUnitPrice
FROM Sales.SalesOrderDetail
WHERE ProductID = 770
GROUP BY ProductID, [UnitPrice], [UnitPriceDiscount]
UNION
SELECT ProductID, [UnitPrice], [UnitPriceDiscount],
       [UnitPrice] * (1 - [UnitPriceDiscount]) AS FinalUnitPrice,
       [UnitPriceDiscount] + 0.10 AS NewUnitPriceDiscount,
       [UnitPrice] * (1 - 0.30) AS NewFinalUnitPrice
FROM Sales.SalesOrderDetail
WHERE UnitPrice = 3399.99
GROUP BY ProductID, [UnitPrice], [UnitPriceDiscount];
```

Let's observe the new query execution plan:

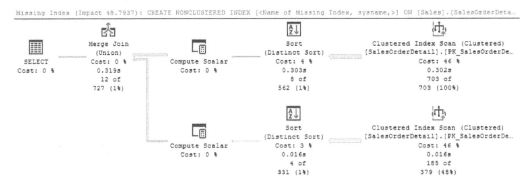

Figure 5.28 – Execution plan for the query using a UNION

Since we now have separate queries, we see a missing index suggestion. The index being suggested is the following, which covers the second query in the union:

```
CREATE NONCLUSTERED INDEX IX_UnitPrice ON [Sales].[SalesOrderDetail] (
    [UnitPrice]
)
INCLUDE (
    [ProductID],
    [UnitPriceDiscount]
);
```

But I know we can also cover the first query in the union. There is already a non-clustered index on ProductID, but it does not cover IX_SalesOrderDetail_ProductID. However, I can change the existing index to make it a covering index with negligible effects on any query that was using the index before:

```
CREATE NONCLUSTERED INDEX IX_SalesOrderDetail_ProductID ON [Sales].
[SalesOrderDetail] (
    [ProductID]
)
INCLUDE (
    [UnitPrice],
    [UnitPriceDiscount]
)
WITH DROP_EXISTING;
```

The new query execution plan is the following:

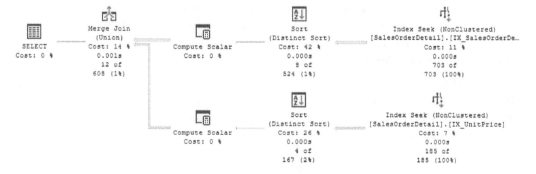

Figure 5.29 – Execution plan for the query using the new index

> **Tip**
>
> If we can verify that the predicates are mutually exclusive and that no repeated rows can exist in the result set, use UNION ALL instead of UNION and avoid the SORT operator seen in the plan. There's more on this in the *UNION ALL versus UNION* section of *Chapter 6, Discovering T-SQL Anti-Patterns in Depth.*

The **QueryTimeStats** for this query execution plan confirm this improved performance: CPU time dropped from 42 ms to 23 ms (45 percent less), and execution time dropped from 287 ms to 2 ms (~99 percent less):

Figure 5.30 – QueryTimeStats for the query execution plan in Figure 5.29

The query execution plan shape now seeks non-clustered indexes. This is a more scalable and better-performing plan than the one scanning the clustered index. Now that we've learned some techniques to optimize OR logic, let's learn a little more about NULL and how it's handled in the SQL Database Engine.

NULL means unknown

In the context of a database, if a column is set to NULL, it effectively means that the value is unknown. If we compare any other value with NULL, the result of that comparison is also unknown. In other words, a value can never be equal to NULL, as NULL is the absence of a value. This means the expression ColumnValue = NULL will never evaluate to true or false; even if ColumnValue is in fact NULL, it will always evaluate to unknown. To detect if a column value is NULL, we must use the special expressions IS NULL or IS NOT NULL rather than = or <>.

> **Note**
>
> This handling of NULL is not unique to the SQL Database Engine, it is based on the ANSI standard handling of NULL values.

Having NULL values in our database is not an anti-pattern in and of itself, but when we assign a meaning to the value NULL in our application, we may face some challenges when it comes to writing performant T-SQL due to the need for special handling of NULL comparisons.

Let's look at an example like this in the AdventureWorks database. The Product table contains information about products that are sold in the shop, but it also contains information about parts that are kept in stock that are not goods for sale. These items will not have a category, so the

ProductSubcategoryID column is NULL for these rows. This makes sense if there truly is no category for these items, but what if we were to say that a value of NULL in the ProductSubcategoryID column really means that these items are in the Parts category because they are unfinished goods. If we want to build a query that returns a list of all the products and includes their category and sub-category, since the sub-category column is NULL for all the parts, we need to embed a function in the join condition in order to handle the special NULL case. In fact, we need to get a bit creative with the T-SQL:

```
SELECT p.ProductID,
p.Name AS ProductName,
c.Name AS Category,
s.Name AS SubCategory
FROM Production.Product p
LEFT JOIN Production.ProductSubcategory s
ON p.ProductSubcategoryID = s.ProductSubcategoryID
INNER JOIN Production.ProductCategory c
ON ISNULL(s.ProductCategoryID, 5) = c.ProductCategoryID
ORDER BY Category, SubCategory;
```

We need to perform a LEFT JOIN between the Product and ProductSubcategory tables in order to include the rows that have a NULL value for ProductSubcategoryID in the Product table, but if we still want to join these NULL rows with the ProductCategory table, we must handle these NULL values in the join condition by using the ISNULL() function. We've hardcoded the value of 5, which is the ProductCategoryID for the new Parts category we added for this example. This would be even more complicated if the value we want to join on is NULL on both sides. In that case, we would need to have a function on both sides of the join to convert the NULL values into something that can actually be compared. In this case, there's a better way we could write this that would prevent NULL handling in the join. Since we know that all the rows with a NULL value for ProductSubcategoryID are in the Parts category, we can handle this in the SELECT list instead. Having an ISNULL() function in the SELECT list does not impact the performance as much because the function call does not interfere with the selectivity estimate, index usage, or plan selection; it's simply executed on the results after they are retrieved:

```
SELECT p.ProductID,
p.Name AS ProductName,
ISNULL(c.Name, 'Parts') AS Category,
s.Name AS SubCategory
FROM Production.Product p
LEFT JOIN Production.ProductSubcategory s
ON p.ProductSubcategoryID = s.ProductSubcategoryID
INNER JOIN Production.ProductCategory c
ON s.ProductCategoryID = c.ProductCategoryID
ORDER BY Category, SubCategory;
```

Let's look at the query plan for these two queries and their estimated cost. Query 1 is the "bad" query with ISNULL() in the join condition, and Query 2 is the "good" query with ISNULL() in the SELECT list:

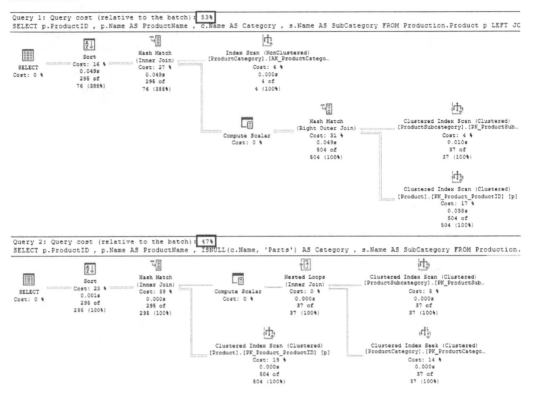

Figure 5.31 – Execution plan for Query 1 (the "bad" query) and Query 2 (the "good" query)

Looking at the **QueryTimeStats** for these two queries, we can see that Query 1 uses three times as much CPU as Query 2:

Query 1		Query 2	
⊟ QueryTimeStats		⊟ QueryTimeStats	
CpuTime	3	CpuTime	1
ElapsedTime	50	ElapsedTime	1

Figure 5.32 QueryTimeStats for the query execution plan in Figure 5.31

We might notice that there is a scan of the Product table in both plans, which leads to an expensive Hash Match. This is because there is no index on the ProductSubcategoryID column in the Product table. Let's add a covering index to that column to see if we can get the plan to be a little better:

```
CREATE NONCLUSTERED INDEX [IX_Product_ProductSubcategoryID] ON
[Production].[Product] (
        [ProductSubcategoryID]
)
INCLUDE (
[Name]
);
```

Now if we run the queries again, we get the following plans and their estimated cost:

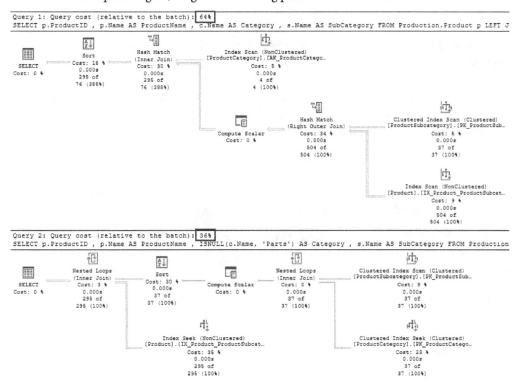

Figure 5.33 – Execution plan for Query 1 and Query 2 using the new index

Query 1 uses the covering index, but because the ISNULL() function prevents the SQL Database Engine from using the predicate as a seek predicate, it has to scan it. Query 2, on the other hand, gets much better with seeks and Nested Loops joins. This is reflected in the **QueryTimeStats** as well:

Query 1			Query 2	
⊟ QueryTimeStats			⊟ QueryTimeStats	
CpuTime	1		CpuTime	1
ElapsedTime	1		ElapsedTime	1

Figure 5.34 – QueryTimeStats for the query execution plan in Figure 5.33

Query 1 goes down to 1 ms, whereas Query 2 stays the same at 1 ms. Keep this in mind when using NULL in our application. NULL means unknown or the absence of a value and requires special handling for comparisons; don't rely on it to represent something concrete. Now that we understand how NULL works, let's move on to another potential performance pitfall – fuzzy string matching.

Fuzzy string matching

When searching for strings in the SQL Database Engine using =, the strings must match exactly for the expression to evaluate to true. If we want to match only part of the string, however, we must use a LIKE operator with wildcards. If we want to search for a pattern anywhere within a string, we need both leading and trailing wildcards. The problem with this is that it prevents us from being able to use an index or accurately estimate the cardinality. An index with a string key is sorted starting with the first character of the string, but if we are searching for a pattern that may appear in the middle of the string, the SQL Database Engine must scan every value and search for the matching pattern in each string in the column. A LIKE operator with a leading wildcard (%a value or %a value%) almost always causes a scan operation.

Consider an example from the AdventureWorks database where we want to find all the Flat Washers in the Product table. We know they all start with "Flat Washer" but there are several different names in the table. If we're not sure whether there are any characters before the words "Flat Washer," we could write the following query:

```
SELECT ProductID, Name AS ProductName, ProductNumber
FROM Production.Product
WHERE Name LIKE '%Flat Washer%';
```

This query would yield the following execution plan:

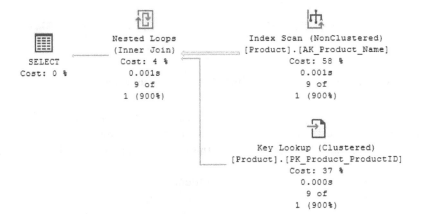

Figure 5.35 – Execution plan for the query

Notice there's an Index Scan, which is the most expensive operator in the plan.

If we look at the result set, we can see that the words "Flat Washer" always appear at the beginning of the string:

	Results		Messages		Execution plan
	ProductID	ProductName	ProductNumber		
1	341	Flat Washer 1	FW-1000		
2	343	Flat Washer 2	FW-1400		
3	346	Flat Washer 3	FW-5160		
4	345	Flat Washer 4	FW-3800		
5	348	Flat Washer 5	FW-7160		
6	342	Flat Washer 6	FW-1200		
7	349	Flat Washer 7	FW-9160		
8	347	Flat Washer 8	FW-5800		
9	344	Flat Washer 9	FW-3400		

Figure 5.36 – Result set for the query

In this case, we don't really need the leading wildcard, so we could re-write the query as follows:

```
SELECT ProductID, Name AS ProductName, ProductNumber
FROM Production.Product
WHERE Name LIKE 'Flat Washer%';
```

And then we can examine the execution plan:

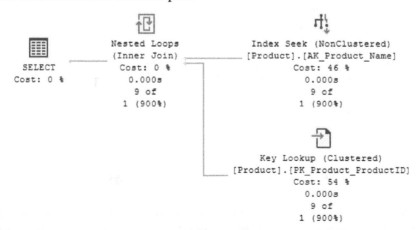

Figure 5.37 – Execution plan for the improved query

The expensive scan is replaced by a more efficient Index Seek.

If you must use a LIKE expression, try to avoid using a leading wildcard if possible. LIKE expressions without a leading wildcard translate into a range scan. If it is not possible to avoid the leading wildcard, we might consider using full text indexes and their accompanying text functions such as CONTAINS to provide better performance for fuzzy string matching, particularly if this is the only filter condition on these queries. Now on to another similar potential query problem – inequality logic.

Inequality logic

Inequality logic is logic that involves negative comparisons such as !=, <>, NOT IN, and NOT LIKE. This type of predicate can be costly because it often results in evaluating each row, which translates to scan operations. Consider the following queries, 1 and 2, from the AdventureWorks database:

```
SELECT BusinessEntityID, FirstName, LastName
FROM Person.Person
WHERE PersonType NOT IN ('EM','SP','IN','VC','GC');
SELECT BusinessEntityID, FirstName, LastName
FROM Person.Person
WHERE PersonType = 'SC';
```

These queries are logically equivalent, since 'SC' is the only PersonType that is not listed in the first query. Out of the box, the execution plans look like this:

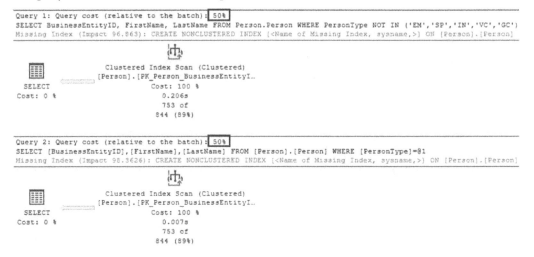

Figure 5.38 – Execution plan for Query 1 and Query 2

At this point, they appear to have the same estimated cost, but notice that both are doing a Clustered Index Scan and there is a missing index suggestion from the SQL Database Engine. This is because there is no index on the PersonType column to support the query. Let's add the following covering index to support this query:

```
CREATE NONCLUSTERED INDEX [IX_Person_PersonType] ON [Person].[Person]
(
        [PersonType] ASC
)
INCLUDE (
        [BusinessEntityID],
        [FirstName],
        [LastName]
);
```

Once we add the index, the SQL Database Engine can leverage it for both queries, but notice that the first query results in a scan of the index, whereas the second query performs a seek. Also note the estimated cost difference between the plans, the first query is much more expensive than the second:

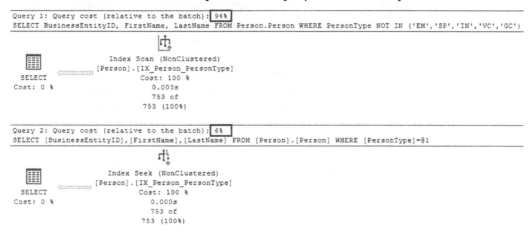

Figure 5.39 – Execution plan for Query 1 and Query 2 using the new index

As we can see, while both queries are logically the same and return the same results, the second query is much more efficient than the first once the proper indexes are in place. If we have the option of writing a filter condition using an equality comparison or an inequality comparison, using the equality comparison is generally better. Now that we've explored a few different ways we can rewrite queries to get better performance, let's look at an anti-pattern related to how the query itself is executed.

EXECUTE versus sp_executesql

There are times when an application must build a T-SQL statement dynamically before executing it on the server. In order to execute a dynamically created T-SQL statement, we can use either the EXECUTE command or the sp_executesql stored procedure. The sp_executesql procedure is the preferred method for executing dynamic T-SQL because it allows us to add parameter markers and thus increases the likelihood that the SQL Database Engine will be able to reuse the plan and avoid costly query compilations.

Here's an example script from the `AdventureWorks` database that builds a dynamic T-SQL statement and executes it via the `EXECUTE` command:

```
DECLARE @sql nvarchar(MAX), @JobTitle nvarchar(50) = N'Sales
Representative';

SET @sql = 'SELECT e.BusinessEntityID, p.FirstName, p.LastName
FROM HumanResources.Employee e
INNER JOIN Person.Person p ON p.BusinessEntityID = e.BusinessEntityID
WHERE e.JobTitle = N''' + @JobTitle + '''';

EXECUTE (@sql);
```

Notice that there is a variable for the `JobTitle` column, but the `EXECUTE` command does not allow parameters, so this variable is appended to the T-SQL string in order to include it in the resulting query. We can reuse the same script by changing `'Sales Representative'` to `'Accountant'` and re-running it, but because the resulting query is not parameterized, the SQL Database Engine will have to compile and cache the query again. We can verify this by examining the `sys.dm_exec_query_stats` **dynamic management view** (**DMV**). Recall from the *Query plan properties of interest* section of *Chapter 3, Exploring Query Execution Plans*, that there is a property called `QueryHash` that contains a value that can identify a query in the cache and will return all the queries that are syntactically equivalent but have different query strings for some reason:

```
SELECT st.text, qs.sql_handle, qs.execution_count
FROM sys.dm_exec_query_stats qs
CROSS APPLY sys.dm_exec_sql_text(qs.sql_handle) st
WHERE qs.query_hash = 0x3A17ADF596F7D5C9;
```

This query returns the following results:

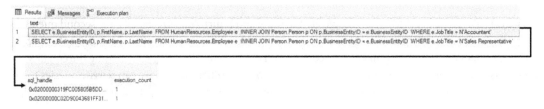

Figure 5.40 – Result set showing different SQL handles for the same query hash

We can see that there are two different queries here, one for each of the different `JobTitle` values, and each has a single execution. Each execution of the script resulted in a separate compilation and a separate cached query plan.

> **Note**
>
> We will discuss sys.dm_exec_query_stats as well as other dynamic management views in more detail in *Chapter 7, Building Diagnostic Queries Using DMVs and DMFs.*

Let's see how we can rewrite this script using sp_executesql instead:

```
DECLARE @sql nvarchar(MAX), @JobTitle nvarchar(50) = N'Sales
Representative';

SET @sql = 'SELECT e.BusinessEntityID, p.FirstName, p.LastName
FROM HumanResources.Employee e
INNER JOIN Person.Person p ON p.BusinessEntityID = e.BusinessEntityID
WHERE e.JobTitle = @p1';

EXEC sp_executesql @sql, N'@p1 nvarchar(50)', @JobTitle;
```

Notice that in this case, we can use the @JobTitle variable as a parameter in the query. If we change the value of @JobTitle to 'Accountant' and run the query again, the SQL Database Engine can reuse the existing execution plan from the cache. We can verify this by running the same query against sys.dm_exec_query_stats with the QueryHash from this new query. This time, the results are different:

Figure 5.41 – Result set showing the same SQL handle for the same query hash and two executions

Notice that the query in the cache has a parameter marker, and the execution count is 2, indicating that the query plan has been reused.

Whenever our application requires dynamic T-SQL for any reason, using the sp_executesql procedure rather than the EXECUTE command is generally more efficient because it will increase the likelihood that the SQL Database Engine can reuse the query plan. Also recall that in the *The importance of parameters* section in the *Understanding Query Processing* chapter, we mentioned that parameters and the use of sp_executesql can also help prevent SQL injection attacks, so it is more secure than using EXECUTE. For these reasons, sp_executesql is the recommended method for executing dynamic T-SQL. Now that we know the proper way to execute dynamic T-SQL, let's look at another common programming problem – composable logic – and how it might actually perform better if written as dynamic T-SQL.

Composable logic

Composable logic is what some developers use to make a single T-SQL statement do more than one thing, which allows us to reuse the same code for multiple tasks. When writing procedural code, reusability is desired because it makes the code more concise and maintainable. It allows developers to create libraries of modules that can be reused in other areas of the application, or even in other applications altogether. In T-SQL, however, there can be a hefty performance penalty for writing generic reusable code.

For the SQL Database Engine to execute a query in the most efficient way, it needs to estimate the cost of the query and choose operators that will return the results in the cheapest way possible. This is all done at **compile-time** based on how the query is written. With composable logic, however, the true cost of the query cannot be known until **runtime** because it is based on variables that change whenever the query is run. This type of generic code causes the SQL Database Engine to generate a generic plan at compile time that will work no matter what the runtime values are. Typically, this plan will not perform well for any combination of runtime values, whereas a specific plan generated for the specific case that is being executed would likely perform much better. Writing T-SQL code for the specific case that it is needed may result in some code duplication and less maintainability, what developers sometimes refer to as **spaghetti code**, but it will almost always provide better performance and scalability.

Consider the following stored procedure, which can be executed in the `AdventureWorks` sample database:

```
CREATE OR ALTER PROCEDURE usp_GetSalesPersonOrders @SalesPerson INT
NULL
AS
BEGIN
    SELECT SalesOrderID, p.FirstName AS SalesFirstName, p.LastName AS
SalesLastName
    FROM Sales.SalesOrderHeader AS soh
    LEFT JOIN Person.Person AS p ON soh.SalesPersonID =
p.BusinessEntityID
    WHERE @SalesPerson IS NULL OR SalesPersonID = @SalesPerson;
END;
```

This is an example of composable logic. If a value is sent for the `@SalesPerson` parameter, we are effectively executing this query:

```
SELECT SalesOrderID, p.FirstName as SalesFirstName, p.LastName as
SalesLastName
FROM Sales.SalesOrderHeader AS soh
LEFT JOIN Person.Person AS p ON soh.SalesPersonID = p.BusinessEntityID
WHERE SalesPersonID = @SalesPerson;
```

If NULL is sent for the @SalesPerson parameter, we are effectively executing this query:

```
SELECT SalesOrderID, p.FirstName as SalesFirstName, p.LastName as
SalesLastName
FROM Sales.SalesOrderHeader AS soh
LEFT JOIN Person.Person p ON soh.SalesPersonID = p.BusinessEntityID;
```

Note that this second query has no WHERE clause. It will return the entire SalesOrderHeader table, including any matching rows from the Person table. This is naturally going to be much more expensive than the first query and should really have a different query plan. Let's look at the query plans and see how the SQL Database Engine would perform each query if written separately:

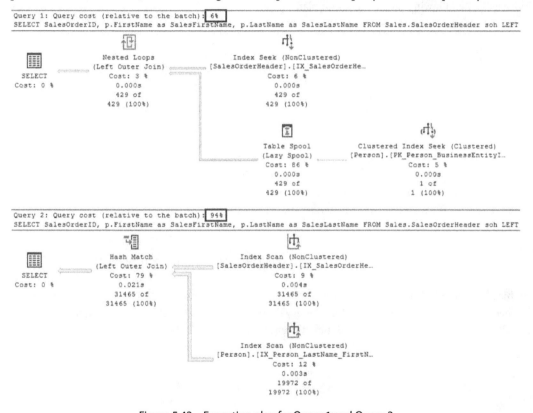

Figure 5.42 – Execution plan for Query 1 and Query 2

As we can see, the estimated cost for Query 1, which uses the @SalesPerson variable in the WHERE clause, is much cheaper than the estimated cost for Query 2, which returns every row in the SalesOrderHeader table. Also, note that Query 1 uses Index Seeks and a Nested Loops join, whereas Query 2 uses Index Scans and a Hash Match. Here are the resulting **QueryTimeStats**:

Query 1		Query 2	
⊟ QueryTimeStats		⊟ QueryTimeStats	
CpuTime	1	CpuTime	27
ElapsedTime	29	ElapsedTime	114

Figure 5.43 – QueryTimeStats for the query execution plans in Figure 5.42

Now let's try executing Query 1 by using the stored procedure that we created earlier:

```
EXECUTE usp_GetSalesPersonOrders @SalesPerson = 279;
```

This yields the following query execution plan:

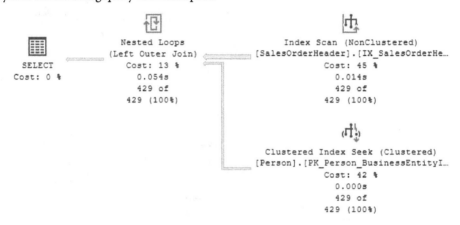

Figure 5.44 – Execution plan for Query 1 using the stored procedure for the first time

In this plan, the SQL Database Engine chooses to use a Nested Loops join, but one of the Index Seeks has become a scan. Also, if we look at the **QueryTimeStats** property of the plan, this plan used 5 ms of CPU time to execute – more than double the amount of time the standalone query used:

⊟ QueryTimeStats	
CpuTime	5
ElapsedTime	55

Figure 5.45 – QueryTimeStats for the query execution plan in Figure 5.44

We can also execute the equivalent of Query 2 using this stored procedure by sending a NULL value for @SalesPerson:

```
EXECUTE usp_GetSalesPersonOrders @SalesPerson = NULL;
```

This execution of the stored procedure will reuse the same plan from the cache, but the runtime is very different:

□ QueryTimeStats
    CpuTime   28
    ElapsedTime   100

Figure 5.46 – QueryTimeStats for the same query execution plan using a NULL parameter

While the difference isn't as much as with Query 1, Query 2 used 28 ms of CPU time versus 27 ms when run as a standalone query. So, the plan generated by this generic stored procedure is worse for both queries than a plan generated for the specific queries.

The situation gets even worse if we happen to execute the stored procedure with @SalesPerson = NULL the first time. We introduced the concept of parameter sniffing in the *The importance of parameters* section in the *Understanding Query Processing* chapter. Composable logic in stored procedures leaves our application even more vulnerable to parameter sniffing issues. Let's look at the plan that is generated if we execute the preceding stored procedure for the first time with a NULL parameter:

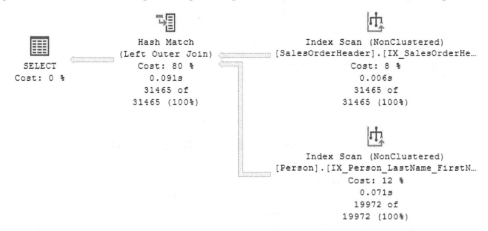

Figure 5.47 – Execution plan for the stored procedure compiled using a NULL parameter

This is effectively the same plan that was generated for Query 2 earlier, and the CPU time is similar at 29 ms. For Query 2, the impact of the composable logic is small, but what happens if we reuse this plan for the @SalesPerson = 279 case? First, the CPU time is even higher than with the first stored procedure plan – 8 ms versus 5 ms:

□ QueryTimeStats
    CpuTime   8
    ElapsedTime   8

Figure 5.48 – QueryTimeStats for the same query execution plan using a non-NULL parameter

We can also see an excessive memory grant warning:

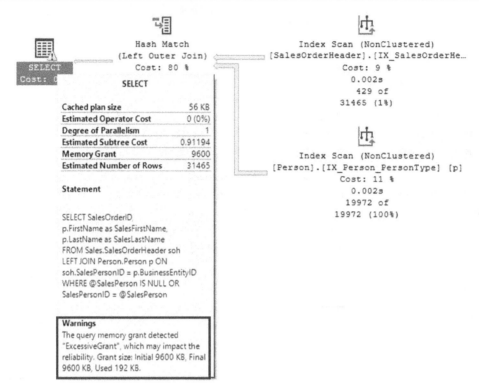

Figure 5.49 – Execution plan for the same query execution plan using a non-NULL parameter

Because of parameter sniffing, the plan created the first time the procedure was run returned a much larger number of rows that necessitated an expensive Hash Match that used a large amount of memory. When using a specific parameter value rather than NULL, the number of rows returned is much smaller, and thus neither the Hash Match nor the memory grant make sense. At compile time, the SQL Database Engine must choose a plan that works for any parameter value that may be sent at runtime. Unfortunately, because of composable logic, the plan chosen is often the wrong one.

The best way to resolve this issue would be to have separate stored procedures for the two queries. The problem with this is that we can end up with many stored procedures that have similar queries and similar names, and code manageability can become an issue. One compromise is to have a single stored procedure with conditional logic outside the query in question. Here's an example of how that would look for these queries:

```
CREATE OR ALTER PROCEDURE usp_GetSalesPersonOrders_better @SalesPerson
INT NULL
AS
BEGIN
    IF @SalesPerson IS NULL
    BEGIN
```

```
        SELECT SalesOrderID, p.FirstName AS SalesFirstName,
p.LastName AS SalesLastName
        FROM Sales.SalesOrderHeader AS soh
        LEFT JOIN Person.Person AS p
ON soh.SalesPersonID = p.BusinessEntityID
    END
    ELSE
    BEGIN
        SELECT SalesOrderID,
p.FirstName AS SalesFirstName,
p.LastName AS SalesLastName
        FROM Sales.SalesOrderHeader AS soh
        LEFT JOIN Person.Person AS p
ON soh.SalesPersonID = p.BusinessEntityID
        WHERE SalesPersonID = @SalesPerson;
    END
END;
```

The code is slightly less readable, but we get the benefit of the right plan at runtime:

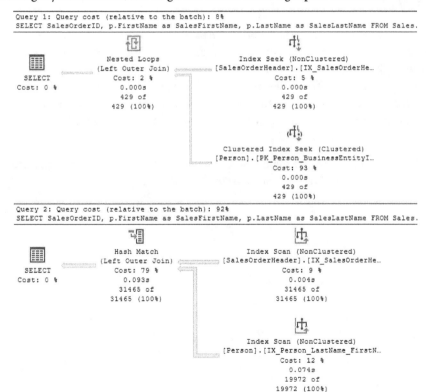

Figure 5.50 – Execution plan for the stored procedure with conditional logic outside the query

This is reflected in the **QueryTimeStats**:

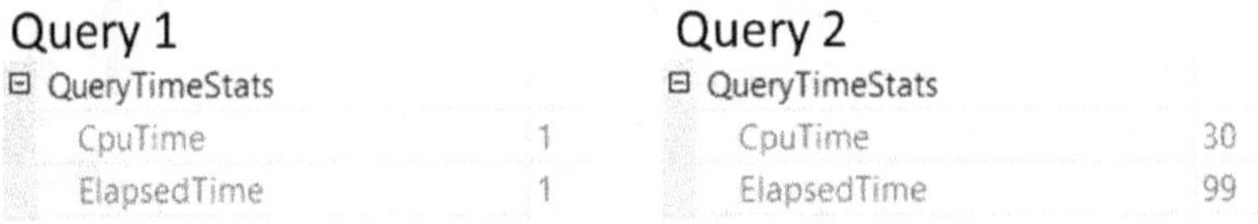

Query 1

QueryTimeStats

| CpuTime | 1 |
| ElapsedTime | 1 |

Query 2

QueryTimeStats

| CpuTime | 30 |
| ElapsedTime | 99 |

Figure 5.51 – QueryTimeStats for the query execution plan in Figure 5.50

Another way to solve this problem would be to use dynamic T-SQL. In the previous section, *EXECUTE versus sp_executesql*, we discussed using `sp_executesql` to execute dynamic T-SQL statements with parameter markers to allow the SQL Database Engine to cache and reuse the plans. If we have composable logic that involves many different options and would generate too many permutations to make conditional logic practical, leveraging dynamic T-SQL is likely the best option. Using the `sp_executesql` procedure allows us to programmatically generate code that is still reusable by the SQL Database Engine, so we get the right plan for the query every time without excessive compile time and cache bloat.

Summary

In this chapter, we reviewed a few T-SQL anti-patterns, such as `SELECT *` syntax, `OR` logic, and functions in our predicates, that are relatively easy to find simply by looking at our T-SQL code and how it is written. The scenarios covered in this chapter are some of the most common examples of patterns that prevent our T-SQL queries from scaling well and maintaining the expected level of performance throughout the lifetime of the application. All are easy to detect, and most have easy workarounds. Therefore, when writing queries, try to avoid these anti-patterns by leveraging some of the techniques we outlined here.

In the next chapter, we will investigate some T-SQL anti-patterns that are a bit more difficult to identify as they require some additional research beyond simply reading the code.

Discovering T-SQL Anti-Patterns in Depth

In *Chapter 5, Writing Elegant T-SQL Queries*, we covered some anti-patterns that may impact query performance that should be obvious just by reading the T-SQL code itself. Now we will move on to some anti-patterns that may require some more in-depth analysis to be identified. These often involve T-SQL that at first glance seems straightforward, but when we dig into the query plan, there may be hidden performance pitfalls such as expensive operations or hidden practices that prevent predicate SARGability.

In this chapter we will cover the following topics:

- Implicit conversions
- Avoiding unnecessary sort operations
- Avoiding UDF pitfalls
- Avoiding unnecessary overhead with stored procedures
- Pitfalls of complex views
- Pitfalls of correlated sub-queries
- Properly storing intermediate results

Technical requirements

The examples used in this chapter are designed for use on SQL Server 2022 and Azure SQL Database, but they should work on versions of SQL Server 2012 and later. The Developer Edition of SQL Server is free for development environments and can be used to run all the code samples. There is also a free tier of Azure SQL Database you can use for testing at https://aka.ms/freedb.

You will need the sample databases `AdventureWorks2016_EXT` (referred to as `AdventureWorks`) and `AdventureWorksDW2016_EXT` (referred to as `AdventureWorksDW`), which can be found on GitHub at `https://github.com/Microsoft/sql-server-samples/releases/tag/adventureworks`. The code used in this chapter can also be found on GitHub at `https://github.com/PacktPublishing/Learn-T-SQL-Querying-Second-Edition/tree/main/ch6`.

Implicit conversions

We introduced the concept of implicit conversions in the chapter *Exploring Query Execution Plans*, particularly in the context of `PlanAffectingConvert` warnings. An implicit conversion happens when the SQL Database Engine needs to compare two values that are not of the same data type. At this point we should understand how to recognize an implicit conversion in our query plans, but what may not always be obvious is how they got there in the first place and how to correct them.

The most obvious cause of implicit conversions is to compare two columns that are not of the same data type. We can easily avoid this by making sure that columns that are related in our database, and thus may be joined, are of the same data type. A common mistake that can cause this situation is where we have some tables that have been created with NVARCHAR strings and some tables that have VARCHAR strings. This may happen because a database was upgraded at some point to support Unicode UTF-16 strings so new tables have NVARCHAR strings, but old tables still have VARCHAR strings, or perhaps some of the old tables were missed when data types were changed. The best resolution in this case is to convert the VARCHAR columns to NVARCHAR so that the data types match.

Another cause of implicit conversions that is not so obvious, but is perhaps the most common, is mismatched parameter data types. This is particularly common when using an **Object-Relational Mapper** (**ORM**) such as **Entity Framework** (**EF**). EF sends queries to the SQL Database Engine as parameterized statements. By default, any strings that are sent as parameters are of NVARCHAR type. This is fine, as long as the strings in the database are stored as NVARCHAR, but if they are stored as VARCHAR, this will lead to implicit conversions of the type that will make any comparisons using these parameters non-SARGable.

Let's look at an example from the `AdventureWorks` database that illustrates this situation. We will build a parameterized query using `sp_executesql` to simulate how an EF query would appear to the SQL Database Engine. All the strings in the AdventureWorks database are stored as NVARCHAR, so we'll need to do some setup to create our scenario here. Using the following queries, let's set up a table called `Product_Narrow`, which will contain a subset of the data in the `Product` table, but with VARCHAR strings instead of NVARCHAR:

```
CREATE TABLE [Production].[Product_Narrow] (
    [ProductID] [int] NOT NULL,
    [Name] [varchar](50) NOT NULL,
    [ProductNumber] [varchar](25) NOT NULL,
    [Color] [varchar](15) NULL,
```

```
        [StandardCost] [money] NOT NULL,
        [ListPrice] [money] NOT NULL,
        [Size] [varchar](5) NULL,
        [SizeUnitMeasureCode] [char](3) NULL,
        [WeightUnitMeasureCode] [char](3) NULL,
        [Weight] [decimal](8, 2) NULL,
        [Class] [char](2) NULL,
        [Style] [char](2) NULL,
        [ProductSubcategoryID] [int] NULL,
        [ProductModelID] [int] NULL,
   CONSTRAINT [PK_Product_Narrow_ProductID] PRIMARY KEY CLUSTERED (
        [ProductID] ASC
));
GO


INSERT Production.Product_Narrow
            (ProductID, Name, ProductNumber, Color, StandardCost,
ListPrice, Size, SizeUnitMeasureCode
            , WeightUnitMeasureCode, Weight, Class, Style,
ProductSubcategoryID, ProductModelID)
SELECT ProductID, Name, ProductNumber, Color, StandardCost, ListPrice,
Size, SizeUnitMeasureCode
            , WeightUnitMeasureCode, Weight, Class, Style,
ProductSubcategoryID, ProductModelID
FROM Production.Product;
CREATE UNIQUE NONCLUSTERED INDEX [AK_Product_Narrow_Name] ON
[Production].[Product_Narrow]
(
        [Name] ASC
);
```

First, let's start with an implicit conversion example that would not trigger a `PlanAffectingConvert` warning. We'll use the original `Product` table for this query:

```
EXEC sp_executesql N'SELECT ProductID, Name, ListPrice, StandardCost
FROM Production.Product
      WHERE Name = @ProductName'
            , N'@ProductName VARCHAR(50)', 'Long-Sleeve Logo Jersey,
XL';
```

The Name column in the `Product` table is stored as a user-defined type called Name, which maps to NVARCHAR(50). Using `sp_executesql`, we sent VARCHAR(50) instead. Here's the query execution plan:

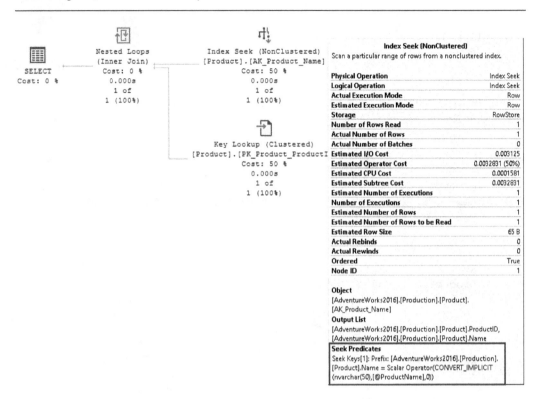

Figure 6.1 – Execution plan using sp_executesql with parameter conversion and no warning

Notice that there is an implicit conversion here, but it didn't produce a warning. This is because the SQL Database Engine converted the parameter, rather than the column. This conversion happened only one time against the literal side of the comparison, so it doesn't affect the plan at all. We can verify this by sending the correct parameter data type:

```
EXEC sp_executesql N'SELECT ProductID, Name, ListPrice, StandardCost
            FROM Production.Product
            WHERE Name = @ProductName'
            , N'@ProductName nvarchar(50)', N'Long-Sleeve Logo
Jersey, XL';
```

Here's the query execution plan – no implicit conversion this time:

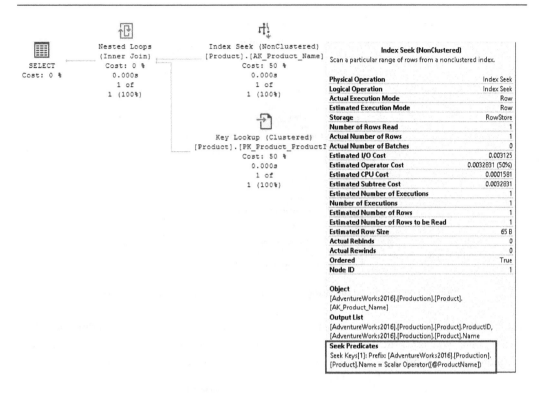

Figure 6.2 – Execution plan using sp_executesql without an implicit conversion

Now let's use our new `Product_Narrow` table to illustrate an implicit conversion that will cause a warning. We'll use the same query, but this time remember that the `Name` column is stored as `VARCHAR(50)` rather than `NVARCHAR(50)`:

```
EXEC sp_executesql N'SELECT ProductID, Name, ListPrice, StandardCost
            FROM Production.Product_Narrow
            WHERE Name = @ProductName'
            , N'@ProductName nvarchar(50)', N'Long-Sleeve Logo
Jersey, XL';
```

The following is our query execution plan, including a warning this time:

Figure 6.3 – Execution plan using sp_executesql with a conversion warning

If we look at the properties of the scan, we'll see there's an implicit conversion, but this time the SQL Database Engine converted the column side of the comparison rather than the literal side as it did in the previous query against the Product table, making the predicate non-SARGable:

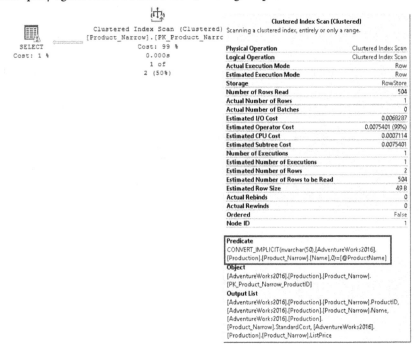

Figure 6.4 – Properties of the Scan operator in the execution plan with a conversion warning

We might be wondering why the SQL Database Engine would choose to do this conversion when it is obviously more expensive than converting the literal side of the comparison. The reason is that the SQL Database Engine must follow the rules of data type precedence when performing an implicit conversion. The SQL Database Engine will convert all the data types involved in the comparison to the data type that has the highest precedence, if the conversion is possible at all. For example, a `DATETIME2` type only implicitly converts to strings and other date- and time-related types. Here's a list of the SQL Database Engine data types in order of their precedence:

1. `user-defined data types` (highest)
2. `sql_variant`
3. `xml`
4. `datetimeoffset`
5. `datetime2`
6. `datetime`
7. `smalldatetime`
8. `date`
9. `time`
10. `float`
11. `real`
12. `decimal`
13. `money`
14. `smallmoney`
15. `bigint`
16. `int`
17. `smallint`
18. `tinyint`
19. `bit`
20. `ntext`
21. `text`
22. `image`
23. `timestamp`
24. `uniqueidentifier`
25. `nvarchar` (including NVARCHAR (MAX))
26. `nchar`
27. `varchar` (including VARCHAR (MAX))
28. `char`
29. `varbinary` (including VARBINARY (MAX))
30. `binary` (lowest)

Notice that NVARCHAR has a higher precedence than VARCHAR. This means that no matter which side of the comparison the VARCHAR value is on, it will always be converted to NVARCHAR, even if it makes the predicate non-SARGable. The solution here is simple: send the correct parameter data type and the conversion will be unnecessary. See the following example with the correct parameter data type:

```
EXEC sp_executesql N'SELECT ProductID, Name, ListPrice, StandardCost
            FROM Production.Product_Narrow
            WHERE Name = @ProductName'
            , N'@ProductName varchar(50)', 'Long-Sleeve Logo
Jersey, XL';
```

When sending the correct data type of VARCHAR(50) for the parameter, no implicit conversion is needed and the SQL Database Engine is able to choose a better plan:

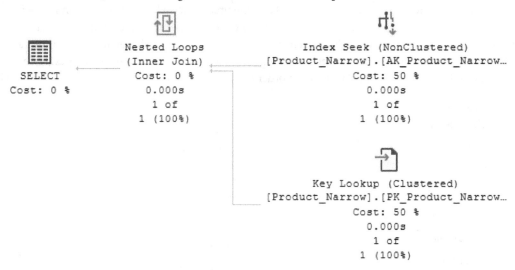

Figure 6.5 – Execution plan using sp_executesql without conversions

This problem is easy to see when the code is all in the database in the form of stored procedures, but when the database code is generated on the client, it may be more difficult to identify. If we see a conversion warning in a query execution plan, be sure to check the ParameterList property and verify that the data types of all the parameters are correct. See the *Exploring Query Execution Plans* chapter for more information on the ParameterList property.

EF is one example of a database code generator vulnerable to this problem, but it is not the only one. With the increasing popularity of code-first database design, this problem is becoming more and more common. It's important to take the time to ensure that the data types chosen for the database match the needs of the application, and even more so that, when possible, the database code is strictly typed based on the actual data types rather than the defaults. Now that we understand how important data types are in avoiding the performance issues associated with implicit conversions, let's move on to learning about sort operations and how to avoid them.

Avoiding unnecessary sort operations

Sort operations in a query plan are very expensive, so we need to avoid anything that might introduce a sort where it is not needed. Using ORDER BY in our query practically guarantees a sort unless we happen to be able to leverage an index and an ordered scan.

> **Tip**
> If your query needs to produce an ordered result set and uses a covering index, ensure the index sort order is the same as the query's desired order. This will increase the likelihood that the SQL Database Engine can leverage the index to order the rows rather than having to do a costly sort operation.

This may be necessary if we need our result set to be returned in a specific order, but if order is not important, this is just overhead.

In this section, we will look at a few examples that may introduce an unnecessary sort operation.

UNION ALL versus UNION

The UNION and UNION ALL syntax is used to combine the results of two separate queries into a single result set. If it is possible for rows to be duplicated between the two queries and we do not want to return duplicate rows, using the UNION syntax will cause the SQL Database Engine to filter out any duplicate rows in the two sets. Doing this requires a sort operation, however, so it is important to only use UNION when necessary. If duplicate values are allowed in the final result set, or if the source results sets cannot have duplicates to begin with – for example, both inputs have unique constraints or primary keys and the sets don't overlap – then using a UNION ALL is more efficient. This avoids introducing implicit sort operations that increase the query cost.

Let's look at an example from the AdventureWorks database. The store is going to have a friends and family sale and we'd like to invite all our customers and vendors to get a special discount on this day. We need to build an email list to send out the promotion, but the information about customers is stored separately from vendors. The easiest way to do this is to create two separate queries and join them using the UNION syntax.

Here's what the query might look like:

```
SELECT 'Customer' AS ContactType, p.FirstName, p.LastName,
e.EmailAddress
FROM Sales.Customer c
INNER JOIN Person.Person p ON c.PersonID = p.BusinessEntityID
INNER JOIN Person.EmailAddress e ON e.BusinessEntityID =
p.BusinessEntityID
WHERE EmailPromotion > 0
UNION
SELECT 'Vendor' AS ContactType, v.FirstName, v.LastName,
v.EmailAddress
FROM Purchasing.vVendorWithContacts v
WHERE EmailPromotion > 0;
```

If we use a UNION, as with the preceding query, this is what the plan looks like:

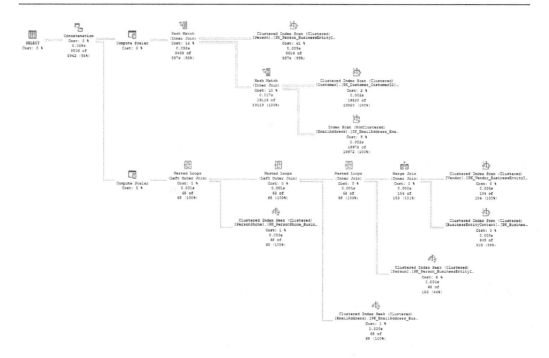

Figure 6.6 – Execution plan using UNION and a concatenation operator

And here are the **QueryTimeStats** for this query:

Figure 6.7 – QueryTimeStats for the plan using UNION and a concatenation operator

There is obviously some opportunity for tuning here as we have several scans and hash matches, which can be eliminated with the addition of an index or two, but notice there is also a sort operation that makes up 95 percent of the estimated cost. This can be eliminated by simply changing the UNION operator to UNION ALL. Unlike UNION, UNION ALL assumes that there is no overlap between the result sets that are being combined – if there are overlaps, then the duplicates will not be eliminated as they would by using UNION. We know that there is no overlap between our vendors and customers, and even there were, we are fine with sending duplicate emails, especially because vendors may receive a different email than customers. Here's the plan for the same query with UNION ALL instead of UNION:

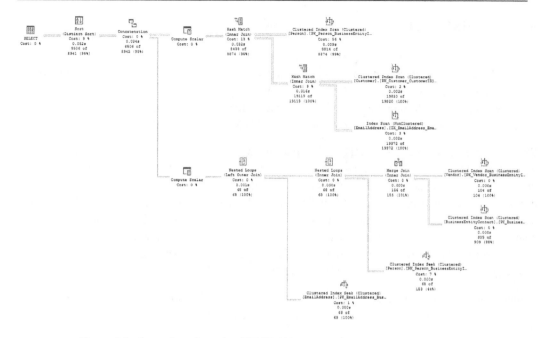

Figure 6.8 – Execution plan using UNION ALL, sort, and concatenation operators

Notice the sort operator is gone now, and the results are the same, but the **QueryTimeStats** have improved:

⊟ QueryTimeStats	
CpuTime	45
ElapsedTime	45

Figure 6.9 – QueryTimeStats for the plan using UNION ALL, sort, and concatenation operators

Both CPU and elapsed time were reduced from 61 ms to 45 ms (an improvement of ~26 percent). When we need to join two or more result sets together, leveraging UNION ALL rather than UNION wherever possible will make our queries more efficient with very little effort on our part.

SELECT DISTINCT

Like the UNION syntax, using DISTINCT in our SELECT query directs the SQL Database Engine to filter out any duplicate rows that may be in the results, which it typically does by introducing a sort operation. If we already have an ORDER BY clause in the query, the sort may be necessary anyway so this would not be additional overhead, but if order is not important, and neither are duplicates, then DISTINCT is unnecessary and the query would likely be cheaper without it.

Rather than blindly applying a DISTINCT operator to our query, it's worth taking some time to investigate why there are duplicate rows in the results. It may be expected and intentional, but getting duplicates in our results when they are not expected often indicates an error condition. It could be due to an incorrectly formed join condition, bad data in the table (for example, incorrect ETL causing duplicate or missing values, or the lack of a unique or primary key allowing duplicate rows), or selecting columns from a table that together are not unique. The outcome is that using DISTINCT can hide these conditions but doesn't solve them. Even if the duplicates are expected, there may be a cheaper way to get the desired results than applying DISTINCT.

Going back to the AdventureWorks database, let's assume that we want to get a list of all the categories and subcategories for products that haven't been discontinued. The most basic way to do this would be the following query:

```
SELECT c.Name AS Category, s.Name AS SubCategory
FROM Production.Product p
INNER JOIN Production.ProductSubcategory s
ON p.ProductSubcategoryID = s.ProductSubcategoryID
INNER JOIN Production.ProductCategory c
ON s.ProductCategoryID = c.ProductCategoryID
WHERE p.DiscontinuedDate IS NULL;
```

Unfortunately, this query by itself will return a lot of duplicate rows because there are many products that have the same category and subcategory. The simplest way to fix this problem is to add DISTINCT to the query:

```
SELECT DISTINCT c.Name AS Category, s.Name AS SubCategory
FROM Production.Product p
INNER JOIN Production.ProductSubcategory s
ON p.ProductSubcategoryID = s.ProductSubcategoryID
INNER JOIN Production.ProductCategory c
ON s.ProductCategoryID = c.ProductCategoryID
WHERE p.DiscontinuedDate IS NULL;
```

This solves the problem, but it also requires the SQL Database Engine to sort all the rows and keep only the unique category and subcategory combinations. Another way to do this is to use an IN or EXISTS predicate in the WHERE clause. Here's an example of what that query might look like:

```
SELECT c.Name AS Category, s.Name AS SubCategory
FROM Production.ProductSubcategory s
INNER JOIN Production.ProductCategory c
ON s.ProductCategoryID = c.ProductCategoryID
WHERE s.ProductSubcategoryID IN (SELECT ProductSubcategoryID
                        FROM Production.Product
                        WHERE DiscontinuedDate IS NULL);
```

This may look more complicated and, on the surface, may seem more expensive, but if we examine the plans we can see that it's cheaper:

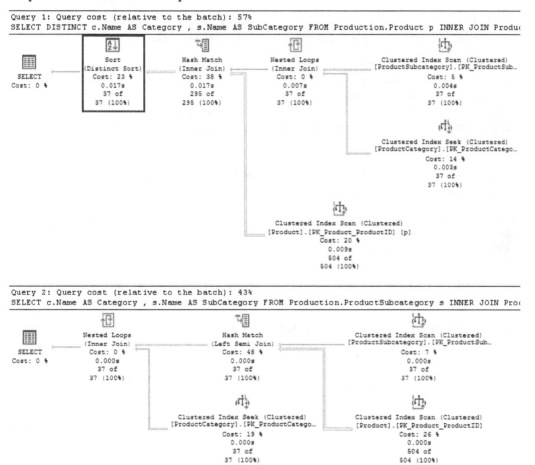

Figure 6.10 – Plan comparison using DISTINCT and a sub-query with IN

Query 1 with DISTINCT in the SELECT clause contains a Sort operator which accounts for 23 percent of the estimated cost. Query 2 which uses the IN clause does not require a sort. This query returns the same results but does so with less effort. While it may be more effort for us to take the time to investigate the query plan and determine whether there's an alternative to adding DISTINCT, we only need to spend that effort once, whereas the SQL Database Engine will have to spend it every time it executes the query.

SELECT TOP 1 with ORDER BY

A very common way to return the maximum or minimum row in a set is to perform a SELECT TOP 1 query with an ORDER BY clause. The problem with this pattern is that it again may result in an unnecessary sort operation. The SQL Database Engine will need to sort all the rows to order them by the desired column, but then return only the first (or last) row in the set. In some cases, it is more efficient to find the minimum or maximum value first, then select the row that is equal to this value.

Let's look at an example from the AdventureWorks database. The following query returns the row with the highest sub-total from the Sales.SalesOrderHeader table:

```
SELECT TOP 1 soh.CustomerID, SalesPersonID, SubTotal, OrderDate, cust.
LastName as CustomerLastName, cust.FirstName as CustomerFirstName
FROM Sales.SalesOrderHeader soh
INNER JOIN sales.Customer c ON c.CustomerID = soh.CustomerID
LEFT JOIN Person.Person cust ON cust.BusinessEntityID = c.CustomerID
ORDER BY SubTotal DESC;
```

Alternatively, for this sample database we could write the query the following way, when we know the sub-query can only return one row:

```
SELECT soh.CustomerID, SalesPersonID, SubTotal, OrderDate, cust.
LastName as CustomerLastName, cust.FirstName as CustomerFirstName
FROM Sales.SalesOrderHeader soh
INNER JOIN sales.Customer c ON c.CustomerID = soh.CustomerID
LEFT JOIN Person.Person cust ON cust.BusinessEntityID = c.CustomerID
WHERE SubTotal = (SELECT MAX(SubTotal) FROM Sales.SalesOrderHeader);
```

Examining the two query plans, we can see that **Query 1** (the TOP 1 plan) is significantly more expensive than **Query 2**, and it includes a costly sort operator:

Query 1: Query cost (relative to the batch): 68%
SELECT TOP 1 soh.CustomerID, SalesPersonID, SubTotal, OrderDate , cust.LastName as CustomerLastName, cust.FirstName as Custome

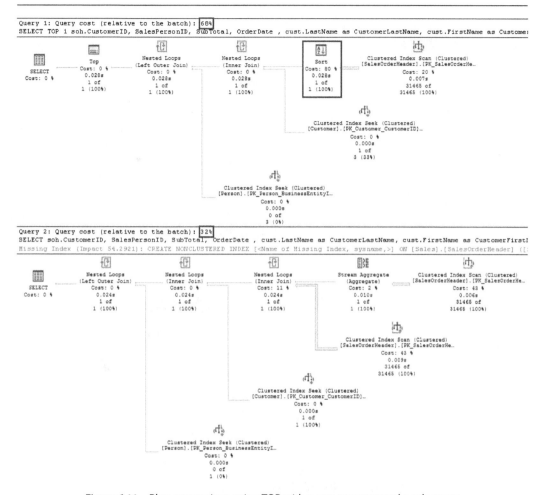

Query 2: Query cost (relative to the batch): 32%
SELECT soh.CustomerID, SalesPersonID, SubTotal, OrderDate , cust.LastName as CustomerLastName, cust.FirstName as CustomerFirst
Missing Index (Impact 54.2921): CREATE NONCLUSTERED INDEX [<Name of Missing Index, sysname,>] ON [Sales].[SalesOrderHeader] ([

Figure 6.11 – Plan comparison using TOP with a sort operator and a sub-query

Notice there is a missing index suggestion for **Query 2** in the preceding plan. If we add this index it can be leveraged by both plans and will eliminate the sort in **Query 1**, but **Query 2** will still be significantly cheaper because it can perform the TOP operation earlier in the plan. The following query plan does not include the expensive sort operator:

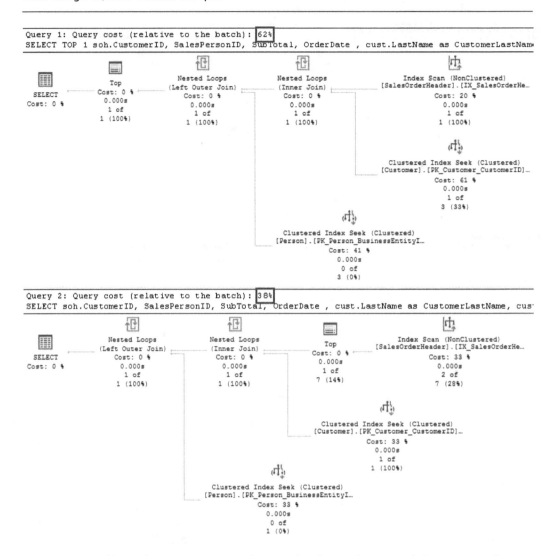

Figure 6.12 – Same plan comparison as in the preceding figure, after creating a supporting index

Keep in mind that not all queries will benefit from removing the TOP 1, but it's worth looking into, especially if the query in question is already very expensive and/or runs frequently. Now that we've discovered some techniques to avoid sorts when using TOP 1 with ORDER BY in our queries, let's learn about user-defined functions and how they influence query performance.

Avoiding UDF pitfalls

Scalar **User-Defined Functions (UDFs)** are a very useful T-SQL programming artifact because they allow a specific routine to be reused very easily. However, these seemingly harmless constructs can be detrimental to performance, because the Query Optimizer does not account for any T-SQL logic inside a UDF, and UDFs are executed for every row in the result set just like a cursor. When using scalar UDFs, there are specific recommendations that apply to UDFs that access system or user data, and recommendations that apply to all UDFs.

An example of a scalar UDF that does not access data was referenced in the chapter *Exploring Query Execution Plans*, in the *Query plan properties of interest* section, as seen in the following code block:

```
CREATE FUNCTION ufn_CategorizePrice (@Price money)
RETURNS NVARCHAR(50)
AS
BEGIN
     DECLARE @PriceCategory NVARCHAR(50)
     IF @Price < 100 SELECT @PriceCategory = 'Cheap'
     ELSE IF @Price BETWEEN 101 and 500 SELECT @PriceCategory = 'Mid
Price'
     ELSE IF @Price BETWEEN 501 and 1000 SELECT @PriceCategory =
'Expensive'
     ELSE IF @Price > 1001 SELECT @PriceCategory = 'Unaffordable'
     RETURN @PriceCategory
END;
```

An example of a query that uses that UDF in the `AdventureWorks` sample database looks like the following:

```
SELECT dbo.ufn_CategorizePrice(UnitPrice),
     SalesOrderID, SalesOrderDetailID, CarrierTrackingNumber,
     OrderQty, ProductID, SpecialOfferID, UnitPrice,
UnitPriceDiscount,
     LineTotal, rowguid, ModifiedDate
FROM Sales.SalesOrderDetail;
```

And note the resulting query execution plan:

Figure 6.13 – Execution plan using a scalar UDF

Evaluating the performance impact of running a UDF in our T-SQL code was not an easy task until the recent versions of the SQL Database Engine. We see that the UDF execution is identified only by the presence of the Compute Scalar operator, and its logic is obfuscated from the query plan. We also observe that it took almost 4 times as much time to execute the UDF (931 ms) than to read the data from the table (275 ms).

Also note that the plan above is not being executed in parallel. This is because by-design, UDFs inhibit the use of parallelism, which may also add to performance problems with certain queries that would be otherwise eligible for parallelism.

We know this scalar UDF doesn't access data by looking at its definition, but the SQL Database Engine doesn't expand the UDF definition at compile time, so the assumption is that the UDF does access data. This adds overhead to UDF execution.

The following query example allows us to see the UDF properties:

```
-- Object accesses system data, system catalogs or virtual system
tables, in the local instance of SQL Server?
SELECT OBJECTPROPERTYEX(OBJECT_id('dbo.ufn_CategorizePrice'),
'SystemDataAccess') AS AccessesSystemData
-- Object accesses user data, user tables, in the local instance of
SQL Server?
SELECT OBJECTPROPERTYEX(OBJECT_id('dbo.ufn_CategorizePrice'),
'UserDataAccess') AS AccessesUserData
-- The precision and determinism properties of the object can be
verified by SQL Server?
SELECT OBJECTPROPERTYEX(OBJECT_id('dbo.ufn_CategorizePrice'),
'IsSystemVerified') AS HasBeenSystemVerified
GO
```

Executing the preceding query yields the following resultset:

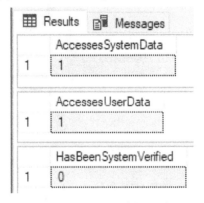

Figure 6.14 – Properties of the scalar UDF

We see the SQL Database Engine takes a pessimistic approach and assumes the scalar UDF we created might access both system and user data, and it has not been system-verified. Especially for UDFs that do not access data (such as the case in this example), always specify the SCHEMABINDING option during the UDF creation, as seen in the following example:

```
CREATE OR ALTER FUNCTION ufn_CategorizePrice (@Price money)
RETURNS NVARCHAR(50)
WITH SCHEMABINDING
AS
BEGIN
     DECLARE @PriceCategory NVARCHAR(50)
     IF @Price < 100 SELECT @PriceCategory = 'Cheap'
     ELSE IF @Price BETWEEN 101 and 500 SELECT @PriceCategory = 'Mid
Price'
     ELSE IF @Price BETWEEN 501 and 1000 SELECT @PriceCategory =
'Expensive'
     ELSE IF @Price > 1001 SELECT @PriceCategory = 'Unaffordable'
     RETURN @PriceCategory
END;
```

This will make the UDF schema-bound and mark the UDF as a deterministic object in the system, allowing the SQL Database Engine to verify the UDF and properly derive its data-access properties.

> **Note**
> For UDFs that are schema-bound, any attempt to change the underlying schema that depends on the UDF will result in an error. But the schema binding option ensures that the UDF will not inadvertently break due to schema changes.

We can use the preceding query example to see the new UDF properties, which now yields the following resultset:

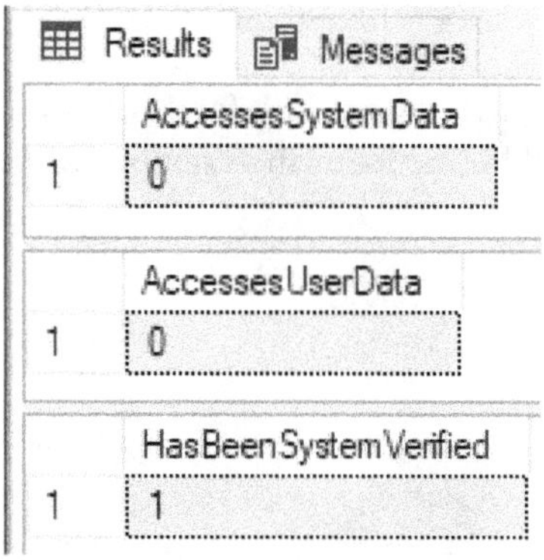

Figure 6.15 – Properties of the schema-bound scalar UDF

In the previous screenshot we can see that the new schema-bound UDF has been system-verified and does not access neither system nor user data. When schema-binding scalar UDFs, the SQL Database Engine can determine in advance whether the UDF accesses system catalogs or virtual system tables, and whether the UDF accesses user tables. In turn, this ensures that the Query Optimizer does not generate any unnecessary operations for query plans involving UDFs that don't access data and avoids having to derive the underlying schema properties for each execution of the UDF.

This schema-bound UDF was verified to not access user tables, and notice the resulting query execution plan:

Figure 6.16 – Execution plan using a schema-bound scalar UDF

In the chapter *Exploring Query Execution Plans*, in the *Query plan properties of interest* section, we referenced an improvement introduced in the SQL Database Engine in SQL Server 2016 SP2 and SQL Server 2017 CU3, where showplan started to include UDF runtime stats in the **QueryTimeStats** property.

Looking at those UDF runtime stats, we see the UDF still has a significant cost (500 ms of elapsed time), although smaller than the non-schema-bound UDF.

Note that the aforementioned object properties can be determined using the following sample query:

```
SELECT OBJECTPROPERTY(object_id, 'IsDeterministic'),
    OBJECTPROPERTY(object_id, 'IsSystemVerified'),
    OBJECTPROPERTY(object_id, 'SystemDataAccess'),
    OBJECTPROPERTY(object_id, 'UserDataAccess'),
    OBJECTPROPERTY(object_id, 'IsSystemVerified')
FROM sys.objects WHERE name = 'ufn_CategorizePrice';
```

When a scalar UDF accesses data, the potential performance implications on SQL Server 2017 or an earlier version are considerable. The following example can be executed in the scope of the AdventureWorks sample database:

```
CREATE OR ALTER FUNCTION dbo.ufn_GetTotalQuantity (@SalesOrderID INT)
RETURNS INT
WITH SCHEMABINDING
AS
BEGIN
DECLARE @Qty INT
```

```
SELECT @Qty = SUM(OrderQty)
FROM Sales.SalesOrderDetail
WHERE SalesOrderID = @SalesOrderID
RETURN (@Qty)
END;
GO


SELECT TOP 5000 *,
      dbo.ufn_GetTotalQuantity (SalesOrderID) AS TotalQty
FROM Sales.SalesOrderHeader;
```

The query generates the following execution plan:

Figure 6.17 – Execution plan using a schema-bound scalar UDF

We can make similar observations regarding the obfuscation of the T-SQL logic inside the UDF. The **QueryTimeStats** for this query execution plan are the following:

QueryTimeStats	
CpuTime	365
ElapsedTime	912
UdfCpuTime	323
UdfElapsedTime	582

Figure 6.18 – QueryTimeStats for the plan using schema-bound scalar UDF

The recommended action to attempt to improve the plan is to surface the expressions inside the UDF to the query itself, in an exercise called inlining the expression. Doing this across all queries that reference the scalar UDF may be hard work, but the effort may be warranted if the performance gains are considerable.

Starting with SQL Server 2019 however, and starting with database compatibility level 150, the SQL Database Engine can automatically inline certain UDF expressions, and account for the UDF logic during query optimization to yield better query plans.

The goal of the **Scalar UDF inlining** feature is to improve performance for queries that invoke scalar UDFs, where the UDF execution is a bottleneck, without any code changes.

> **Note**
>
> A team of researchers at Microsoft's Gray Systems Lab developed the Froid framework for inlining UDF constructs into parent queries. The Froid paper can be accessed at http://www.vldb.org/pvldb/vol11/p432-ramachandra.pdf.

An object property can be used to determine whether a scalar UDF is can be made inline (`inlineable`) for any given version of the SQL Database Engine, using the following sample query:

```sql
SELECT is_inlineable, inline_type
FROM sys.sql_modules
WHERE object_id = OBJECT_ID('ufn_CategorizePrice');
```

The full list of requirements for a scalar UDF to be inlined is available in the documentation page for the feature and has grown throughout several Cumulative Updates for SQL Server 2019.

By simply changing the `AdventureWorks` database compatibility level from 130 to 150, notice the resulting query execution plan where all the scalar UDF logic is now visible:

Figure 6.19 – Execution plan showing the scalar UDF was inlined

The **QueryTimeStats** for this inlined execution plan are considerably better than before, both in CPU time and elapsed time:

QueryTimeStats	
CpuTime	59
ElapsedTime	619

Figure 6.20 – QueryTimeStats for the plan using schema-bound scalar UDF

Now that we've learned some techniques to make our user-defined functions more efficient, let's move on to a similar discussion about stored procedures.

Avoiding unnecessary overhead with stored procedures

In stored procedures, use the SET NOCOUNT ON notation even when there's a requirement to return the current row count during execution, as in the following example:

```
CREATE OR ALTER PROCEDURE [dbo].[uspStocksPerWorkOrder] @WorkOrderID
[int]
AS
BEGIN
SET NOCOUNT ON;
     SELECT wo.StockedQty, wor.WorkOrderID
     FROM Production.WorkOrder AS wo
     LEFT JOIN Production.WorkOrderRouting AS wor
ON wo.WorkOrderID = wor.WorkOrderID
     WHERE wo.WorkOrderID = @WorkOrderID;
END;
```

When SET NOCOUNT is ON, the count indicating the number of rows affected by a T-SQL statement is not returned to the application layer, which provides a performance boost.

> **Note**
>
> The @@ROWCOUNT function will still be incremented even with SET NOCOUNT ON.

To put this to a test, we can use the ostress utility and simulate a client application executing the same stored procedure 1,000 times over 10 concurrent connections, as seen in the following command:

```
ostress.exe -S<my_server_name> -E -dAdventureWorks -Q"EXEC [dbo].
[uspStocksPerWorkOrder] 117" -n10 -r1000
```

> **Note**
>
> ostress is a free command line tool that is part of the **Replay Markup Language** (**RML**) Utilities for SQL Server. This tool can be used to simulate the effects of stressing a SQL instance by using ad hoc queries or pre-saved .sql script files.

Executing the preceding command three times yields the following elapsed time information:

OSTRESS exiting normally, elapsed time: 00:00:31.057

OSTRESS exiting normally, elapsed time: 00:00:31.484

OSTRESS exiting normally, elapsed time: 00:00:31.476

We can see a stable elapsed time between executions. Now if we recreate the stored procedure to remove the SET NOCOUNT ON and execute the same command three times, it yields the following elapsed time information:

OSTRESS exiting normally, elapsed time: 00:00:33.771

OSTRESS exiting normally, elapsed time: 00:00:33.824

OSTRESS exiting normally, elapsed time: 00:00:34.097

Again, we get consistent results but higher elapsed time throughout the test runs. For stored procedures that do not return large datasets such as the case here, or for stored procedures that contain T-SQL loops, setting NOCOUNT to ON can provide a significant performance boost: network traffic is reduced because the SQL Database Engine doesn't send the **DONE_IN_PROC** token stream for each statement in the code. This may not be noticeable in singleton executions, but when a stored procedure is executed multiple times, the scale effect is usually measurable.

Also, strive to validate input parameters early in the T-SQL code. Doing this allows early determination of whether data access operations can run, instead of encountering issues after much work has already been done, wasting resources. Using the previous example, adding an IF condition prevents data access if the incoming parameter is null for a column that doesn't accept null values by design:

```
CREATE OR ALTER PROCEDURE [dbo].[uspStocksPerWorkOrder] @WorkOrderID
[int]
AS
BEGIN
SET NOCOUNT ON;
     IF @WorkOrderID IS NOT NULL
     BEGIN
          SELECT wo.StockedQty, wor.WorkOrderID
          FROM Production.WorkOrder AS wo
          LEFT JOIN Production.WorkOrderRouting AS wor
ON wo.WorkOrderID = wor.WorkOrderID
          WHERE wo.WorkOrderID = @WorkOrderID;
     END;
END;
```

While these simple changes may seem small, they can add up to a lot across an application that relies heavily on stored procedures, especially on a busy production system. Another place where small changes can add up to big gains is with views. In the next section, we'll examine some best practices around complex views.

Pitfalls of complex views

Views are often used with the same intent as **User-Defined Functions (UDFs)** – to allow easy re-use of what could otherwise be a complex expression to inline in our T-SQL query. Often developers build a view that will serve multiple queries, and then just select from that view with different SELECT statements and different filters, be those joins or search predicates. However, what may look like a seemingly harmless T-SQL construct may be detrimental for query performance if the underlying view is complex.

Imagine that in the AdventureWorks sample database, a developer built an all-encompassing view that gets data on all company employees, as in the following example:

```
CREATE OR ALTER VIEW [HumanResources].[vEmployeeNew]
AS
SELECT e.[BusinessEntityID], p.[Title], p.[FirstName], p.[MiddleName],
      p.[LastName], p.[Suffix], e.[JobTitle], pp.[PhoneNumber],
      pnt.[Name] AS [PhoneNumberType], ea.[EmailAddress],
p.[EmailPromotion],
      a.[AddressLine1], a.[AddressLine2], a.[City], sp.[Name] AS
[StateProvinceName],
      a.[PostalCode], cr.[Name] AS [CountryRegionName]
FROM [HumanResources].[Employee] AS e
INNER JOIN [Person].[Person] AS p
ON p.[BusinessEntityID] = e.[BusinessEntityID]
INNER JOIN [Person].[BusinessEntityAddress] AS bea
ON bea.[BusinessEntityID] = e.[BusinessEntityID]
INNER JOIN [Person].[Address] AS a
ON a.[AddressID] = bea.[AddressID]
INNER JOIN [Person].[StateProvince] AS sp
ON sp.[StateProvinceID] = a.[StateProvinceID]
INNER JOIN [Person].[CountryRegion] AS cr
ON cr.[CountryRegionCode] = sp.[CountryRegionCode]
INNER JOIN [Person].[PersonPhone] AS pp
ON pp.BusinessEntityID = p.[BusinessEntityID]
INNER JOIN [Person].[PhoneNumberType] AS pnt
ON pp.[PhoneNumberTypeID] = pnt.[PhoneNumberTypeID]
INNER JOIN [Person].[EmailAddress] AS ea
ON p.[BusinessEntityID] = ea.[BusinessEntityID];
```

This view may have been built as an encapsulation for a recurrent query, making it just an easily referenceable artifact. But later, another developer needs to build a report with a simplified org chart, and the following query is executed using the preexisting view:

```
SELECT Title, FirstName, MiddleName, LastName, Suffix, JobTitle
FROM [HumanResources].[vEmployeeNew];
```

Notice the resulting query execution plan:

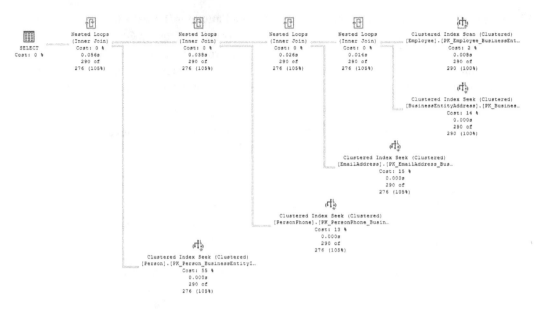

Figure 6.21 – Execution plan using the view previously created

And its **QueryTimeStats** property:

QueryTimeStats	
CpuTime	6
ElapsedTime	56
Reason For Early Termination Of Statement Optimization	Time Out

Figure 6.22 – QueryTimeStats for the plan using the view previously created

Also notice the information concerning how the Query Optimizer got to this plan (seen in the **Reason for Early Termination Of Statement Optimization** property in showplan): a timeout means that the best available plan found before the Query Optimizer timeout hit was used. The immediate conclusion is that the query is probably too complex and the optimization space too wide to run through it all before the internal timeout is reached.

The fact is the plan accesses five tables to retrieve data from each one, even though the columns in the SELECT clause are present in a small subset of the tables (just two, in this case). Each table in the query execution plan outputs 290 rows, therefore incurring I/O for each table.

What if we could simplify the query, having the report query only the required data? To do this, we replace the query referencing the view with a query that only accesses the required tables:

```
SELECT Title, FirstName, MiddleName, LastName, Suffix, JobTitle
FROM HumanResources.Employee AS e
INNER JOIN [Person].[Person] AS pp ON e.BusinessEntityID =
pp.BusinessEntityID;
```

Note the resulting query execution plan:

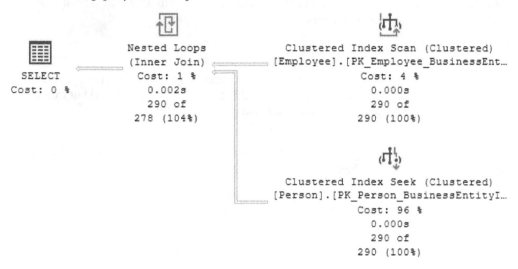

Figure 6.23 – Execution plan accessing only the required tables instead of the view

And its **QueryTimeStats** property:

QueryTimeStats	
CpuTime	2
ElapsedTime	3
Reason For Early Termination Of Statement Optimization	Good Enough Plan Found

Figure 6.24 – QueryTimeStats for the plan accessing only the required tables instead of the view

The result is a simpler and faster plan. Also notice the information seen in the **Reason for Early Termination Of Statement Optimization** showplan property: the optimization search space was smaller and so was covered inside the internal timeout period, resulting is the good-enough plan seen earlier.

This is an example of how our workload may be incurring higher costs because certain shortcuts were used at development time – in this case, using an all-encompassing view that doesn't fit all usage scenarios – which may even limit the Query Optimizer ability to search for a more optimal plan. Simplification is the key action in these cases – only query for what we want to query, and no more. The performance and scalability of our workload will speak for itself. This is similar to what we discussed in the *Composable logic* section of *Chapter 5, Writing Elegant T-SQL Queries* – writing generic code saves development time, but the potential trade-off is poor performance during execution.

Another less efficient but valid option is to create a unique clustered index on the view and ensure the SQL Database Engine accesses the view itself, rather than expanding it.

> **Note**
> Expanding the view is the action of opening the view definition and using the tables defined inside the view, rather than accessing the view itself. This is done for every view but can be optionally skipped for indexed views, also known as materialized views.

To create an indexed view, we must first recreate the view as schema-bound by adding the `WITH SCHEMABINDING` keyword to the view definition:

```
CREATE OR ALTER VIEW [HumanResources].[vEmployeeNew]
WITH SCHEMABINDING
AS
(…)
```

And then create the following index:

```
CREATE UNIQUE CLUSTERED INDEX IX_vEmployeeNew
ON [HumanResources].[vEmployeeNew] (
       [BusinessEntityID]

);
```

> **Note**
> A view without an index contains no data, it's simply the definition of a query stored as an object. Once an index is created on the view, however, the results of the view are physically stored as a database object, as if we had created a new table. This results in additional storage requirements and overhead when updating data in the base tables that are referenced by the view.

To ensure the view is used directly by the Query Optimizer, we can add the `NOEXPAND` table hint, as seen as in the following example:

```
SELECT Title, FirstName, MiddleName, LastName, Suffix, JobTitle
FROM [HumanResources].[vEmployeeNew] WITH (NOEXPAND);
```

Notice the resulting query execution plan and **QueryTimeStats**:

Figure 6.25 – Execution plan using the view using NOEXPAND

⊟ QueryTimeStats
    CpuTime   1
    ElapsedTime   27

Figure 6.26 – QueryTimeStats for the plan using the view using NOEXPAND

While this is not as optimal as querying only for the data we need for the report, creating an indexed view is a valid strategy for improving query performance, as we can see by comparing the preceding **QueryTimeStats** with the **QueryTimeStats** in the first query using the non-indexed view: CPU time dropped from 6 ms to 1 ms (~84 percent less), and execution time dropped from 56 ms to 27 ms (~52 percent less). The estimated cost for each plan is also clearly different as seen next, whereby using the indexed view in **Query 1** is significantly more efficient than **Query 2**:

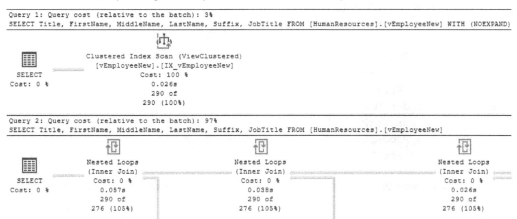

Figure 6.27 – Comparison of execution plans using the view with and without NOEXPAND

While in this case we used the NOEXPAND table hint, if a view is indexed then the Query Optimizer may choose to do indexed view matching automatically, a process whereby the view is used directly rather than expanding it to access the underlying tables. This process can also be forced by using the NOEXPAND table hint as we did in this example.

> **Note**
> Before SQL Server 2016 Service Pack 1, only Enterprise Edition could do *indexed view matching*: the NOEXPAND hint was required to use indexed views in Standard Edition. Azure SQL Database doesn't require the NOEXPAND hint to make use of **indexed view matching**.

The SQL Database Engine will automatically create statistics on an indexed view when the NOEXPAND table hint is used. If we see a plan that is using indexed views and notice a plan warning about missing statistics, then either use the hint or manually create the missing statistics.

Now that we understand how complex views can impact performance and how to make them more efficient, let's move on to another common but sometimes problematic pattern, correlated sub-queries.

Pitfalls of correlated sub-queries

It is not uncommon to use sub-queries to express certain predicates inline in queries, but developers must keep in mind that joins are frequently better than correlated sub-queries. The following query examples can be executed in the scope of the AdventureWorks sample database:

```
SELECT wo.StockedQty, wo.WorkOrderID, wor.ActualCost
FROM Production.WorkOrder AS wo
INNER JOIN Production.WorkOrderRouting AS wor ON wo.WorkOrderID = wor.
WorkOrderID
WHERE wor.WorkOrderID = 12345;
SELECT wo.StockedQty, wo.WorkOrderID,
        (SELECT wor.ActualCost
            FROM Production.WorkOrderRouting AS wor
            WHERE wor.WorkOrderID = 12345)
FROM Production.WorkOrder AS wo
WHERE wo.WorkOrderID IN
        (SELECT wor.WorkOrderID
            FROM Production.WorkOrderRouting AS wor
            WHERE wor.WorkOrderID = 12345);
```

These yield different query plans but the same resultsets, where the plan with the correlated sub-queries is more expensive:

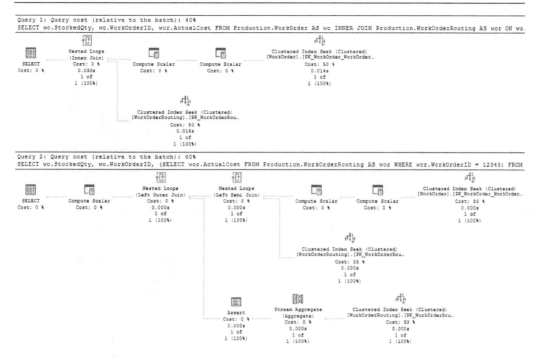

Figure 6.28 – Comparison of execution plans where one uses a sub-query

The estimated cost for each plan is clearly different, and use of the join emerges as the favorite as it is significantly more efficient than the correlated sub-query.

This is another pattern that is often encountered when using database code generation tools such as Entity Framework. With these tools it may not be a simple task to change the code that is generated, but in some cases, you may be able to introduce a stored procedure or view to influence the generated code. While it may take some extra time and understanding of the data model to express the logic as joins rather than sub-queries, the effort often pays off, especially for queries that are executed frequently. Another area where some extra effort can pay big dividends is using intermediate result sets to simplify complex business logic. Let's examine some ways we can make this technique more efficient.

Properly storing intermediate results

There are times when a query can become very complex, either because of a complicated database schema or because of complex business logic in the query, or both. In these cases, it may be easier to write the query in parts and store intermediate query results so that they can be used in a later query. This can make the query more readable, but it can also help the SQL Database Engine create a better query execution plan. There are different ways to store intermediate query results – this section will look at a few different options along with some of the considerations for when and where to use them.

Using table variables and temporary tables

Table variables and temporary tables serve the same basic principle: to store an intermediate resultset to be used by a subsequent query. Database developers use these to break down complex joined queries that typically are not very efficient.

> **Tip**
>
> We have mentioned before about how the way a query is written can severely compromise the SQL Database Engine's ability to optimize the query efficiently in the little time it has to do it.

This means that a complex T-SQL query can be broken down into simpler T-SQL statements that store intermediate results before being used to join with other tables. Imagine a developer needs to build a query in the `AdventureWorks` sample database that returns the sales quota data by year for each salesperson. This requires intermediate calculations that cannot be easily expressed with a joined query. Instead, a developer can use table variables to store intermediate results and then use a simple joined query, as seen in the following example:

```
DECLARE @Sales_TV TABLE (
     SalesPersonID int NOT NULL,
     TotalSales money,
     SalesYear smallint
);
-- Populate the first Table Variable
INSERT INTO @Sales_TV
SELECT SalesPersonID, SUM(TotalDue) AS TotalSales,
     YEAR(OrderDate) AS SalesYear
FROM Sales.SalesOrderHeader
WHERE SalesPersonID IS NOT NULL
GROUP BY SalesPersonID, YEAR(OrderDate);
-- Define the second Table Variable, which stores sales quota data by
year for each salesperson.
DECLARE @Sales_Quota_TV TABLE (
     BusinessEntityID int NOT NULL,
     SalesQuota money,
     SalesQuotaYear smallint
);
INSERT INTO @Sales_Quota_TV
SELECT BusinessEntityID, SUM(SalesQuota) AS SalesQuota,
     YEAR(QuotaDate) AS SalesQuotaYear
FROM Sales.SalesPersonQuotaHistory
GROUP BY BusinessEntityID, YEAR(QuotaDate)
-- Define the outer query by referencing columns from both Table
Variables.
```

```
SELECT CONCAT(FirstName, ' ', LastName) AS SalesPerson, SalesYear,
 FORMAT(TotalSales,'C','en-us') AS TotalSales, SalesQuotaYear,
 FORMAT (SalesQuota,'C','en-us') AS SalesQuota,
 FORMAT (TotalSales -SalesQuota, 'C','en-us') AS Amt_Above_or_Below_
Quota
FROM @Sales_TV AS Sales_TV
INNER JOIN @Sales_Quota_TV AS Sales_Quota_TV
    ON Sales_Quota_TV.BusinessEntityID = Sales_TV.SalesPersonID
    AND Sales_TV.SalesYear = Sales_Quota_TV.SalesQuotaYear
INNER JOIN Person.Person
    ON Person.BusinessEntityID = Sales_Quota_TV.BusinessEntityID
ORDER BY SalesPersonID, SalesYear;
```

Notice the resulting query execution plan with three queries:

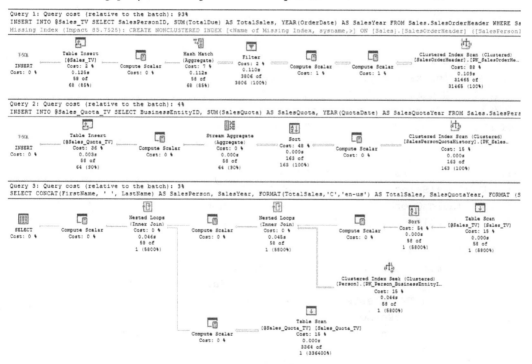

Figure 6.29 – Execution plan using table variables

Alternatively, temporary tables can be used, as seen in the following example:

```
DROP TABLE IF EXISTS #Sales_TT;
CREATE TABLE #Sales_TT (
     SalesPersonID int NOT NULL,
     TotalSales money,
```

```
        SalesYear smallint
) ;
-- Populate the first Temp Table
INSERT INTO #Sales_TT
SELECT SalesPersonID, SUM(TotalDue) AS TotalSales,
      YEAR(OrderDate) AS SalesYear
FROM Sales.SalesOrderHeader
WHERE SalesPersonID IS NOT NULL
GROUP BY SalesPersonID, YEAR(OrderDate);
-- Define the second Temp Table, which stores sales quota data by year
for each sales person.
DROP TABLE IF EXISTS #Sales_Quota_TT;
CREATE TABLE #Sales_Quota_TT (
      BusinessEntityID int NOT NULL,
      SalesQuota money,
      SalesQuotaYear smallint
) ;
INSERT INTO #Sales_Quota_TT
SELECT BusinessEntityID, SUM(SalesQuota) AS SalesQuota,
      YEAR(QuotaDate) AS SalesQuotaYear
FROM Sales.SalesPersonQuotaHistory
GROUP BY BusinessEntityID, YEAR(QuotaDate)
-- Define the outer query by referencing columns from both Temp
Tables.
SELECT CONCAT(FirstName, ' ', LastName) AS SalesPerson, SalesYear,
 FORMAT(TotalSales,'C','en-us') AS TotalSales, SalesQuotaYear,
 FORMAT (SalesQuota,'C','en-us') AS SalesQuota,
 FORMAT (TotalSales -SalesQuota, 'C','en-us') AS Amt_Above_or_Below_
Quota
FROM #Sales_TT AS Sales_TT
INNER JOIN #Sales_Quota_TT AS Sales_Quota_TT
      ON Sales_Quota_TT.BusinessEntityID = Sales_TT.SalesPersonID
      AND Sales_TT.SalesYear = Sales_Quota_TT.SalesQuotaYear
INNER JOIN Person.Person
      ON Person.BusinessEntityID = Sales_Quota_TT.BusinessEntityID
ORDER BY SalesPersonID, SalesYear;
```

Notice the resulting query execution plan with three queries. Comparing Query 1 and Query 2 from the table variable and temporary table examples, we see the plan is the same on both, except for the type of object where the data is inserted.

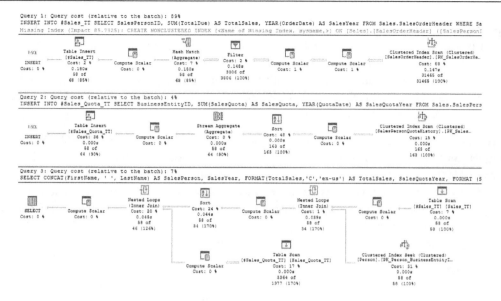

Figure 6.30 – Execution plan using temporary table

However, notice how the plans for Query 3 in both examples are different. Notice especially the differences in the information of how many actual rows versus estimated rows flowed through the operators in each plan. In the table variable case, we see the estimations are always 1, whereas in the temporary table case they are either completely accurate (i.e., the actual rows and estimated rows match) or are much closer to each other (3,364 actual of 1,977 estimated rows).

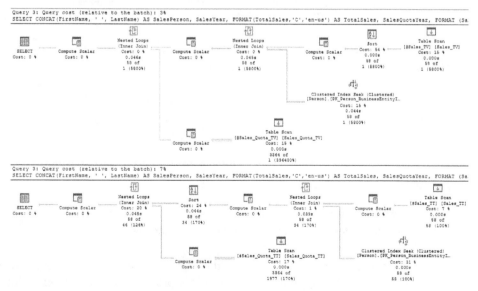

Figure 6.31 – Comparison of Query 3 in two plans, using a table variable or a temporary table

This is because the SQL Database Engine supports automatic statistics creation on temporary tables, as well as manual statistics creation and update, which the Query Optimizer can use. Up to and including SQL Server 2017, table variables are runtime objects only and are compiled together with all other statements, before any of the statements that populate the table variables even execute. For this reason, the Query Optimizer uses a default estimation of one row for table variables since the row count is not available at compile time.

However, in SQL Server 2019 and under database compatibility level 150, the **Table Variable Deferred Compilation** feature is available. With this feature, the compilation of a statement that references a table variable that doesn't exist is deferred until the first execution of the statement, just as is done for temporary tables. In effect, this means that table variables are materialized on their first use, and the Query Optimizer uses the row count in the first materialization of the table variable to create a query plan. See the following example of Query 3 running in SQL Server 2017, and then in SQL Server 2019.

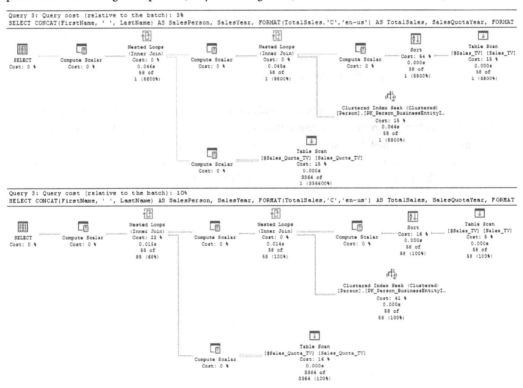

Figure 6.32 – Comparison of Query 3 in two plans using either the table
variable deferred compilation feature versus a temporary table

While in this case the plan doesn't materially change, the estimated and actual rows match when using SQL Server 2019's deferred compilation of Table Variables, providing the Query Optimizer the opportunity to create a query plan with better estimate memory requirements, which translates into improved resource usage.

Using Common Table Expressions (CTEs)

Common Table Expressions (CTEs) are runtime constructs to derive an inline intermediate result set from a query. This means that a complex T-SQL query can be broken down into simpler T-SQL statements that store intermediate results before joining with other tables or other CTEs that had been previously defined in the T-SQL statement. For example, take the two following queries that can be executed in the AdventureWorks sample database:

```
WITH Sales_CTE (SalesPersonID, SalesOrderID, SalesYear)
AS
(
  SELECT SalesPersonID, SalesOrderID, YEAR(OrderDate) AS SalesYear
  FROM Sales.SalesOrderHeader
  WHERE SalesPersonID IS NOT NULL
)
SELECT SalesPersonID, COUNT(SalesOrderID) AS TotalSales, SalesYear
FROM Sales_CTE
GROUP BY SalesYear, SalesPersonID
ORDER BY SalesPersonID, SalesYear;
GO
SELECT SalesPersonID, COUNT(SalesOrderID) AS TotalSales,
YEAR(OrderDate) AS SalesYear
FROM Sales.SalesOrderHeader
WHERE SalesPersonID IS NOT NULL
GROUP BY YEAR(OrderDate), SalesPersonID
ORDER BY SalesPersonID, SalesYear;
GO
```

The queries generate the following execution plans:

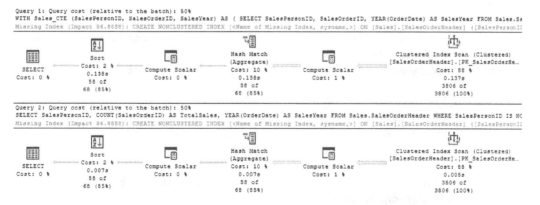

Figure 6.33 – Execution plans for queries listing the total sales per year and by salesperson

These yield matching query plans because they express the same set of conditions and were optimized the same way. However, CTEs can be very useful to express conditions that become impossible to express with a joined query, such as recursive queries or queries that reference nested result sets.

The following example is a different way of building a query that can be executed in the `AdventureWorks` sample database and builds a CTE that is then referenced by another CTE before being joined with the `Person.Person` table:

```
WITH Sales_CTE (SalesPersonID, TotalSales, SalesYear)
AS
-- Define the first CTE query.
(
 SELECT SalesPersonID, SUM(TotalDue) AS TotalSales,
         YEAR(OrderDate) AS SalesYear
 FROM Sales.SalesOrderHeader
 WHERE SalesPersonID IS NOT NULL
 GROUP BY SalesPersonID, YEAR(OrderDate)
)

,
-- Define the second CTE query, which returns sales quota data by year
for each sales person.
Sales_Quota_CTE (BusinessEntityID, SalesQuota, SalesQuotaYear)
AS
(
     SELECT BusinessEntityID, SUM(SalesQuota) AS SalesQuota,
          YEAR(QuotaDate) AS SalesQuotaYear
     FROM Sales.SalesPersonQuotaHistory
     GROUP BY BusinessEntityID, YEAR(QuotaDate)
)
-- Define the outer query by referencing columns from both CTEs and a
Table.
SELECT CONCAT(FirstName, ' ', LastName) AS SalesPerson, SalesYear,
 FORMAT(TotalSales,'C','en-us') AS TotalSales, SalesQuotaYear,
 FORMAT (SalesQuota,'C','en-us') AS SalesQuota,
 FORMAT (TotalSales -SalesQuota, 'C','en-us') AS Amt_Above_or_Below_
Quota
FROM Sales_CTE
INNER JOIN Sales_Quota_CTE
ON Sales_Quota_CTE.BusinessEntityID = Sales_CTE.SalesPersonID
     AND Sales_CTE.SalesYear = Sales_Quota_CTE.SalesQuotaYear
INNER JOIN Person.Person
ON Person.BusinessEntityID = Sales_Quota_CTE.BusinessEntityID
ORDER BY SalesPersonID, SalesYear;
```

Notice the resulting query execution plan with one single query, unlike the table variable and temporary table variants:

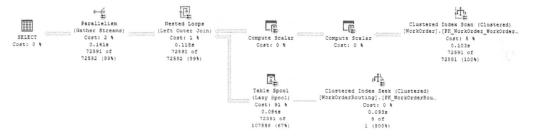

Figure 6.34 – Execution plan for a single query listing the total sales per year and by salesperson

CTEs can be a very efficient alternative for driving Query Optimizer choices that improve performance. In the chapter *Exploring Query Execution Plans* in the *Query plan operators of interest* section, we had the following example of a query executed in the AdventureWorks sample database:

```
SELECT WO.WorkOrderID, WO.ProductID, WO.OrderQty, WO.StockedQty,
WO.ScrappedQty, WO.StartDate, WO.EndDate, WO.DueDate,
WO.ScrapReasonID, WO.ModifiedDate, WOR.WorkOrderID,
    WOR.ProductID, WOR.LocationID
FROM Production.WorkOrder AS WO
LEFT JOIN Production.WorkOrderRouting AS WOR
ON WO.WorkOrderID = WOR.WorkOrderID AND WOR.WorkOrderID = 12345;
```

The query generates the following execution plan:

Figure 6.35 – Execution plan for the query listing orders

Where we can see its **QueryTimeStats** property:

QueryTimeStats	
CpuTime	247
ElapsedTime	713

Figure 6.36 – QueryTimeStats for the plan

Notice the **Table Spool** operator, which we know at this point is something developers must attempt to avoid. We can't always avoid these, for example a spool that enforces Halloween protection is unlikely to be removable. But in this case, refactoring the query to move the part that required the spool to a CTE and including the join predicate seeking on the scalar value 12345 allows us to eliminate the spool:

```
;WITH cte AS (
SELECT WorkOrderID, ProductID, LocationID
FROM Production.WorkOrderRouting WHERE WorkOrderID = 12345
)
SELECT WO.WorkOrderID, WO.ProductID, WO.OrderQty, WO.StockedQty,
WO.ScrappedQty, WO.StartDate, WO.EndDate, WO.DueDate,
WO.ScrapReasonID, WO.ModifiedDate, WOR.WorkOrderID,
      WOR.ProductID, WOR.LocationID
FROM Production.WorkOrder AS WO LEFT JOIN cte AS WOR
ON WO.WorkOrderID = WOR.WorkOrderID
GO
```

Verify the new execution plan:

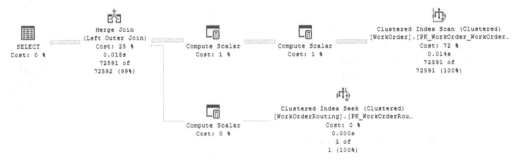

Figure 6.37 – Execution plan for the query listing orders now using a CTE

Its **QueryTimeStats** property is as follows:

Figure 6.38 – QueryTimeStats for the plan using a CTE

Because of the CTE use, the Query Optimizer found that a **Merge Join** is a good-enough join algorithm, and better than a **Nested Loops**, which is why the **Spool** is eliminated in this case. And the plan becomes cheap enough to avoid exceeding the cost threshold for parallelism configuration, which means it is executed in serial.

Let's compare the preceding **QueryTimeStats** with the **QueryTimeStats** in the first query using the non-indexed view: the CPU time dropped from 247 ms to 46 ms (~81 percent less), and execution time dropped from 713 ms to 46 ms (~93 percent less). For such a simple query, this means we not only improved the singleton execution and CPU time, but also removed any use of `tempdb`. This in turn improved the scalability of the workload by using fewer resources and reducing the overall concurrency in the workload.

Summary

This chapter covered some performance pitfalls that are not always obvious when writing T-SQL queries. Using the knowledge and tools covered in earlier chapters together with the anti-patterns discussed in this chapter, we should now be able to dig deeper into our query execution plans and uncover issues that have the potential to impact performance and scalability before they reach production. Up to now, we have been focusing on how to write efficient, performant T-SQL code, but what if the code is already written and we are faced with identifying these issues in an existing system?

In the next and final part of the book, we will investigate some of the tools available to us that help identify and troubleshoot issues with our T-SQL query performance.

Part 3:
Assembling Our Query
Troubleshooting Toolbox

This part introduces all the diagnostics artifacts and tools that ship with the SQL Database Engine and SQL Server Management Studio for query performance troubleshooting.

This part has the following chapters:

- *Chapter 7, Building Diagnostic Queries Using DMVs and DMFs*
- *Chapter 8, Building XEvent Profiler Traces*
- *Chapter 9, Comparative Analysis of Query Plans*
- *Chapter 10, Tracking Performance History with Query Store*
- *Chapter 11, Troubleshooting Live Queries*
- *Chapter 12, Managing Optimizer Changes*

7

Building Diagnostic Queries Using DMVs and DMFs

Dynamic management views (**DMVs**) and **dynamic management functions** (**DMFs**) expose relevant real-time information that can unlock the secrets of T-SQL execution and SQL Database Engine health, even on a live production server. There are hundreds of DMVs and DMFs (collectively referred to as DMVs) available in the SQL Database Engine, and while they are mostly documented, it may not be obvious how they can be used by database developers and administrators to troubleshoot performance both in production systems and during the development process.

In this chapter, we will start by enumerating some of the DMVs that are most relevant for both T-SQL developers and database administrators alike to troubleshoot T-SQL query performance. Building on this information, we will provide real-world examples to explore how to use DMVs to troubleshoot different poor-performance scenarios, as well as give us the information needed to begin building our own DMV scripts. This chapter covers the following topics:

- Introducing DMVs
- Exploring query execution DMVs
- Exploring query plan cache DMVs
- Troubleshooting common scenarios with DMV queries

Technical requirements

The examples used in this chapter are designed for use on SQL Server 2022 and Azure SQL Database, but they should work on any version of SQL Server, 2012 or later. The Developer edition of SQL Server is free for development environments and can be used to run all the code samples. There is also a free tier of Azure SQL Database you can use for testing at `https://aka.ms/freedb`.

You will need the sample databases `AdventureWorks2016_EXT` (referred to as `AdventureWorks`) and `AdventureWorksDW2016_EXT` (referred to as `AdventureWorksDW`), which can be found on GitHub at `https://github.com/Microsoft/sql-server-samples/releases/tag/adventureworks`. Code samples for this chapter can also be found on GitHub at `https://github.com/PacktPublishing/Learn-T-SQL-Querying-Second-Edition/tree/main/ch6`.

Introducing DMVs

SQL Server 2005 introduced a new concept in the Database Engine – the **SQL Operating System (SQLOS)**. The SQLOS is an abstraction layer that encapsulates all the low-level resource management and monitoring tasks that the SQL Database Engine must perform while providing an **application programming interface** (**API**) for other components of the Database Engine to leverage these services. Not only does this centralization of resource management code make the SQL Database Engine more efficient, but it also provides a central location for monitoring various aspects of Database Engine performance. DMVs take advantage of this centralized architecture by providing the user with a mechanism to view this information in a way that is lightweight and accurate.

DMVs allow the user to query memory structures in SQLOS. Some DMVs show information that is only relevant for the specific point in time at which they are queried, while other DMVs show cumulative information that goes back to the last time the SQL Database Engine service was started. Because they are querying in-memory structures, most DMVs do not retain any information between restarts of the SQL Database Engine service.

Hundreds of DMVs can be used to monitor everything from memory consumption to query performance, as well as features of the SQL Database Engine such as replication, Resource Governor, and availability groups. In this chapter, we will be focusing on DMVs that are relevant for troubleshooting T-SQL query performance, as well as some other performance issues that are relevant when monitoring query execution.

Exploring query execution DMVs

Several different DMVs may be relevant when analyzing the activity that is currently happening in a SQL Database Engine. In this section, we will cover a few of the most common DMVs, along with some examples of the information that they can provide.

sys.dm_exec_sessions

The `sys.dm_exec_sessions` DMV lists information about all the sessions that are currently active on the server. This includes both user sessions and system sessions, and it also includes idle sessions that are connected but are not currently executing any queries.

> **Tip**
>
> Idle sessions can be identified by looking for rows that have a status of `sleeping`. When using connection pooling especially, it is common to have several user sessions in a `sleeping` status.

This DMV can be used to view information that is relevant to the session, such as `login_name`, `host_name`, `program_name`, and other properties that would be set at the session level. This can be helpful when trying to identify which applications might be connected to the server, and which databases those applications are connected to. It shows current information only, so once a session is no longer active, it will not be visible in the view.

Here is a sample query that can be executed against `sys.dm_exec_sessions`:

```
SELECT session_id, login_time, host_name, program_name, login_name,
status, last_request_start_time, db_name(database_id) AS [db_name]
FROM sys.dm_exec_sessions
WHERE session_id = 93;
```

The following screenshot shows an example of the results when running this query from **SQL Server Management Studio (SSMS)**:

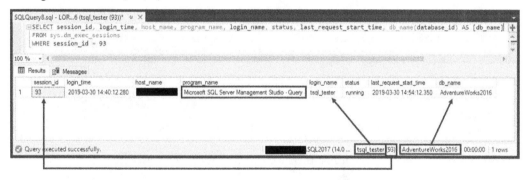

Figure 7.1 – Results of a query on sys.dm_exec_sessions

There are a few interesting things to note here. The first is `session_id`. This is important because it will help identify this session in other DMVs.

> **Tip**
>
> We can use the `is_user_process` column of `sys.dm_exec_sessions` to determine whether a session is generated by the system (`is_user_process = 0`) or by a user (`is_user_process = 1`), but most system sessions have a session ID less than `50`. This is a shortcut that can help us distinguish between user and system sessions in other views that contain `session_id`. In newer versions of the SQL Database Engine, there may be system sessions with an ID greater than `50`, but they will typically have a status of `background`.

When we run a query in SSMS, we might notice that the status bar at the bottom contains information such as our login name, the server we are connected to, and the database name. The number in parentheses next to our login name is our `session_id`. We can see this same information in `sys.dm_exec_sessions`, along with the `program_name` **Microsoft SQL Server Management Studio – Query**, indicating the session is coming from a query window in SSMS. If we are investigating a long-running query in a production SQL Database Engine, this information can help us identify where that query is coming from and who is executing it.

sys.dm_exec_requests

When we execute a T-SQL statement or batch on the server, it is called a `request`. This DMV lists all the requests that are currently active on the server. Once a batch completes and the results have been consumed by the client who made the request, it will no longer appear in this view, even if the session that generated it is still active. We can join this view to `sys.dm_exec_sessions` through the `session_id` column to obtain information about the session such as `program_name` and `login_time`, as well as information about the query execution such as `cpu_time`, `total_elapsed_time`, and `logical_reads`. This DMV displays information that is current for the moment in time at which it was queried, so the results returned will likely be different each time it is run.

For example, the following query will give us information about queries that are currently executing:

```
SELECT r.session_id, r.start_time, s.program_name, r.status,
r.command, r.sql_handle, r.statement_start_offset, r.statement_end_
offset, r.database_id
FROM sys.dm_exec_requests r
INNER JOIN sys.dm_exec_sessions s ON s.session_id = r.session_id
WHERE r.session_id > 50
    AND r.status IN ('running', 'runnable', 'suspended');
```

As we can see in the following screenshot, there are two queries currently executing from SSMS:

	session_id	start_time	program_name	status	command
1	93	2019-03-30 16:32:11.080	Microsoft SQL Server Management Studio - Query	running	SELECT
2	101	2019-03-30 16:32:07.780	Microsoft SQL Server Management Studio - Query	suspended	SELECT

sql_handle	statement_start_offset	statement_end_offset	database_id
0x020000002FD31338CFAA1C9D87AF90E16372F6A26330882...	0	652	30
0x0200000012B271257D955C46339A0A23FFA5C49BE0DE31...	0	3460	26

Figure 7.2 – Results of a query on sys.dm_exec_requests and sys.dm_exec_sessions

> **Note**
>
> Refer to *Chapter 1, Understanding Query Processing*, for a discussion of the various states that a query will cycle through during execution. Filtering out sessions that have a status other than running, runnable, or suspended will allow us to focus on user sessions only.

We can gain a lot of information from this view about the performance of a request as well, such as CPU consumption, elapsed time in milliseconds, and I/O. The following query shows some of the relevant performance-related columns:

```
SELECT session_id, status, cpu_time, total_elapsed_time, logical_
reads, reads, writes
FROM sys.dm_exec_requests
WHERE session_id > 50
    AND status IN ('running', 'runnable', 'suspended');
```

The following screenshot shows the results of this query:

	session_id	status	cpu_time	total_elapsed_time	logical_reads	reads	writes
1	62	running	4306	4306	233878	0	241
2	63	running	2487	2507	162912	9	245
3	64	runnable	6059	6085	291462	9	241
4	65	running	2	2	228	0	0

Figure 7.3 – Results of a query on sys.dm_exec_requests

sys.dm_exec_sql_text

The sys.dm_exec_sql_text DMF is a helper function that can be used in conjunction with any DMV that contains the sql_handle column to retrieve the text of a query. We can select from this system table-valued function by passing a valid sql_handle as a parameter, but it is most commonly used via the CROSS APPLY operation in combination with queries against either sys. dm_exec_requests or sys.dm_exec_query_stats.

Building on our example from the previous section, we can use the CROSS APPLY operator to retrieve the text of the queries that are running, as in the following query:

```
SELECT r.session_id, r.start_time, s.program_name, r.status, r.st.text
AS statement_text, r.statement_start_offset, r.statement_end_offset,
r.database_id
FROM sys.dm_exec_requests r
INNER JOIN sys.dm_exec_sessions s ON s.session_id = r.session_id
CROSS APPLY sys.dm_exec_sql_text(r.sql_handle) st
WHERE r.session_id > 50
    AND r.status IN ('running', 'runnable', 'suspended');
```

This query yields the results illustrated in the following screenshot:

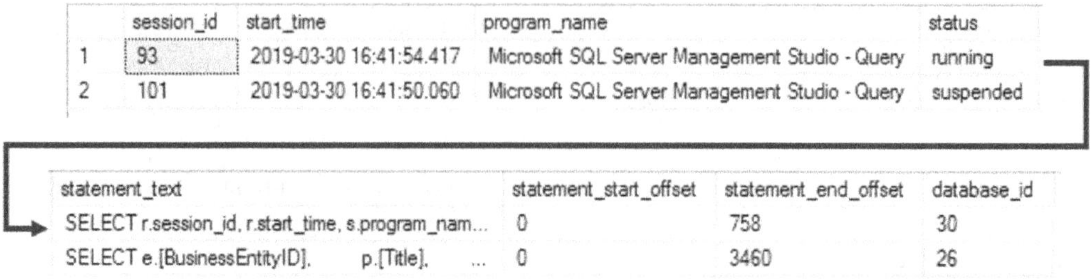

	session_id	start_time	program_name	status
1	93	2019-03-30 16:41:54.417	Microsoft SQL Server Management Studio - Query	running
2	101	2019-03-30 16:41:50.060	Microsoft SQL Server Management Studio - Query	suspended

statement_text	statement_start_offset	statement_end_offset	database_id
SELECT r.session_id, r.start_time, s.program_nam...	0	758	30
SELECT e.[BusinessEntityID]. p.[Title]. ...	0	3460	26

Figure 7.4 – Results of a query using sys.dm_exec_sql_text

Alternatively, we can copy one of the values for `sql_handle` that we obtained from the first sample query in the `sys.dm_exec_requests` section and execute this DMF as a standalone query:

```
SELECT *
FROM sys.dm_exec_sql_
text(0x020000002EED8B2B6539C6D9CB85FAAA57145FECF54E1DA
70000000000000000000000000000000000000000);
```

This query yields the following results:

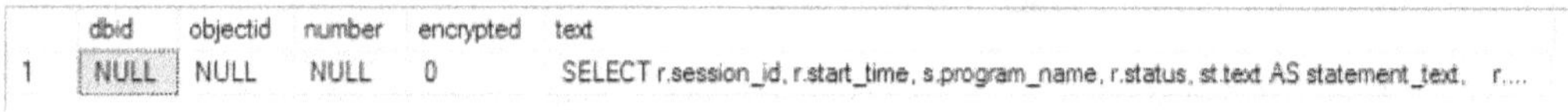

	dbid	objectid	number	encrypted	text
1	NULL	NULL	NULL	0	SELECT r.session_id, r.start_time, s.program_name, r.status, st.text AS statement_text, r....

Figure 7.5 – Results of a query on sys.dm_exec_sql_text for a specific handle

As we can see, the `text` column contains the text of the first sample query we executed in the `sys.dm_exec_requests` section.

sys.dm_os_waiting_tasks

Every request that is submitted to the SQL Database Engine is broken down into one or more tasks, depending on whether parallelism is involved. As we mentioned previously in the *Query execution essentials* section of *Chapter 1, Understanding Query Processing*, each task that is involved in processing the query is assigned to a worker thread, and these threads are used to complete the work of the query on the CPUs. Throughout the execution of a query, the various threads will cycle through the statuses `running`, `runnable`, and `suspended` as they process the different operations required to complete the query. When a task needs to wait for a resource, it goes into the `suspended` state. This is relevant information when troubleshooting query performance because it indicates contention for a resource of some kind. The `sys.dm_os_waiting_tasks` DMV lists all the tasks that are active within the server, but are in the suspended state, meaning they are waiting for a resource. This view contains information such as `wait_type`, which is helpful when analyzing what is contributing to a query's execution time. This information is also available at the request level via `sys.dm_exec_requests` as we discussed earlier in this chapter, but when a query is running in parallel, the information listed at the request level may not be giving us a full picture of what is going on at the individual thread level.

Let's change the columns we select from `sys.dm_exec_requests` to show more information about the current status of the queries that are executing:

```
SELECT r.session_id, r.start_time, r.status, r.sql_handle,
       r.wait_type, r.wait_time, r.wait_resource
FROM sys.dm_exec_requests r
WHERE r.session_id > 50
    AND r.status IN ('running', 'runnable', 'suspended')
```

The following screenshot illustrates the results of this query:

	session_id	start_time	status	sql_handle	wait_type	wait_time	wait_resource
1	93	2019-03-30 16:51:43.440	running	0x020000007AF71800029A4291F7CA5C915B33445EDB18C13...	NULL	0	
2	101	2019-03-30 16:51:25.067	suspended	0x0200000012B271257D955C46339A0A23FFA5C49BE0DE31...	CXPACKET	18025	

Figure 7.6 – Results of query getting requests from user sessions and their current request state

Note that `session_id 101` is currently in the `suspended` state, which means it is waiting for a resource. The `wait_type` column contains the value `CXPACKET`. This wait type indicates that the query is running in parallel, but we're only getting information from one of the threads in `sys.dm_exec_requests`, the coordinator thread. If we want to know what all the suspended threads that are involved in this query execution are doing, we need to join the `sys.dm_os_waiting_tasks` DMV to get the task-level detail:

```
SELECT r.session_id, t.exec_context_id, t.blocking_exec_context_id,
r.start_time, r.status, r.sql_handle, t.wait_type, t.wait_duration_ms
FROM sys.dm_exec_requests r
LEFT JOIN sys.dm_os_waiting_tasks t ON r.session_id = t.session_id
WHERE r.session_id > 50
    AND r.status IN ('running', 'runnable', 'suspended')
ORDER BY t.exec_context_id
```

Note that a left join is used in this query because it is possible to have rows in `sys.dm_exec_requests` that have no waiting tasks, but we still want them to appear in our results. This yields the following results:

	session_id	exec_context_id	blocking_exec_context_id	start_time	status
1	93	NULL	NULL	2019-03-30 17:05:31.207	running
2	101	0	18	2019-03-30 17:05:26.297	suspended
3	101	1	12	2019-03-30 17:05:26.297	suspended
4	101	2	13	2019-03-30 17:05:26.297	suspended
5	101	3	11	2019-03-30 17:05:26.297	suspended
6	101	4	15	2019-03-30 17:05:26.297	suspended
7	101	5	9	2019-03-30 17:05:26.297	suspended
8	101	6	13	2019-03-30 17:05:26.297	suspended
9	101	7	13	2019-03-30 17:05:26.297	suspended
10	101	8	9	2019-03-30 17:05:26.297	suspended

sql_handle	wait_type	wait_duration_ms
0x02000000E0B2B83399C76C847B5AE78710EE50522B9CB9B...	NULL	NULL
0x0200000012B271257D955C46339A0A23FFA5C49BE0DE31...	CXPACKET	4612
0x0200000012B271257D955C46339A0A23FFA5C49BE0DE31...	CXCONSUMER	481
0x0200000012B271257D955C46339A0A23FFA5C49BE0DE31...	CXCONSUMER	526
0x0200000012B271257D955C46339A0A23FFA5C49BE0DE31...	CXCONSUMER	118
0x0200000012B271257D955C46339A0A23FFA5C49BE0DE31...	CXCONSUMER	4255
0x0200000012B271257D955C46339A0A23FFA5C49BE0DE31...	CXCONSUMER	37
0x0200000012B271257D955C46339A0A23FFA5C49BE0DE31...	CXCONSUMER	335
0x0200000012B271257D955C46339A0A23FFA5C49BE0DE31...	CXCONSUMER	300
0x0200000012B271257D955C46339A0A23FFA5C49BE0DE31...	CXCONSUMER	148

Figure 7.7 – Results of a query getting requests from user sessions including thread detail

We can see that session 93 was in the running state, so the fields from sys.dm_os_waiting_tasks are NULL for this row. For session 101, the parallel query, there are several rows returned with different values for exec_context_id and blocking_exec_context_id. These show the various tasks that make up the request, and which tasks are blocking them, along with wait_type and wait_duration_ms. Note that while sys.dm_exec_requests showed only CXPACKET for the wait type, there are in fact several tasks waiting on CXCONSUMER as well. The task with exec_context_id = 0 is the coordinator thread; the rest of the tasks are the ones doing actual work.

> **Tip**
> A detailed discussion about waits is beyond the scope of this book, but if we would like more information about wait types, search the SQL Database Engine documentation for the sys.dm_os_wait_stats DMV. This DMV shows cumulative wait information since the server was last started. The documentation for this DMV contains a reference for the various wait types and what they mean.

Exploring query plan cache DMVs

Another set of DMVs that are helpful when troubleshooting T-SQL query performance is the query plan cache-related DMVs. While the execution DMVs we discussed in the previous section contain point-in-time information that changes frequently, these DMVs contain information about queries that are currently in the plan cache, which can contain information back to when the server was last restarted, depending on how long the query plans remain in the cache.

> **Note**
> The amount of time a plan remains in the cache depends on several factors such as memory pressure, recompilation, and schema changes. Provided that the server has been online for some time and no cache-flushing events have occurred, such as changing **max degree of parallelism**, or manually clearing the plan cache by running ALTER DATABASE SCOPED CONFIGURATION CLEAR PROCEDURE_CACHE, these plan cache DMVs should give you a good idea of the overall query performance on the server.

Before describing the DMVs in more detail, it's important to understand how query execution plans are stored. Query execution plans are stored as a batch, which means that all the statements that were submitted to the server as a single request are stored as a single plan object. An example of a batch might be a single stored procedure or a group of T-SQL queries submitted in a single request.

> **Tip**
> If running a query from SSMS, the GO command serves as a batch separator. All the T-SQL statements between GO commands make up a single batch. Note that GO is not a T-SQL statement itself; it simply directs SSMS to submit the preceding statements to the Database Engine as a batch.

A plan object will have a plan_handle, which is a hexadecimal value that uniquely identifies the object. The text of the batch will also have a handle called sql_handle, which can be used to identify the T-SQL query itself and retrieve the batch text. Within that batch, there will be one or more statements. Each statement is identified by a statement_start_offset and statement_end_offset which are byte offsets from the beginning of the batch text that point to the beginning and end of the statement within the batch. We can use these offsets to extract the individual queries from a batch, typically by using a SUBSTRING function. Keep these concepts in mind as we explore the various plan cache DMVs.

sys.dm_exec_query_stats

The sys.dm_exec_query_stats DMV displays cumulative query execution statistics for all the queries that are currently in the cache. As we observed in the previous section, the sys.dm_exec_requests DMV shows query performance while the query is executing. Once the query is complete, sys.dm_exec_query_stats is incremented with this new execution information. While query execution plans are stored as a batch, this DMV lists one row per statement, so there may be multiple rows with the same plan_handle and sql_handle. These rows will have a different statement_start_offset and statement_end_offset to distinguish between the statements in the same batch.

Many different query performance metrics can be gathered with this DMV. This sample query highlights a few of the more common ones:

```
SELECT st.text, qs.plan_handle, qs.last_execution_time, qs.execution_
count, qs.total_worker_time AS total_cpu_time,
qs.total_worker_time/qs.execution_count AS average_cpu_time,
qs.total_logical_reads, qs.total_logical_reads/qs.execution_count AS
average_logical_reads, qs.total_elapsed_time, (qs.total_elapsed_time/
qs.execution_count)/1000000 AS average_elapsed_time_sec
FROM sys.dm_exec_query_stats qs
CROSS APPLY sys.dm_exec_sql_text(qs.sql_handle) st
WHERE qs.sql_handle =
0x0200000022D4D930BD648A1C5BA9320D2448C8F7CFCEF3D
60000000000000000000000000000000000000000;
```

In this case, we've used the instance of sql_handle that we retrieved earlier from the sample query against sys.dm_exec_requests. This query yields the following results:

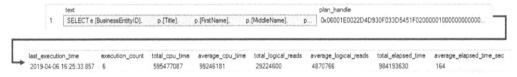

Figure 7.8 – Results of query getting query performance metrics for a specific sql_handle

Based on the execution_count value in the results, we can see that this query plan has been executed six times since it entered the cache. The columns that start with total_ are cumulative for all six executions, so we can calculate the average by dividing by execution_count. Also, note that all times are in microseconds, so in order to get the average execution time in seconds, we calculated the average first by dividing total_elapsed_time by execution_count, then we divided by 1,000,000 to convert microseconds to seconds. In addition to totals, each metric also has columns for minimum and maximum values across all executions, as well as the value for the last execution.

> **Tip**
>
> In the *Troubleshooting common scenarios with DMV queries* section, we will cover some additional columns that are specific to certain performance scenarios, but a comprehensive list of the columns returned by this DMV can be found by searching for the sys.dm_exec_query_stats documentation page.

sys.dm_exec_procedure_stats

The sys.dm_exec_procedure_stats DMV is like sys.dm_exec_query_stats in that it contains cumulative execution statistics for query plans in the cache, but at the stored procedure level rather than the query level. Stored procedures may contain T-SQL code constructs other than queries such as conditional logic, variable assignments, and function calls. These constructs consume resources, but they aren't accounted for in sys.dm_exec_query_stats because they aren't queries. This DMV can be used to determine the total resource consumption of the procedure as a whole, including code that is not accounted for in sys.dm_exec_query_stats.

The following example shows a stored procedure that contains some conditional logic as well as a WAITFOR command that causes the execution to wait for the specified amount of time before proceeding to the next statement in the procedure:

```
CREATE OR ALTER PROCEDURE uspGetEmployeeByDepartment @Department
nvarchar(50)
AS
SELECT *
FROM HumanResources.vEmployeeDepartment
WHERE Department = @Department
IF @Department = N'Engineering'
    WAITFOR DELAY '00:00:10'
GO
```

We can execute this stored procedure a few times in the AdventureWorks sample database with a few different values for @Department, and then use the following query to see the execution statistics:

```
SELECT object_name(object_id, database_id) AS proc_name, plan_handle,
execution_count, min_elapsed_time, max_elapsed_time
FROM sys.dm_exec_procedure_stats
WHERE object_id = object_id('uspgetEmployeeByDepartment')
```

This query returns the following results:

	proc_name	plan_handle	execution_count	min_elapsed_time	max_elapsed_time
1	uspGetEmployeeByDepartment	0x05001E008116D84AA0BC768B1F02000001000000000000...	22	2119	10008883

Figure 7.9 – Results of a query getting query performance metrics for a specific stored procedure

Notice the difference between the minimum and maximum elapsed time. This is because the WAITFOR command only executes when @Department = N'Engineering' so these executions take over 10 seconds, whereas other parameter values take much less time, only about the time it takes to execute the query. We can confirm this by using the value from the plan_handle column to look up the statements in sys.dm_exec_query_stats:

```
SELECT st.text, qs.statement_start_offset, qs.statement_end_offset,
```

```
qs.execution_count, qs.min_elapsed_time, qs.max_elapsed_time
FROM sys.dm_exec_query_stats qs
CROSS APPLY sys.dm_exec_sql_text(qs.sql_handle) st
WHERE plan_handle = 0x05001E008116D84AA0BC768B1F0
20000010000000000000000000000000000000000000000000000000000000000;
```

This query returns the following results:

	text	statement_start_offset	statement_end_offset	execution_count	min_elapsed_time	max_elapsed_time
1	CREATE PROCEDURE uspGetEmployeeByDepartment @Dep...	152	316	22	2061	211117

Figure 7.10 – Results of a query getting performance metrics for statements in a specific stored procedure

Notice that while the minimum elapsed time for the query alone is close to the minimum elapsed time of the entire procedure, the maximum elapsed time is an order of magnitude smaller. This is because the WAITFOR command is not part of the query, and thus its execution time is not included here.

There are two other DMVs that are like sys.dm_exec_procedure_stats called sys.dm_exec_trigger_stats and sys.dm_exec_function_stats. These DMVs can be used to view execution statistics for triggers and functions respectively, in the same way sys.dm_exec_procedure_stats is used for stored procedures.

sys.dm_exec_query_plan

The sys.dm_exec_query_plan DMF is another helper function like sys.dm_exec_sql_text that retrieves the estimated execution plan based on a plan_handle. We can call sys.dm_exec_query_plan on its own with a valid plan_handle, or we can leverage CROSS APPLY with views such as sys.dm_exec_query_stats that contain a plan_handle column.

The value that is returned in the query_plan column is in XML format but querying this view in SSMS will show the XML as a link. When clicked, the link will open as a graphical plan in a new tab.

We can use the instance of plan_handle we found earlier in the sys.dm_exec_procedure_stats section to retrieve the estimated plan for the uspGetEmployeeByDepartment stored procedure, as in the following example:

```
SELECT query_plan
FROM sys.dm_exec_query_plan(0x05001E008116D84AA0BC768B1F0
20000010000000000000000000000000000000000000000000000000000000000);
```

The following screenshot shows the results of this query:

	query_plan
1	<ShowPlanXML xmlns="http://schemas.microsoft.com...

Figure 7.11 – Results of query getting the plan for a specific plan_handle

If we click the link displayed in the results, the following query execution plan opens in a new window:

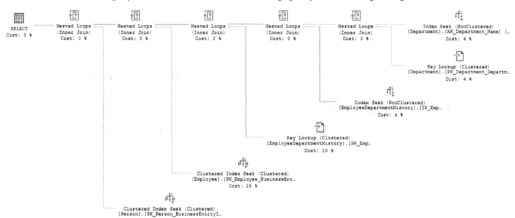

Figure 7.12 – Query plan for the uspGetEmployeeByDepartment stored procedure

There are some cases where even if the plan is still in the cache and we have a valid `plan_handle`, `sys.dm_exec_query_plan` returns a NULL value for the plan. In most cases, the reason for this is that the query that generated the plan is very complex and has many nested elements within it. Due to a limitation with the XML data type that only allows for 128 levels of nested elements, these complex plans cannot be returned via `sys.dm_exec_query_plan`. If we face this situation, we can attempt to use the `sys.dm_exec_text_query_plan` function instead. This function returns the plan as `NVARCHAR(max)` rather than XML. The text returned is XML data, but since the `NVARCHAR(max)` datatype doesn't have any formatting, it isn't affected by the nesting limitation. Query plans retrieved this way will not be clickable, so we will need to copy the XML data from the column, paste it into a new window (either SSMS or some other text editor), and save it as a `.sqlplan` file. Once we have this file, we can double-click it and SSMS will open it as a graphical plan.

The following query can be used to retrieve the same plan using `sys.dm_exec_text_query_plan`:

```
SELECT query_plan
FROM sys.dm_exec_text_query_plan(0x05001E008116D84AA0BC768B1F0
200000100000000000000000000000000000000000000000000000000000, 152,
316);
```

Note that this function takes two additional parameters, which are `statement_start_offset` and `statement_end_offset`. These values can also be obtained from `sys.dm_exec_query_stats`. This query returns the following results:

	query_plan
1	<ShowPlanXML xmlns="http://schemas.microsoft.com...

Figure 7.13 – Results of query getting the plan for a specific statement
inside the uspGetEmployeeByDepartment stored procedure

As we can see, the results are essentially the same as sys.dm_exec_query_plan, except there is no hyperlink.

sys.dm_exec_cached_plans

The sys.dm_exec_cached_plans DMV can be used to view all the query execution plans that are currently in the cache. Unlike sys.dm_exec_query_stats, which contains information about the execution of the query, this DMV contains information about the plan object itself, including things such as the size of the plan, the type of plan (for example, stored procedure, prepared statement, ad hoc query, and so on), and the number of times the plan has been used. Also, since plans are stored as a batch, this DMV will have only one row per plan, rather than one row per statement as in sys.dm_exec_query_stats.

Here's an example of a query against sys.dm_exec_cached_plans:

```
SELECT TOP 10 plan_handle, usecounts, size_in_bytes, objtype, query_
plan
FROM sys.dm_exec_cached_plans
CROSS APPLY sys.dm_exec_query_plan(plan_handle)
ORDER BY size_in_bytes DESC;
```

Note in the preceding query example that we can CROSS APPLY the sys.dm_exec_query_plan DMF with this DMV in order to retrieve the plan. This query yields the following results, ordered by the size of the plan, largest first:

	plan_handle	usecounts	size_in_bytes	objtype	query_plan
1	0x06000100EE9461139082C37DB9010000010000000000000...	15	2138112	Adhoc	<ShowPlanXML xmlns="http://schemas.microsoft.com...
2	0x0600090023769005D051C27DB9010000010000000000000...	107	835584	Prepared	NULL
3	0x06000400FE012E12B0DDB0E7B8010000010000000000000...	2	819200	Prepared	<ShowPlanXML xmlns="http://schemas.microsoft.com...
4	0x06001E00FE012E1260BFFAC0B8010000010000000000000...	38	819200	Prepared	<ShowPlanXML xmlns="http://schemas.microsoft.com...
5	0x06001A002376900590C2C27DB9010000010000000000000...	1	770048	Prepared	NULL
6	0x0600010044A7DF07104AC37DB9010000010000000000000...	15	679936	Adhoc	NULL
7	0x05000400BD2C136AB033669FB8010000010000000000000...	1	630784	Proc	<ShowPlanXML xmlns="http://schemas.microsoft.com...
8	0x0500FF7F99F756F09031C27DB9010000010000000000000...	31	598016	Proc	<ShowPlanXML xmlns="http://schemas.microsoft.com...
9	0x0600040056CDA83760DF8396B8010000010000000000000...	10	573440	Prepared	<ShowPlanXML xmlns="http://schemas.microsoft.com...
10	0x0600010056CDA837603F26BAB8010000010000000000000...	4	565248	Prepared	<ShowPlanXML xmlns="http://schemas.microsoft.com...

Figure 7.14 – Results of a query getting the top 10 largest plans in a cache

This is just a simple example that returns the 10 largest plans in the cache. In the next section, we will look at a few more comprehensive queries that leverage sys.dm_exec_cached_plans.

Troubleshooting common scenarios with DMV queries

Now that we have reviewed some of the DMVs that are relevant for examining query performance, we can look at how to combine these views into larger queries that target specific troubleshooting scenarios.

> **Note**
>
> Many of the examples in this chapter are derived from queries on the Tiger Toolbox on GitHub (`https://aka.ms/tigertoolbox`). For more examples and comprehensive DMV scripts, be sure to download and explore this repository.

Investigating blocking

Blocking is a very common scenario in many database systems. This is what happens when one query holds exclusive access to a resource that another query also requires. It is normal for some blocking to occur, but severe blocking can cause major performance issues and should be investigated. When troubleshooting query performance, it's a good idea to check for blocking first to see if queries are slow because they are expensive, or because they are being blocked by some other workload.

The key DMVs for investigating blocking are `sys.dm_exec_requests` and `sys.dm_os_waiting_tasks`. As we discussed previously, these DMVs show us which queries are currently running and what state they are in. They also have columns that will indicate which sessions may be causing blocking.

The following example shows a simple query that can be used to look for blocking on the system:

```
SELECT s.session_id, s.last_request_end_time, ISNULL(r.status,s.
status) AS status, s.database_id, r.blocking_session_id, r.wait_type,
r.wait_time, r.wait_resource, s.open_transaction_count
FROM sys.dm_exec_sessions s
LEFT JOIN sys.dm_exec_requests r ON r.session_id = s.session_id
WHERE s.is_user_process = 1;
```

The following screenshot shows an example of the results this query might generate on a system that has blocking:

	session_id	last_request_end_time	status	database_id	blocking_session_id	wait_type	wait_time	wait_resource	open_tr
1	51	2019-04-07 11:14:30.527	running	30	0	NULL	0		0
2	54	2019-04-07 11:08:42.263	sleeping	1	NULL	NULL	NULL	NULL	0
3	61	2019-04-06 17:44:40.757	sleeping	30	NULL	NULL	NULL	NULL	0
4	62	2019-04-06 17:28:33.773	sleeping	1	NULL	NULL	NULL	NULL	0
5	63	2019-04-07 15:48:51.190	sleeping	26	NULL	NULL	NULL	NULL	0
6	73	2019-04-07 11:13:16.480	sleeping	30	NULL	NULL	NULL	NULL	0
7	97	2019-04-07 10:19:30.173	suspended	26	0	WAITFOR	3300229		0
8	99	2019-04-07 10:54:09.127	suspended	30	109	LCK_M_S	1221379	KEY: 30:72057594048086016 (61a06abd401c)	0
9	100	2019-04-07 11:14:30.530	sleeping	26	NULL	NULL	NULL	NULL	0
10	101	2019-04-07 11:11:18.217	sleeping	1	NULL	NULL	NULL	NULL	0
11	102	2019-04-07 11:13:36.327	suspended	26	0	WRITELOG	0		1
12	103	2019-04-07 11:13:36.327	suspended	26	125	PAGELATCH_EX	0	26:1:157921	2
13	104	2019-04-06 17:32:39.947	sleeping	26	NULL	NULL	NULL	NULL	0
14	105	2019-04-07 11:13:36.327	suspended	26	0	WRITELOG	0		1
15	106	2019-04-06 17:04:05.573	sleeping	1	NULL	NULL	NULL	NULL	0
16	107	2019-04-07 11:13:36.330	suspended	26	0	WRITELOG	0		1
17	108	2019-04-07 11:13:36.327	suspended	26	111	PAGELATCH_EX	0	26:1:157921	2
18	109	2019-04-07 10:54:06.477	sleeping	30	NULL	NULL	NULL	NULL	1

Figure 7.15 – Results of a query getting current blocked sessions

Notice that session 99 has a status of suspended, which indicates it's waiting for something. The wait_type column shows a value of LCK_M_S, which means the session is waiting on a shared lock. The wait_resource column gives some information about what resource the session is trying to lock – it's a key (as in a key of an index), in database 30, with hobt_id of 72057594048086016.

> **Note**
>
> The hobt_id identifier stands for **Heap** or **B-Tree ID**. This is the identifier for a single partition of an object, either a table, an index, or column store segments.

We can reference system catalog views in the database to determine which object the lock request is for. The following query will return the index that is causing this blocking situation:

```
SELECT object_name(p.object_id) AS [object_name], p.index_id, i.name
AS index_name, partition_number
FROM sys.partitions p
INNER JOIN sys.indexes i ON i.object_id = p.object_id AND i.index_id =
p.index_id
WHERE p.hobt_id = 72057594048086016;
```

This will return the following results in the AdventureWorks sample database:

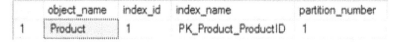

	object_name	index_id	index_name	partition_number
1	Product	1	PK_Product_ProductID	1

Figure 7.16 – Results of the example query showing the index where blocking is occurring

The `blocking_session_id` column shows a value of `109`, which means that session 109 is the session that is currently holding this resource and therefore blocking session 99. Interestingly, session 99 has a status of `sleeping`, which means it is not currently executing a query, but `open_transaction_count` is 1, which means it started a transaction but hasn't committed or rolled back the transaction. This is what is sometimes referred to as an **orphaned session**; it can happen when an application generates an unhandled exception, and the transaction doesn't get cleaned up. In this case, there's not much we can do to resolve the blocking situation naturally, so we typically need to kill the orphaned session (session 109), which should allow the blocked session (session 99) to proceed.

> **Tip**
>
> Other wait types may cause blocking, such as `PAGELATCH_EX`, which can be seen in the previous screenshot. These wait types are not user objects such as tables and indexes, they are pages that are an internal resource.

We can still get more information about these resources using a new DMF in SQL Server 2019 called `sys.dm_db_page_info`. Using `wait_resource 26:1:157921` from the previous screenshot, we can generate the following query to determine which page this resource references:

```
SELECT *
FROM sys.dm_db_page_info (26,1,157921,'LIMITED');
```

In this case, the blocking scenario was quite simple, one session was blocking one other session. In some cases, blocking can be very complex and form what's called a **blocking chain**. A blocking chain is hierarchical, one session blocks another session, and that session in turn blocks another session, and so forth. In this case, the session that starts the blocking chain is called the **head blocker**. This complex blocking is difficult to diagnose using a simple query such as the one we referenced here. In this case, we can use a more comprehensive query such as can be found in the Tiger Toolbox (`http://aka.ms/uspWhatsUp`), or by using a tool such as Activity Monitor in SSMS. We can read more about Activity Monitor in *Chapter 11, Troubleshooting Live Queries*.

We may notice in the preceding screenshot showing a blocking situation, that there are other sessions that are `suspended` but have a value of 0 for `blocking_session_id`. These sessions are waiting for a resource, but it's not considered blocking because the resource is not one that is owned by another session. These are typically system resources such as the disk, memory, or CPU. In this case, `wait_type` is `WRITELOG`, which means the session is waiting to write to the transaction log on disk.

Cached query plan issues

As we discussed earlier in the *sys.dm_exec_query_stats* section, the SQL Database Engine maintains execution statistics for all the queries that are currently in the cache. There is a wealth of information in this DMV that we can use to troubleshoot several different query performance-related issues. We will cover a few issues here, but be sure to reference the BPCheck script in the Tiger Toolbox (`https://aka.ms/bpcheck`) for a more comprehensive example of queries to identify these scenarios and others.

Single-use plans (query fingerprints)

In the *EXECUTE vs. sp_executesql* section of *Chapter 5, Writing Elegant T-SQL Queries*, we discussed how to send ad hoc T-SQL queries to the SQL Database Engine in a way that allows for plan reuse (also see the *Plan caching and re-use* section in *Chapter 1, Understanding Query Processing*, for the importance of plan reuse). If we are not sure whether or not our application is successfully parameterizing queries and leveraging plan reuse, we can use the `query_hash` column in `sys.dm_exec_query_stats` (known as the **query fingerprint**) to identify queries that are logically equivalent but have different entries in the cache. Queries that have the same `query_hash` but different values for the `sql_handle` column are stored as separate objects but are effectively the same query.

The following sample query can be used to identify single-use or low-use plans:

```
SELECT qs.query_hash, Query_Count = COUNT(DISTINCT sql_handle),
Executions = SUM(execution_count), CPU = SUM(qs.total_worker_time),
Reads = SUM(qs.total_logical_reads), Duration = SUM(qs.total_elapsed_
time), Sample_Query = MAX(st.text)
FROM sys.dm_exec_query_stats qs
CROSS APPLY sys.dm_exec_sql_text(qs.sql_handle) st
GROUP BY qs.query_hash
HAVING COUNT(DISTINCT sql_handle) > 5 --> Can be any number, depending
on our tolerance for duplicate queries
ORDER BY Query_Count DESC;
```

The results of this query are shown in the following screenshot:

	query_hash	Query_Count	Executions	CPU	Reads	Duration	Sample_Query
1	0x952BEAE65388AE04	8	22	246903	86509	285116	SELECT p.BusinessEntityID, p.FirstName, p.LastNa...

Figure 7.17 – Results of a query getting single-use or low-use plans

The results show a single row where `Query_Count` is 8. This means that the cache currently contains eight different queries that have the same `query_hash` and therefore are effectively the same query. If we look at the `Sample_Query` column, we'll find the following query:

```
SELECT p.BusinessEntityID, p.FirstName, p.LastName, e.EmailAddress
FROM Person.Person p
INNER JOIN Person.EmailAddress e ON p.BusinessEntityID =
e.BusinessEntityID
WHERE PersonType = 'IN' AND EmailPromotion = 1;
```

As we can see, this query does not have any parameter markers. There are three different ways we can fix this:

- Create a stored procedure and have the application call that instead.
- Parameterize the query by using `sp_executesql` or parameter objects from the database connection library.
- Turn on **Forced Parameterization**.

If there are only one or two queries like this, it may be easy enough to fix them by modifying the code using either method 1 or 2. If there are hundreds of queries that need to be parameterized, it might be worth turning on **Forced Parameterization** to temporarily correct the issue until the application can be re-written, using the following T-SQL command:

```
ALTER DATABASE CURRENT SET PARAMETERIZATION FORCED WITH NO_WAIT;
```

It may also be worth enabling the **Optimize for Ad hoc Workloads** server setting to prevent plan cache bloating for workloads that contain many single-use ad hoc batches, using the following T-SQL command:

```
EXEC sys.sp_configure N'optimize for ad hoc workloads', N'1';
GO
RECONFIGURE WITH OVERRIDE;
GO
```

These are also useful if the application is developed by a third-party software vendor, and we do not have the ability to change the code.

Finding resource-intensive queries

If the SQL Database Engine is experiencing resource contention such as high CPU consumption or heavy I/O, or we simply want to find queries that are resource intensive, we can use `sys.dm_exec_query_stats` to list out the top resource-consuming queries that are currently in the cache. There are several different metrics available via `sys.dm_exec_query_stats`, such as CPU, logical reads, and elapsed time, which we can sort to obtain a list of queries that consume large amounts of these resources.

The following query will list out the top 10 queries by average CPU consumption in the cache:

```
WITH queries AS
(SELECT TOP 10 [execution_count],
[total_worker_time]/[execution_count] AS [Avg_CPU_Time],
[total_elapsed_time]/[execution_count] AS [Avg_Duration],
[total_logical_reads]/[execution_count] AS
[Avg_Logical_Reads],
ISNULL([Total_grant_kb]/[execution_count], -1) AS [Avg_Grant_KB],
ISNULL([Total_used_grant_kb]/[execution_count], -1) AS [Avg_Used_
Grant_KB],
plan_handle, sql_handle
FROM sys.dm_exec_query_stats
ORDER BY [Avg_CPU_Time] DESC)
SELECT st.[text], qp.query_plan, queries.*
FROM queries
OUTER APPLY sys.dm_exec_query_plan(queries.plan_handle) AS qp
OUTER APPLY sys.dm_exec_sql_text(queries.sql_handle) AS st;
```

This query yields the following results:

	text	query_plan	execution_count
1	SELECT e.[BusinessEntityID], p.[Title], p.[First...	<ShowPlanXML xmlns="http://schemas.microsoft.com...	1
2	SELECT e.[BusinessEntityID], p.[Title], p.[First...	<ShowPlanXML xmlns="http://schemas.microsoft.com...	1
3	SELECT e.[BusinessEntityID], p.[Title], p.[First...	<ShowPlanXML xmlns="http://schemas.microsoft.com...	1
4	SELECT target_data FROM sys.dm_xe_session_ta...	<ShowPlanXML xmlns="http://schemas.microsoft.com...	1
5	SELECT st.[text], qp.query_plan, q.* FROM (SELECT T...	<ShowPlanXML xmlns="http://schemas.microsoft.com...	1
6	SELECT st.[text], qp.query_plan, q.* FROM (SELECT T...	<ShowPlanXML xmlns="http://schemas.microsoft.com...	1
7	(@used_memory_count_ratio float) select /* {5552be2b-...	NULL	2
8	(@ph varbinary(64))select query_plan from sys.dm_exec_...	<ShowPlanXML xmlns="http://schemas.microsoft.com...	1
9	WITH profiled_sessions as (SELECT DISTINCT sessio...	<ShowPlanXML xmlns="http://schemas.microsoft.com...	47
10	(@_msparam_0 nvarchar(4000),@_msparam_1 nvarchar...	<ShowPlanXML xmlns="http://schemas.microsoft.com...	1

Avg_CPU_Time	Avg_Duration	Avg_Logical_Reads	Avg_Grant_KB	Avg_Used_Grant_KB	plan_handle	sql_handle
247019338	332544264	4870724	115520	7056	0x060005009292E20390A2...	0x020000009292E2038A...
191279733	418772142	4870753	115520	7056	0x060005009292E2039042...	0x020000009292E2038A...
190289745	417717910	4870738	115520	7056	0x060005009292E203F048...	0x020000009292E2038A...
437101	811505	226	1200	104	0x060001008604D91CE068...	0x020000008604D91CA9...
215396	706739	70	1024	16	0x06001E00E2D5B9318069...	0x02000000E2D5B931C9...
199686	643946	56	1024	16	0x06001E00A411CC156077...	0x02000000A411CC15C5...
17927	17928	1043	1248	32	0x06000D00A0BC3739106A...	0x02000000A0BC3739D6...
13321	37580	4	0	0	0x06000100DDDAB12810B...	0x02000000DDDAB128B...
9512	37428	80	0	0	0x06000200C37C8B1110D9...	0x02000000C37C8B117D...
8054	69519	1496	1024	16	0x06001E0056CDA837E0B...	0x0200000056CDA8373E...

Figure 7.18 – Results of a query getting the top 10 queries by average CPU use in cache

Notice that many of the queries in the results have only a single execution. Tuning these queries would make them faster, but if they're only executed occasionally, this may not have a large impact on the overall server performance. If we want to reduce CPU consumption on the server as a whole, we might consider changing the query to sort by `total_worker_time` rather than the calculated `Avg_CPU_Time` column. This would bring queries to the top that are both high-CPU consumers and are executed frequently.

We can use this same query to examine other aspects of server performance. If we want to find slow queries, sort by `Avg_Duration`. If we want to find I/O intensive queries, sort by `Avg_Logical_Reads` or `total_logical_reads`. If we want to find queries that use a large amount of memory, sort by `Avg_Grant_KB` or `total_grant_kb`. We can find more queries like these in the BPCheck script in the Tiger Toolbox (`https://aka.ms/bpcheck`), or we can experiment with our own queries using the example in this section as a starting point.

Queries with excessive memory grants

In *Chapter 3*, *Exploring Query Execution Plans*, we covered a few different topics regarding memory grants, particularly in the *Query plan properties of interest* section. It is important for the SQL Database Engine to get memory grants correct. If a query asks for more memory than it needs, other queries may be stuck waiting for a memory grant even though this memory is not actually being used. Similarly, if the query asks for less memory than it needs, it could end up spilling to disk, which will slow it down significantly. In the previous section, *Finding resource intensive queries*, we explored the different ways to sort results from `sys.dm_exec_query_stats` to surface queries that consume a large amount of resources. We can also use these columns to do more complex computations that will allow us to identify queries that have an excessive memory grant.

The following query is a modification of the example we showed in the *Finding resource intensive queries* section:

```
WITH queries AS
    (SELECT TOP 10 [execution_count],
    [total_worker_time]/[execution_count] AS [Avg_CPU_Time],
     [total_elapsed_time]/[execution_count] AS [Avg_Duration],
     [total_logical_reads]/[execution_count] AS [Avg_Logical_Reads],
    ISNULL([total_grant_kb]/[execution_count], -1) AS [Avg_Grant_KB],
    ISNULL([total_used_grant_kb]/[execution_count], -1) AS [Avg_Used_
Grant_KB],
    COALESCE((((([total_used_grant_kb] * 100.00) / NULLIF([total_grant_
kb],0))), 0) AS [Grant2Used_Ratio],
    plan_handle, sql_handle
    FROM sys.dm_exec_query_stats
    WHERE total_grant_kb/execution_count > 1024 AND execution_count >
1
    ORDER BY [Grant2Used_Ratio])
```

```
SELECT st.[text], qp.query_plan, queries.*
FROM queries
OUTER APPLY sys.dm_exec_query_plan(queries.plan_handle) AS qp
OUTER APPLY sys.dm_exec_sql_text(queries.sql_handle) AS st;
```

In this query, we added a new column called `Grant2Used_Ratio`, which is a calculation of the percent of the memory grant that was actually used. The lower this ratio, the further off the memory grant estimate was, which means a large amount of memory is being wasted. Looking at the `WHERE` clause in the example, we can see that we are filtering out single execution queries and queries that have a very small memory grant (1 KB or less).

The following screenshot shows sample results from this query:

	text	query_plan	execution_count
1	DECLARE @xmlMessage XML DECLARE @x XML SELECT ...	<ShowPlanXML xmlns="http://schemas.microsoft.com...	30
2	SELECT DISTINCT Name FROM Production.Product WHERE ...	<ShowPlanXML xmlns="http://schemas.microsoft.com...	2
3	SELECT DISTINCT Name FROM Production.Product WHERE ...	<ShowPlanXML xmlns="http://schemas.microsoft.com...	19
4	SELECT DISTINCT Name FROM Production.Product AS p W...	<ShowPlanXML xmlns="http://schemas.microsoft.com...	13
5	SELECT DISTINCT Name FROM Production.Product WHERE ...	<ShowPlanXML xmlns="http://schemas.microsoft.com...	3
6	SELECT ProductID, AVG(UnitPrice) AS 'Average Price' FROM ...	<ShowPlanXML xmlns="http://schemas.microsoft.com...	8
7	SELECT ProductID FROM Sales.SalesOrderDetail GROUP BY...	<ShowPlanXML xmlns="http://schemas.microsoft.com...	4
8	SELECT ProductID FROM Sales.SalesOrderDetail WHERE U...	<ShowPlanXML xmlns="http://schemas.microsoft.com...	2
9	SELECT AVG(OrderQty) AS 'Average Quantity', NonDiscountS...	<ShowPlanXML xmlns="http://schemas.microsoft.com...	13
10	SELECT ProductID, SpecialOfferID, AVG(UnitPrice) AS 'Average...	<ShowPlanXML xmlns="http://schemas.microsoft.com...	16

Avg_CPU_Time	Avg_Duration	Avg_Logical_Reads	Avg_Grant_KB	Avg_Used_Grant_KB	Grant2Used_Ratio	plan_handle	sql_handle
1311	1397	0	1517744	0	0.000000000000000	0x06001A000151451C90A2C...	0x020000000151451C51C5...
926	927	17	1056	104	9.848484848484848	0x06001A005C2E4725C0A7F...	0x020000005C2E47254813...
1024	1024	17	1056	104	9.848484848484848	0x06001A005C2E472560DF5...	0x020000005C2E47254813...
1041	13490	17	1056	104	9.848484848484848	0x06001A00163F4C0050DAA...	0x02000000163F4C00F1A1...
1051	1051	17	1056	104	9.848484848484848	0x06001A005C2E472560DF9...	0x020000005C2E47254813...
18587	22375	1266	1632	328	20.098039215686274	0x06001A009A588104E09A1...	0x020000009A588104D026...
76778	101549	1266	1616	328	20.297029702970297	0x06001A00910D5C12909C1...	0x02000000910D5C12355...
79075	79743	1266	1616	328	20.297029702970297	0x06001A00863A5632B0516...	0x02000000863A5632A3D2...
109090	169823	1266	3792	920	24.261603375527426	0x06001A007E8D690830B6E...	0x020000007E8D6908C614...
272490	490791	1266	2704	688	25.443786982248520	0x06001A00032AC613B0AEE...	0x02000000032AC613EF1A...

Figure 7.19 – Results of a query getting the top 10 queries by average grant size in cache

The top query in this result has `Grant2Used_Ratio` of 0, which is the worst it can possibly be. In this case, the query requested 1.5 GB of memory and didn't use any of it! This is a query that we would want to tune as soon as possible. The rest of the queries in the list have low percentages, but their `Avg_Grant_KB` values are not very high, so they may not be as big of a problem as the first query. We can experiment with different predicates in the `WHERE` clause and different sorting columns to find different issues with memory grants using the sample query in this section as a starting point.

Mining XML query plans

As we mentioned in the *sys.dm_exec_query_plan* section, query execution plans are stored as XML, and the `sys.dm_exec_query_plan` DMV returns them as a proper XML data type. This allows us to leverage **XML Path Language** (**XPath**) to generate queries that can search for elements and attributes within the query execution plans. Using these XPath queries, or **XQueries**, we can search for common query performance issues across all the query execution plans in the cache, rather than having to examine each graphical plan individually. In this section, we will cover a few common scenarios, but be sure to reference the `Mining-PlanCache` section of the Tiger Toolbox (`https://aka.ms/tigertoolbox`) for more examples.

> **Tip**
> The queries shown in this section can be used individually to search for specific issues, but running the entire BPCheck script from the Tiger Toolbox (`https://aka.ms/bpcheck`) will gather all this information and more in a single resultset.

Plans with missing indexes

In the *Query plan properties of interest* section of *Chapter 3, Exploring Query Execution Plans*, we discussed the `MissingIndexes` property. If this property exists in a query execution plan, it means that there is at least one index that the SQL Database Engine could have benefitted from that does not exist.

The following query uses DMVs to list all the missing index suggestions since the last restart:

```
SELECT DB_NAME(d.database_id) as [database_name], OBJECT_NAME(d.
object_id, d.database_id) AS object_name, total_cost_savings =
ROUND(s.avg_total_user_cost * s.avg_user_impact * (s.user_seeks +
s.user_scans),0) /100, s.avg_total_user_cost, s.avg_user_impact,
s.user_seeks, s.user_scans, d.equality_columns, d.inequality_columns,
d.included_columns
FROM sys.dm_db_missing_index_groups g
INNER JOIN sys.dm_db_missing_index_group_stats s on s.group_handle =
g.index_group_handle
INNER JOIN sys.dm_db_missing_index_details d on d.index_handle =
g.index_handle
ORDER BY total_cost_savings DESC;
```

Sample results for this query can be seen in the following screenshot:

	database_name	object_name	total_cost_savings	avg_total_user_cost	avg_user_impact	user_seeks	user_scans	equality_columns	inequality_columns	included_columns
1	AdventureWorks2016CTP3	SalesOrderDetailBulk	23434.52	67.2765925805513	78.63	443	0	NULL	[ProductID]	[OrderQty], [UnitPrice], [UnitPriceDiscount]
2	AdventureWorks2016_EXT	SalesOrderDetail	297.72	3.59327503977793	36.5	227	0	[ProductID]	NULL	[OrderQty], [UnitPrice], [UnitPriceDiscount]
3	AdventureWorks2016_EXT	SalesOrderDetail	180.29	1.69672937411795	57.75	184	0	NULL	[UnitPrice]	[ProductID], [LineTotal]
4	AdventureWorks2016	Person	157.11	3.10548731539778	90.34	56	0	[PersonType], [EmailPromotion]	NULL	[FirstName], [LastName]
5	AdventureWorks2016_EXT	SalesOrderDetail	100.23	1.17768299416184	88.65	96	0	NULL	[CarrierTrackingNumber]	NULL
6	AdventureWorks2016_EXT	SalesOrderDetail	98.06	1.21672150262773	83.95	96	0	NULL	[OrderQty]	[ProductID], [UnitPrice]
7	AdventureWorks2016_EXT	SalesOrderDetail	98.06	1.32619431562189	77.02	96	0	NULL	[UnitPrice]	[OrderQty], [ProductID]
8	AdventureWorks2016_EXT	SalesOrderDetail	86.42	1.83201991110446	53	89	0	NULL	[UnitPrice]	[OrderQty], [ProductID], [LineTotal]
9	AdventureWorks2016	Person	5.6	2.85557850074074	98.05	2	0	[PersonType]	NULL	[FirstName], [LastName]
10	AdventureWorks2016	Person	5.58	2.88154210074074	96.86	2	0	NULL	[PersonType]	[FirstName], [LastName]

Figure 7.20 – Results of query listing all the missing index suggestions

This is useful for getting an overall idea of all the missing index suggestions across all the queries on the server, but on a busy server with many applications and databases, this may be overwhelming. Also, while this gives us the ability to sort the index suggestions by potential impact, there is no way to determine which queries may benefit from these indexes. Also, in some cases, the index suggestion may not be practical. Looking at the query execution plan that generated the missing index suggestion may reveal an even better index that would improve the query performance even more, and perhaps be useable by multiple queries.

> **Tip**
>
> Use the BPCheck script from the Tiger Toolbox (`https://aka.ms/bpcheck`) to learn about missing indexes that may be required in a database. BPCheck can optionally generate the index creation scripts for the missing indexes that are expected to have a very high impact using a scoring method. BPCheck can warn if two missing indexes would be redundant if created; for example, if one suggested index is already a subset of another suggested index.

The following query can be used to look for any query execution plans that have the `MissingIndex` property:

```
WITH XMLNAMESPACES (DEFAULT 'http://schemas.microsoft.com/
sqlserver/2004/07/showplan'),
PlanMissingIndexes AS (SELECT query_plan, cp.usecounts, cp.refcounts,
cp.plan_handle
FROM sys.dm_exec_cached_plans cp WITH (NOLOCK)
CROSS APPLY sys.dm_exec_query_plan(cp.plan_handle) tp
WHERE cp.cacheobjtype = 'Compiled Plan' AND tp.query_plan.exist('//
MissingIndex')=1)
SELECT c1.value('(//MissingIndex/@Database)[1]', 'sysname') AS
database_name,
c1.value('(//MissingIndex/@Schema)[1]', 'sysname') AS [schema_name],
c1.value('(//MissingIndex/@Table)[1]', 'sysname') AS [table_name],
c1.value('@StatementText', 'VARCHAR(4000)') AS sql_text,
c1.value('@StatementId', 'int') AS StatementId, pmi.usecounts, pmi.
refcounts,
c1.value('(//MissingIndexGroup/@Impact)[1]', 'FLOAT') AS impact,
REPLACE(c1.query('for $group in //ColumnGroup for $column in $group/
Column where $group/@Usage="EQUALITY" return string($column/@Name)').
value('.', 'varchar(max)'),'] [', '],[') AS equality_columns,
REPLACE(c1.query('for $group in //ColumnGroup for $column in $group/
Column where $group/@Usage="INEQUALITY" return string($column/@
Name)').value('.', 'varchar(max)'),'] [', '],[') AS inequality_
columns,
REPLACE(c1.query('for $group in //ColumnGroup for $column in $group/
Column where $group/@Usage="INCLUDE" return string($column/@Name)').
value('.', 'varchar(max)'),'] [', '],[') AS include_columns, pmi.
query_plan, pmi.plan_handle
FROM PlanMissingIndexes pmi
CROSS APPLY pmi.query_plan.nodes('//StmtSimple') AS q1(c1)
WHERE pmi.usecounts > 1
ORDER BY c1.value('(//MissingIndexGroup/@Impact)[1]', 'FLOAT') DESC
OPTION(RECOMPILE, MAXDOP 1);
```

The following screenshot shows sample results for this query:

	database_name	schema_name	table_name	sql_text	StatementId	usecounts	refcounts	impact
1	[AdventureWorks2016]	[Person]	[Person]	SELECT BusinessEntityID, FirstName, LastN...	1	4	2	96.8582
2	[AdventureWorks2016]	[Person]	[Person]	: SELECT BusinessEntityID, FirstName, Las...	2	4	2	96.8582

equality_columns	inequality_columns	include_columns	query_plan	plan_handle
[PersonType]	[PersonType]	[FirstName],[LastName],[FirstName],[LastName]	<ShowPlanXML xmlns="http://schemas.microsoft.com...	0x06001E000DA44507203D4...
[PersonType]	[PersonType]	[FirstName],[LastName],[FirstName],[LastName]	<ShowPlanXML xmlns="http://schemas.microsoft.com...	0x06001E000DA44507203D4...

Figure 7.21 – Results of a query showing plans that have the MissingIndex property

As the results show, this query allows us to gather the same information that the DMVs provide, but include the query execution plan so that further analysis can be done before we create any of the indexes suggested.

> **Tip**
>
> Executing XQueries can be very expensive, particularly on a busy server that has a very large procedure cache. Avoid running this type of query directly on a production server. If we would like to analyze a production workload, it is best to dump the XML query plans into a table on the production server, and then backup or detach the database and restore or attach it on a test server for analysis. Also note that this is why the OPTION(RECOMPILE, MAXDOP 1) clause has been added to each of these queries.

Plans with warnings

In the *Query plan properties of interest* section of *Chapter 3, Exploring Query Execution Plans*, we covered warnings, which can occur in a query execution plan at either the plan level or the operator level. We can leverage XQueries to identify plans with warnings as well.

The following query will find query execution plans that have a plan-level warning:

```
WITH XMLNAMESPACES (DEFAULT 'http://schemas.microsoft.com/
sqlserver/2004/07/showplan'),
WarningSearch AS (SELECT qp.query_plan, cp.usecounts, cp.objtype,
wn.query('.') AS StmtSimple, cp.plan_handle
FROM sys.dm_exec_cached_plans cp WITH (NOLOCK)
CROSS APPLY sys.dm_exec_query_plan(cp.plan_handle) qp
CROSS APPLY qp.query_plan.nodes('//StmtSimple') AS p(wn)
WHERE wn.exist('//Warnings') = 1 AND wn.exist('@QueryHash') = 1)
SELECT StmtSimple.value('StmtSimple[1]/@StatementText',
'VARCHAR(4000)') AS sql_text,
StmtSimple.value('StmtSimple[1]/@StatementId', 'int') AS StatementId,
CASE WHEN c2.exist('@UnmatchedIndexes[. = "1"]') = 1 THEN
'UnmatchedIndexes'
WHEN (c4.exist('@ConvertIssue[. = "Cardinality Estimate"]') = 1 OR
c4.exist('@ConvertIssue[. = "Seek Plan"]') = 1) THEN 'ConvertIssue_'
+ c4.value('@ConvertIssue','sysname') END AS warning, ws.objtype,
ws.usecounts, ws.query_plan, ws.plan_handle
FROM WarningSearch ws
CROSS APPLY StmtSimple.nodes('//QueryPlan') AS q1(c1)
CROSS APPLY c1.nodes('./Warnings') AS q2(c2)
CROSS APPLY c1.nodes('./RelOp') AS q3(c3)
OUTER APPLY c2.nodes('./PlanAffectingConvert') AS q4(c4)
OPTION(RECOMPILE, MAXDOP 1);
```

The following screenshot shows sample results for this query:

	sql_text	StatementId	warning	objtype	usecounts	query_plan	plan_handle
1	SELECT * FROM #tmpSales WHERE SalesOrderID = 44360	1	ConvertIssue_Cardinality Estimate	Adhoc	2	<ShowPlanXML xmlns="http://sch...	0x06001E00108F8C24203D797BF5...
2	SELECT * FROM #tmpSales WHERE SalesOrderID = 44360	1	ConvertIssue_Seek Plan	Adhoc	2	<ShowPlanXML xmlns="http://sch...	0x06001E00108F8C24203D797BF5...

Figure 7.22 – Results of a query showing plans that have a plan-level warning

We can also use a similar query to find warnings at the operator level. The following query will find query execution plans that have an operator-level warning:

```
WITH XMLNAMESPACES (DEFAULT 'http://schemas.microsoft.com/
sqlserver/2004/07/showplan'),
WarningSearch AS (SELECT qp.query_plan, cp.usecounts, cp.objtype,
wn.query('.') AS StmtSimple, cp.plan_handle
FROM sys.dm_exec_cached_plans cp WITH (NOLOCK)
CROSS APPLY sys.dm_exec_query_plan(cp.plan_handle) qp
CROSS APPLY qp.query_plan.nodes('//StmtSimple') AS p(wn)
WHERE wn.exist('//Warnings') = 1 AND wn.exist('@QueryHash') = 1)
SELECT StmtSimple.value('StmtSimple[1]/@StatementText',
'VARCHAR(4000)') AS sql_text,
StmtSimple.value('StmtSimple[1]/@StatementId', 'int') AS StatementId,
c1.value('@PhysicalOp','sysname') AS physical_op,
c1.value('@LogicalOp','sysname') AS logical_op,
CASE WHEN c2.exist('@NoJoinPredicate[. = "1"]') = 1 THEN
'NoJoinPredicate'
WHEN c3.exist('@Database') = 1 THEN 'ColumnsWithNoStatistics' END AS
warning, ws.objtype, ws.usecounts, ws.query_plan, ws.plan_handle
FROM WarningSearch ws
CROSS APPLY StmtSimple.nodes('//RelOp') AS q1(c1)
CROSS APPLY c1.nodes('./Warnings') AS q2(c2)
OUTER APPLY c2.nodes('./ColumnsWithNoStatistics/ColumnReference') AS
q3(c3)
OPTION(RECOMPILE, MAXDOP 1);
```

The following screenshot shows sample results for this query:

	sql_text	StatementId	physical_op	logical_op	warning	objtype	usecounts	query_plan	plan_handle
1	SELECT [CarrierTrackingNumber] FROM Sales.SalesO...	1	Clustered Index Scan	Clustered Index Scan	ColumnsWithNoStatistics	Adhoc	6	<ShowPlanXML xmlns="...	0x06001E00F42F8B07D...
2	--USE [master] --GO --ALTER DATABASE [Adventure...	1	Clustered Index Scan	Clustered Index Scan	ColumnsWithNoStatistics	Adhoc	3	<ShowPlanXML xmlns="...	0x06001E009CD2B5316...
3	SELECT [CarrierTrackingNumber] FROM Sales.Sales...	1	Clustered Index Scan	Clustered Index Scan	ColumnsWithNoStatistics	Adhoc	2	<ShowPlanXML xmlns="...	0x06001E009AC32B3B1...

Figure 7.23 – Results of a query showing plans that have an operator-level warning

Use these queries to start experimenting with finding different warnings in our query plans. We can change the predicates in these queries to look for any of the warnings outlined in *Chapter 3, Exploring Query Execution Plans*.

Plans with implicit conversions

In the previous section, *Plans with warnings*, we looked at an XQuery that will find plans that have conversion warnings at the plan level. If we want to find query execution plans that have implicit conversions anywhere in the plan, whether or not they generate a `PlanAffectingConvert` warning, we can use an XQuery that looks specifically for implicit conversions.

The following query will find query execution plans that have implicit conversions in any of the operators within the plan:

```
WITH XMLNAMESPACES (DEFAULT 'http://schemas.microsoft.com/
sqlserver/2004/07/showplan'),
Convertsearch AS (SELECT qp.query_plan, cp.usecounts, cp.objtype,
cp.plan_handle, cs.query('.') AS StmtSimple
FROM sys.dm_exec_cached_plans cp WITH (NOLOCK)
CROSS APPLY sys.dm_exec_query_plan(cp.plan_handle) qp
CROSS APPLY qp.query_plan.nodes('//StmtSimple') AS p(cs)
WHERE cp.cacheobjtype = 'Compiled Plan'
AND cs.exist('@QueryHash') = 1
AND cs.exist('.//ScalarOperator[contains(@ScalarString, "CONVERT_
IMPLICIT")]') = 1
AND cs.exist('.[contains(@StatementText, "Convertsearch")]') = 0)
SELECT c2.value('@StatementText', 'VARCHAR(4000)') AS sql_text,
c2.value('@StatementId', 'int') AS StatementId,
c3.value('@ScalarString[1]','VARCHAR(4000)') AS expression,
ss.usecounts, ss.query_plan, ss.plan_handle
FROM Convertsearch ss
CROSS APPLY query_plan.nodes('//StmtSimple') AS q2(c2)
CROSS APPLY c2.nodes('.//ScalarOperator[contains(@ScalarString,
"CONVERT_IMPLICIT")]') AS q3(c3)
OPTION(RECOMPILE, MAXDOP 1);
```

The following screenshot shows sample results for this query:

	sql_text		StatementId	expression	usecounts	query_plan	plan_handle
1	BEGIN	DELETE TOP(@batch_size) sys.syscom...	20	CONVERT_IMPLICIT(bigint,[@batch_size],0)	1	<ShowPlanXML xmlns="htt...	0x0500FF7F99F756F0B0...
2	BEGIN	DELETE TOP(@batch_size) sys.syscom...	20	CONVERT_IMPLICIT(bigint,[@batch_size],0)	1	<ShowPlanXML xmlns="htt...	0x0500FF7F99F756F0A0...
3	BEGIN	DELETE TOP(@batch_size) sys.syscom...	20	CONVERT_IMPLICIT(bigint,[@batch_size],0)	1	<ShowPlanXML xmlns="htt...	0x0500FF7F99F756F010...
4	BEGIN	DELETE TOP(@batch_size) sys.syscom...	20	CONVERT_IMPLICIT(bigint,[@batch_size],0)	1	<ShowPlanXML xmlns="htt...	0x0500FF7F99F756F0B0...
5	BEGIN	DELETE TOP(@batch_size) sys.syscom...	20	CONVERT_IMPLICIT(bigint,[@batch_size],0)	1	<ShowPlanXML xmlns="htt...	0x0500FF7F99F756F050...

Figure 7.24 – Results of a query showing plans that have implicit conversion warnings

Leveraging this query will help us identify queries that are comparing two values with different data types, either because of incorrect parameter types, or mismatched data types in the database schema itself.

Plans with lookups

One of the quickest ways to tune a query is to add a covering index. As we discussed in *Chapter 3, Exploring Query Execution Plans*, the presence of a lookup in a query execution plan indicates that a query is not covered. We can leverage this same XQuery method to find query execution plans that contain a lookup anywhere in the plan.

The following query will find query execution plans that have a lookup:

```
WITH XMLNAMESPACES (DEFAULT 'http://schemas.microsoft.com/
sqlserver/2004/07/showplan'),
Lookupsearch AS (SELECT qp.query_plan, cp.usecounts, ls.query('.') AS
StmtSimple, cp.plan_handle
FROM sys.dm_exec_cached_plans cp (NOLOCK)
CROSS APPLY sys.dm_exec_query_plan(cp.plan_handle) qp
CROSS APPLY qp.query_plan.nodes('//StmtSimple') AS p(ls)
WHERE cp.cacheobjtype = 'Compiled Plan'
AND ls.exist('//IndexScan[@Lookup = "1"]') = 1
AND ls.exist('@QueryHash') = 1)
SELECT StmtSimple.value('StmtSimple[1]/@StatementText',
'VARCHAR(4000)') AS sql_text,
StmtSimple.value('StmtSimple[1]/@StatementId', 'int') AS StatementId,
c1.value('@NodeId','int') AS node_id,
c2.value('@Database','sysname') AS database_name,
c2.value('@Schema','sysname') AS [schema_name],
c2.value('@Table','sysname') AS table_name,
'Lookup - ' + c1.value('@PhysicalOp','sysname') AS physical_
operator, c2.value('@Index','sysname') AS index_name, c3.value('@
ScalarString','VARCHAR(4000)') AS predicate, ls.usecounts, ls.query_
plan, ls.plan_handle
FROM Lookupsearch ls
CROSS APPLY query_plan.nodes('//RelOp') AS q1(c1)
CROSS APPLY c1.nodes('./IndexScan/Object') AS q2(c2)
OUTER APPLY c1.nodes('./IndexScan//ScalarOperator[1]') AS q3(c3)
-- Below attribute is present either in Index Seeks or RID Lookups so
it can reveal a Lookup is executed
WHERE c1.exist('./IndexScan[@Lookup = "1"]') = 1
AND c2.value('@Schema','sysname') <> '[sys]'
OPTION(RECOMPILE, MAXDOP 1);
```

The following screenshot shows sample results from this query:

	sql_text	StatementId	node_id	database_name	schema_name	table_name	physical_operator
1	SELECT * FROM Person.Person WHERE Last...	1	3	[AdventureWorks2016]	[Person]	[Person]	Lookup - Clustered Index Seek

index_name	predicate	usecounts	query_plan	plan_handle
[PK_Person_BusinessEntityID]	[AdventureWorks2016].[Person].[Person].[BusinessEntityID]	10	<ShowPlanXML xmlns="...	0x06001E0064DDB728E0...

Figure 7.25 – Results of a query showing plans that have a lookup

While we can't add covering indexes to all queries, this sample XQuery can help us identify areas where our index strategy can be improved, and hopefully reveal targeted indexes that may benefit multiple queries.

Summary

While the examples in this chapter are only a small sample, hopefully at this point, we can see how DMVs and DMFs can be a powerful troubleshooting tool when it comes to diagnosing query performance issues. They are lightweight, easy to use, and provide a breadth of information that is useful for zeroing in on the performance issues that were covered in *Chapter 5, Writing Elegant T-SQL Queries*, and *Chapter 6, Discovering T-SQL Anti-Patterns in Depth*.

While DMVs are great for point-in-time and cumulative analysis, there are some issues that can only be diagnosed by catching queries and related data in real time. This is where tracing with **Extended Events (XEvents)** is useful. In the next chapter, we will introduce XEvents and discuss how to set up the new XEvent profiler trace that can capture all the queries that are executed against a server in real time.

Building XEvent Profiler Traces

In *Chapter 7, Building Diagnostic Queries Using DMVs and DMFs*, we learned how to gain insights into query performance using the built-in system views. This information is valuable, but because these views mostly represent the current point in time, they are not always sufficient to answer every question we have about the performance of our queries. In this chapter, we will introduce **Extended Events (XEvents)**, the lightweight infrastructure that exposes relevant just-in-time information from every component of the SQL Database Engine, focusing on those related to T-SQL execution. We will explore real-world examples of how to use these XEvents to troubleshoot different poor performance scenarios, leverage collection and analysis tools such as the XEvent Profiler, SQL LogScout and **Replay Markup Language (RML)** utilities for event analysis, and drop a note on the infamously deprecated SQL Server Profiler.

In this chapter, we're going to cover the following main topics:

- Introducing XEvents
- Getting up and running with the XEvent Profiler
- Remote collection with SQL LogScout
- Analyzing traces with RML Utilities

Technical requirements

The examples used in this chapter are designed for use on SQL Server 2022 and Azure SQL Database, but they should work on any version of SQL Server, 2012 or later. The Developer Edition of SQL Server is free for development environments and can be used to run all the code samples. There is also a free tier of Azure SQL Database you can use for testing at `https://aka.ms/freedb`.

You will need the `AdventureWorks2016_EXT` (referred to as `AdventureWorks`) and `AdventureWorksDW2016_EXT` (referred to as `AdventureWorksDW`) sample databases, which can be found on GitHub at `https://github.com/Microsoft/sql-server-samples/releases/tag/adventureworks`. Code samples for this chapter can also be found on GitHub at `https://github.com/PacktPublishing/Learn-T-SQL-Querying-Second-Edition/tree/main/ch8`.

Introducing XEvents

When we connect to the SQL Database Engine and run a query, it fires a series of events – a user logs in, a connection is established, a query begins executing, a plan is found in the cache, a plan is recompiled, and a query completes execution (these are just a few examples). Virtually everything that happens within the Database Engine is an event.

While **Dynamic Management Views (DMVs)** are powerful tools, they don't always give a complete picture of what is going on within the engine. Most DMVs provide a snapshot in time, a picture of what is going on the moment they are queried. They may have some history that goes back to the last time the server was restarted, but even then, the information is typically cumulative; they can't tell us what the server looked like a few minutes before, and they can't tell us the events that led up to the current state. This is where tracing comes in. Tracing allows us to capture all the occurrences of one or more events on the server over a period of time, and store that data in a target location, typically a file on disk, for later analysis.

The XEvents engine provides a mechanism to consume events, collect related data, and direct them to a target for later analysis. The events themselves are defined at various points in the Database Engine code that are significant for some reason.

Using XEvents to trace these significant database events can give you a much greater level of detail than DMVs, but the cost to the server is higher. While the XEvents engine is relatively lightweight compared to other tracing mechanisms such as SQL Trace, it still generates overhead on the server and should only be used when this level of detail is required.

There are a few terms that are important to understand before we begin creating XEvent traces:

- A **package** is a container for a group of XEvents objects (events, actions, filters, etc.) that are related in some way. There are three packages in the SQL Database Engine – `package0` (the default package), `sqlserver`, and `sqlos`.

- An **event** is a point of interest in the SQL Database Engine code. When an event fires, it means that the code in question was reached, and any information that is relevant to that event is captured. There are hundreds of events in the SQL Database Engine, far too many to list here, but we will cover some T-SQL performance-related events in this chapter and a few of the remaining chapters in the book.

- A **channel** is a categorization of events by intended audience. There are four channels in the SQL Database Engine:

  - **Admin** – General events that are targeted to administrators, such as `cpu_threshold_exceeded` and `xml_deadlock_report`.

  - **Operational** – Events used to diagnose a problem, such as `blocked_process_report` and `server_memory_change`.

  - **Analytic** – Events that are used in performance investigations, such as `sql_batch_completed` and `rpc_completed`.

  - **Debug** – Events that are used for deep troubleshooting and debugging such as `inaccurate_cardinality_estimate`. These events are generally reserved for use when working with Microsoft Support. They can be especially expensive to consume and should be used with caution.

- A **category** (also known as a keyword) is a finer-grain categorization used to identify events that pertain to a specific component or area of the Database Engine.

- A **target** is where the event output is directed. The SQL Database Engine supports six targets:

  - **Event file** – A file on disk. This is the most common, and the one we will use most often when creating XEvent traces.

  - **Ring buffer** – This is a circular in-memory buffer, meaning when the buffer is full, the oldest events are overwritten.

  - **Event counter** – This target simply counts the occurrences of an event, rather than capturing the data for the event.

  - **Histogram** – This is like the event counter target in that it counts occurrences, but the histogram target allows us to sort events into buckets based on data available in the event. This is useful for something like the `wait_info` event where we might want to count the number of waits by the `wait_type` event field.

  - **Event pairing** – This target allows us to pair events such as login and logout so that we can identify events that don't occur as a matched set.

  - **Event Tracing for Windows (ETW)** – ETW is a common framework that is used to correlate traces across applications running on Windows or with the operating system itself.

- An **action** is a response to an event firing. Typically, this is additional data that we want to collect that's not a part of the event data itself.

- A **session** is the definition of the XEvent collection that we want to perform. In a session, we define the events we want to collect, the target, the actions, and any predicates we might want to apply to filter the events that are captured.

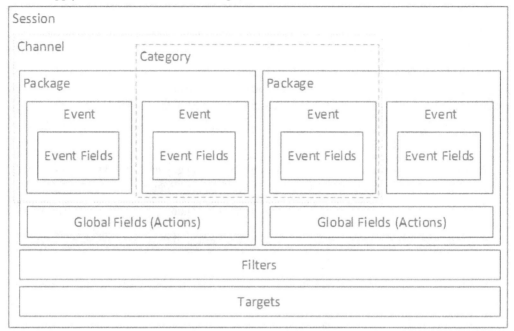

Figure 8.1: Hierarchy of XEvents objects

Now that we've got our terms defined, let's look at an example of how we can use XEvents to analyze database activity. Assume that a group within our company is about to release a new application that they want us to validate. The developers have used some sort of database code generator, so there are no stored procedures in the database for us to review. To get an idea of the queries that the application generates and the performance of those queries, we want to trace all the query activity against the server while the application is being tested in pre-production.

For this example, we'll use **SQL Server Management Studio** (**SSMS**) to create and analyze an XEvent session. To get started, expand the **Extended Events** section under the **Management** folder in **Object Explorer**. Right-click on **Sessions** and choose **New Session…**, as shown in the following screenshot:

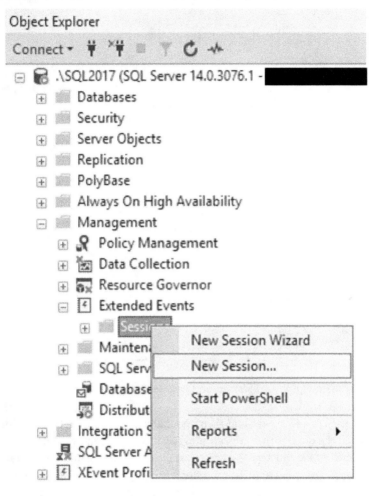

Figure 8.2: SSMS Object Explorer window showing the Extended Events > Sessions context window

In the **New Session** window, type in a name for our session, as shown in the following screenshot:

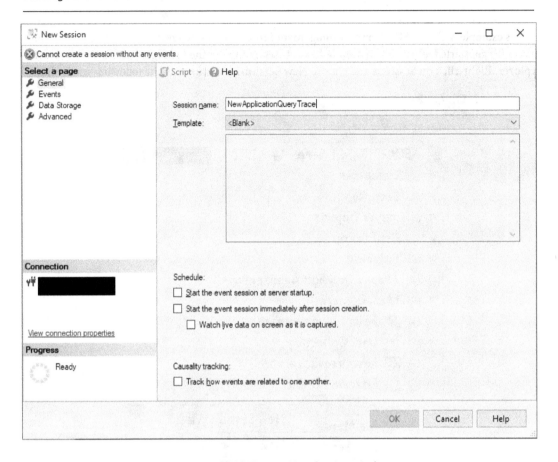

Figure 8.3: SSMS XEvents New Session window

Click on the **Events** page to add events, and then optionally add actions and filter predicates. Since we want to capture all the queries that are executing against the server, we'll need two events at a minimum: `rpc_completed` and `sql_batch_completed`. **RPC** stands for **Remote Procedure Call**. When an application executes a stored procedure using a procedure object, it comes through as an RPC. This is also the event we would see if we ran a query via `sp_executesql`, or if we built a parameterized query from client code using a database connectivity library such as **Open Database Connectivity** (**ODBC**). If we send an ad hoc query to the server using `EXECUTE`, or by sending a text query string, the query will be a SQL batch rather than an RPC. There are events for both starting and completing a batch or an RPC, but if all we want to know are the queries that are executing and the performance metrics for those queries, the completed events are enough.

In the following screenshot, we are typing `completed` into the search box to find the desired events:

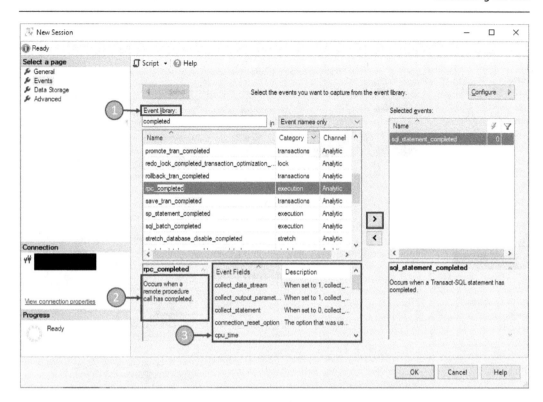

Figure 8.4: SSMS XEvents New Session window showing the Events selection page

In this screenshot, we can see the following:

1. The search box used to locate events that contain the search term in the name – this is where we typed `completed`.

2. The name and description of the selected event.

3. The event fields that the selected event collects by default, including a description of each field.

After we select the events we want, we then click the right arrow to add them to the session. Once we have added all the events, we can click the **Configure** button to add any actions and filter predicates that we might want.

In the event configuration window, we can add any additional fields that we'd like to collect (actions) when the event fires. Since we are not familiar with the applications working on the server, it might be worthwhile to collect `client_app_name` so we can see the various applications that are running queries against the server. Each event is configured separately, so if we want to collect the same actions for all the events, we need to select all the events in the **Selected events** box, as shown in the following screenshot:

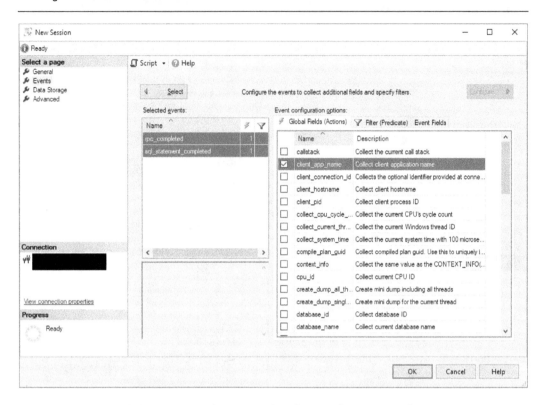

Figure 8.5: SSMS XEvents New Session window showing the Events configuration page

In most cases, the event fields that are part of the event are enough to provide the data needed for analysis. Try to avoid adding a large number of actions if possible. Gathering this data is extra work that must be done for each event whenever it fires, so adding too many actions can cause extra overhead on the server.

Once we have added the desired actions, click the **Filter (Predicate)** tab to add any predicates. This allows us to filter the events that will be passed to the target. While filtering out events can keep the size of our target down, it does not reduce the overhead of the session as each event must be processed to apply the filter. In this case, we're only interested in the queries that are coming from the application, not system sessions. To keep system sessions out of our trace, we can add a filter to both events to capture only events where is_system = 0. Again, the events are configured separately, so we can apply different filters to each event. In this case, we want the same filter for both so we will select both events, as shown in the following screenshot:

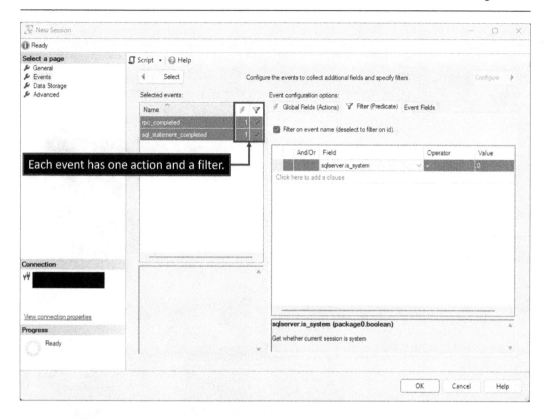

Figure 8.6: SSMS XEvents New Session window showing the Events filter configuration page

As we can see here, we've added our filter to both events. The lightning bolt column indicates actions, and the funnel column indicates filters. Each event has one action configured and a filter applied.

At this point, we could click **OK** and start the session, but then the only way to view the events would be to watch the session live in real time. This wouldn't allow us to do much analysis of the data, so we want to add a target to the session before we create it. We will add a file target so that we can save the event data and then analyze it on another server later. To do this, click the **Data Storage** page in the **Select a page** window, then click **Click here to add a target**, and finally, choose `event_file` from the target **Type** drop-down list. Once we choose `event_file`, several configurable properties appear below the **Targets** window. We can choose the file name and location, maximum size, whether a new file should be created when the file is full (file rollover), and the maximum number of files. In this case, we will keep the default values and the files will be created in the default log directory for SQL Server, for example, `C:\Program Files\Microsoft SQL Server\MSSQL14.SQL2017\MSSQL\Log`. This is shown in the following screenshot:

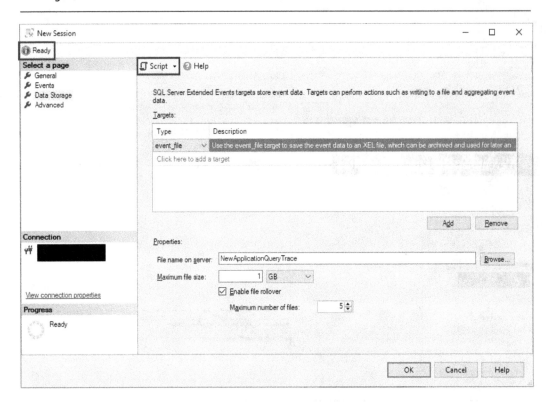

Figure 8.7: SSMS XEvents New Session window showing the Data Storage page

With a maximum file size of 1 GB and a maximum number of 5 files, we will retain up to 5 GB of event data. Once the maximum of five files is reached, if the trace is still running, the oldest trace file will be removed when a new file is created to maintain the maximum of five files.

> **Note**
>
> You can use an event file target in Azure SQL Database by creating a storage container in Azure and creating a database-scoped credential to allow the SQL Database Engine to connect to the storage container. Specific instructions for creating XEvent sessions in Azure SQL Database can be found at `https://aka.ms/AzureSQLDBXEvents`.

As we can see from the previous screenshot, all the required elements have been configured so the session is marked as **Ready** and will be created once we click **OK**. Before we do that, it's worth clicking the **Script** button so we can see what the equivalent T-SQL is to create this session. Using T-SQL to configure a session is another option that allows us to save the definition of the session for use on other servers. The following code block shows the T-SQL script that will create this event session:

```
CREATE EVENT SESSION [NewApplicationQueryTrace] ON SERVER
ADD EVENT sqlserver.rpc_completed(
```

```
    ACTION(sqlserver.client_app_name)
    WHERE ([sqlserver].[is_system]=(0))),
ADD EVENT sqlserver.sql_batch_completed(
    ACTION(sqlserver.client_app_name)
    WHERE ([sqlserver].[is_system]=(0)))
ADD TARGET package0.event_file(SET
filename=N'NewApplicationQueryTrace')
GO
```

At this point, we can either run the script or click **OK** on the **New Session** window to create the session. Since we did not check the **Start the event session immediately after session creation** box when we configured the event session, we'll now need to manually start and stop it once we're ready to test the application. Again, we can do this either via T-SQL or through SSMS. From SSMS, find the session in the **Management | Extended Events | Sessions** folder, right-click, and choose **Start Session**, as shown in the following screenshot:

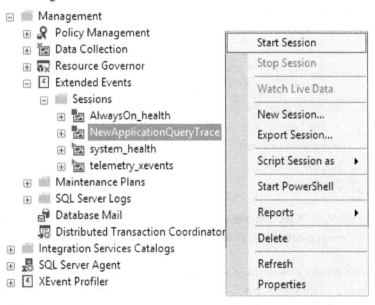

Figure 8.8: SSMS Object Explorer window showing the Extended Events | Sessions context window

The following script will start the session via T-SQL:

```
ALTER EVENT SESSION NewApplicationQueryTrace ON SERVER
STATE = start;
```

Once the session has started, we can instruct the testing team to begin testing the application. Once the team has notified us that they have completed their test, we can stop the session in a similar manner; right-click on the session and click **Stop Session** or run the following T-SQL script:

```
ALTER EVENT SESSION NewApplicationQueryTrace ON SERVER
STATE = stop;
```

At this point, we are ready to do some analysis of the data collected. Expand the **NewApplicationQueryTrace** session and there should be a single target, **package0.event_file**. Right-click on this file and click **View Target Data…**, as shown in the following screenshot:

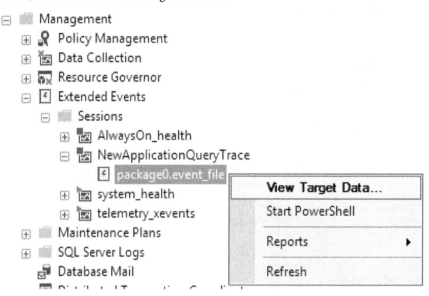

Figure 8.9: SSMS Object Explorer window showing the Extended Events | Sessions
| NewApplicationQueryTrace | package0.event_file context window

This opens the event file as a new tab in SSMS. The tab has a summary view at the top that shows the list of events ordered by their timestamp. Clicking any of the events in the summary view displays the details of that event in the **Details** tab below. By default, only the name (event name) and timestamp columns are displayed in the summary view, but you can right-click on any of the fields in the **Details** tab and click **Show Column in Table** to display the field as a column in the summary view above. This is all shown in the following screenshot:

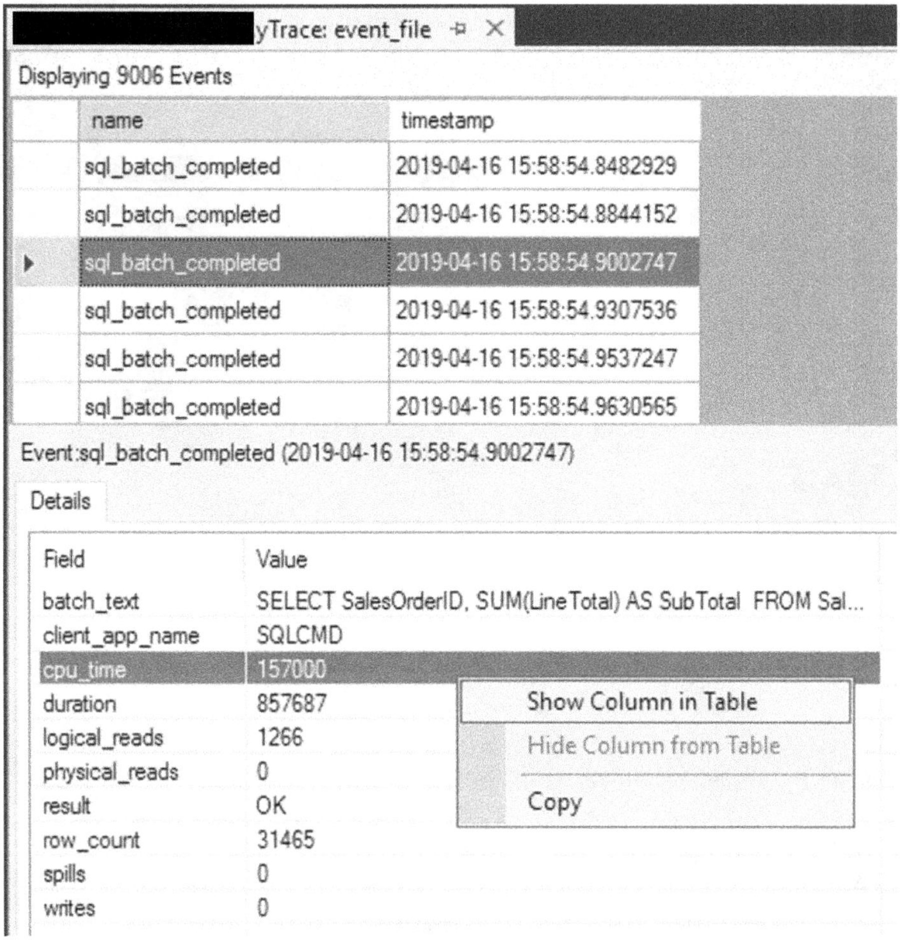

Figure 8.10: SSMS event_file tab showing both summary and Details windows
along with the context menu for the cpu_time event field

Once you have the desired fields displayed, you can use either the **Extended Events** menu or the toolbar to filter, group, aggregate, and search for data within the XEvent results, as shown in the following screenshot:

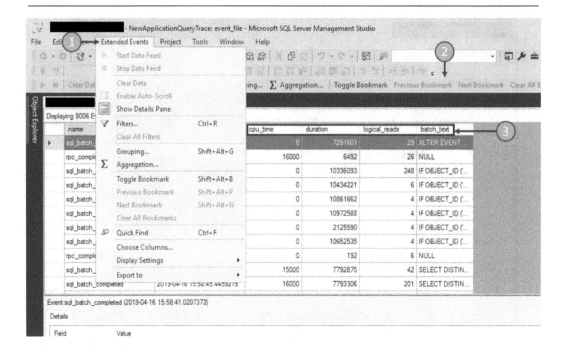

Figure 8.11: Extended Events menu and toolbar in SSMS

In the preceding screenshot, we can see the following:

1. The **Extended Events** menu that appears when an XEvent data viewer tab is opened.

2. The XEvents toolbar that appears when an XEvent data viewer tab is opened.

3. Additional fields that were added from the **Details** tab.

> **Tip**
>
> Depending on the screen resolution and the width of the SSMS window, we may or may not be able to see the entirety of the XEvents toolbar. If only one or two buttons are visible, we can use the mouse to pull the toolbar down to a new line so that the entire bar is visible.

While SSMS has a rich set of features that allows you to analyze XEvents data within the UI, when there are many events or we need to do more extensive analysis on the trace as a whole, it may be easier and more efficient to use another tool to do the analysis for us. In the *Analyzing traces with RML Utilities* section later in this chapter, we will introduce such a tool.

In this section, we have done a very high-level introduction to tracing with XEvents. Many of the scenarios we have described throughout the book can be detected and analyzed by collecting events such as `query_post_execution_showplan` to retrieve an actual execution plan, `statement_recompile` to detect statements that are recompiling frequently, `blocked_process_report` to detect blocking, and many, many more. We will cover a few more events in the remainder of the book, but a great way to get started is to open the **New Session** window in SSMS and begin browsing the available events along with their descriptions, to get an idea of the breadth of information that can be collected using this method.

Getting up and running with XEvent Profiler

Those of us who have been working with SQL Server for some time are likely to have experience with SQL Server Profiler. Profiler is a tool that has been around since the early versions of SQL Server and leverages the SQL Trace infrastructure to provide event-based monitoring of SQL Server. While it has been deprecated since SQL Server 2012, many users still prefer it over XEvents due to its ease of use, familiarity, and the rich set of tools that have been built over the years to capture, analyze, and replay trace data.

While SQL Server Profiler is still available in the product, its use has declined over the years as XEvents gained feature parity. Starting with SQL Server 2012, all the events that can be captured with Profiler can also be captured with XEvents, and with less overhead on the server. In fact, XEvents have a much wider range of events than Profiler and a rich set of actions that can be captured along with the events to provide much more detail than Profiler. Also, XEvents have more flexibility in configuration with the ability to apply filters at the event level, more complex targets, and the ability to support multiple targets in a single session.

Given that XEvents are a more powerful and lighter-weight way to monitor SQL Server, why are users still using SQL Server Profiler? The answer is most often either ease of use or lack of knowledge about XEvents. Since Profiler has been available for much longer, the tools that go along with it have been as well, so users have become familiar with them. The good news is that most of these tools now support XEvents as well, so we can continue to use all the tools we are familiar with, but still leverage the power and performance of XEvents. In the last few sections of this chapter, we will discuss some of the complementary tools that help us work with XEvents to profile our applications and servers.

One of the benefits of SQL Server Profiler was that it was very easy to get a trace going quickly. With all its built-in templates, we can open the tool, click **Start**, and we're up and running. This is very handy if there's an ongoing problem that we need to diagnose quickly.

All the templates that were available in Profiler are available in XEvents, and we can access them from the **New Session** window, as shown in the following screenshot:

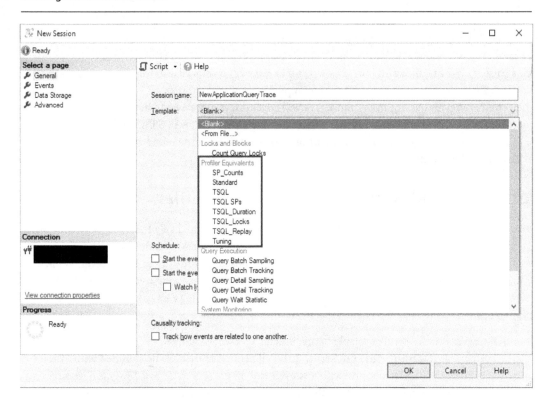

Figure 8.12: SSMS XEvents New Session window showing the Profiler Equivalents templates

The only problem with setting up an XEvent session is that it requires a few more steps than creating a live Profiler trace. Once we add the template, we then need to check the box for **Start the event session immediately after session creation** and **Watch live data on screen as it is captured** or add a target. Once the session is running, only the `name` and `timestamp` fields will be visible in the viewer, so we'll need to select the events and add any additional fields we want to view. This can take quite a bit of time, so if we're trying to catch something quickly, by the time we get this set up, we could miss it.

By leveraging the XEvent Profiler in SSMS, with a few clicks, we can be up and running with a live XEvent trace that gives us a similar experience to SQL Server Profiler. At the bottom of **Object Explorer** in SSMS, we'll see a folder called **XEvent Profiler**. Expanding this folder will show us two options for traces – **Standard** and **TSQL** – which map to the Profiler templates with the same names. Simply right-click the desired template and click **Launch Session**, as shown in the following screenshot:

Figure 8.13: SSMS Object Explorer window with the XEvent Profiler | Standard context menu

This will start up the session using the selected template, open a live data XEvent viewer that contains the same columns we would see in Profiler, and start displaying events, as shown in the following screenshot:

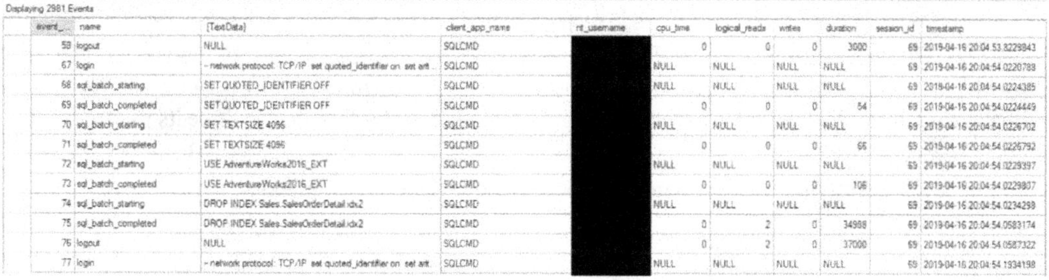

Figure 8.14: Sample results from a Standard XEvent Profiler trace

In short, XEvent Profiler gives us a quick and easy way to see what's happening on a server in real time, with less overhead than SQL Server Profiler.

Remote collection with SQL LogScout

While configuring an XEvent session is simple enough when you have access to the server, if you find yourself in a situation where you need to analyze server or application performance remotely, XEvents can be a challenge. As we discussed in the *Introducing XEvents* section, we can save the XEvent session as a script file and send it to someone to run, but to analyze the data, we'll need a file target, and configuring one requires knowledge of the disk layout of the system. Also, we would need to ensure that the person we send the script to has at least basic SQL Database Engine knowledge such as how to open, edit, and execute a T-SQL script along with the rights to create an XEvent session. If the person who has access to the server is not a database professional, this might be a challenge.

This is the type of troubleshooting that Microsoft Support must do every day. To make the job easier, they created a tool called **SQL LogScout**, which is available to the public on GitHub. If you open a case with Microsoft Support, you may be asked to download and run this tool, but it's also a useful tool to use for your own troubleshooting. You can find everything you need to get started with SQL LogScout at `https://aka.ms/sqllogscout`, but we'll cover some of the basics here.

> **Note**
>
> SQL LogScout is specifically designed to collect data from a server (virtual or physical) hosting one or more SQL Server instances, so this section applies to SQL Server only. You can collect similar data from Azure SQL Database using the built-in diagnostics; learn more at `https://aka.ms/AzureSQLDBMonitorTune`.

SQL LogScout is a configurable tool that can collect various diagnostic information from SQL Server and from the server on which it is running (either Windows or Linux). It can be used to collect things such as **Performance Monitor** (**Perfmon**), DMV output, SQL error logs, Windows event logs, custom T-SQL scripts, and more – including XEvents. The tool is based on PowerShell and can be run from the command line, from PowerShell, or even with a **graphical user interface** (**GUI**). Like its predecessor, **PSSDiag**, everything it collects is written to a folder called `output` in the same directory it runs from. This folder can then be zipped and sent to Microsoft Support for analysis.

> **Tip**
>
> SQL LogScout can be downloaded from `https://aka.ms/get-sqllogscout`, but if you happen to be running SQL Server on an Azure VM using a SQL Server Marketplace image, the tool will already be available on the VM by default in the `C:\SQLServerTools` folder.

The download for SQL LogScout consists of a .zip file that contains a bin folder with all the supporting files and scripts, and the main SQL_LogScout.cmd script file. These files need to be placed on the local machine where SQL Server is running. XEvent traces can become large depending on how busy the server is, so be sure you are running SQL LogScout from a folder that has several gigabytes of space available. It is not a good idea to put the collector on a drive that hosts SQL Server data or transaction log files, as we do not want to generate unnecessary I/O on these drives and potentially cause a performance issue on the server.

The easiest way to run the collector is to open an elevated Command Prompt and run the SQL_LogScout command. There are several parameters that you can use, which are all documented in the Readme.htm file in the bin folder and at https://aka.ms/sqllogscout, but for our purposes, we will use the GUI to view the main options. After running the SQL_LogScout command, you will be asked whether you would like to use GUI mode; type Y to launch GUI mode, as shown in the following screenshot:

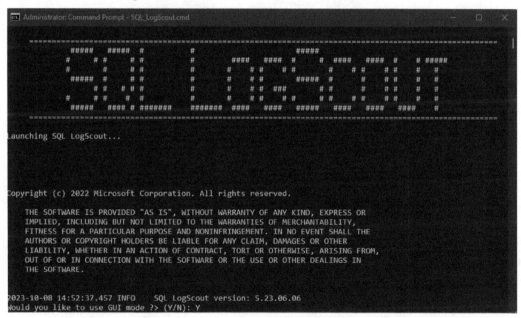

Figure 8.15: Elevated Command Prompt running the SQL LogScout script showing the GUI mode prompt

After hitting *Enter*, the GUI window will open on the screen, as shown here:

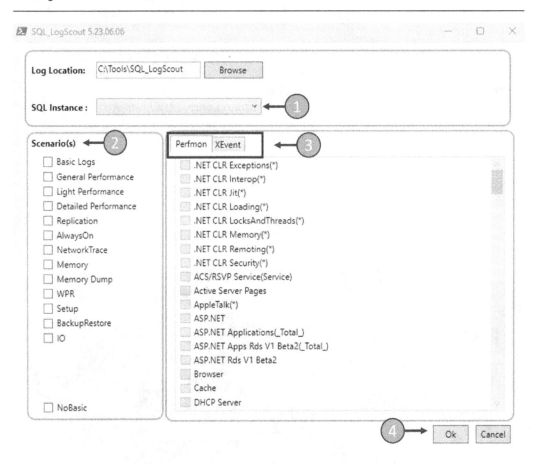

Figure 8.16: The SQL LogScout GUI

Let's examine the various options that can be configured using this tool:

1. The **SQL Instance** dropdown is populated with the SQL Server instances found on the local machine. Choose the instance you wish to monitor here; you can only monitor one instance at a time.

2. The **Scenario(s)** list allows us to choose one or more troubleshooting scenarios that will enable various collectors in the tool. **General Performance** will get what is needed to troubleshoot the most common scenarios. **Light Performance** will configure a very lightweight XEvent trace, like the one we collected in the *Introducing XEvents* section of this chapter. **Detailed Performance** will configure a much heavier trace that includes the query_post_execution_showplan event. This gives us everything we need to troubleshoot a query performance issue, but it can consume a large amount of resources on the server and shouldn't be run for more than a few minutes at a time.

3. On the right side of the window are two tabs that contain configuration options for the **Perfmon** and **XEvent** collectors. The scenario(s) chosen will determine which counters and events are collected, but you can use these tabs to customize the collection according to your needs.

4. Once everything is configured as desired, click the **Ok** button to return control to the command window and begin collection.

After clicking **Ok**, SQL LogScout will begin collecting the requested data and you will see the following output in the command window:

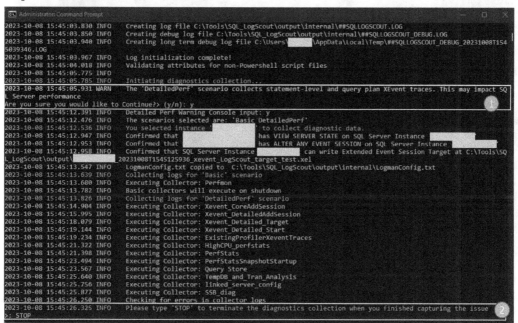

Figure 8.17: Command window showing the output generated by the SQL LogScout tool

A couple of things to note about this window are as follows:

1. If you choose the **Detailed Performance** collector, you will get a warning about the potential performance impact on the server. You must type Y to acknowledge this warning before SQL LogScout will continue collecting.

2. After the green line that states **Please type 'STOP' to terminate the diagnostics collection...** is shown, the collector is gathering data.

Once the issue has been reproduced or the required data is collected, type STOP to stop the collector. When the collector is stopped, some additional data will be gathered, then the script will complete, and the SQL LogScout command window should look like the following screenshot:

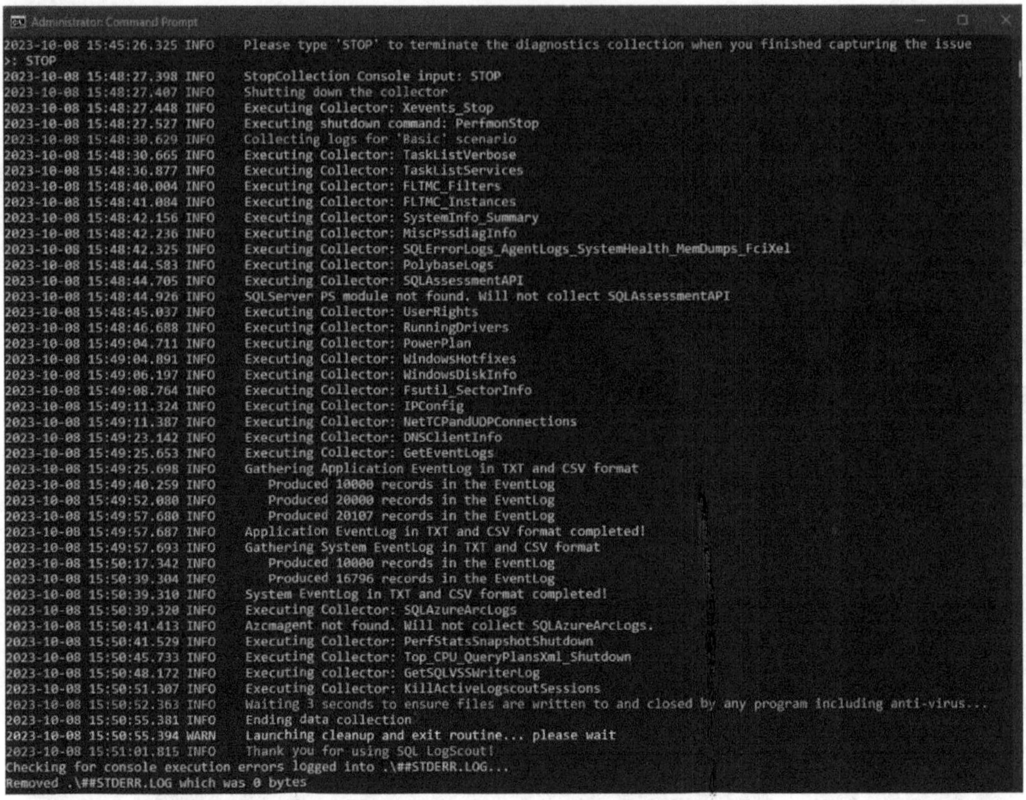

Figure 8.18: Command window showing the output of the SQL LogScout tool after it has been stopped

Once the collector has stopped, you can then go to the location of the collector and find the folder named `output`; zip the folder and move the results to another machine for analysis or to upload to Microsoft Support. We can then manually review the data by opening the XEvent trace files in SSMS and the other various files in a text editor, or we can use a tool such as RML Utilities to automatically analyze the XEvent data and produce a report that we can review instead. In the next section, we will explore RML Utilities and see how we can use it to analyze XEvent trace files quickly and easily.

> **Tip**
>
> A great tool for analyzing SQL LogScout data is SQL Nexus. This is another tool created and maintained by Microsoft Support that can not only run and display results for RML Utilities but also has some great reports for other output files that SQL LogScout generates. You can find SQL Nexus on GitHub at `https://aka.ms/SQLNexus`.

Analyzing traces with RML Utilities

RML Utilities is a suite of tools that can be used to analyze and replay SQL Database Engine workloads. We first introduced the RML Utilities in *Chapter 6, Discovering T-SQL Anti-Patterns in Depth*, in the *Avoiding unnecessary overhead with stored procedures* section where we used the **ostress** tool to simulate a multithreaded workload on the server. The input to **ostress** can be a single query or T-SQL script, but ostress can also take a prepared trace file (either SQL Trace or XEvents) as input. This allows you to capture a workload from a production server, and then replay that workload on a test server so that you can experiment with various settings or performance tuning options – or even test how a new version of the SQL Database Engine would perform with the same workload.

Another tool that is part of RML Utilities is **ReadTrace**. The **ReadTrace** tool is used to analyze and prepare traces for replay via ostress, but it can also be used to do a general analysis of an XEvent trace. Together with its native **Reporter** tool, RML Utilities can be used to extract and aggregate relevant data from the trace, and then present it in a way that allows you to quickly zero in on poor-performing queries, or other potential performance issues on the server and/or with the application.

In this section, we will explore using ReadTrace and Reporter to analyze the XEvent trace we captured via SQL LogScout in the previous section, *Remote collection with SQL LogScout*.

The first thing we need to do to begin the analysis is to run the ReadTrace tool with the XEvents output from our SQL LogScout collection. Once we have downloaded and installed RML Utilities from `https://aka.ms/RMLUtilities`, we find some helpful shortcuts in the **Start** menu, as shown in the following screenshot:

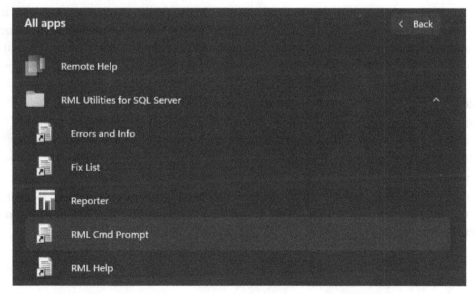

Figure 8.19: Windows Start menu showing the RML Utilities for SQL Server program group

ReadTrace is a command-line tool, but there is a shortcut called **RML Cmd Prompt** that will automatically open a Command Prompt in the correct location. From here, you can run the `ReadTrace /?` command to get some information about the various commands and switches that are available, as well as some examples of how to run the tool. We are doing a basic analysis of XEvent data for the purpose of performance troubleshooting, not to replay the trace, so the following sample command can be used:

```
ReadTrace -S<servername>\<instancename> -E -IC:\PSSDIAG\
output\SERVERNAME_20231008T1545148475_xevent_LogScout_
target_0_133412787193700000.xel -f -dNewApplicationPerf -T28 -T29
```

Let's look at the switches used in the example:

- `-S` is the SQL Server that ReadTrace will connect to for the purposes of loading and aggregating the trace data.

- `-E` indicates we should connect to the server with a trusted connection (Windows authentication).

- `-I<filename>` is the first `.xel` trace file to be imported. If the trace rolled over and multiple files were generated, ReadTrace will automatically read all the `.xel` files in the same sequence.

- `-f` indicates that individual session-level RML files should not be created. These are required for replay, but not for analyzing the trace for performance.

- `-d` is the database name that will be created and will contain the trace analysis data once the process is complete.

- `-T28` and `-T29` are trace flags that disable validation of events collected. As long as we are using SQL LogScout to collect the traces, we should have the events we need for performance analysis, and using these trace flags can help avoid some validation errors that may prevent a successful import of the files.

> **Note**
>
> RML Utilities can be installed on any Windows machine, client, or server, but it needs to connect to either a local or remote SQL Server database to perform and save its analysis. Installing on a production server is not recommended.

Depending on the size of the trace file(s), this may take several minutes to complete. Once it is complete, review the output to look for any errors that may have occurred, then close the **RML Cmd Prompt** window.

If the trace files were successfully processed, the **Reporter** tool will automatically open and display the **Performance Overview** report. If it does not open for some reason, or to view reports for a collection that was done in the past, we can open **Reporter** from the **Start** menu. When it is opened this way, the first screen is a configuration screen where we can enter connection information.

In the **Server Name** and **Baseline Database** fields, we enter the SQL Database Engine instance name and database name where we had directed the ReadTrace output, as shown in the following screenshot:

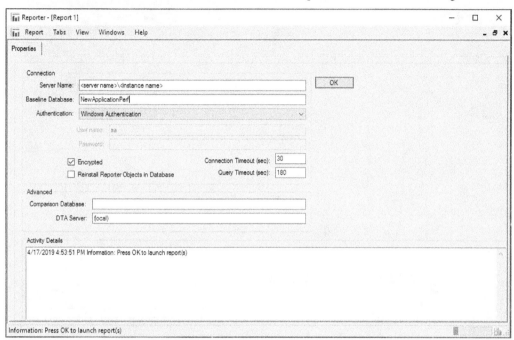

Figure 8.20: RML Utilities Reporter tool window showing the Properties tab

When we click **OK**, the Reporter tool will open the **Performance Overview** report, as shown in the following screenshot:

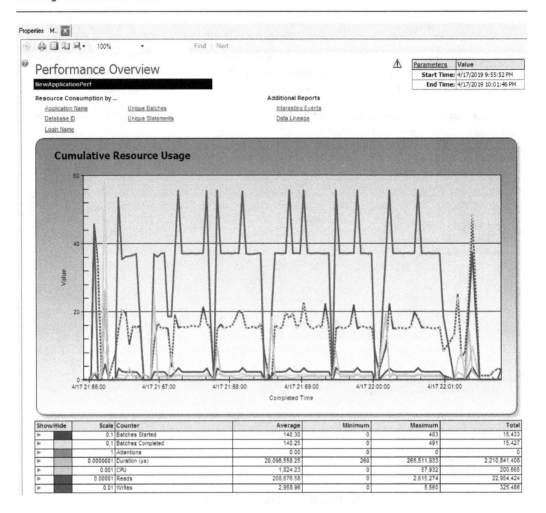

Figure 8.21: RML Utilities Reporter tool window showing the Performance Overview report

This report gives us some overall statistics about the workload, such as the number of batches started and batches completed, along with resource consumption. This information is graphed over time so we can get an idea of the overall workload pattern. At the top, there are several hyperlinks that will open other more detailed reports in new tabs. This allows us to switch between the reports as we analyze the data.

> **Tip**
>
> If the links do not work, you may need to install a hotfix for the Visual Studio Report Viewer, which is one of RML's dependencies. This hotfix can be found at `https://support.microsoft.com/kb/2549864`.

Exploring the various reports will give us a good picture of what was happening on the server while the trace was running. Covering all the reports is out of scope for this book, but one worth mentioning, and perhaps the most useful one, is the **Top Unique Batches** report. This report presents the top unique batches that ran during the trace, along with several metrics for each query. The following screenshot shows an example of this report:

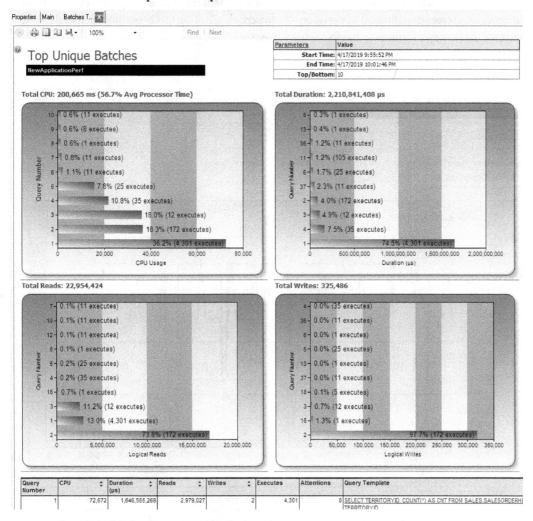

Figure 8.22: RML Utilities Reporter tool window showing the Top Unique Batches report

The graphs at the top of the report show the top queries by each metric: **CPU**, **Duration**, **Reads**, and **Writes**. The list of queries is first sorted by CPU and assigned a number based on their position in the list. Query Number 1 has the highest total CPU, Query Number 2 the next, and so on.

The other three graphs sort the list by their respective metrics using the numbers assigned based on the CPU ranking. As you can see in the previous screenshot, Query Number 1 had the highest total CPU and total duration but did not have the highest reads or writes. Also note that these metrics are a total across all executions of the query. The number of executions is also indicated in the graph.

Each of the queries is listed below the graphs ordered by CPU ranking, and as we can see at the bottom of the previous screenshot, the text of the query is a hyperlink. Clicking this hyperlink opens a detailed report for that query, as shown in the following screenshot:

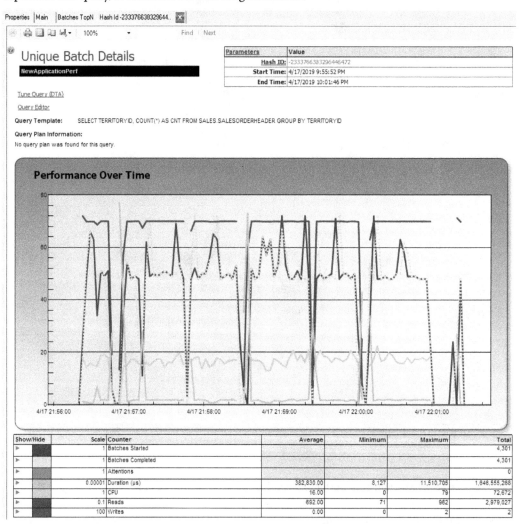

Figure 8.23: RML Utilities Reporter tool window showing the
Unique Batch Details report for the selected query

This report allows us to see more detailed metrics for the query in question, including average, minimum, and maximum numbers for each of the various metrics, as well as the performance of the query graphed over the time of the collection. The **Query Editor** hyperlink at the top of the report allows us to open the query in an SSMS query editor window so we can examine the T-SQL and begin tuning the query using the knowledge we have gained in this book.

> **Tip**
>
> In the GitHub Tiger Toolbox (`http://aka.ms/tigertoolbox`) in the `SQL Nexus and ReadTrace Analysis Scripts` folder, we can find scripts that allow us to extract interesting information from the ReadTrace database that is not available through the default reports.

As we can see, RML Utilities provides us with a few simple tools that make the work of analyzing XEvent traces quick and easy. Together with SQL LogScout, we can easily gather the data we need to diagnose any number of T-SQL performance issues, even without direct access to the server where the queries are running.

Summary

In this chapter, we reviewed the Extended Events engine in the SQL Database Engine and how you can leverage XEvent traces to gather detailed data about query execution and performance. We also discussed the various free tools from Microsoft that can be used to configure, capture, and analyze XEvent traces quickly and easily. Together with DMVs, we now have several tools in our toolbelt that can be used to diagnose and troubleshoot the various issues covered throughout the book.

In the next chapter, we will review yet another tool that is part of SQL Server designed to help diagnose query performance issues – using SSMS for the analysis of query plans.

9

Comparative Analysis of Query Plans

In *Chapter 3, Exploring Query Execution Plans*, we discussed how to access query plans, how to navigate a query plan, and what properties we can look for when analyzing query performance issues. **SQL Server Management Studio** (**SSMS**) has rich UI features to make query plan analysis easier. This chapter will introduce the query plan comparison and query plan analysis functionalities in SSMS to help streamline the process of troubleshooting certain classes of issues with query performance.

In this chapter, we will cover the following topics:

- Query plan comparison
- Query plan analysis

Technical requirements

The examples used in this chapter are designed for use on SQL Server 2022 and Azure SQL Database, but they should work on any version of SQL Server that is 2012 or later. The Developer edition of SQL Server is free for dev environments and can be used to run all the code samples. There is also a free tier of Azure SQL Database you can use for testing at `https://aka.ms/freedb`.

You will need the sample databases `AdventureWorks2016_EXT` (referred to as `AdventureWorks`) and `AdventureWorksDW2016_EXT` (referred to as `AdventureWorksDW`), which can be found on GitHub at `https://github.com/Microsoft/sql-server-samples/releases/tag/adventureworks`. Code samples for this chapter can also be found on GitHub at `https://github.com/PacktPublishing/Learn-T-SQL-Querying-Second-Edition/tree/main/ch9`.

Query plan comparison

Throughout their careers, database professionals are likely to encounter some of the following scenarios:

- Troubleshooting point-in-time performance regressions. In other words, the scenario where a query was meeting performance expectations, but after an incident it started to slow down. Finding the root cause may uncover opportunities to tune queries that prevent regressions from reoccurring.

- Determine what the impact of rewriting a T-SQL query is. For example, when tuning a query, it may be required to rewrite it in part or as a whole. Does it actually perform better?

- Determine the impact of changing or adding a schema object such as an index.

For all these scenarios, typically we must compare query plans to determine what differences may help explain what changed between the plans. For example, what are the differences between plan A – a plan from a query that has regressed in the production system – and plan B – a plan from the same query that was tuned in a **development** (**dev**) machine using a copy of the same database?

In the following example, we captured the plan for a query that was not performing as expected in production – when compared to dev tests. The plan was captured using one of the methods described in the *Exploring query plan cache DMVs* section of *Chapter 7, Building Diagnostic Queries Using DMVs and DMFs*. That query plan was saved as a `.sqlplan` file, and we can open it with SSMS in the dev environment. The following screenshot shows the captured query plan:

```
Query 1: Query cost (relative to the batch): 0%
EXEC usp_GetSalesOrderDetailToDate '2014-3-28 00:00:00'
```

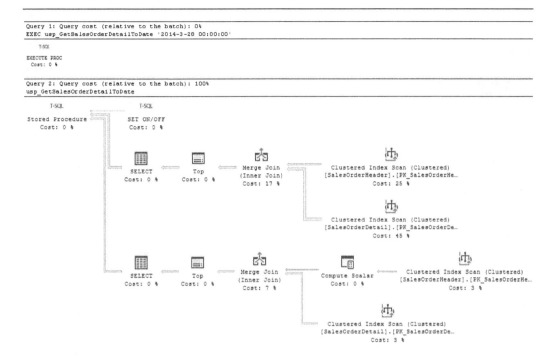

Figure 9.1: Query execution plan as captured from a plan cache DMV

In the following screenshot, we can see more details of the queries inside the stored procedure:

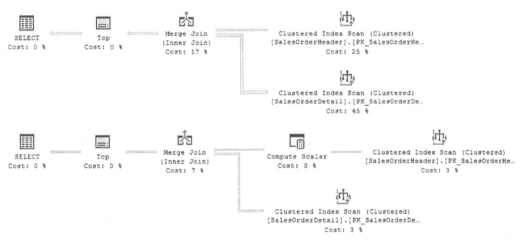

Figure 9.2: Close-up of the query section of the execution plan shown in Figure 9.1

The stored procedure in the preceding query plan is executing in the AdventureWorks sample database, and is created as in the following example:

```
CREATE OR ALTER PROCEDURE usp_GetSalesOrderDetailToDate @FromDate
DATETIME
AS
SET NOCOUNT ON;
SELECT TOP 1500 h.SalesOrderID, h.RevisionNumber, h.OrderDate,
       h.OnlineOrderFlag, h.PurchaseOrderNumber, h.DueDate,
       h.ShipDate, h.Status, h.AccountNumber, h.CustomerID
FROM Sales.SalesOrderHeader AS h
INNER JOIN Sales.SalesOrderDetail AS d ON h.SalesOrderID =
d.SalesOrderID
WHERE h.OrderDate >= @FromDate;
SELECT TOP 100 h.SalesOrderID, h.RevisionNumber, h.OrderDate,
       h.OnlineOrderFlag, h.PurchaseOrderNumber, h.DueDate,
       h.ShipDate, h.Status, h.AccountNumber, h.CustomerID
FROM Sales.SalesOrderHeader AS h
INNER JOIN Sales.SalesOrderDetail AS d ON h.SalesOrderID =
d.SalesOrderID
WHERE h.TotalDue > 1000;
```

Only the first query in the stored procedure depends on parameters. We can see the parameter with which this stored procedure was compiled in the **Parameter List** section of the plan's properties. This provides us with our first hypothesis to test: is this issue related to parameter sniffing? And if so, would updating statistics provide a different plan?

Figure 9.3: Properties window of the example execution plan showing Parameter List

---

Note

We discussed the topic of parameter sniffing in the *The importance of parameters* section in *Chapter 1, Understanding Query Processing*, and *Query plan properties of interest* in *Chapter 3, Exploring Query Execution Plans*.

In a production-like dev machine, we can execute the stored procedure with the compiled value `'2014-3-28 00:00:00'` using the following T-SQL command:

```
EXECUTE usp_GetSalesOrderDetailToDate '2014-3-28 00:00:00'
```

This yields the following query execution plan:

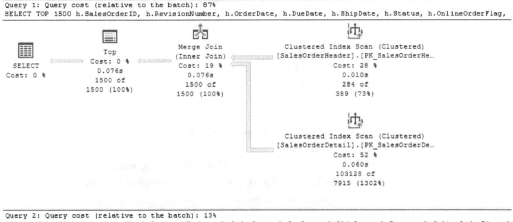

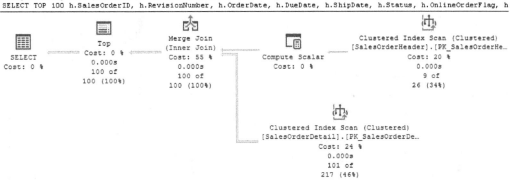

Figure 9.4: Execution plan for the example stored procedure

We want to compare this query execution plan (an actual execution plan) with the query plan from production (an estimated execution plan). We need to determine whether this was a valid execution as it relates to production. Are the plans in both environments being compiled in the same way? The plan shapes are similar, but we need to have more evidence than that.

In the past, we would need two monitors for this comparison, but not in more recent versions of SSMS. To compare the plan we just got with the previously saved `.sqlplan` file, right-click anywhere in the query execution plan, and the following menu pops up:

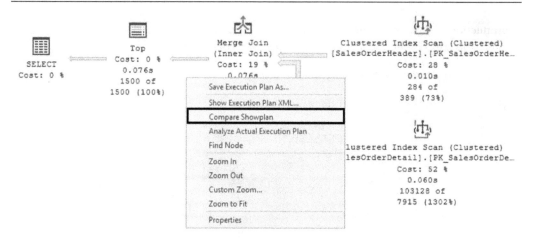

Figure 9.5: Query execution plan with context menu showing the Compare Showplan option

Clicking the **Compare Showplan** menu option opens an **Open file** dialog, where we can search for and open the required `.sqlplan` file. In turn, this opens the new **Showplan Comparison** tab:

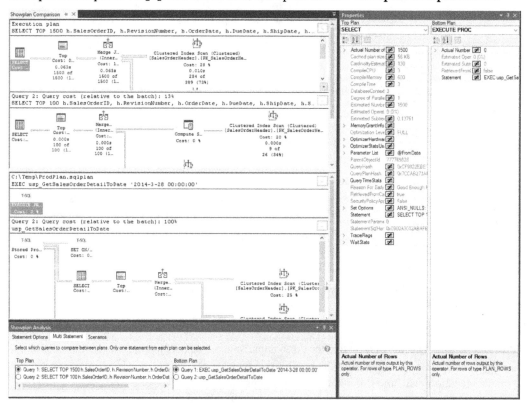

Figure 9.6: SSMS Showplan Comparison tab

> **Tip**
>
> The SSMS query plan comparison feature can open `.sqlplan` files from any version of the SQL Database Engine, starting with SQL Server 2008. Also, this feature can be used completely disconnected from any instance of the SQL Database Engine, when comparing two previously saved `.sqlplan` files.

What are the components of query plan comparison we see on the screen? We will go through each one.

First, there's the split window with the compared plans. At the top, we have the query execution plan (the actual execution plan), identified as **Execution plan**, and at the bottom, we have the `ProdPlan.sqlplan` file that had been previously saved (the estimated execution plan).

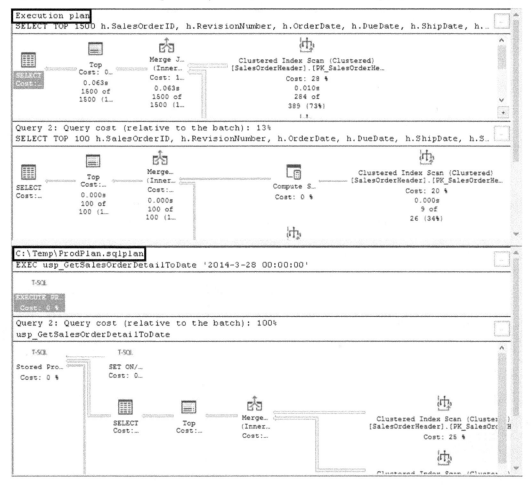

Figure 9.7: Split execution plan window showing the current query
execution plan along with the saved plan from disk

Normally, when two query execution plans are compared, the same region on each plan is highlighted with the same color and outline pattern. When we click on one colored region in any compared plan, the **UI** will center the other plan on the matching region. In this case, we can't see that behavior just yet. We'll see why further ahead.

Also, depending on whether we use a tall/vertical monitor instead of a wide/horizontal monitor, right-clicking any area of a plan shows the following menu, where the split comparison tab can be toggled from the default top/bottom to left/right:

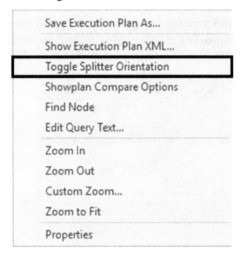

Figure 9.8: Query execution plan context menu showing the Toggle Splitter Orientation option to toggle between top/bottom and left/right comparison windows

Second, the **Showplan Analysis** window will open in the scope of the **Multi Statement** tab. Here, we can select which statement pair to compare. By default, each plan opens in the scope of **Query 1**. The default nomenclature of the plans is **Top Plan** and **Bottom Plan**, signifying their position in the comparison tab. If the comparison window orientation has been toggled from the default, then this will be displayed as **Left Plan** and **Right Plan**.

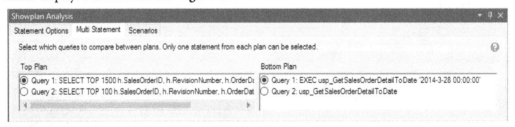

Figure 9.9: Showplan Analysis window showing the Multi Statement tab

The **Statement Options** tab allows us to configure the plan comparison experience, such as whether to ignore the database names when comparing plans, which is useful when comparing plans between a production environment and dev, where the dev database has a different name, for example, if the production database is called `AdventureWorks`, and `AdventureWorksDev` in the dev environment, but the schema of both databases is the same.

Third, the **Properties** comparison window opens in the scope of the root node for the compared statements. The nomenclature of the plans here is also **Top Plan** and **Bottom Plan**, or **Left Plan** and **Right Plan** if the comparison window orientation has been toggled from the default. Each property on either side that is either not matched to a counterpart on the other side, or whose existing counterpart has a different value, will show the mathematical symbol for difference ($\neq$). Only top-level and first-level nested properties are compared. Beyond the first nesting level, properties are not compared and must be manually expanded and compared.

Figure 9.10: Query execution plan properties window showing both
Top Plan and Bottom Plan from the plan comparison

Notice that in the preceding screenshot, hardly any property is actually comparable because the starting point for any plan comparison – the root node of the first query in both plans – is different in both plans. In the top plan, the root node is a SELECT statement, and in the bottom plan, the root node is an EXECUTE PROC statement. Why?

That is because the query plan captured in production is a cached plan from a stored procedure and as such it has extra elements, as compared to the actual execution plan for the stored procedure we got from the dev environment.

Take a look at the following screenshot: the top plan shows the two query statements separately as **Query 1** and **Query 2**, whereas the bottom plan has both query statements consolidated under **Query 2** and the execute command under **Query 1**. The latter is what we see for cached plans from stored procedures or user-defined functions.

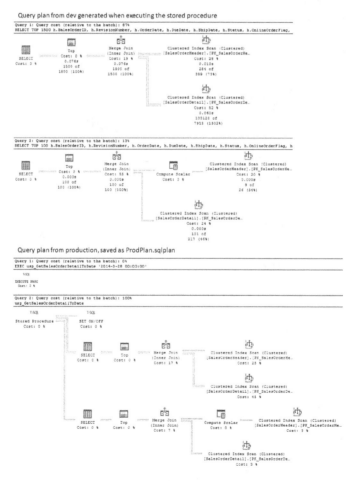

Figure 9.11: Comparison of execution plans when captured from a live exeuction versus being saved from a cached plan DMV

To compare the correct statements – in this case, comparing the estimated plan and the actual plan for a stored procedure – we need to use a multi-step process. First, we need to go back to the **Multi Statement** tab and select **Query 1** from the top plan, and **Query 2** from the bottom plan, as seen in the following screenshot:

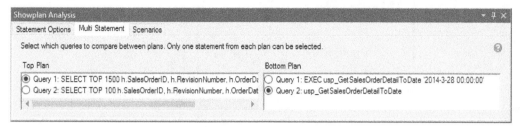

Figure 9.12: Showplan Analysis window showing the Multi Statement
tab with the desired statement comparison chosen

This resets the comparison window to highlight similar areas in both plans, so we can start comparing what has happened in the same context for both plans. Only data processing operators such as seeks, scans, and joins are accounted for when searching for similar regions. Also, the same table must be used in the matching region of the plan.

In the following screenshot, we can see the matched regions between the compared plans. In the top plan, we selected **Query 1** to compare. In the bottom plan, we selected **Query 2**, which actually contains two separate queries, and thus has two matching regions. We know these two regions don't belong to the same query in this example – only one relates to the first query in the stored procedure – but they both have a join with two inputs on the same tables (remember, plan comparison ignores Compute Scalar), making them similar enough to be matched.

Execution plan
SELECT TOP 1500 h.SalesOrderID, h.RevisionNumber, h.OrderDate, h.DueDate, h.ShipDate, h.

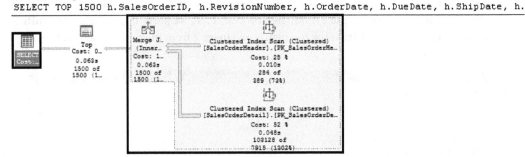

Query 2: Query cost (relative to the batch): 13%
SELECT TOP 100 h.SalesOrderID, h.RevisionNumber, h.OrderDate, h.DueDate, h.ShipDate, h.S

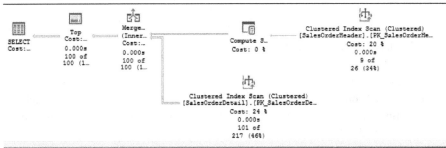

C:\Temp\ProdPlan.sqlplan
EXEC usp_GetSalesOrderDetailToDate '2014-3-28 00:00:00'

T-SQL

Query 2: Query cost (relative to the batch): 100%
usp_GetSalesOrderDetailToDate

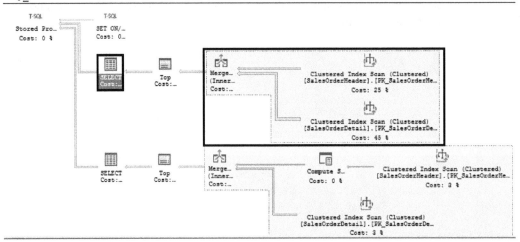

Figure 9.13: Query plan comparison showing highlighting of related regions

If we wanted to compare the second queries in each batch, we would need to return to the **Multi Statement** tab and choose **Query 2** from the top plan and **Query 2** again from the bottom plan.

We'll focus on comparing the highlighted regions of both plans, as shown in the previous screenshot. But before doing that, we want to know whether there are any compilation differences between production and dev that can lead us down the wrong investigation path. To do that, we compare the root nodes (SELECT) on both plans. Click on the root node (SELECT) of the **Top Plan**, and manually click on the corresponding SELECT statement of the **Bottom Plan**, as seen in the previous screenshot.

Looking at the following **Properties** window, we can compare properties that can help answer our question: are we looking at equivalent query plans?

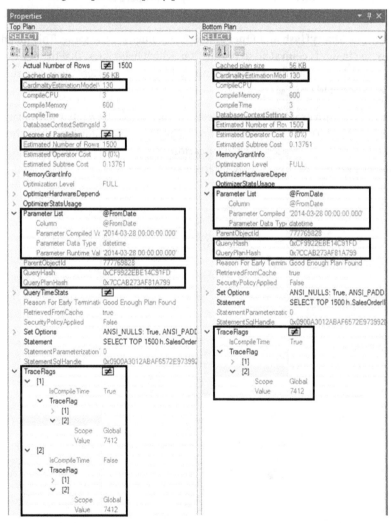

Figure 9.14: Properties window showing relevant regions highlighted for both the top and bottom plans

Both plans have the same **CardinalityEstimationModelVersion** (**130**) and **Estimated Number of Rows**. The **TraceFlags** property is signaled as being different between plans. Expanding them reveals that's not the case, it's just that the top plan is an actual execution plan, and thus it has both **IsCompileTime | True and IsCompileTime | False**, whereas the bottom plan – a cached plan or estimated execution plan – only has **IsCompileTime | True**. But the actual trace flags are the same on both environments (showing only trace flag **7412** in the preceding screenshot) and none impact the Query Optimizer.

> Tip
> Refer to the *Query plan properties of interest* section of *Chapter 3, Exploring Query Execution Plans*, for a run-down of most of the relevant showplan properties.

More importantly, the **QueryHash** and **QueryPlanHash** values are the same. This means that the plan we are analyzing in dev is equivalent to production, which helps attest that the dev environment is good enough to dig deeper into the standing hypothesis: are we experiencing a parameter sniffing issue? And are statistics outdated?

A quick look in the **OptimizerStatsUsage** property in both plans shows that both plans used the same set of statistics objects (only three statistics are expanded in the following screenshot) and that no statistics require updating – notice the **ModificationCount** value is **0** and **SamplingPercent** is **100** – so in principle, we can rule out outdated statistics as a problem.

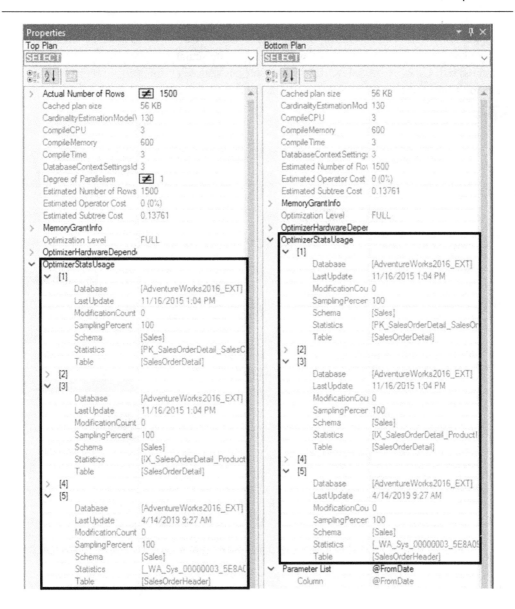

Figure 9.15: Properties window showing the OptimizerStatsUsage
property highlighted in both the top and bottom plans

Now we are confident that whatever investigations and recommendations we do in the dev environment are likely to be applicable to production. Looking back at the actual execution plan, it's evident that the clustered index scan on the **SalesOrderDetail** table has skewed estimations – it returned 103,128 of 7,915 rows, which is over 1,300 percent of what had been estimated.

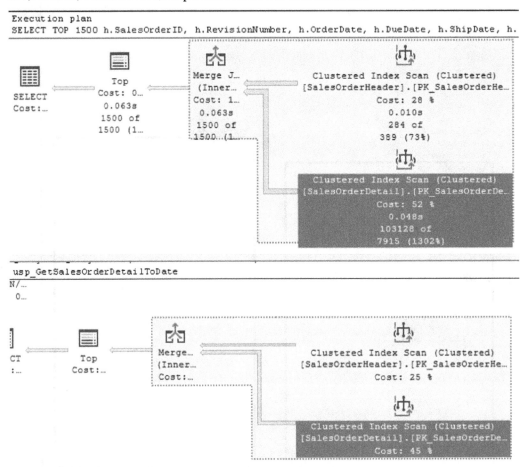

Figure 9.16: Query plan comparison highlighting the SalesOrderDetail clustered index scan operator

This may very well be a parameter sniffing issue. So, next, we clear the plans from the plan cache, and try with different parameters, as seen in the following examples:

```
ALTER DATABASE SCOPED CONFIGURATION CLEAR PROCEDURE_CACHE;
GO
EXEC usp_GetSalesOrderDetailToDate '2014-5-28 00:00:00'
GO
ALTER DATABASE SCOPED CONFIGURATION CLEAR PROCEDURE_CACHE;
```

```
GO
EXEC usp_GetSalesOrderDetailToDate '2013-5-28 00:00:00'
GO
```

These examples yield the following query execution plans, which do not differ from the query plan we saved from the production environment, nor from the query execution plan produced for the first compiled value:

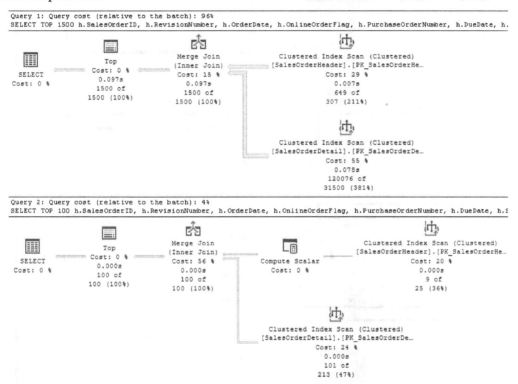

Figure 9.17: Query plan comparison for the example procedure
after recompiling to check for parameter sniffing

It is not parameter sniffing. But the answer lies somewhere in the query plan. Focus on the overly skewed clustered index scan and its properties. As seen in the following screenshot, the bottom plan (production) has a severe skew between the **Estimated Number of Rows** and the **Estimated Number of Rows to be Read** (7,915 of 121,317 rows) values. The top plan (dev) has the same estimation skews, but these are not confirmed by runtime data: comparing **Actual Number of Rows** with **Number of Rows Read** shows these are equal. We have seen this pattern in the *Understanding predicate SARGability* section of *Chapter 4, Indexing for T-SQL Performance*. Could this be a predicate pushdown-related problem? Notice there aren't seek predicate properties in the clustered index scan, so there isn't any predicate involved here.

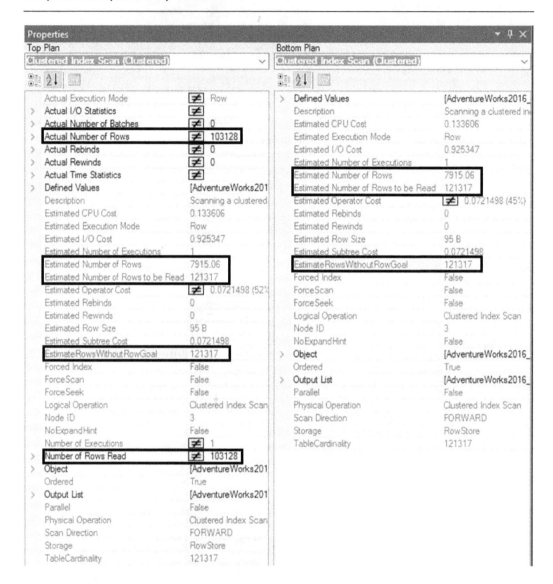

Figure 9.18: Properties window showing various estimated row properties
highlighted, including EstimateRowsWithoutRowGoal

However, notice another property: **EstimateRowsWithoutRowGoal**. We discussed this property in the *Query plan properties of interest* section of *Chapter 3, Exploring Query Execution Plans*.

EstimateRowsWithoutRowGoal shows that if a row goal wasn't used, the Query Optimizer would account for 103,128 rows to be processed rather than just 7,915. That would be much closer to the 121,317 rows that were actually read.

> **Note**
>
> When a query uses a TOP, IN, or EXISTS clause, the FAST query hint, or a SET ROWCOUNT statement, this causes the Query Optimizer to search for a query plan that will quickly return a smaller number of rows – this is called row goal optimization.

When the row goal is very low and a join is required, the Query Optimizer will use nested loop joins because its initial cost (the cost to produce the first row) is relatively low. However, when the row goal is larger, other types of joins might be preferred. For example, a Hash Match join is usually a good choice when the SQL Database Engine needs to join larger inputs. Although it has a higher initial cost because it must build a hash table before any rows can be returned, once the hash table is built, the Hash Match join is generally cheaper. But if the two join inputs are sorted on their join predicate, a Merge join is usually the cheapest.

We can disable the Query Optimizer row goal technique and see whether that has a positive effect. Starting with SQL Server 2016 SP1, this can be done at the query level using the DISABLE_OPTIMIZER_ ROWGOAL use hint, or trace flag 4138 for earlier versions.

> **Tip**
>
> Starting with SQL Server 2022, the **Cardinality Estimation** (CE) Feedback feature will automatically evaluate whether disabling the Query Optimizer row goal technique will have a positive effect on the given query. We touched on the CE Feedback feature in the *Understanding the query optimization workflow* section of *Chapter 2, Mechanics of the Query Optimizer*.

Before we change the stored procedure to add the hint, save the actual execution plan from the stored procedure execution in the dev environment to a .sqlplan file. We will need it to do a final comparison. Then change the stored procedure, as seen in the following example:

```
ALTER PROCEDURE usp_GetSalesOrderDetailToDate @FromDate DATETIME
AS
SET NOCOUNT ON;
SELECT TOP 1500 h.SalesOrderID, h.RevisionNumber, h.OrderDate,
      h.OnlineOrderFlag, h.PurchaseOrderNumber, h.DueDate,
      h.ShipDate, h.Status, h.AccountNumber, h.CustomerID
FROM Sales.SalesOrderHeader AS h
INNER JOIN Sales.SalesOrderDetail AS d ON h.SalesOrderID =
d.SalesOrderID
WHERE h.OrderDate >= @FromDate
OPTION (USE HINT('DISABLE_OPTIMIZER_ROWGOAL'));
SELECT TOP 100 h.SalesOrderID, h.RevisionNumber, h.OrderDate,
      h.OnlineOrderFlag, h.PurchaseOrderNumber, h.DueDate,
      h.ShipDate, h.Status, h.AccountNumber, h.CustomerID
FROM Sales.SalesOrderHeader AS h
```

```
INNER JOIN Sales.SalesOrderDetail AS d ON h.SalesOrderID =
d.SalesOrderID
WHERE h.TotalDue > 1000;
```

Then we execute the stored procedure again as in the following example:

```
ALTER DATABASE SCOPED CONFIGURATION CLEAR PROCEDURE_CACHE;
GO
EXECUTE usp_GetSalesOrderDetailToDate '2014-3-28 00:00:00';
```

We now need to compare the resulting query execution plan with the `DevPlan.sqlplan` file we saved earlier. The Plan Comparison window opens, as seen in the following screenshot, in the scope of **Query 1** and the first occurrence of a similar region or operator.

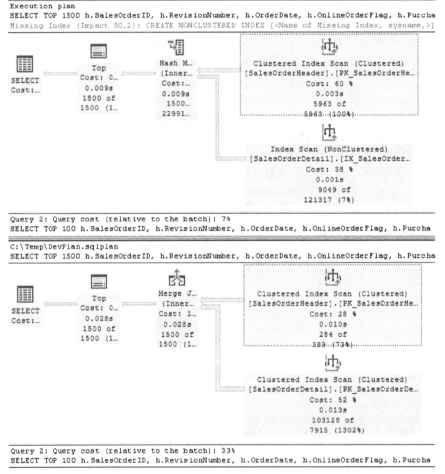

Figure 9.19: Query plan comparison with the new stored procedure
showing both similarities and differences highlighted

Note that for this comparison, we also want to highlight differences, not only the default similar regions or operators. For that purpose, we can go to the **Statement Options** tab in the **Showplan Analysis** window and check the **Highlight operators not matching similar segments** box, after which the operators that don't match between plans are highlighted in yellow.

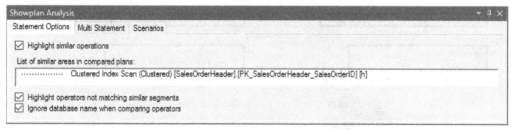

Figure 9.20: Showplan Analysis Statement Options window showing the
Highlight operators not matching similar segments checkbox checked

Back to the previous Plan Comparison window, we see the execution plans for **Query 1** are different. The join type between both tables has changed from a Merge join to a Hash Match join, which executes much faster (9 ms instead of 28 ms). Hash Matches are usually a good choice when the SQL Database Engine needs to join larger inputs, which, now that we have removed the row goal optimization, we can verify here.

The only similar region between plans is the clustered index scan on the SalesOrderHeader table, but where before it was the outer table for a Merge join, it's now the Build table for the Hash Match join. While this operator returns fewer rows in the bottom plan (the original query) than in the top plan (the hinted query), it also takes longer to execute (10 ms instead of 3 ms). This can be explained by looking at the compared properties of both operators in the following screenshot:

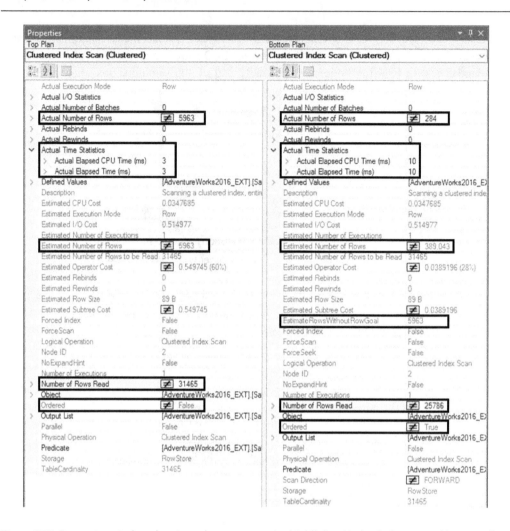

Figure 9.21: Properties window showing relevant properties highlighted in both the top and bottom plans

In the preceding screenshot, we can see the following:

- The **Actual Number of Rows** value after the [h].[OrderDate] >= [@FromDate] predicate is applied changed from 284 in the bottom plan to 5,963 in the top plan

- The **Number of Rows Read** (before the predicate is applied) value changed from 25,786 in the bottom plan to 31,465 in the top plan (this is the full **TableCardinality**)

- Yet we see in **Actual Time Statistics** that the scan is faster in the top plan. Why?

- Both the **Actual Number of Rows** and **Estimated Number of Rows** values in the top plan match the **EstimateRowsWithoutRowGoal** value in the bottom plan. This was expected when we purposefully hinted at the row goal optimization.

  The scan of the bottom plan is slower because it has the **Ordered** property set to `True`, which indicates that the scan needs to enforce an explicit order to guarantee that the Merge join has the required sorted input. At the Storage Engine level, this means enforcing that all rows are read in their logical order, following a linked list of index leaf level pages ordered by index key order – rather than their physical order, the page allocation order.

  The scan of the top plan has the **Ordered** property set to `False`, which indicates the rows are read by following the index leaf level pages physical order. This explains that while the scan in the top plan reads more rows than the bottom plan, it is faster by reading all pages in order of physical allocation.

And what about the other index that is now identified as a difference? The clustered index scan on the `SalesOrderDetail` table was replaced by a non-clustered index scan. In the following plan comparison screenshot, we can see the following:

- While the bottom plan (the original query) has a big underestimation of the actual number of rows (103,128 compared to 7,915 estimated rows), the top plan (the hinted query) has an overestimation (9,049 actual rows compared to121,317 estimated rows)

- However, the scan in the top plan executed in 1 ms, whereas the scan in the bottom plan executed in 13 ms

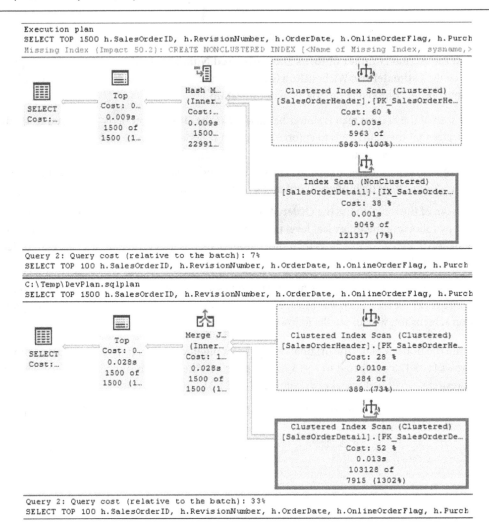

Figure 9.22: Query plan comparison with the new stored procedure showing the non-clustered index scan in the top plan versus the clustered index scan in the bottom plan

But even if the SQL Database Engine had to scan the entire non-clustered index as it did with the clustered index in the previous plan, it would still be faster with the new plan. Why? We can see information about the indexes in `SalesOrderDetail` using the following T-SQL query example:

```
SELECT t.name AS TableName, i.name AS IndexName,
      i.type_desc, p.rows, a.total_pages, a.used_pages,
      CONVERT(DECIMAL(19,2),ISNULL(a.used_pages,0))*8/1024 AS
DataSizeMB,
      ips.index_depth, ips.avg_record_size_in_bytes
FROM sys.allocation_units AS a
```

```
INNER JOIN sys.partitions AS p ON p.hobt_id = a.container_id AND
a.type = 1
INNER JOIN sys.indexes AS i ON i.object_id = p.object_id
    AND i.index_id = p.index_id
INNER JOIN sys.tables AS t ON t.object_id = p.object_id
CROSS APPLY sys.dm_db_index_physical_stats (DB_ID(), p.object_id,
i.index_id, NULL, 'SAMPLED') AS ips
WHERE t.name = 'SalesOrderDetail';
```

The following screenshot shows the resultset for the query example:

	TableName	IndexName	type_desc	rows	total_pages	used_pages	DataSizeMB	index_depth	avg_record_size_in_bytes
1	SalesOrderDetail	PK_SalesOrderDetail_SalesOrderID...	CLUSTERED	121317	1505	1290	10.0781250	3	80.06
2	SalesOrderDetail	AK_SalesOrderDetail_rowguid	NONCLUSTERED	121317	657	495	3.8671875	3	28
3	SalesOrderDetail	IX_SalesOrderDetail_ProductID	NONCLUSTERED	121317	424	308	2.4062500	2	16

Figure 9.23: Results of the example metadata query showing the indexes of the SalesOrderDetail table

When compared to the clustered index, we can see that even if the SQL Database Engine had to scan the full non-unique, non-clustered index IX_SalesOrderDetail_ProductID, that would amount to 2.4 MB of I/O instead of 10 MB for a full scan of the clustered index, which would be consistently better. The size difference is explained by the average record size for the non-clustered index being 16 bytes versus 80 bytes for the clustered index. Now that we've learned how to use the plan comparison tool in SSMS to help troubleshoot query performance by comparing two plans with each other, let's look at another helpful tool that can guide our query performance troubleshooting – the query plan analyzer.

Query plan analyzer

So far, we have had to analyze query plans by correlating information in plan and operator properties to create working hypotheses on how to solve query performance issues. One constant throughout all these troubleshooting scenarios has to do with comparing estimated rows with actual rows flowing through the operators in a query plan. This is because significant differences between estimated and actual rows usually expose cardinality estimation issues, which speak to several possible causes, from outdated statistics to parameter sniffing or even out-of-model constructs such as **User-Defined Functions (UDFs)** or **Multi-Statement Table-Valued Functions (MSTVFs)**.

Depending on the query performance problem, it may not be easy to even start troubleshooting, especially in complex plans. This is exactly why SSMS has a plan analysis tool, and this can jump-start our query performance troubleshooting efforts.

In the following example, we will examine a query that was not performing as expected in production. Specifically, one stored procedure that's executed many times a minute was thought to be abnormally slow, because the application that used it was not responding properly.

First, we tried running the stored procedure in the dev environment using sample data and couldn't find any major issues with the resulting query plan, nor its performance. This must mean that whatever is happening can only be found in production. What is needed to proceed with troubleshooting is an actual execution plan, and so we used **Extended Events** (**XEvents**) to capture the query execution plan for the offending stored procedure using the `query_post_execution_showplan` XEvent – not an easy proposition given collecting this XEvent itself generates overhead. We will discuss several other ways of collecting the actual execution plan in a much more lightweight fashion in *Chapter 11, Troubleshooting Live Queries*.

The captured query execution plan is the following:

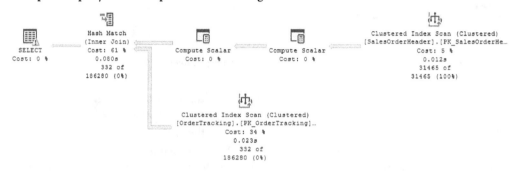

Figure 9.24: Query execution plan of the problem stored procedure

The stored procedure in the preceding query execution plan is in the `AdventureWorks` sample database, and is created as follows:

```
CREATE OR ALTER PROCEDURE usp_SalesTracking @UpdatedOn datetime
AS
SET NOCOUNT ON;
SELECT *
FROM Sales.SalesOrderHeader AS soh
INNER JOIN Sales.OrderTracking AS ot ON ot.SalesOrderID = soh.
SalesOrderID
WHERE ot.EventDateTime >= @UpdatedOn;
GO
```

With the plan open, right-click anywhere in the query execution plan, and the following menu pops up:

Figure 9.25: Query execution plan context menu showing the Analyze Actual Execution Plan menu option

Clicking the **Analyze Actual Execution Plan** menu option opens a new window docked on the bottom – **Showplan Analysis**:

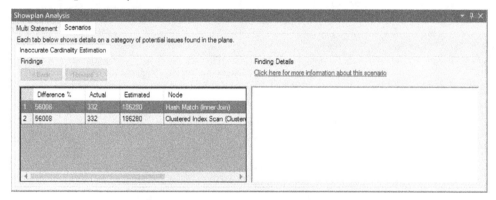

Figure 9.26: Scenarios tab of the Showplan Analysis window

Inside the window, there is a **Scenarios** tab – a placeholder for future scenarios if there's user demand for them – on which we find the **Inaccurate Cardinality Estimation** tab.

> **Note**
>
> At the time of this revision, Microsoft is no longer investing in this feature in favor of the new CE Feedback feature introduced in SQL Server 2022. We touched on CE Feedback in the *Understanding the query optimization workflow* section of *Chapter 2, Mechanics of the Query Optimizer*. You can read more about CE Feedback at https://aka.ms/CEFeedback.

If we click on the link to the right under **Finding Details**, we get a popup that explains what this scenario is all about:

"One of the most important inputs for the Query Optimizer to choose an optimal execution plan is the estimated number of rows to be retrieved per operator. These estimations model the amount of data to

be processed by the query, and therefore drive cost estimation. Changes in the estimated number of rows is one of the most frequent reasons for the Query Optimizer to pick different query plans.

This scenario helps you to find differences in estimated number of rows between two execution plans, scoped to the operators that perform similar data processing, and suggests possible causes for those differences, as well as possible workarounds to improve the estimates. Note that this automation may not identify all operators, their differences, or all possible root causes. So while the information displayed here is a tentative mitigation opportunity to resolve an issue identified by this scenario, it should still help in analyzing root causes of plan difference."

As it suggests, it will try to find hotspots in the query execution plan that have to do with patterns of inaccurate cardinality estimation and two such findings are already on the left side of the window. As shown in the following screenshot, selecting any of the findings will center the plan on the offending operator – in this case, the clustered index scan:

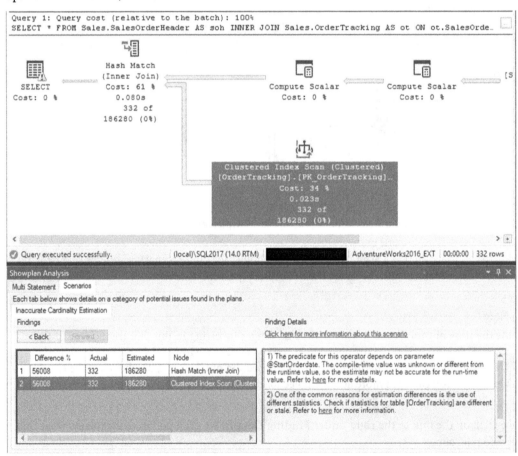

Figure 9.27: Scenarios tab of the Showplan Analysis window showing one of the findings highlighted in both the analysis window and the corresponding query plan

We should always start by analyzing findings that are related to data reading operators such as seeks and scans, and then move up the query plan tree to aggregates and joins. The clustered index scan in the plan has a 56,000 percent difference between the actual and estimated row numbers (332 compared to 186,280). Notice the **Finding Details** section to the right. Two possible reasons for the misestimation are as follows:

- The plan analyzer found a predicate in this scan that depends on a parameter whose runtime value is different from the compile-time value, or that the compile-time value is NULL. This constitutes a case of bad parameter sniffing.

- Clicking the link at the end of the finding (the word **here**) opens a pop-up window with detailed background information about bad parameter sniffing and how to mitigate it.

Because it's common to have misestimations based on wrong or outdated statistics, the query plan analyzer suggests we need to look at whatever statistics are loaded for this plan and verify whether they need to be updated. Again, clicking the link at the end of the finding (the word **here**) opens a pop-up window with background information.

We can start with suggestion 2 because it's very easy to determine using an actual execution plan. On the plan root node (SELECT), open the properties window to analyze the **OptimizerStatsUsage** property. As seen in the following screenshot, no statistics require updating – notice the **ModificationCount** value is **0**; however, several statistics related to the OrderTracking table have only 30 percent sampling. This may be an issue – if it's possible to update statistics with a higher sampling ratio, especially for tables whose data distribution is not uniform, that is always a good choice.

Figure 9.28: Properties window of the query plan showing the OptimizerStatsUsage property

If updating statistics with a larger sample is not doable for now (maybe the tables have millions of rows and updating with a larger sample could cause problems), we can move on to suggestion 1, where it points to bad parameter sniffing.

> **Note**
>
> We discussed the topic of parameter sniffing in the *The importance of parameters* section in *Chapter 1, Understanding Query Processing*, and *Query plan properties of interest* in *Chapter 3, Exploring Query Execution Plans*.

This is also easy enough to investigate: open the properties window to analyze the **Parameter List** property. As seen in the following screenshot, the parameter with which the stored procedure was compiled and optimized is not the same as the parameter runtime value.

Parameter List	@UpdatedOn
Column	@UpdatedOn
Parameter Compiled Value	'2011-07-31 00:00:00.000
Parameter Data Type	datetime
Parameter Runtime Value	'2014-06-30 00:00:00.000

Figure 9.29: Properties window of the query plan showing the Parameter List property

This means that at its first execution, the plan was optimized for the '2011-07-31 00:00:00.000' data value and that the plan was cached for subsequent use.

> **Note**
>
> Before moving on, we save the current plan to a .sqlplan file because we may need it later to compare with other plans.

Executing the stored procedure with the compiled value yields the following query execution plan:

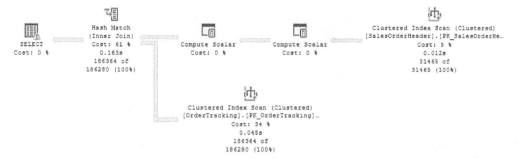

Figure 9.30: Query plan for the stored procedure when executed with the compiled value of the parameter

A quick analysis shows that all operators have perfect estimations – the actual rows are the same as the estimated rows. This confirms that the currently cached plan is optimized for the first incoming parameter, which is an older date. But if the parameter used in the first compilation wasn't the most used, but instead more recent dates are often used as parameters, the reasonable hypothesis is that compiling the stored procedure and executing it for the first time using a common parameter will yield a different plan.

We can test this using the following example, which creates a new test stored procedure that is not called by the application:

```
CREATE OR ALTER PROCEDURE usp_SalesTracking_Test @UpdatedOn datetime
AS
SET NOCOUNT ON;
SELECT *
FROM Sales.SalesOrderHeader AS soh
INNER JOIN Sales.OrderTracking AS ot ON ot.SalesOrderID = soh.
SalesOrderID
WHERE ot.EventDateTime >= @UpdatedOn;
GO
EXECUTE usp_SalesTracking_Test '2014-6-30 00:00:00'
GO
```

Executing the new stored procedure with the common value yields the following query execution plan:

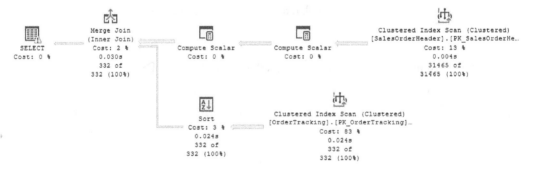

Figure 9.31: Query plan for the test stored procedure executed with the more common parameter value

This is a very different plan that also executed faster. We can use the plan comparison feature we discussed in the previous section to quickly find the main differences between the plan we just got and the previously saved `ParamSniffingInvestigation.sqlplan` file. The comparison window looks like the following:

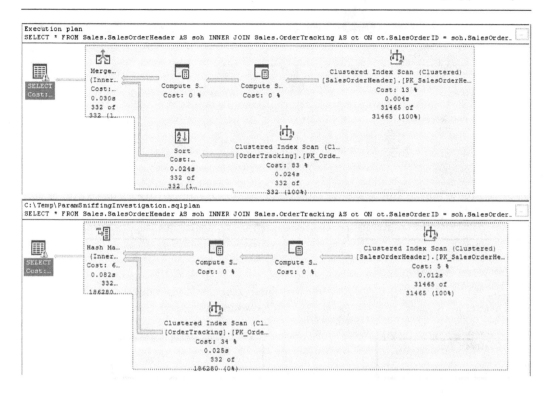

```
Execution plan
SELECT * FROM Sales.SalesOrderHeader AS soh INNER JOIN Sales.OrderTracking AS ot ON ot.SalesOrderID = soh.SalesOrder...
```

```
C:\Temp\ParamSniffingInvestigation.sqlplan
SELECT * FROM Sales.SalesOrderHeader AS soh INNER JOIN Sales.OrderTracking AS ot ON ot.SalesOrderID = soh.SalesOrder...
```

Figure 9.32: Query plan comparison between the original plan and the new test stored procedure plan

The plans are similar, with a couple of interesting observations to be made:

- The clustered index scan on the OrderTracking table has accurate estimations that match the common case of returning fewer records – the estimated rows match the actual rows returned

- The previous Hash Match join (the bottom plan compiled with a parameter value of '2011-7-31 00:00:00') turned to a Merge join (the top plan compiled with a parameter value of '2014-6-30 00:00:00'), due to the corrected estimations

Opening the properties of the root nodes (SELECT) shows additional relevant information that speaks to the need to optimize for the common case, as seen in the following screenshot:

- The **QueryTimeStats** value for each query shows that optimizing for the common value (the top plan) executes faster than reusing the plan from production (the bottom plan), compiled with an older date: 32 ms instead of 81 ms.

- The **Memory Grant** value is also much lower in the top plan (1.9 MB) than in the bottom plan (76 MB). Expanding the **MemoryGrantInfo** section would reveal that of the 76 MB, the bottom plan only used 7 MB.

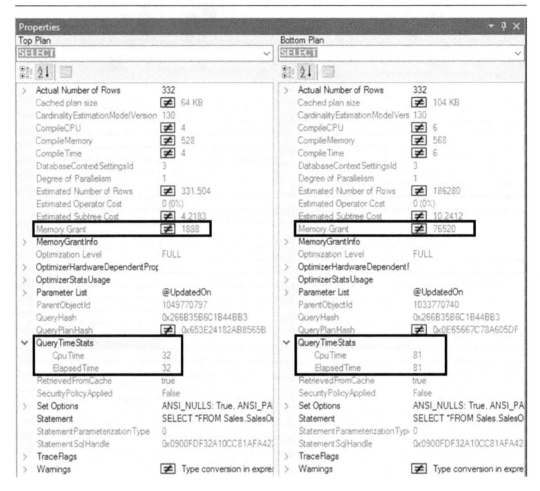

Figure 9.33: Properties window for the query plan comparison between
the original plan and the test stored procedure plan

We discussed the effects on concurrency of having memory grant misestimations in the *Query plan properties of interest* section of *Chapter 3, Exploring Query Execution Plans*, and how to mine the plan cache for other such concurrency inhibitors in the *Troubleshooting common scenarios with DMV queries* section of *Chapter 7, Building Diagnostic Queries Using DMVs and DMFs*.

Having proven that this is a case of bad parameter sniffing, a few options are available to remediate the issue in production:

- Rewrite the stored procedure to add the OPTION (RECOMPILE) hint. With this hint, a plan is calculated every time the stored procedure is executed and optimized for the current incoming parameter value.

- Rewrite the stored procedure to add the OPTION (OPTIMIZE FOR (@UpdatedOn = '2014-6-30 00:00:00')) hint. With this hint, even after recompiling, the stored procedure will be optimized for the common value – a recent date that we chose.

- Rewrite the stored procedure to add the OPTION (OPTIMIZE FOR UNKNOWN) hint. This will create a generic plan that may not be necessarily optimized for any incoming parameter.

> **Tip**
> This currently has the same effect as rewriting the stored procedure to assign the parameter value to a local variable and using that within the query rather than the parameter directly. However, this is simply a side effect of the way local variables affect the optimization process, and not explicitly directing the Query Optimizer to turn off parameter sniffing.

- If most queries in a database had a bad parameter sniffing issue, then disabling parameter sniffing may be a mitigation when hinting all the code is not feasible. To do this at the database level, use the database-scoped PARAMETER_SNIFFING configuration in the following T-SQL command:

```
ALTER DATABASE SCOPED CONFIGURATION SET PARAMETER_SNIFFING =
OFF;
```

To do this at the system level, use the DBCC TRACEON (4136, -1) T-SQL command to enable trace flag 4136 globally. Note that enabling a global trace flag requires sysadmin privileges and can't be used on Azure.

Summary

In the *Query plan comparison* section, we were able to take a query plan from the production environment that was not performing as expected and validate that when running the same query in the dev environment with a production-like database we were able to get a consistent reproduction of the issue. Then, through comparative analysis of the cached query plan from production (an estimated execution plan) and the actual execution plan from dev, we could create hypotheses from the data we observed until we found the root cause. Last, we tested a fix for the root cause of the issue by hinting at queries, which again, by comparing plans, determined that the new plan was better than the old plan, which should now be implemented in production.

In the *Query plan analyzer* section, we were able to take a query plan that had been captured in the production environment through an XEvent trace and get started on finding what could be negatively affecting performance by using this new feature. This allowed us to find significant differences between estimated and actual rows in the affected query execution plan and directed us to investigate a bad parameter sniffing problem, which turned out to be confirmed. After that, we were given several strategies to deal with the problem to bring back to production and definitively mitigate the issue.

In the next chapter, we will look at a tool called the Query Store that can help capture query plans and identify query performance regressions.

10

Tracking Performance History with Query Store

This chapter will introduce the Query Store, which is effectively a flight recorder for the SQL Database Engine T-SQL executions, allowing performance tracking over time and analysis of workload trends through rich-UI reports that are included with **SQL Server Management Studio** (**SSMS**).

We will also see how Query Store integrates with Query Plan Comparison, which was covered in *Chapter 9, Comparative Analysis of Query Plans*, for a complete **user interface** (**UI**)-driven workflow for query performance insights. This chapter covers the following topics:

- Introducing the Query Store
- Tracking expensive queries
- Fixing regressed queries
- Features that rely on the Query Store

Technical requirements

The examples used in this chapter are designed for use on SQL Server 2022 and Azure SQL Database, but they should work on any version of SQL Server 2012 or later. The Developer Edition of SQL Server is free for development environments and can be used to run all the code samples. There is also a free tier of Azure SQL Database that you can use for testing at `https://aka.ms/freedb`.

You will need the `AdventureWorks2016_EXT` (referred to as `AdventureWorks`) and `AdventureWorksDW2016_EXT` (referred to as `AdventureWorksDW`) sample databases, which can be found on GitHub at `https://github.com/Microsoft/sql-server-samples/releases/tag/adventureworks`. Code samples for this chapter can also be found on GitHub at `https://github.com/PacktPublishing/Learn-T-SQL-Querying-Second-Edition/tree/main/ch10`.

Introducing the Query Store

The requirement to track query performance statistics over time has been a longtime request by SQL Database Engine users because it unlocks the ability to go back in time and understand trends and point-in-time occurrences. Maybe a point-in-time issue with the database caused our company website to glitch, or a critical application slows down periodically without a predictable pattern, or we noticed that part of our workload is much slower after an upgrade to a new version of the SQL Database Engine. Barring any hardware problems, all these scenarios can usually be boiled down to one common cause – *query plan optimization choices*. This led to the creation of the **Query Store** – an effective flight recorder for our databases that's available in SQL Server (starting with SQL Server 2016) and Azure SQL Database, including Managed Instance.

Recall what we discussed on the process of query optimization in *Chapter 1, Understanding Query Processing*, and specifically the role of cardinality estimation discussed in *Chapter 2, Mechanics of the Query Optimizer*: the SQL Database Engine can consider many plans during the query optimization process and so, when a problem happens, being able to backtrack historical information to understand whether there were changes to the query plans of slow queries is fundamental.

We have seen queries that allow us to mine the plan cache to get all types of important information in the *Exploring query plan cache DMVs* section of *Chapter 7, Building Diagnostic Queries Using DMVs and DMFs*, but those alone are not enough to help answer three pressing questions during a performance troubleshooting exercise:

- Which query or set of queries slowed down from a previous moment in time?

- What was the previous query plan that worked better than the current plan in the cache?

- Is there a way I can force the plan to look more like the "good" plan? Can I use a plan guide, for example? We will see how a plan guide can be used in *Chapter 11, Troubleshooting Live Queries*, in the *Activity Monitor gets new life* section.

To answer these questions, the Query Store captures query plans and runtime execution statistics in the user database. Storing information on disk means that, unlike most DMVs, its information is available after a restart, database upgrade, and query plan recompilations. With all of this, Query Store makes it easier to find performance regressions and mitigate them literally with one click of a button – we'll show this later in this chapter in the *Fixing regressed queries* section – which is a process that can take hours or days with other means, such as collecting traces and analyzing them manually. Query Store also unlocks the ability to identify top resource-consuming queries and analyze performance trends across workloads, putting database professionals in the driving seat when it comes to learning about recurring patterns and finding tuning opportunities to optimize our T-SQL queries.

Inner workings of the Query Store

When a query is compiled, its query text and plan (the same plan that gets stored in the plan cache) are captured in Query Store's memory structures to minimize I/O overhead. When the query's first execution completes (and any subsequent execution), runtime execution statistics are also stored in memory. In the background, an asynchronous process runs to bucketize the information in time interval aggregates and stores all this data in internal tables that reside in the user database. Both the aggregation time intervals and storage for on-disk tables are configurable, and we will cover them in the next section of this chapter.

Storing internal tables in the user database means that the QS is a single-database performance tracking system that stays with database backups and database clones. This is a powerful capability because we can get a database backup that includes its Query Store from one system and analyze the performance data in another system.

> **Note**
>
> Database clones refer to schema-only databases created with the DBCC CLONEDATABASE command. This operation creates a database with empty tables and indexes but maintains all programmability objects such as stored procedures and functions, as well as statistics objects and the Query Store. This becomes a powerful tool during cases of remote assistance for query optimization-related issues.

On top of Query Store's memory and disk tables, there are system views to access all the information that is stored on both dimensions of data that's collected: query compilation and query execution time information. The QS system views exist in Azure SQL Database and SQL Server.

The SQL Server 2022 QS system views can be seen in the following screenshot, which we will use throughout this chapter:

Figure 10.1: SSMS IntelliSense window showing some of the SQL Server 2022 QS system views

In turn, SSMS has a rich UI experience on Query Store that's built on top of the system views. The available SSMS Query Store reports can be accessed under each database in the Query Store folder, as seen in the following screenshot:

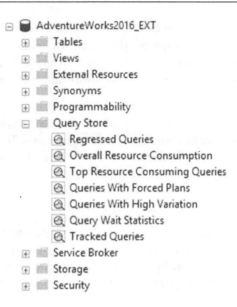

Figure 10.2: SSMS Object Explorer showing the built-in Query Store reports

The following diagram outlines the Query Store architecture discussed in this section:

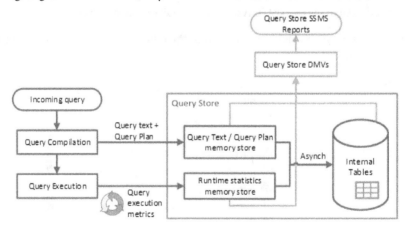

Figure 10.3: Diagram depicting the Query Store architecture

Configuring the Query Store

Azure SQL Database has the Query Store enabled by default. In SQL Server 2022, the Query Store is enabled by default for new databases, but any databases that were migrated from older systems will maintain the Query Store state from the version from which they migrated. In SQL Server 2016, 2017, and 2019, it must be enabled manually. This can be done in two different ways:

- Using T-SQL, as seen in the following example for the `AdventureWorks2016` sample database:

```
USE [master]
GO
ALTER DATABASE [AdventureWorks2016]
SET QUERY_STORE = ON;
GO
ALTER DATABASE [AdventureWorks2016]
SET QUERY_STORE (OPERATION_MODE = READ_WRITE);
```

- Using SSMS, when we right-click on a database name in **Object Explorer**, select **Properties**, select the **Query Store** page, and change **Operation Mode** from **Off** to **Read Write**, as seen in the following screenshot:

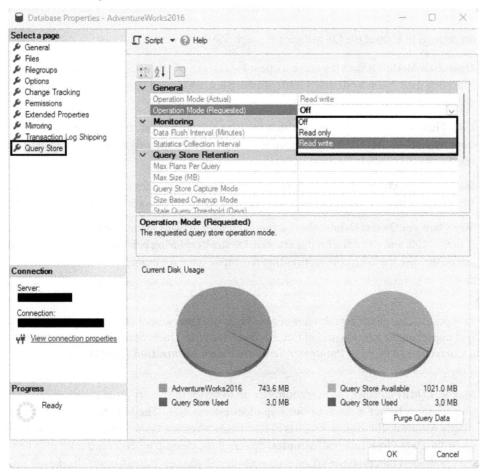

Figure 10.4: SSMS Database Properties window showing the Query Store properties

In the previous screenshot, we can see the full size of the database (**743.6 MB**) and how much of that size is used by Query Store (**3.0 MB**). From the current Query Store size limit (**1024.0 MB**), we can also see how much is used (**3.0 MB**).

While the Query Store is disabled by default in older versions of SQL Server, it can be enabled via the `model` database. This will ensure that each new database will inherit the enabled Query Store settings from the `model` database. However, QS options cannot be set for the `model` database via SSMS. T-SQL must be used, as seen in the following example:

```
USE [master]
GO
ALTER DATABASE [model] SET QUERY_STORE = ON;
GO
ALTER DATABASE [model] SET QUERY_STORE (OPERATION_MODE = READ_WRITE);
```

As for the settings to control the QS behavior through SSMS, they are as follows:

- **Operation Mode**: Defines the current operational status of QS, such as whether it is currently collecting data. It can be disabled (**Off**), disabled but not cleared (**Read only**), and enabled for data collection (**Read write**).

- **Data Flush Interval (Minutes)**: Defines the frequency to persist collected runtime statistics from memory to disk tables. The default is **15** minutes (**900** seconds internally), which is what Microsoft recommends for most systems.

- **Statistics Collection Interval**: Defines the time interval buckets for aggregation. The default is **1** hour (**60** minutes internally). Microsoft doesn't recommend a lower value for 24x7 operation.

- **Max Plans per Query**: Defines the maximum number of plans maintained for each query. The default is **200**, and when the limit is reached, QS stops capturing new plans for that query. This can be the case for stored procedures that recompile often for example.

> **Tip**
> If you choose to change the default value of **Max Plans per Query**, keep in mind that it will have a direct impact on the effectiveness of features that rely on the Query Store, such as **Automatic Plan Correction** (APC) and **Parameter Sensitive Plan Optimization** (PSPO).

- **Max Size (MB)**: Defines the maximum size up to which the Query Store can grow inside the user database before it starts to clean up older information. The **Max Size (MB)** limit isn't strictly enforced. The storage usage is checked only when the QS writes data to disk, which is set by the **Data Flush Interval (Minutes)** option. If the cleanup process cannot keep up before the QS space is full, then the QS operation mode will change to **Read only**. The default up to SQL Server 2017 is **100** MB, increased to **1** GB in SQL Server 2019.

- **Query Store Capture Mode**: Defines the amount of query information collected. Query Store can collect information on all queries (**All**), only queries that execute regularly (**Auto**), or no queries whatsoever (**None**). The default is **All** up to SQL Server 2017 (but highly recommended to use **Auto** instead), and changes to **Auto** in SQL Server 2019 – the same as Azure SQL Database. The **All** setting can be used sporadically for point-in-time troubleshooting, but we have other methods of collecting query plan information that don't aggregate data, which we discuss in *Chapter 11, Troubleshooting Live Queries*.

- **Size Based Cleanup Mode**: Defines whether the internal cleanup task removes the oldest queries and their related runtime statistics from the Query Store using a **least recently used** (**LRU**) algorithm. The cleanup task wakes up when the size of QS on-disk tables reaches 90 percent of the defined maximum. The cleanup task stops when approximately 20 percent of the defined maximum is free. The default is **Auto** but can also be **Off**, in which case the QS operation mode will change to **Read only** when the size limit is reached.

- **Stale Query Threshold (Days)**: Defines the duration that runtime statistics must be kept per collected query. For queries that haven't been executed over the defined time, its runtime statistics are evicted. The default is **30 days**. Consider the time that we need to reasonably keep query execution history. For example, if our workload roughly repeats itself every other week, we can lower this configuration value to **15 days** because we should only need to keep about 2 weeks of data to investigate any issues.

- **Wait Stats Capture Mode**: Defines whether wait stats should be captured (**On**) or not (**Off**). The default is **On**. A detailed discussion about waits is outside the scope of this book, but if more information about the various wait types is needed, the SQL Database Engine documentation about waits is on the page for the `sys.dm_os_wait_stats` DMV. This DMV shows cumulative wait information since the server was last started.

  However, QS does not collect detailed information per individual wait type name. Instead, QS groups wait types per category, such as Lock, CPU, Tran Log IO, Network IO, Buffer IO, Latch, and numerous others. The mapping between Query Store wait categories and real wait type names is available in the SQL Database Engine documentation page for the system view, `sys.query_store_wait_stats`.

Microsoft also recommends enabling two global trace flags that improve QS behavior on typical production systems:

- **Trace flag 7745**: Used to prevent QS data from having to be written to disk in case of a failover or shutdown, which would otherwise delay the failover or shutdown. However, this causes QS data that has not been persisted to disk yet to be lost (up to the time that was defined by **Data Flush Interval**), but typically, this is not critical. This is the default behavior in Azure SQL Database.

- **Trace flag 7752**: Up to SQL Server 2017, this trace flag is used to allow asynchronous load of the Query Store during database startup operations. The default synchronous load can delay database startup until the Query Store is fully available, which may not be warranted for production databases where uptime is more valuable than synchronous availability of monitoring data. Starting with SQL Server 2019, this trace flag is not needed because asynchronous load becomes the default behavior. This is also the default behavior in Azure SQL Database.

We can see the options in the following screenshot, where the defaults were changed to the recommended values, just after we changed **Operation Mode** to **Read write**:

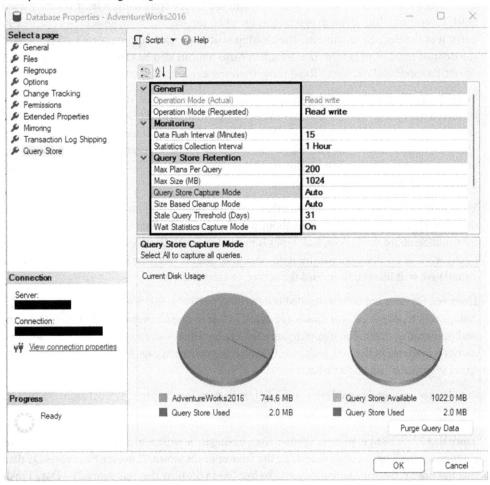

Figure 10.5: SSMS Database Properties window showing Query
Store settings with their recommended values

We can also use T-SQL, as shown in the following example:

```
USE [master]
GO
ALTER DATABASE [AdventureWorks2016] SET QUERY_STORE = ON;
GO
ALTER DATABASE [AdventureWorks2016] SET QUERY_STORE (
    OPERATION_MODE = READ_WRITE,
    DATA_FLUSH_INTERVAL_SECONDS = 900,
    INTERVAL_LENGTH_MINUTES = 60,
    MAX_STORAGE_SIZE_MB = 1000,
    QUERY_CAPTURE_MODE = AUTO,
    SIZE_BASED_CLEANUP_MODE = AUTO,
    MAX_PLANS_PER_QUERY = 200,
    WAIT_STATS_CAPTURE_MODE = ON,
    CLEANUP_POLICY = (STALE_QUERY_THRESHOLD_DAYS = 90)
    );
```

SQL Server 2019 introduced a new **Operation Mode** called **Custom**. When it's enabled, you can fine-tune data collection in a server by specifying additional Query Store configurations using the **Query Store Capture Policy** setting. The new **Custom** settings define what happens during the internal capture policy time threshold: a time boundary during which the configurable conditions are evaluated and, if any are true, the query is eligible to be captured by Query Store. The new settings are as follows:

- **Stale Capture Policy Threshold**: Defines the time window for which one or more of the other Query Store capture policy OR conditions need to occur for a query to be captured in the Query Store. While the default is **1 day**, it can be set as low as **1 hour**, and up to **7 days**. As you evaluate changes from the default value, it's important to be mindful that lowering the value will increase the load on Query Store, because it is likely that more queries will be captured.

- **Execution Count**: Defines the number of times a query must be executed within the time window configured in **Stale Capture Policy Threshold** for the query to be considered for capture. The default is **30**, which means that if using all default configurations, a query must execute at least 30 times in one day to be captured in the Query Store.

- **Total Compile CPU Time (ms)**: Defines the total cumulative CPU time a query must spend during compilation within the time window configured in **Stale Capture Policy Threshold** for the query to be considered for capture. The default is **1000**, which means that if using all default configurations, a query must accumulate at least one second of CPU time during query compilation in one day to be captured in the Query Store.

- **Total CPU Time (ms)**: Defines the total cumulative CPU time a query must spend in execution within the time window configured in **Stale Capture Policy Threshold** for the query to be considered for capture. The default is **100**, which means that if using all default configurations, a query must accumulate at least 100 ms of CPU time during query execution in one day to be captured in the Query Store.

From the T-SQL example we used previously, the full syntax available in SQL Server 2019 and later becomes the following:

```
USE [master]
GO
ALTER DATABASE [AdventureWorks2016] SET QUERY_STORE = ON
GO
ALTER DATABASE [AdventureWorks2016] SET QUERY_STORE (
     OPERATION_MODE = READ_WRITE,
     DATA_FLUSH_INTERVAL_SECONDS = 900,
     INTERVAL_LENGTH_MINUTES = 60,
     MAX_STORAGE_SIZE_MB = 1000,
     QUERY_CAPTURE_MODE = CUSTOM,
     SIZE_BASED_CLEANUP_MODE = AUTO,
     MAX_PLANS_PER_QUERY = 200,
     WAIT_STATS_CAPTURE_MODE = ON,
     CLEANUP_POLICY = (STALE_QUERY_THRESHOLD_DAYS = 90),
     QUERY_CAPTURE_POLICY = (
          EXECUTION_COUNT = 30
          TOTAL_COMPILE_CPU_TIME_MS = 1000
          TOTAL_EXECUTION_CPU_TIME_MS = 100
          )
     );
```

> **Note**
>
> If using SQL Server 2016, ensure that Cumulative Update 2 of Service Pack 2 is installed at a minimum. This update included several scalability fixes for Query Store that are part of SQL Server 2017 and later.

When Query Store is configured according to the best practices we discussed in this chapter, it can be enabled 24x7. When QS is always enabled, it can start providing value to every database professional who ever had to invest countless hours in query performance troubleshooting resulting from plan changes related to data distribution changes, or even configuration changes with SQL Server. We'll discuss some of the ways database professionals can make use of the valuable information stored in the QS later in this chapter, but first, let's learn about some of the ways the database engine itself can use the QS.

Tracking expensive queries

Query Store only collects plans for **Data Manipulation Language** (**DML**) statements such as SELECT, INSERT, UPDATE, DELETE, MERGE, and BULK INSERT, as these are the T-SQL statements that will be responsible for most of our SQL Database Engine's resource usage. Most **database administrators** (**DBAs**) and database reliability engineers are constantly looking for ways to optimize resource usage; after all, if T-SQL queries are using just the resources they need (CPU, I/O, and memory), then the SQL Database Engine is operating at peak efficiency and allows for maximum concurrency with its current hardware resources.

This brings us to one of the main benefits of Query Store: tracking our workload heavy hitters – the most resource-consuming queries. With this exercise, we may be able to uncover tuning opportunities that, if successful, further improve the efficiency of the server's resource usage.

To generate enough workload in our AdventureWorks database, we will be using an application called QueryStoreSimpleDemo.exe, available in the Microsoft GitHub sample repository at https://github.com/Microsoft/sql-server-samples/blob/master/samples/features/query-store. When this executable is started, we are prompted to enter the SQL Database Engine instance we want to connect to and one of several sample workloads that are available, as seen in the following screenshot. For now, we will use the L option.

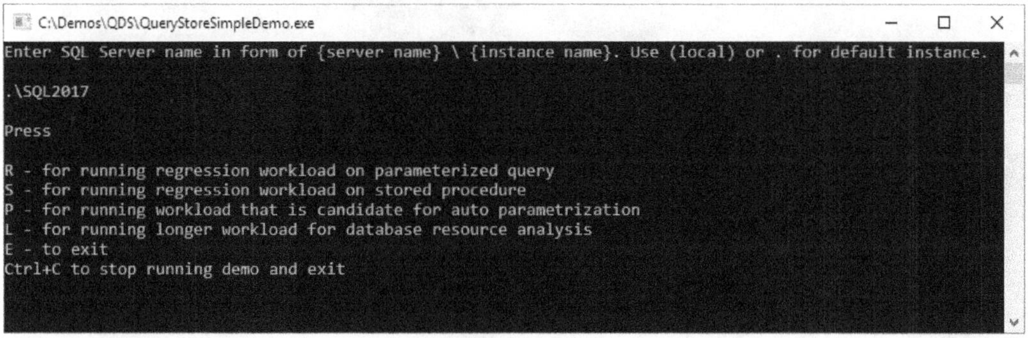

Figure 10.6: Command window showing the QueryStoreSimpleDemo.exe application running

To have relevant data for our exercise, we leave the workload executing for about one hour at least, to allow considerable resources to be used and tracked and have a production-like data collection available in Query Store. Then, we can start by using some of the reports and system views to understand the behavior of the workload over our AdventureWorks sample database. We will start by double-clicking on the **Top Resource Consuming Queries** SSMS report, highlighted in the following screenshot:

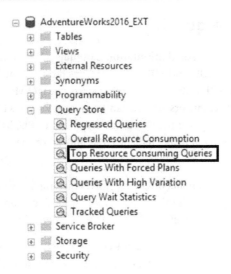

Figure 10.7: SSMS Object Explorer showing the Top Resource Consuming Queries report

This opens the report in a new window tab, as seen in the following screenshot:

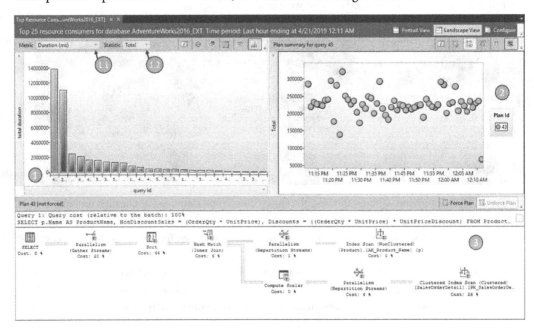

Figure 10.8: Top Resource Consuming Queries Query Store report in SSMS

Let's explore what this report can show us. The top-left quadrant (marked as **1** in the preceding screenshot) displays the top 25 resource consumers for our database. Just above it, we see two dropdowns that allow us to change the following:

- **Metric**: The setting by which the charts are drawn (marked as **1.1** in the preceding screenshot), from the default **Duration (ms)** to any other metric available, as seen in the following screenshot detail.

- **Statistic**: The aggregation used for the chosen metric (marked as **1.2** in the preceding screenshot) with the default being **Total**, but others are available such as average (**Avg**), maximum (**Max**), minimum (**Min**), and standard deviation (**Std Dev**).

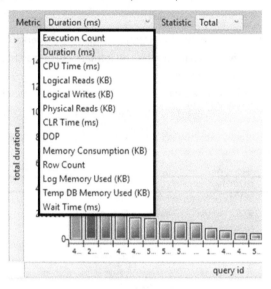

Figure 10.9: Top Resource Consuming Queries Query Store report detail showing
the Metric dropdown with the default Duration (ms) highlighted

For example, assume our server is CPU-bound: it makes sense to change the metric to **CPU Time (ms)** so we can see those queries and analyze them for tuning opportunities. Other scenarios are possible; for example, if we've detected waiting queries and suspect parallelism may be misused in the workload, then we change the metric to **DOP** to find queries that operate with a high degree of parallelism and may be waiting too much. Or maybe memory is the concern, and so using the **Memory Consumption (KB)** metric is the starting point.

The top-right quadrant (marked as **2** in *Figure 10.8*) displays the **plan summary** for the chosen query – namely, its distribution throughout the timeline. If more than one plan exists for the query in scope, we'll see different colors for each **Plan Id** number. We will explore other options available here later in this section.

The bottom (marked as **3** in *Figure 10.8*) displays the **query plan** – the same as the cached query plan. Given that we know query plan choices drive resource usage, this is an important resource to have available. There are no runtime metrics in the query plan – this is not an actual execution plan, but we can explore runtime information about this plan by playing with the top-left quadrant view.

The top-left quadrant can also be displayed in a tabular format organized by the chosen metric, which makes it easier to see actual numbers to correlate with the query plans. To change the view, we click the button highlighted in the following screenshot:

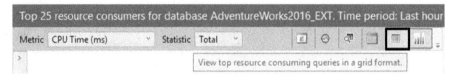

Figure 10.10: Detailed view of the Top Resource Consuming Queries Query Store report displaying the menu bar with the grid format view button highlighted

This changes the report to the following view (notice we also changed the metric to **CPU Time (ms)**):

	query id	object id	object name	query sql text	▼ total cpu time	execution count	plan count
1	20	0		SELECT 'Total income is', ((OrderQty * UnitPrice) * (1...	3482732.11	3299	1
2	43	0		SELECT p.Name AS ProductName, NonDiscountSal...	3041406.6	3306	1
3	3	0		SELECT 'Customer' AS ContactType, p.FirstName, p....	1872006.05	23769	1
4	44	0		SELECT ProductID, SpecialOfferID, AVG(UnitPrice) AS...	844163.39	3299	1
5	40	0		SELECT SalesOrderID, SUM(LineTotal) AS SubTotal F...	689287.44	3299	1
6	10	0		SELECT ProductID, [UnitPrice], [UnitPriceDiscount], ...	683700.08	23769	1
7	51	0		SELECT ProductID, AVG(OrderQty) AS AverageQuant...	652663.78	3299	1
8	52	0		SELECT ProductID, Total = SUM(LineTotal) FROM Sa...	572168.81	3299	1
9	53	0		SELECT ProductID, SUM(LineTotal) AS Total FROM S...	562768.74	3299	1
10	46	0		SELECT AVG(OrderQty) AS 'Average Quantity', Non...	291700.66	3299	1
11	48	0		SELECT ProductID FROM Sales.SalesOrderDetail GR...	208529.41	3299	1
12	54	0		SELECT ProductID, LineTotal FROM Sales.SalesOrder...	203791.23	3299	1
13	5	0		SELECT ProductID, OrderQty, SUM(LineTotal) AS Tot...	172340.82	3299	1

Figure 10.11: Top-left quadrant of the Top Resource Consuming Queries Query Store report displaying grid view

Notice that query ID 20 is the heaviest in terms of total CPU time. We can also see the same information programmatically, using the system views that the report also leverages, as shown in the following sample query:

```
SELECT TOP 25 q.query_id, qt.query_sql_text,
    SUM(rs.count_executions) AS total_execution_count,
    AVG(rs.avg_rowcount) AS avg_rowcount,
    CAST(AVG(rs.avg_duration/1000) AS decimal(8,2)) AS avg_duration_
ms,
    CAST(AVG(rs.avg_cpu_time/1000) AS decimal(8,2)) AS avg_cpu_time_
ms,
```

```
        CAST(AVG(rs.avg_query_max_used_memory/8) AS decimal(8,2)) AS avg_
query_max_used_memory_KB,
        CAST(AVG(rs.avg_physical_io_reads/8) AS decimal(8,2)) AS avg_
physical_io_reads_KB,
        CAST(AVG(rs.avg_logical_io_reads/8) AS decimal(8,2)) AS avg_
logical_io_reads_KB,
        CAST(AVG(rs.avg_logical_io_writes/8) AS decimal(8,2)) AS avg_
logical_io_writes_KB
FROM sys.query_store_query_text AS qt
INNER JOIN sys.query_store_query AS q ON qt.query_text_id = q.query_
text_id
INNER JOIN sys.query_store_plan AS p  ON q.query_id = p.query_id
INNER JOIN sys.query_store_runtime_stats AS rs ON p.plan_id = rs.plan_
id
WHERE execution_type = 0
GROUP BY q.query_id, qt.query_sql_text
ORDER BY avg_cpu_time_ms DESC;
```

This returns the following result set ordered by average CPU time. Not surprisingly, query ID 20 is the heaviest:

	query_id	query_sql_text	total_execution_count	avg_rowcount	avg_duration_ms
1	20	SELECT 'Total income is', ((OrderQty * UnitPrice) * (1.0 - ...	11338	121317	3384.34
2	89	SELECT u.name AS [Name], u.principal_id AS [ID], ISN...	4	22	1107.48
3	119	SELECT q.query_id, qt.query_text_id, qt.query_sql_text, ...	1	8136	3086.32
4	43	SELECT p.Name AS ProductName, NonDiscountSales...	11337	121317	4241.63
5	131	SELECT TOP 25 q.query_id, qt.query_sql_text. SU...	1	25	846.22
6	121	SELECT q.query_id, qt.query_sql_text, wait_category_d...	1	225	979.92
7	135	SELECT TOP 25 q.query_id, qt.query_sql_text. SU...	1	25	750.58
8	120	SELECT q.query_id, qt.query_text_id, qt.query_sql_text, ...	1	223	640.94
9	127	SELECT q.query_id, qt.query_sql_text, wait_category_d...	1	236	1054.82
10	147	SELECT 'Total income is', ((OrderQty * UnitPrice) * (1.0 - ...	1	121317	705.61

avg_cpu_time_ms	avg_query_max_used_memory_KB	avg_physical_io_reads_KB	avg_logical_io_reads_KB	avg_logical_io_writes_KB
1061.00	525.00	0.00	169.75	0.00
1033.33	0.00	0.00	24.00	0.00
974.10	485.25	62.75	16929.50	2071.50
927.36	523.00	0.00	169.75	0.00
614.09	408.88	0.00	186.38	0.00
611.17	335.50	0.00	134.00	0.00
594.03	424.00	0.00	191.00	0.00
588.11	485.25	0.00	21284.88	2390.25
573.53	346.50	0.00	172.75	0.00
515.47	525.00	0.00	169.75	0.00

Figure 10.12: Results of the sample query showing top CPU queries from the Query Store DMVs

We can also see the top 25 queries by their average wait time using the following sample query:

```
SELECT TOP 25 q.query_id, qt.query_sql_text, wait_category_desc,
    SUM(ws.total_query_wait_time_ms) AS total_query_wait_time_ms,
    AVG(ws.avg_query_wait_time_ms) AS avg_query_wait_time_ms
FROM sys.query_store_query_text AS qt
INNER JOIN sys.query_store_query AS q ON qt.query_text_id = q.query_text_id
INNER JOIN sys.query_store_plan AS p ON q.query_id = p.query_id
INNER JOIN sys.query_store_wait_stats AS ws ON p.plan_id = ws.plan_id
WHERE ws.wait_category_desc NOT IN ('Unknown', 'Idle')
AND ws.execution_type = 0
GROUP BY q.query_id, qt.query_sql_text, ws. wait_category_desc
ORDER BY avg_query_wait_time_ms DESC;
```

This returns the following result set, where query ID 20 is the second query with the most wait time. Notice it is a parallelism-related wait:

	query_id	query_sql_text	wait_category_desc	total_query_wait_time_ms	avg_query_wait_time_ms
1	43	SELECT p.Name AS ProductName, NonDiscountSales ...	Parallelism	340353788	28911.5003290672
2	20	SELECT 'Total income is', ((OrderQty * UnitPrice) * (1.0 - ...	Parallelism	259237557	22032.4774165844
3	147	SELECT 'Total income is', ((OrderQty * UnitPrice) * (1.0 - ...	Parallelism	4899	4899
4	119	SELECT q.query_id, qt.query_text_id, qt.query_sql_text, ...	Other Disk IO	1406	1406
5	89	SELECT u.name AS [Name], u.principal_id AS [ID], ISNU...	Preemptive	4413	1103.25
6	130	SELECT TOP 25 q.query_id, qt.query_sql_text, SU...	CPU	1035	1035
7	122	SELECT q.query_id, qt.query_sql_text, SUM(rs.cou...	CPU	941	941
8	138	SELECT TOP 25 q.query_id, qt.query_sql_text, SU...	CPU	802	802
9	43	SELECT p.Name AS ProductName, NonDiscountSales ...	CPU	8681128	737.939639723995
10	43	SELECT p.Name AS ProductName, NonDiscountSales ...	Network IO	7769547	659.022727884016

Figure 10.13: Results of the sample query showing queries with
the most wait time from the Query Store DMVs

While using the system view can prove to be a powerful tool, if the rich UI experience that's available in SSMS reports is preferred, a **Query Wait Statistics** report is also available. Opening it provides the view seen in the following screenshot, where we confirm that parallelism waits are the most prevalent in the workload:

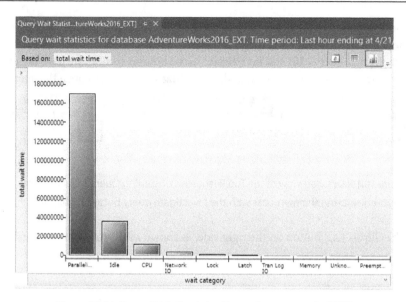

Figure 10.14: Query Wait Statistics Query Store report in SSMS

Clicking in the first bar (**Parallelism**) opens a second view with the details for that wait category, as seen in the following screenshot. It confirms what we'd seen in the waits DMV – query ID 20 is the second highest in wait times:

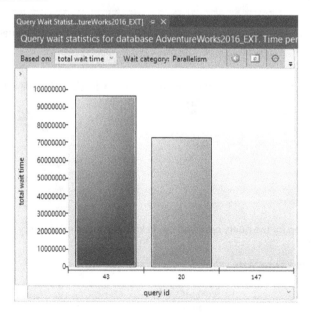

Figure 10.15: Query Wait Statistics drilldown report showing queries with the most parallelism waits

Now, we have a clear notion of the heavy hitters that need investigation, and the working hypothesis that tuning these will drive down CPU usage and alleviate my CPU-bound server. Back in the QS report, let's take the first query (**20**) and investigate. In the bottom section, we have the query plan; we can click the magnifier button, as shown in the following screenshot, to open the query text:

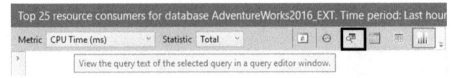

Figure 10.16: Detailed view of the Top Resource Consuming Queries Query Store
report displaying the menu bar with the investigate query button highlighted

We can click the ellipsis (**…**) button on the right side, as shown in the following screenshot, for the same purpose:

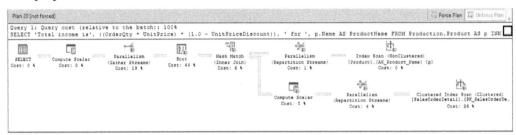

Figure 10.17: Query plan view of the Top Resource Consuming Queries
Query Store report displaying the ellipsis button

Once the query opens in a new session window, we can execute to get the following actual execution plan:

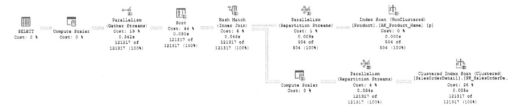

Figure 10.18: Execution plan for the query retrieved by clicking the investigate query button in Query Store

We can also get the **QueryTimeStats** values for this plan:

Figure 10.19: QueryTimeStats for the example query

Now that we have the query execution plan, in the `WaitStats` property, we confirm that this query waited mostly on `CXPACKET`, which is a parallelism wait, just like it was reported in Query Store:

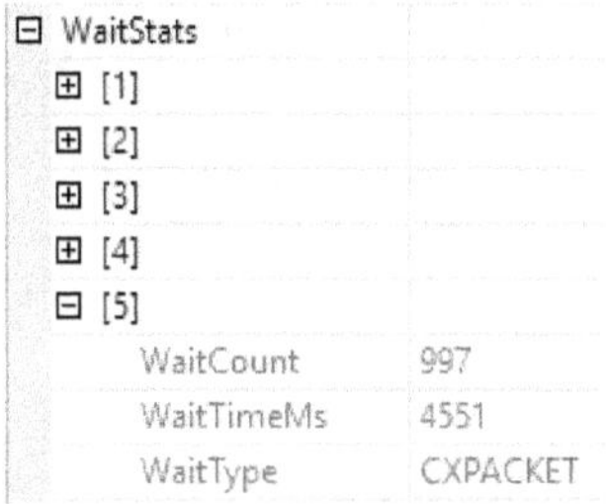

Figure 10.20: WaitStats for the example query showing CXPACKET waits

We also have a Clustered Index Scan on the `SalesOrderDetail` table. The query only needs three columns from this table so it is a relevant subset, but there's no index that can cover the query. However, we see that the existing `IX_SalesOrderDetail_ProductID` index already covers the join predicate on the `ProductID` column. Given that there are no other predicates on the query, and we need three extra columns just for `SELECT`, we can add them to this index as `INCLUDE` columns. The hypothesis is that if the SQL Database Engine uses a narrower index, it can optimize I/O, which in turn has tangible effects on CPU usage as well. And given that the new columns are not interfering with the key of the existing index, any other queries that need it won't be too affected and we should be able to address our current heavy hitter query. The index can be changed using the following query example:

```
CREATE NONCLUSTERED INDEX IX_SalesOrderDetail_ProductID ON [Sales].
[SalesOrderDetail] (
        [ProductID] ASC
)
INCLUDE (
        [OrderQty],
        [UnitPrice],
        [UnitPriceDiscount]
) WITH DROP_EXISTING;
```

After creating the index, we execute the query again to get the following actual execution plan, using the new index. Notice the plan no longer executes in parallel because it became cheap enough not to exceed the **Cost Threshold for Parallelism** configuration. And because of the lower cost to access data in both tables, Hash Match was replaced with Nested Loops, which is cheaper, and Sort has gone now because both indexes are sorted on the required key order:

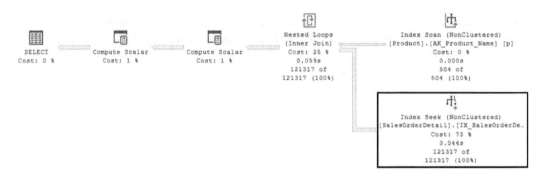

Figure 10.21: Execution plan for the example query after the new index was created

The **QueryTimeStats** values for this plan reflect the lower resource usage: CPU time dropped from 514 ms to 265 ms (~49 percent less), and execution time dropped from 704 ms to 570 ms (20 percent less):

QueryTimeStats	
CpuTime	265
ElapsedTime	570

Figure 10.22: QueryTimeStats for the execution plan with the new index

And without parallelism, there are no more parallelism waits for this query. By cutting CPU usage in half, we were successful in tuning this query. The next step would be to continue with the other heavy hitters until the CPU is reduced to an acceptable level.

Fixing regressed queries

Parameters are fundamental drivers of the query optimization process. We discussed the topic of parameter sensitivity, known as parameter sniffing, in the *The importance of parameters* section in *Chapter 1, Understanding Query Processing*, and the *Query plan properties of interest* section in *Chapter 3, Exploring Query Execution Plans*.

This brings us to the other main benefit of Query Store: tracking plan changes over time – in other words, regressions from parameter-sensitive plans. With this exercise, we want to make sure the volatility that can come with parameter-sensitive plans is addressed, and that the plan that is used is the one that's best for most uses, if not all. If successful, we will address the complaints we've been getting that sometimes the application just slows down for a few minutes and then recovers.

To generate enough workload in our AdventureWorks database, again, we will use the QueryStoreSimpleDemo.exe application, available in the Microsoft GitHub sample repository at https://github.com/Microsoft/sql-server-samples/blob/master/samples/features/query-store. When this executable is started, we are prompted to enter the SQL Database Engine instance we want to connect to, and one of several sample workloads that are available, as shown in the following screenshot. For now, we will use the S option.

```
C:\Demos\QDS\QueryStoreSimpleDemo.exe                                    —    □    ×
Enter SQL Server name in form of {server name} \ {instance name}. Use (local) or . for default instance.

.\SQL2017

Press

R - for running regression workload on parameterized query
S - for running regression workload on stored procedure
P - for running workload that is candidate for auto parametrization
L - for running longer workload for database resource analysis
E - to exit
Ctrl+C to stop running demo and exit
```

Figure 10.23: Command window showing the QueryStoreSimpleDemo.exe application running

To have relevant data for our exercise, we leave the workload executing for about 15 to 20 minutes at least – although less than that already produces visible results. Then, we can start to understand the behavior of the workload over the `AdventureWorks` sample database. We can start by double-clicking on the **Queries With High Variation** SSMS report, highlighted in the following screenshot:

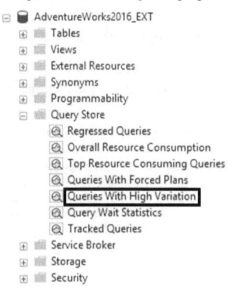

Figure 10.24: SSMS Object Explorer showing the Queries With High Variation built-in Query Store report

Then, the report opens in a new window, as shown in the following screenshot, in which we changed to the standard deviation (**Std Dev**) statistic:

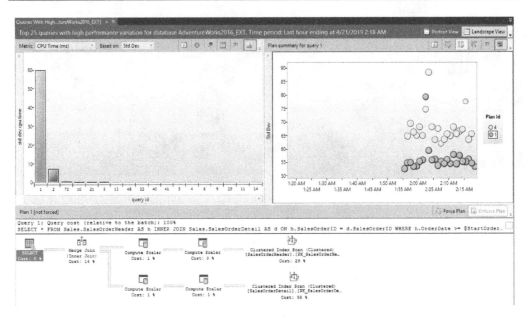

Figure 10.25: Queries With High Variation Query Store report in SSMS

Immediately we see that query ID 1 has two plans being tracked (top-right quadrant) with widely different performance. Query ID 1 is the query with the widest variance between executions (top-left quadrant) running in our SQL Server.

We can click on each plan (**4** and **1**) but we can also use **Plan Comparison** for the job. We discussed this tool as a standalone in *Chapter 9, Comparative Analysis of Query Plans*, but it can also be used from within Query Store. To do that, hold down the *Shift* key and click on both IDs in the **Plan Id** legend; after they're selected, as shown in the following screenshot, click the **Plan Comparison** button:

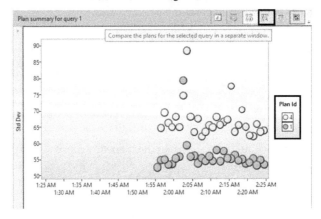

Figure 10.26: Top-right quadrant of the Queries With High Variation Query Store report showing the plan summary for query 1 with the two Plan IDs selected and the Plan Comparison button highlighted

The comparison window appears as shown in the following screenshot:

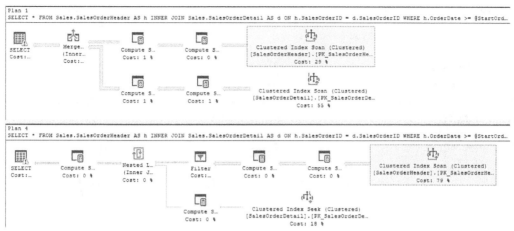

Figure 10.27: Plan Comparison window showing the two selected Plan IDs

Notice that the only similarity between the plans is a Clustered Index Scan on the `SalesOrderHeader` table. Everything else is different: the data reader on the `SalesOrderDetail` tables changes from Clustered Index Scan in Plan ID 1 to Clustered Index Seek in Plan ID 4, which affects the type of join. Plan ID 1 has a Merge Join that changes to Nested Loops on Plan ID 1. Looking at the compared **Properties** window, we can see why the plans are different: the plans were compiled with different parameters, so this is a case of parameter sensitivity.

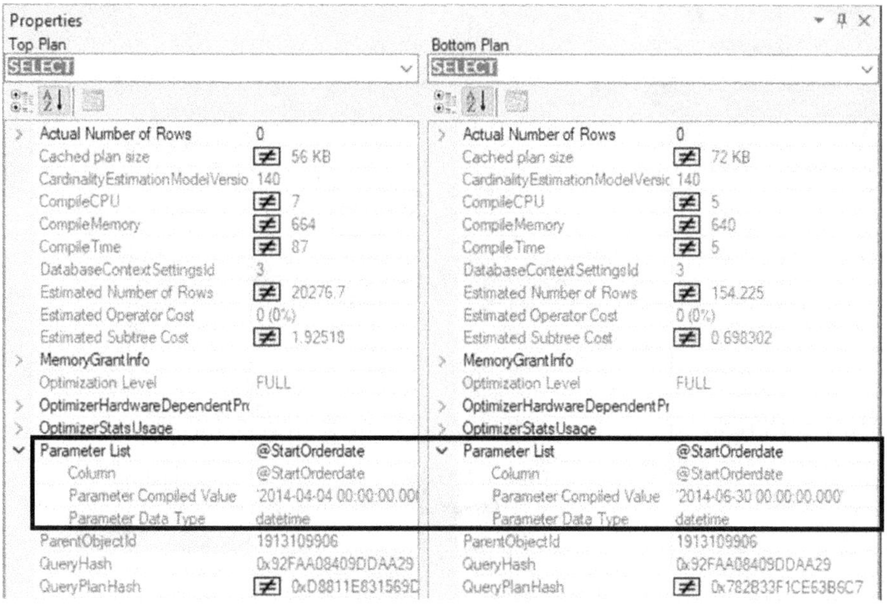

Figure 10.28: Properties for the two plans from the Plan Comparison window

And because we have `ParentObjectId` in the query plan, the following example tells us the queries in the comparison are executed in the context of the `usp_SalesFromDate` stored procedure:

```
SELECT OBJECT_NAME(1913109906);
```

We have covered several techniques to deal with this scenario in the *Query Plan Comparison* section of *Chapter 9, Comparative Analysis of Query Plans*, but in the meantime, the application is unstable. This is where Query Store proves its worth again. We can select Plan ID 1, which is consistently better, as seen in the report, and click the **Force Plan** button, as shown in the following screenshot:

Figure 10.29: Menu bar on the plan window of the Queries With High
Variation Query Store report highlighting the Force Plan button

With just one click, we stabilized the application by forcing the better plan, and minutes later, we refreshed the report to see that Plan ID 4 is no longer used. Notice in the following screenshot that the forced plan shows a checkmark to signal it's been forced. Also notice that the **Unforce Plan** button became available in case we ever need to let the query optimization process run again – for example, if we applied one of the mitigation techniques by making code changes with a `CREATE OR ALTER PROCEDURE`.

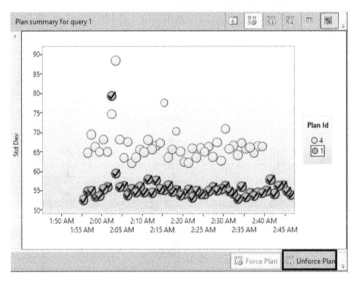

Figure 10.30: Plan summary for query 1 window with the forced Plan
ID selected and the Unforce Plan button highlighted

If we had to force several plans in our work to minimize application issues over time, it could be easy to lose track of which plans are forced. That's why SSMS also includes a **Queries With Forced Plans** report, which looks like the following screenshot:

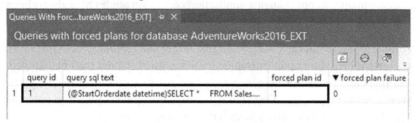

Figure 10.31: Queries With Forced Plans report in SSMS

This report will allow you to track all the queries that have plans forced by the Query Store.

Features that rely on the Query Store

When the QS was first introduced in SQL Server 2016, it was turned off by default to avoid potential impact on production workloads, as Microsoft just didn't know how it would behave with the millions of workload permutations executing out in the wild. Over time, there have been numerous scalability improvements, and better default settings were introduced in Azure and SQL Server 2019, both from customer input and Microsoft Engineering's own experience with the QS. This resulted in the ability to have QS turned on by default for new databases, starting with SQL Server 2022.

Having the QS enabled by default is great for database professionals, but perhaps more importantly, it becomes part of an entire feedback system that gives the SQL Database Engine rich information about query performance. Some of that information can be used to ensure the Query Optimizer can shortcut certain decisions, learn from past performance degradation patterns, and make queries more efficient over time. In this section, we're going to cover a few of these innovations that are available in Azure SQL Database and SQL Server 2022.

Query Store for readable secondary replicas

With the advent of Always On availability group read-scaleout replicas, it's become common to run different workloads against read-only replicas of a database. However, the QS was only tracking workloads executing on the primary replica. This means that the QS was essentially blind to the wealth of data specific to read-only workloads, and users blind to the insights it could provide. With SQL Server 2022, the QS can be enabled on secondary replicas. Query data is captured on the secondary, shipped to the primary's QS, and persisted there with the scope of the replica it applies to. It also means that plan forcing becomes available for the scope of secondary replicas, including the ability to force or unforce a plan for all replicas, or only for read-only replicas in an Availability Group.

Query Store hinting

SQL Server 2022 introduces the ability to hint queries through the QS, which replaces plan guides as a way to shape query plans without changing application code. Plan guides have always been a useful but not easily managed nor easily implemented method to apply hints.

But why apply hints to queries in the Database Engine rather than source code? Query hints can be used to enforce certain behaviors upon a given query when that behavior can't be changed through a query rewrite. There are scenarios where there's no source code access to make changes to a query, such as the case of a vendor application. Or there's dynamically generated code via an **object-relational mapper** (**ORM**). Therefore, the ability to still force certain behaviors at compile time or even at execution time in a targeted manner is an invaluable method to mitigate some classes of performance issues.

With hints, we can limit the **maximum degree of parallelism** (**MaxDOP**) for specific queries, force a Hash Match oin instead of a Nested Loops join, or limit the memory grant size for a bulk operation.

Because the QS is enabled by default for new databases in SQL Server 2022 and enabled for several years now in Azure SQL Database, this feature is readily available for shaping query plans and behavior without changing application code, with the improved manageability of the QS. Hints applied through the QS hints are persisted, which means they survive restarts.

To use hints through the QS, we must find the `query_id` of the query to modify, execute the `sp_query_store_set_hints` stored procedure with the query ID and new `USE HINT` query hint string to apply to the query, and that's it. The list of supported hints can be accessed using the `sys.dm_exec_valid_use_hints` DMV.

Here's an example of finding and setting a hint to limit the MaxDOP for a query referencing the `Sales.SalesOrderDetail` table in `AdventureWorks`:

```
SELECT query_sql_text, q.query_id
FROM sys.query_store_query_text qt
INNER JOIN sys.query_store_query q ON qt.query_text_id = q.query_text_
id
WHERE query_sql_text like N'%FROM Sales.SalesOrderDetail%';
GO
EXEC sp_query_store_set_hints 46006, N'OPTION(MAXDOP 1)';
```

If I later need to also force a specific Query Optimization compatibility level for the same query and keep the `MAXDOP` hint, then the full set of hints must be set for the query:

```
EXEC sp_query_store_set_hints 46006, N'OPTION(MAXDOP 1, USE
HINT(''QUERY_OPTIMIZER_COMPATIBILITY_LEVEL_120''))';
```

And removing all hints for the query is simple enough with this example:

```
EXEC sp_query_store_clear_hints 46006;
```

You can use the example queries to create a wrapper and automate QS hinting throughout your SQL environment for well-known queries that you previously determined must be hinted.

> **Note**
>
> Query Store hints are also the visible implementation artifact of the **CE Feedback** feature, which we discussed in *Chapter 2, Mechanics of the Query Optimizer*. CE Feedback uses documented query hints to force a given CE model assumption when a regression is detected, and the SQL Database Engine tests its applicability through a test-and-verify principle.

Parameter Sensitive Plan Optimization

We introduced the **Parameter Sensitive Plan Optimization** (**PSPO**) feature in *Chapter 1*. While PSPO is not dependent on the QS for its common use cases, when QS is enabled, plan variants are captured and have their own `query_id`. This means the QS is required to force a plan for a query variant and to use hints for plan variants.

Automatic Plan Correction

Automatic Plan Correction (**APC**), previously named **Automatic Plan Regression Correction** (**APRC**), was introduced in SQL Server 2017. APC automatically identifies query execution plans that have regressed – for example, when CPU use for the query changed by orders of magnitude – and fixes the regression by forcing the last known good plan, the plan that existed before the regression occurred. This means that DBAs and database reliability engineers can avoid a middle-of-the-night call about some query that regressed due to a plan change.

And what if you need to know when APC made some change while you were sleeping or otherwise occupied? The list of detected plan choice regressions, and whether APC acted on them, can be accessed using the `sys.dm_db_tuning_recommendations` **DMV**. While data in this DMV is not persisted and, therefore, is not available after a restart, forced plans are persisted in the QS, which means they survive restarts. So, in this scenario, you might not know why the plan was reverted, but you can still see the various plans that exist for a given `query_id` and determine when the plan change happened.

> **Note**
>
> The forcing mechanism is through the execution of the `sp_query_store_force_plan` stored procedure, which can be used manually as well.

APC can be enabled using T-SQL, as seen in the following example for the `AdventureWorks` sample database:

```
USE [master]
GO
ALTER DATABASE [AdventureWorks2016]
SET AUTOMATIC_TUNING (FORCE_LAST_GOOD_PLAN = ON);
```

APC's most common use case is the correction of a parameter-sensitive query scenario that originated a plan flip: a recompilation leads to caching and reuse of a query plan that's not deemed good for most of the use cases of that parameterized query, causing a perceived regression. In this case, the last known good plan is forced to fix the regression. Note that APC doesn't negate PSPO though; it merely changes the scope of its action to cover plan variants, as these are standalone queries for the context of the Query Store.

Degree of parallelism feedback

The use of parallel processing is very useful for many queries, especially those reading large amounts of data and doing different types of data aggregations or sorting. While there is a documented Parallelism physical operator in `showplan` – the Exchange Iterator – internally in the SQL Database Engine, parallelism is implemented as if it were two operators: **producers** that push data to consumers, and **consumers** that may have to wait for data from producers. That is important to know because, with perfect parallelism, all threads would read the same number of rows, and there should be no waits between producer and consumer threads, as each thread produces its rowset.

However, in the real world, we can observe several parallelism waits, which occur when the Database Engine is trying to synchronize the Exchange Iterator as it handles data streams (as stated in the product documentation, it can "*distribute streams, gather streams, and repartition streams logical operations*"), or getting a required buffer such as when fetching rows from an Index Scan.

> **Tip**
> Starting with SQL Server 2022 and in Azure SQL Database, CXPACKET and CXCONSUMER waits are accrued by data reading operators only, such as Index Scan or Sort, whereas CXSYNC_PORT and CXSYNC_CONSUMER are accrued specifically for Exchange Iterator synchronization tasks.

For example, for an Index Scan producing one million rows executing in parallel, when there are four CPUs available, it is said the query is executing with a **degree of parallelism** (**DOP**) of four. Each thread reading rows would be expected to read 250,000 rows, and if there is no blocking, finish almost simultaneously.

> **Note**
>
> For any operator executing in parallel, the number of threads spawned is the same as *DOP +*
> *1*: the threads reading their part of the rowset, plus the coordinating thread that is responsible
> for coordinating the data stream from each individual thread doing the reads.

Therefore, the use of parallelism becomes inefficient when the imbalance between threads leads to
wait times that are so high that they offset the benefits of parallel execution. In other words, if 1 of the
4 threads actually reads 700,000 rows while each of the other threads only reads 100,000 rows, this
imbalance means that the coordinating thread (producer) has to wait for the longer running thread
to complete, accruing CXPACKET waits.

And so, it becomes easier to understand how producer waits are the ones that may require attention,
while consumer waits are inevitable as a passive consequence of longer-running producers. A leading
cause is inaccurate cardinality estimations, which can be observed in a query execution plan when the
number of estimated and actual rows processed has a significant difference. One of the most common
strategies to address excess CXPACKET waits if inaccurate cardinality estimations are present is to
update statistics. Otherwise, forcing a specific (lower) MaxDOP value through a query hint is the other
common approach. If inefficient parallelism is widespread in a given database workload, a database
engineer may be tempted to just reduce the MaxDOP server or database configuration, which affects
all workloads: your queries suffering from inefficient parallelism will likely improve, at the cost of
some analytical queries that would benefit from higher parallelism becoming less efficient.

> **Note**
>
> Before SQL Server 2019, the default value for MaxDOP is set to **0** in both Server and Database
> configurations. This means using all available schedulers if a query is eligible for parallelism.
> Starting with SQL Server 2019, the default MaxDOP is calculated at setup time based on available
> processors and NUMA configuration and is set to **8** in Azure SQL Database.

Inefficient parallelism, where one size doesn't fit all, is precisely the scenario where **DOP Feedback**
becomes a fundamental feature to ensure optimal parallelism for most queries. The goal of the feature
is to increase overall concurrency and reduce waits significantly, even if it slightly increases elapsed
time for a given query.

DOP Feedback will identify parallelism inefficiencies for repeating queries, based on CPU time, elapsed
time, and waits. If parallelism usage is deemed inefficient, DOP Feedback will *lower* DOP for the query
from whatever is the configured DOP for the next execution, down to a minimum of two, and *verify*
whether it helps. In its current implementation, DOP will be adjusted using a stepped approach where
the steps are multiples of 4, picking the next closest DOP from the current DOP. Verified feedback is
persisted in the QS, so the optimal DOP for a given query survives restarts.

What if lowering the DOP does more harm? DOP Feedback will detect regressions and revert to the last known good DOP for the query. If an application or user cancels a query, it will also be deemed a regression.

So, is DOP Feedback using a QS hint? No, the MAXDOP query hint is not used because using query hints would force a plan recompilation, but adjusting DOP through DOP Feedback doesn't recompile plans. It uses an internal mechanism not accessible or usable otherwise.

What if data distribution changes and the previously optimal DOP value for a query is no longer valid? DOP Feedback's current stable feedback is re-verified upon plan recompilation. It may be readjusted back to a higher DOP value, or continue to be lowered from the last stable value, but the Server and Database MaxDOP setting will always be upheld as the ceiling.

Optimized plan forcing

As we discussed in *Chapter 1, Understanding Query Processing*, query compilation and optimization is a multi-phased process of quickly generating a "good-enough" query execution plan. The overall query execution time always includes time spent in compilation, which can at times be time and resource-consuming in terms of CPU and memory.

The SQL Database Engine caches query plans for reuse, which reduces much of the compilation overhead for repeating queries. However, query plans can be evicted from the plan cache due to restarts or memory pressure, which means subsequent calls to the same query will require a full new compilation, meaning the benefit is no longer present.

Sometimes "compile storms" may happen, which are occasions when a SQL Database Engine is restarted, and when application database calls resume, they cause numerous plans to be simultaneously compiled within a short period of time. This concurrent compilation activity drives up CPU usage, memory, and even compile blocking: all can impact query execution time.

With SQL Server 2022 and in Azure SQL Database, **Optimized Plan Forcing** (**OPF**) reduces compilation overhead for repeating queries, although in its current version, it works only for queries *forced* through the QS, either by the user or by APC.

After a plan is compiled and stored for a forced query, a **compilation replay script** (**CRS**) will persist key compilation steps to shortcut a recompilation of that plan whenever needed, at a fraction of the cost of a would-be full new compilation.

> **Note**
>
> The CRS is not user-visible. Also, OPF is compatible with Query Store hints and supports Query Store secondary replicas (a preview feature).

While OPF doesn't solve compile storms scenarios for SQL Server 2022 or in Azure SQL Database at the time this book is written, the feature does show promise that compile storms may be solvable in a future iteration of this feature.

Summary

This chapter covered the important topic of storing query performance statistics in the flight recorder, which is the Query Store, which allows us to access query plans and their runtime statistics, along with how they change over time. With what we've learned so far in all the previous chapters of this book (especially in *Chapter 3, Exploring Query Execution Plans*, about what information lies inside query plans), we can now more easily find resolutions for performance problems. We can easily identify plans that must be tuned, or for quick mitigation, just return to a known good plan that had been stored in Query Store. We also learned how the Query Store enables several helpful features that allow the Query Optimizer to automatically detect and correct common query performance issues.

Finally, we covered how to use either system views or SSMS to uncover the highest resource-consuming queries executing in our databases and help us quickly find and fix query performance issues that are related to plan changes, which greatly simplifies query performance troubleshooting. But it also provides performance stability across SQL Database Engine upgrades when following the recommended database compatibility level upgrade process, which we will discuss in the *Understanding where QTA is needed* section of *Chapter 12, Managing Optimizer Changes*.

In the next chapter of the book, we will investigate how to troubleshoot a different kind of query performance issue for which the tools and methods we have covered so far may not be helpful: long-running queries.

Troubleshooting Live Queries

During our career as a database professional, we likely encounter cases where a runaway query takes hours to complete or doesn't even complete by any reasonable time measurement. How do we troubleshoot cases such as this?

A query execution plan can help provide a conclusive explanation of query performance issues. But to get a query execution plan there is one requirement a long-running query can't easily meet: **query completion**.

If the query takes a long time to complete or never actually does, then how can we troubleshoot these cases? And what happens if we take that production query back to our development server and it runs fine? That means there is a set of conditions that can only be reproduced in the production server, be that the size of the database, the data distribution statistics, or even the availability of resources such as memory or CPU. Therefore, the ability to analyze a query execution plan while the query is executing is something many SQL Server professionals have been requesting for a long time.

This chapter will introduce the **Query Profiling Infrastructure** that exposes real-time query execution plans, which enable scenarios such as production systems troubleshooting. We will explore real-world examples of how to leverage rich-UI tools for query performance troubleshooting: **Live Query Statistics** as a standalone case, or as part of the **Activity Monitor** functionality of **SQL Server Management Studio (SSMS)**.

In this chapter, we're going to cover the following main topics:

- Using Live Query Statistics
- Understanding the need for lightweight profiling
- Activity Monitor gets new life

Technical requirements

The examples used in this chapter are designed for use on SQL Server 2022 and Azure SQL Database, but they should work on any version of SQL Server, 2012 or later. The Developer Edition of SQL Server is free for development environments and can be used to run all the code samples. There is also a free tier of Azure SQL Database that you can use for testing at `https://aka.ms/freedb`.

You will need the sample databases `AdventureWorks2016_EXT` (referred to as `AdventureWorks`) and `AdventureWorksDW2016_EXT` (referred to as `AdventureWorksDW`), which can be found on GitHub at `https://github.com/Microsoft/sql-server-samples/releases/tag/adventureworks`. Code samples for this chapter can also be found on GitHub at `https://github.com/PacktPublishing/Learn-T-SQL-Querying-Second-Edition/tree/main/ch11`.

Using Live Query Statistics

To meet the need to analyze a query execution plan while the query is executing, **Live Query Statistics** (**LQS**) was introduced with the SQL Server 2016 release of SSMS, adding rich visuals by animating the in-flight execution plan to allow more immediate and precise identification of hot spots in a plan during query execution.

To see LQS in action, open a new query window in SSMS, in which we can use the following example query from *Chapter 2, Mechanics of the Query Optimizer*. This could be a previously identified long-running query that was created to troubleshoot and tune:

```
SELECT e.[BusinessEntityID], p.[Title], p.[FirstName],
    p.[MiddleName], p.[LastName], p.[Suffix], e.[JobTitle],
    pp.[PhoneNumber], pnt.[Name] AS [PhoneNumberType],
    ea.[EmailAddress], p.[EmailPromotion], a.[AddressLine1],
    a.[AddressLine2], a.[City], sp.[Name] AS [StateProvinceName],
    a.[PostalCode], cr.[Name] AS [CountryRegionName],
p.[AdditionalContactInfo]
FROM [HumanResources].[Employee] AS e
INNER JOIN [Person].[Person] AS p
    ON RTRIM(LTRIM(p.[BusinessEntityID])) = RTRIM(LTRIM(e.
[BusinessEntityID]))
INNER JOIN [Person].[BusinessEntityAddress] AS bea
    ON RTRIM(LTRIM(bea.[BusinessEntityID])) = RTRIM(LTRIM(e.
[BusinessEntityID]))
INNER JOIN [Person].[Address] AS a
    ON RTRIM(LTRIM(a.[AddressID])) = RTRIM(LTRIM(bea.[AddressID]))
INNER JOIN [Person].[StateProvince] AS sp
    ON RTRIM(LTRIM(sp.[StateProvinceID])) = RTRIM(LTRIM(a.
[StateProvinceID]))
INNER JOIN [Person].[CountryRegion] AS cr
```

```
        ON RTRIM(LTRIM(cr.[CountryRegionCode])) = RTRIM(LTRIM(sp.
[CountryRegionCode]))
LEFT OUTER JOIN [Person].[PersonPhone] AS pp
        ON RTRIM(LTRIM(pp.BusinessEntityID)) = RTRIM(LTRIM(p.
[BusinessEntityID]))
LEFT OUTER JOIN [Person].[PhoneNumberType] AS pnt
        ON RTRIM(LTRIM(pp.[PhoneNumberTypeID])) = RTRIM(LTRIM(pnt.
[PhoneNumberTypeID]))
LEFT OUTER JOIN [Person].[EmailAddress] AS ea
        ON RTRIM(LTRIM(p.[BusinessEntityID])) = RTRIM(LTRIM(ea.
[BusinessEntityID]));
```

To see the query progress for the query while it executes on the `AdventureWorks` sample database, click on the **Include Live Query Statistics** button, as shown in the following screenshot:

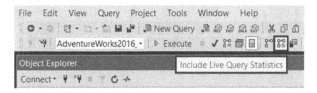

Figure 11.1: SQL Server Management Studio toolbar with the
Include Live Query Statistics button highlighted

When the query execution starts, the **Live Query Statistics** tab appears, showing the in-flight query execution plan.

As the query execution progresses in the following plan, we can see the following:

1. **Solid lines** connecting two operators, indicating areas of the plan that are complete.

2. **Dotted and animated lines** connecting two operators, indicating areas of the plan that are still in flight.

3. Operators with their **elapsed time stopped**, indicating they have finished processing rows.

4. Operators with their **elapsed time continuing to tick**, indicating they are still processing rows.

5. The **overall query elapsed time**.

6. The **estimated query progress displayed as a percentage**. This is an on-the-fly calculation based on the estimated rows versus the actual rows that have already been processed. This calculation is just an indicator that can be accurate enough if the plan doesn't have severe skew between the estimated and actual number of rows. However, for severely skewed estimations, this can be inaccurate, and will not show the expected linear progress.

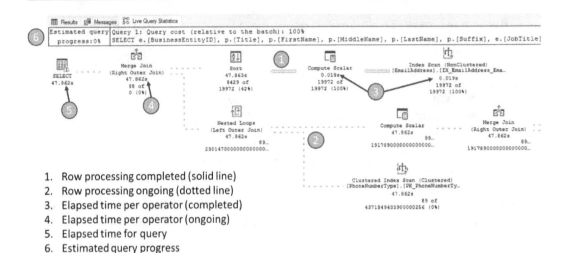

1. Row processing completed (solid line)
2. Row processing ongoing (dotted line)
3. Elapsed time per operator (completed)
4. Elapsed time per operator (ongoing)
5. Elapsed time for query
6. Estimated query progress

Figure 11.2: Live Query Statistics window for the example query

For all query plan operators, we can also see the actual number of rows processed versus the estimated number of rows, together with the percentage of actual rows versus estimated rows.

For example, the Index Scan of the previous plan reads 19,972 of 19,972 rows (100%), which means that estimations were completely accurate compared to the actual rows processed by that operator. But for the Clustered Index Scan, we see it is currently in progress, and reading row 89 of 1,371,849,433,900,000,256 estimated rows (yes, over one quintillion rows). Given that the PhoneNumberType table has only 290 rows and the scan happens once, the misestimation is obvious.

> **Tip**
>
> Even though LQS was released with SQL Server 2016's SSMS, we can use any modern version of SSMS, such as version 17 or later, to connect to any SQL Server instance and use LQS, starting with SQL Server 2014.

LQS is an SSMS UI feature that provides visualization over data stored in the sys.dm_exec_query_profiles DMV. The following query is an example that allows programmatic access to the same information SSMS rendered as a graphical showplan. Note the long-running query was executing in session ID 97, therefore the predicate on session_id = 97.

```
SELECT node_id, physical_operator_name, SUM(row_count) AS row_count,
    SUM(estimate_row_count) AS estimate_row_count,
    CAST(SUM(row_count)*100 AS float) /
SUM(estimate_row_count) AS operator_progress
FROM sys.dm_exec_query_profiles
```

```
WHERE session_id = 97
GROUP BY node_id, physical_operator_name
ORDER BY node_id;
```

The result set for the query shows the following information:

- Each individual operator in the plan (node IDs) that processes rows of data. This excludes operators such as Compute Scalar. Note that node ID 0 corresponds to the top left operator (Merge Join) just before the root node (SELECT) in the graphical query plan, node ID 1 is the Sort at the outer side of the Merge join, node ID 2 is the NonClustered Index Scan leading up to that Sort, node ID 3 is the Nested Loops join at the inner side of the Merge Join, and so on and so forth.

- A snapshot of the current row count for the moment the DMV was invoked.

- The estimated row count for each operator.

- A calculation that provides the current operator progress.

The following screenshot shows the resultset for the sys.dm_exec_query_profiles example:

	node_id	physical_operator_name	row_count	estimate_row_count	operator_progress
1	0	Merge Join	59	9223372036854775807	6.39679281766448E-16
2	1	Sort	5520	19972	27.6386941718406
3	3	Index Scan	19972	19972	100
4	4	Nested Loops	60	23014732682044800000	2.60702571821786E-15
5	6	Merge Join	60	19178943854072578560	3.12843086963098E-15
6	7	Sort	5626	19972	28.1694372120969
7	9	Index Scan	19972	19972	100
8	10	Merge Join	61	959859044513641	6.3550997772708E-12
9	11	Sort	5732	19972	28.7001802523533
10	13	Clustered Index Scan	19972	19972	100
11	14	Merge Join	62	480602358407	1.29004776850252E-08
12	15	Sort	63	290	21.7241379310345
13	17	Clustered Index Scan	290	290	100
14	18	Nested Loops	5812	16572494870	3.50701571826765E-05
15	19	Nested Loops	5812	696323303	0.000834669753972028
16	20	Nested Loops	5812	38470900	0.0151075228289434
17	21	Sort	5813	19614	29.6369939838891
18	23	Index Scan	19614	19614	100
19	24	Table Spool	114002424	384708996	29.6334177743013
20	26	Index Scan	19614	19614	100
21	27	Table Spool	1051972	6963232900	0.0151075228289434
22	29	Clustered Index Scan	181	181	100
23	30	Table Spool	1383256	165724946114	0.000834669753972028
24	32	Index Scan	238	238	100
25	33	Clustered Index Scan	60	3835788770814515714	1.56421543481549E-15

Figure 11.3: Resultset for the sys.dm_exec_query_profiles example query

In summary, using the LQS feature is extremely useful for a scenario where we have a previously identified query that runs with poor performance in a production **very large database** (**VLDB**) but has no issues running in a development machine with a smaller dataset. Often, restoring a VLDB outside a production environment is a non-starter, and so troubleshooting in production is the only viable option.

Understanding the need for lightweight profiling

If you are asking yourself why you would want to know about an obscure Database Engine component named **Query Profiling Infrastructure**, then read on. Not many database professionals know it by name, but most have dealt with it when they need to troubleshoot query performance issues in a production environment. When a SQL Server performance issue occurs, one of the first requirements is to understand which queries are being executed and how system resources are being used, and one of the most important artifacts anyone can use to find out more about queries that are executing is query plans.

Analyzing a query plan, also known as an **estimated execution plan**, means that we're only looking at what SQL Server estimated should be a good-enough plan to return the intended results efficiently. But since an estimated plan is missing runtime data for analysis, it can't truly provide a conclusive explanation for many query performance issues. Recall what we covered about the query compilation and optimization process in *Chapter 1, Understanding Query Processing*, and more specifically how SQL Server estimates work, as discussed in *Chapter 2, Mechanics of the Query Optimizer*: estimations drive optimizer choices, and when these estimations are wrong, then the generated plans are inefficient.

So, what is needed is a query execution plan, also known as an **actual execution plan**. These allow us to see runtime data that is crucial to uncover hot spots in the plan, such as the actual number of rows processed by a query operator.

This runtime information has been accessible for many years and many different versions of SQL Server, but at a very high cost. Collecting runtime data on queries adds overhead to the query execution itself – the SQL Server team measured a 75 percent overhead with a TPC-C-like workload – which is why this information is not readily available all the time.

> **Note**
> TPC-C is a standard **Online Transaction Processing** (**OLTP**) workload that is used to benchmark database systems. You can find out more about TPC-C at http://www.tpc.org/tpcc.

The high cost of this data collection is grounded in the need to enable the standard version of the Query Profiling Infrastructure, the **Standard Query Execution Statistics Profile Infrastructure**, or **Standard Profiling** for short, which must be enabled to collect information about query execution plans, namely the number of actual rows flowing through operators, as well as CPU and I/O usage. Standard Profiling can be enabled globally to collect information for all queries, or for a single session and query.

To collect query execution plans for a single query using Standard Profiling, the following methods are available:

- Use SET STATISTICS XML ON or SET STATISTICS PROFILE ON before a T-SQL query is executed – we covered these commands in the *Accessing a query plan* section of *Chapter 4, Exploring Query Execution Plans*

- **Live Query Statistics** – this feature was covered in the previous section of this chapter

To collect query execution plans for all queries using Standard Profiling, one of the following methods can be used:

- Using the **query_post_execution_showplan** Extended Event (**XEvent** or **XE**) in an XEvent trace. We discussed XEvents in *Chapter 9, Building XEvent Profiler Traces*.

- Using the **Showplan XML** trace event in SQL Trace and SQL Server Profiler. However, these methods are deprecated and should not be used in SQL Server 2012 or newer versions, where the more complete and less intrusive XEvents are available.

SQL Server 2014 SP2 and SQL Server 2016 introduced a lightweight version of the Query Profiling Infrastructure that exists side-by-side with Standard Profiling, the new **Lightweight Query Execution Statistics Profiling Infrastructure**, or **Lightweight Profiling** (**LWP**) for short. LWP has evolved over time to hold true to its name and concentrate on the fundamental task of democratizing access to the equivalent of an actual execution plan – which is an essential artifact for query performance troubleshooting. The SQL Server team measured a 1.5 to 2 percent overhead with a TPC-C-like workload – a significant improvement from Standard Profiling. Lightweight Profiling can also be enabled globally to collect information for all queries, or for a single session and query.

To collect query execution plans for a single query using Lightweight Profiling, use the QUERY_PLAN_PROFILE query hint in conjunction with a trace that captures the query_plan_profile XEvent. We will show how this XEvent can be used in more detail later in this section.

> **Note**
>
> Clicking the **Live Query Statistics** button in SSMS enables Standard Profiling for that single query, irrespective of whether Lightweight Profiling is enabled globally and already populating the sys.dm_exec_query_profiles DMV. In this case, the DMV is populated using Standard Profiling for that query only, and Lightweight Profiling is used for all other queries.

To collect query execution plans for all queries using Lightweight Profiling, one of the following methods can be used:

- Enable **trace flag 7412 globally** in SQL Server 2016 and SQL Server 2017. If our SQL Server instance is not already CPU-bound and can withstand the 1.5-to-2 percent overhead as a trade-off to having always available runtime data for every query in every session, then it is a recommended best practice to enable this trace flag at startup. To enable the trace flag globally, but not at startup, use the following T-SQL command: `DBCC TRACEON (7412, -1)`. When Lightweight Profiling is enabled globally, the `sys.dm_exec_query_profiles` DMV is populated for all queries that are being executed.

- Using the `query_thread_profile` or `query_post_execution_plan_profile` XEvents in an XEvent trace. We will discuss how to use these XEvents in more detail later in this section.

Starting with SQL Server 2019, LWP is enabled by default, and trace flag 7412 is not needed. However, LWP can be disabled at the database level setting the database scoped configuration `LIGHTWEIGHT_QUERY_PROFILING` to OFF using the following T-SQL command: `ALTER DATABASE SCOPED CONFIGURATION SET LIGHTWEIGHT_QUERY_PROFILING = OFF;`

So, what is available in a query execution plan that is obtained through LWP? How is that plan different from one obtained using Standard Profiling? Why is the term "equivalent of an actual execution plan" being used here? These are all pertinent questions that we will answer in this chapter.

From SQL Server 2014 through SQL Server 2017, the noticeable difference between Standard Profiling and Lightweight Profiling is that LWP did not collect per-operator CPU runtime information because tracking CPU usage across queries is one of the aspects that added so much overhead to Standard Profiling. Per-operator CPU usage isn't necessarily fundamental information when we are troubleshooting a query performance issue. For these SQL Server versions, LWP still collects per-operator I/O usage information and actual row counts – this is the important information. At the query level, LWP still collects information about overall CPU and elapsed time, memory grant usage, runtime warnings, and actual **Degree of Parallelism (DOP)**.

> **Note**
> If both Query Profiling Infrastructures are enabled simultaneously, then Standard Profiling takes precedence over Lightweight Profiling, for the scope in which each is enabled. For example, if LWP is enabled globally, but then we use `SET STATISTICS XML ON` for a specific query, that query's execution plan will use Standard Profiling instead.

Starting with SQL Server 2019, LWP was revised to specifically exclude per-operator I/O runtime information by default – only per-operator row counts are reported. This was done after finding that in very extreme cases, even tracking I/O could introduce overhead that would make LWP not stay true to its principle of being lightweight. LWP still collects the same query-level information as it did in previous versions.

> **Tip**
>
> If we require per-operator I/O information to be collected with LWP and have tested its impact on our SQL Server, we can enable trace flag 7415 to restore per-operator I/O metrics as available in SQL Server 2016 and SQL Server 2017.

Diagnostics available with Lightweight Profiling

Because it became cheaper to collect information about query execution plans with LWP, this allowed several diagnostics artifacts to be added to SQL Server: XEvents and **Dynamic Management Functions (DMFs)**. We will discuss all these new diagnostics and how to use them for the remainder of this section.

The query_thread_profile XEvent

SQL Server 2016 Service Pack 1 introduced a new XEvent named `query_thread_profile`. Unlike the `query_post_execution_showplan` XEvent that uses only Standard Profiling, `query_thread_profile` uses Lightweight Profiling by default. Also, unlike `query_post_execution_showplan`, `query_thread_profile` doesn't output a query execution plan as a single `showplan` XML file – it outputs one event per operator and thread with the same execution statistics that are expected in a query execution plan. This means that it can be quite verbose, but since it's based on Lightweight Profiling rather than Standard Profiling, it can be used for a longer period of time than was possible with `query_post_execution_showplan`.

The following example shows a session that uses this XEvent:

```
CREATE EVENT SESSION [PerfStats_Node] ON SERVER
ADD EVENT sqlserver.query_thread_profile(
    ACTION(sqlos.scheduler_id, sqlserver.database_id, sqlserver.is_
system,
sqlserver.plan_handle, sqlserver.query_hash_signed, sqlserver.query_
plan_hash_signed,
sqlserver.server_instance_name,sqlserver.session_id, sqlserver.
session_nt_username, sqlserver.sql_text)
    )
    ADD TARGET package0.event_file(
        SET filename=N'C:\Temp\PerfStats_Node.xel',
max_file_size=(50), max_rollover_files=(2)
    )
WITH (MAX_MEMORY=4096 KB, EVENT_RETENTION_MODE=ALLOW_SINGLE_EVENT_
LOSS,
MAX_DISPATCH_LATENCY=30 SECONDS, MAX_EVENT_SIZE=0 KB, MEMORY_
PARTITION_MODE=NONE,
    TRACK_CAUSALITY=OFF,STARTUP_STATE=OFF);
```

To see the output this XEvent produces, execute the following query in the `AdventureWorks` sample database:

```
ALTER EVENT SESSION [PerfStats_Node] ON SERVER STATE = start;
GO
SELECT COUNT(*)
FROM Sales.SalesOrderDetail AS sod
INNER JOIN Sales.SalesOrderHeader AS soh ON soh.SalesOrderID = sod.
SalesOrderID
GROUP BY soh.Status;
GO
ALTER EVENT SESSION [PerfStats_Node] ON SERVER STATE = stop;
GO
```

The resulting file can be opened using SSMS as seen in the following screenshot. Note that the same XEvent session and query were executed in SQL Server 2017 and SQL Server 2019 for comparison between the versions:

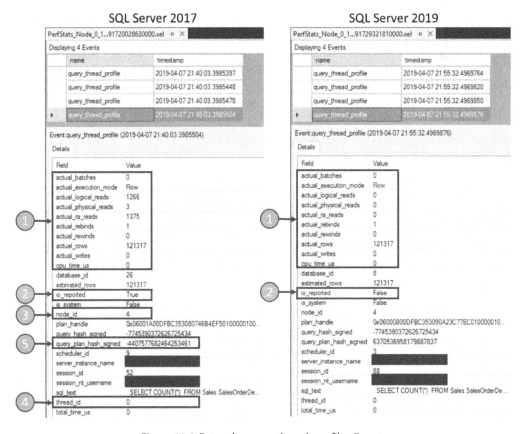

Figure 11.4: Example query_thread_profile xEvent

> **Note**
> The examples in this chapter compare SQL Server 2017 with SQL Server 2019 as this is when the relevant Lightweight Profiling changes were made. SQL Server 2022 has some additional fields, such as `actual_page_server_ra_reads`, `actual_page_server_reads`, and several `hpc_*` fields. These new event fields reference Azure SQL Database Hyperscale and HPC architectures are not relevant for the discussions in this chapter, so we have elected to keep the SQL Server 2019 examples.

Notice that for one single query execution, this XEvent fired four times, once for each operator that processes data in the query plan. Let's focus on the last XEvent fired for this session. In it, we can find the following information:

- Runtime data that includes the number of actual rows read by this operator (node ID) that matches the `RunTimeCountersPerThread` showplan element we discussed in the *Operator-level properties* section of *Chapter 4, Exploring Query Execution Plans*. Notice that the CPU time is zero because LWP doesn't collect per-operator CPU metrics. As expected in the SQL Server 2019 example, the per-operator I/O metrics are also not populated.

- The **io_reported** action indicates whether I/O is reported in the XEvent or not. As expected, it's **True** for SQL Server 2014 through SQL Server 2017 and **False** starting with SQL Server 2019.

- The current node ID in this case is 4. This information will be used to map this node ID when we look at a graphical query plan.

- As mentioned, this XEvent fires once per operator and thread. In this example trace, we only have one XEvent per node ID, and each node ID shows a thread ID zero. When an operator only fires one XEvent, this thread ID will always be zero, and this means the operator executed in serial, meaning on a single scheduler. If an operator executes in parallel, for example, with a DOP of 4, then five such XEvents are fired for a single operator: one for the coordinator thread and one per each of the four child threads.

- The query plan hash that is needed to retrieve the query plan from the cache is useful for mapping the text-only XEvent data to a graphical query plan.

> **Tip**
> Starting with SQL Server 2014 SP2 and SQL Server 2016, use the `query_hash_signed` and `query_plan_hash_signed` actions instead of the `query_hash` and `query_plan_hash` actions to correlate data from XEvent collections with DMVs such as `sys.dm_exec_requests` and `sys.dm_exec_query_stats`. The `query_hash` and `query_plan_hash` actions are not the same data types as the respective columns in the DMVs, which doesn't allow the expected correlation.

The node IDs can be searched in the graphical execution plan so we can get more clarity on all the operator types in this plan. We can use the query plan hash to get the graphical plan from the cache using the following query in SSMS:

```
SELECT qp.query_plan
FROM sys.dm_exec_query_stats qs
CROSS APPLY sys.dm_exec_query_plan(qs.plan_handle) qp
WHERE CAST(qs.query_plan_hash AS BIGINT) = -4407577682464253461;
```

This returns the following result set:

	query_plan
1	<ShowPlanXML xmlns="http://schemas.microsoft.com...

Figure 11.5: Results of the example query showing a link to the graphical query execution plan

Clicking on the link in the results tab opens the graphical plan, and now it's time to start mapping the XEvent session runtime information with the cached plan. To do this, we use the **Node Search** feature in SSMS. Right-click anywhere in the plan and click on **Find Node**:

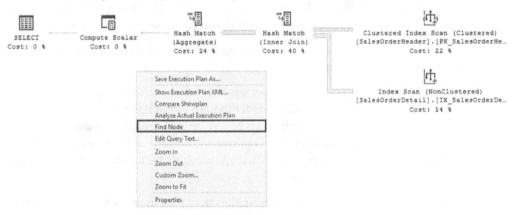

Figure 11.6: Graphical query plan retrieved by the example query

This feature allows me to search for any property that exists in the showplan XML file, as shown in the following screenshot:

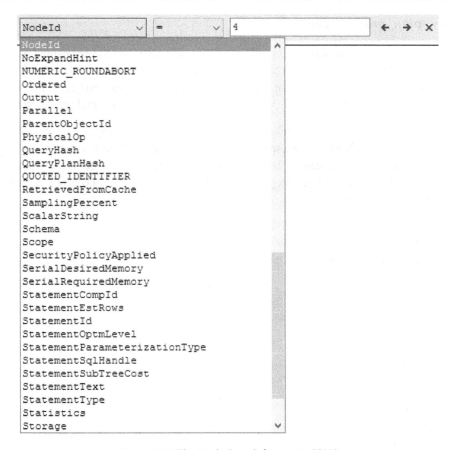

Figure 11.7: The Node Search feature in SSMS

Searching for `NodeId = 4` immediately focuses on the Non-Clustered Index Scan that represents node ID 4 in the following query plan:

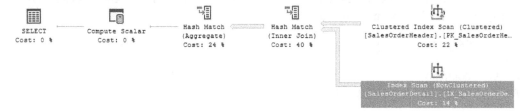

Figure 11.8: Results of the node search showing the Index Scan (NodeId = 4) highlighted

Correlating this with the data in the XEvent, I now know this Index Scan read 121,317 rows, in 1,266 logical reads, and 1,375 read-aheads. This XEvent is very useful for collecting runtime query data at scale, which may be worth the time-consuming task of doing this correlation exercise.

The query_plan_profile XEvent

SQL Server 2016 SP2 CU3 and SQL Server 2017 CU11 introduced a new XEvent named query_ plan_profile. This XEvent outputs the equivalent of a query execution plan like the query_ post_execution_showplan XEvent. Unlike the query_post_execution_showplan Xevent, which uses Standard Profiling, query_plan_profile uses Lightweight Profiling by default.

The query_plan_profile XEvent allows a very targeted plan collection that can be used for a longer period of time to gather data for a specific query execution and doesn't require any object or statement filtering in the XEvent session. This is because the XEvent only fires for a query or queries that are using the USE HINT ('QUERY_PLAN_PROFILE') hint. The following is an example session that uses this XEvent:

```
CREATE EVENT SESSION [PerfStats_LWP_Plan_Single] ON SERVER
ADD EVENT sqlserver.query_plan_profile(
    ACTION(sqlos.scheduler_id, sqlserver.database_id, sqlserver.is_
system,
sqlserver.plan_handle, sqlserver.query_hash_signed, sqlserver.query_
plan_hash_signed,
sqlserver.server_instance_name,sqlserver.session_id, sqlserver.
session_nt_username, sqlserver.sql_text)
    )
    ADD TARGET package0.event_file(
        SET filename=N'C:\Temp\PerfStats_LWP_Plan_Single.xel',
max_file_size=(50), max_rollover_files=(2)
    )
WITH (MAX_MEMORY=4096 KB, EVENT_RETENTION_MODE=ALLOW_SINGLE_EVENT_
LOSS,
MAX_DISPATCH_LATENCY=30 SECONDS, MAX_EVENT_SIZE=0 KB, MEMORY_
PARTITION_MODE=NONE, TRACK_CAUSALITY=OFF,STARTUP_STATE=OFF);
```

To see the output this XEvent produces, we need to set up our example. Creating the following stored procedure in the AdventureWorks sample database allows us to later use this XEvent as we would probably do in a production environment:

```
CREATE OR ALTER PROCEDURE [Sales].[CountSalesOrderByStatus]
AS
SELECT COUNT(*)
FROM Sales.SalesOrderDetail AS sod
```

```
INNER JOIN Sales.SalesOrderHeader AS soh
    ON soh.SalesOrderID = sod.SalesOrderID
GROUP BY soh.Status;
```

In a production system, most likely we will not be able to alter the existing stored procedure to add the required hint. The same would happen if a query we want to track is generated by an application and we can't change the query at its origin. The solution is to use a plan guide to add the hint, as shown in the following example created for the `Sales.CountSalesOrderByStatus` stored procedure:

```
EXEC sp_create_plan_guide
@name = N'Guide1',
@stmt = 'SELECT COUNT(*)
FROM Sales.SalesOrderDetail AS sod
INNER JOIN Sales.SalesOrderHeader AS soh
    ON soh.SalesOrderID = sod.SalesOrderID
GROUP BY soh.Status;',
@type = N'OBJECT',
@module_or_batch = N'Sales.CountSalesOrderByStatus',
@params = NULL,
@hints = N'OPTION (USE HINT (''QUERY_PLAN_PROFILE''))';
```

Now we can execute the following example query in the `AdventureWorks` sample database:

```
ALTER EVENT SESSION [PerfStats_LWP_Plan_Single] ON SERVER STATE =
start;
GO
EXEC Sales.CountSalesOrderByStatus;
GO
ALTER EVENT SESSION [PerfStats_LWP_Plan_Single] ON SERVER STATE =
stop;
GO
```

The resulting file can be opened using SSMS, as shown in the following screenshot:

Figure 11.9: Example of the query_plan_profile xEvent

The XEvent contains runtime data for the overall query, including the duration in microseconds, memory grant information, and the actual DOP that was used: 1, meaning the query executed in serial.

To see the plan itself, click on the **Query Plan** tab. Note that the same XEvent session and query was executed in SQL Server 2017 and SQL Server 2019 for comparison between the versions:

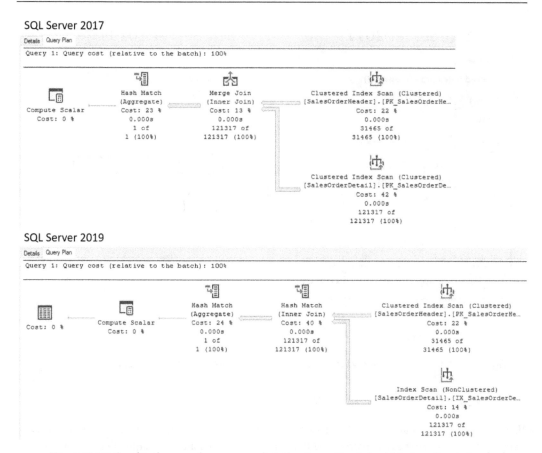

Figure 11.10: Graphical query plans accessed via the Query Plan tab within the xEvent viewer

Notice that the plans don't have any reference to the statement text that was executed: this is already present in the XEvent itself, and so this information can be removed from the captured plan to make the collection more lightweight. Furthermore, the SQL Server 2019 plan contains one extra operator – the Cost root node – which has information that is usually found in a root node of a query execution plan, which was discussed in the *Query plan properties of interest* section in *Chapter 3, Exploring Query Execution Plans*.

When we look at the properties for node ID 4 – the Non-Clustered Index Scan – they include the number of actual rows read by this operator (node ID), which can also be seen below the operator icon as the number of actual rows versus the number of estimated rows that flowed through the operator (121,317 of 12,1317). However, in the SQL Server 2019 example we see the I/O metrics are not present because LWP in SQL Server 2019 doesn't collect I/O information by default, as shown in the following screenshot:

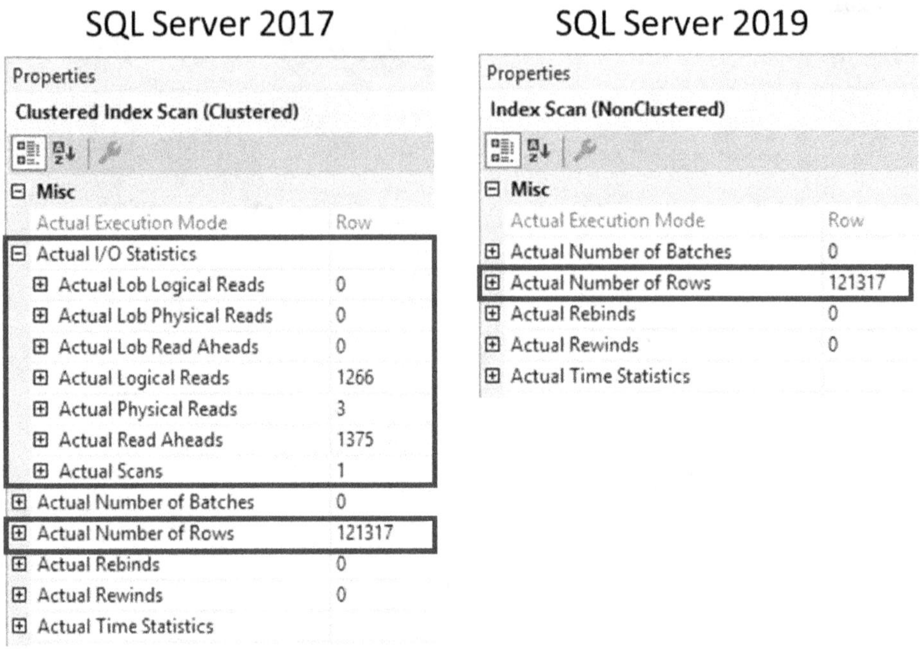

SQL Server 2017

Properties

Clustered Index Scan (Clustered)

Misc	
Actual Execution Mode	Row
⊟ Actual I/O Statistics	
⊞ Actual Lob Logical Reads	0
⊞ Actual Lob Physical Reads	0
⊞ Actual Lob Read Aheads	0
⊞ Actual Logical Reads	1266
⊞ Actual Physical Reads	3
⊞ Actual Read Aheads	1375
⊞ Actual Scans	1
⊞ Actual Number of Batches	0
⊞ Actual Number of Rows	121317
⊞ Actual Rebinds	0
⊞ Actual Rewinds	0
⊞ Actual Time Statistics	

SQL Server 2019

Properties

Index Scan (NonClustered)

Misc	
Actual Execution Mode	Row
⊞ Actual Number of Batches	0
⊞ Actual Number of Rows	121317
⊞ Actual Rebinds	0
⊞ Actual Rewinds	0
⊞ Actual Time Statistics	

Figure 11.11: Properties window for the Non-Clustered Index Scan in the example query plan

The query_post_execution_plan_profile XEvent

SQL Server 2017 Cumulative Update 14 and SQL Server 2019 introduced a new XEvent named `query_post_execution_profile` that can be used to collect the equivalent of an actual execution plan for all queries, much like the `query_post_execution_showplan` XEvent. Unlike the `query_plan_profile` XEvent, `query_post_execution_profile` is not bound to a query hint, but it also uses Lightweight Profiling by default. The following is an example session that uses this XEvent:

```
CREATE EVENT SESSION [PerfStats_LWP_Plan_All] ON SERVER
ADD EVENT sqlserver.query_post_execution_plan_profile(
    ACTION(sqlos.scheduler_id, sqlserver.database_id, sqlserver.is_
system,
sqlserver.plan_handle, sqlserver.query_hash_signed, sqlserver.query_
plan_hash_signed,
```

```
sqlserver.server_instance_name,sqlserver.session_id, sqlserver.
session_nt_username, sqlserver.sql_text)
     )
     ADD TARGET package0.event_file(
          SET filename=N'C:\Temp\PerfStats_LWP_Plan_All.xel',
max_file_size=(50), max_rollover_files=(2)
     )
WITH (MAX_MEMORY=4096 KB, EVENT_RETENTION_MODE=ALLOW_SINGLE_EVENT_
LOSS,
MAX_DISPATCH_LATENCY=30 SECONDS, MAX_EVENT_SIZE=0 KB, MEMORY_
PARTITION_MODE=NONE,
     TRACK_CAUSALITY=OFF,STARTUP_STATE=OFF);
```

To see the output this XEvent produces, execute the following example query in the `AdventureWorks` sample database:

```
ALTER EVENT SESSION [PerfStats_LWP_Plan_All] ON SERVER STATE = start;
GO
SELECT COUNT(*)
FROM Sales.SalesOrderDetail AS sod
INNER JOIN Sales.SalesOrderHeader AS soh
     ON soh.SalesOrderID = sod.SalesOrderID
GROUP BY soh.Status;
GO
ALTER EVENT SESSION [PerfStats_LWP_Plan_All] ON SERVER STATE = stop;
GO
```

The resulting file can be opened using SSMS, as shown in the following screenshot:

Figure 11.12: XEvent viewer showing the query_post_execution_plan_profile xEvent

The XEvent contains the same runtime data we had observed for the `query_plan_profile` XEvent. This makes sense because these XEvents are very close implementations, minus the binding to a query hint on `query_plan_profile`. Therefore, as expected when we click in the **Query Plan** tab, the observations for SQL Server 2017 and SQL Server 2019 query execution plans are also the same as in the previous chapter for the `query_plan_profile` XEvent.

The sys.dm_exec_query_statistics_xml DMF

SQL Server 2016 SP1 introduced a new DMF named `sys.dm_exec_query_statistics_xml` that uses Lightweight Profiling by default, but also works if Standard Profiling is enabled. This DMF outputs the query execution plan as a snapshot of the current in-flight request. As such, this query execution plan will have transient runtime statistics captured at the moment the DMF was invoked.

The ability to programmatically access the query execution plan for any running request is a leap forward for scenarios where we must troubleshoot a long-running query. In this case, we can use this DMF, or Live Query Statistics – which we discussed in the first section of this chapter.

Let's look at a practical example of using this new DMF. The following example was used in *Chapter 2, Mechanics of the Query Optimizer*, and was saved into a file named `ProblemQuery.sql`:

```
SELECT e.[BusinessEntityID], p.[Title], p.[FirstName],
    p.[MiddleName], p.[LastName], p.[Suffix], e.[JobTitle],
    pp.[PhoneNumber], pnt.[Name] AS [PhoneNumberType],
    ea.[EmailAddress], p.[EmailPromotion], a.[AddressLine1],
    a.[AddressLine2], a.[City], sp.[Name] AS [StateProvinceName],
    a.[PostalCode], cr.[Name] AS [CountryRegionName],
p.[AdditionalContactInfo]
FROM [HumanResources].[Employee] AS e
INNER JOIN [Person].[Person] AS p
    ON RTRIM(LTRIM(p.[BusinessEntityID])) = RTRIM(LTRIM(e.
[BusinessEntityID]))
INNER JOIN [Person].[BusinessEntityAddress] AS bea
    ON RTRIM(LTRIM(bea.[BusinessEntityID])) = RTRIM(LTRIM(e.
[BusinessEntityID]))
INNER JOIN [Person].[Address] AS a
    ON RTRIM(LTRIM(a.[AddressID])) = RTRIM(LTRIM(bea.[AddressID]))
INNER JOIN [Person].[StateProvince] AS sp
    ON RTRIM(LTRIM(sp.[StateProvinceID])) = RTRIM(LTRIM(a.
[StateProvinceID]))
INNER JOIN [Person].[CountryRegion] AS cr
    ON RTRIM(LTRIM(cr.[CountryRegionCode])) = RTRIM(LTRIM(sp.
[CountryRegionCode]))
LEFT OUTER JOIN [Person].[PersonPhone] AS pp
    ON RTRIM(LTRIM(pp.BusinessEntityID)) = RTRIM(LTRIM(p.
[BusinessEntityID]))
LEFT OUTER JOIN [Person].[PhoneNumberType] AS pnt
    ON RTRIM(LTRIM(pp.[PhoneNumberTypeID])) = RTRIM(LTRIM(pnt.
[PhoneNumberTypeID]))
LEFT OUTER JOIN [Person].[EmailAddress] AS ea
    ON RTRIM(LTRIM(p.[BusinessEntityID])) = RTRIM(LTRIM(ea.
[BusinessEntityID]));
```

We can use the `ostress` utility and simulate a client application executing the same long-running query over 10 concurrent connections, as seen in the following command:

```
ostress.exe -S<my_server_name> -E -dAdventureWorks -iProblemQuery.sql
-n10 -r1000
```

> **Note**
>
> `ostress` is a free command line tool that is part of the **Replay Markup Language** (**RML**) utilities for SQL Server. This tool can be used to simulate the effects of stressing a SQL Server instance by using ad hoc queries or `.sql` script files.

While the workload is executing, we can join `sys.dm_exec_query_statistics_xml` with other DMVs, such as `sys.dm_exec_requests`, `sys.dm_exec_sessions`, and `sys.dm_exec_connections`. The following query uses the `sys.dm_exec_requests` DMV as a starting point, since I'm looking to get the current state of the execution plan for an in-flight request:

```
SELECT er.session_id, er.start_time, er.status, er.database_id,
    er.wait_type, er.last_wait_type, er.cpu_time, er.total_elapsed_
time,
    er.logical_reads, er.granted_query_memory, er.dop,
    st.text, qsx.query_plan
FROM sys.dm_exec_requests AS er
CROSS APPLY sys.dm_exec_sql_text(plan_handle) AS st
CROSS APPLY sys.dm_exec_query_statistics_xml(session_id) AS qsx;
```

This query returns the following results:

	session_id	start_time	status	database_id	wait_type	last_wait_type	cpu_time
1	66	2019-04-08 17:59:42.517	runnable	26	NULL	SOS_SCHEDULER_YIELD	24
2	75	2019-04-08 17:59:42.497	runnable	26	NULL	SOS_SCHEDULER_YIELD	32
3	77	2019-04-08 17:59:42.377	running	26	NULL	SOS_SCHEDULER_YIELD	78
4	81	2019-04-08 17:59:42.610	running	26	NULL	SOS_SCHEDULER_YIELD	20
5	83	2019-04-08 17:59:42.637	running	26	NULL	RESERVED_MEMORY_AL...	10
6	84	2019-04-08 17:59:42.597	running	26	NULL	SOS_SCHEDULER_YIELD	32
7	85	2019-04-08 17:59:42.703	runnable	26	NULL	SOS_SCHEDULER_YIELD	11
8	86	2019-04-08 17:59:42.687	runnable	26	NULL	SOS_SCHEDULER_YIELD	28
9	88	2019-04-08 17:59:42.680	running	26	NULL	RESERVED_MEMORY_AL...	43
10	112	2019-04-08 17:59:42.567	running	1	NULL	SOS_SCHEDULER_YIELD	81

total_elapsed_time	logical_reads	granted_query_memory	dop	text	query_plan
48	235	3422	1	SELECT e.[BusinessEntityID], ...	<ShowPlanXML xmlns="http://schema...
91	272	3422	1	SELECT e.[BusinessEntityID], ...	<ShowPlanXML xmlns="http://schema...
228	4427	3422	1	SELECT e.[BusinessEntityID], ...	<ShowPlanXML xmlns="http://schema...
20	204	3422	1	SELECT e.[BusinessEntityID], ...	<ShowPlanXML xmlns="http://schema...
18	98	3422	1	SELECT e.[BusinessEntityID], ...	<ShowPlanXML xmlns="http://schema...
93	263	3422	1	SELECT e.[BusinessEntityID], ...	<ShowPlanXML xmlns="http://schema...
21	125	3422	1	SELECT e.[BusinessEntityID], ...	<ShowPlanXML xmlns="http://schema...
55	281	3422	1	SELECT e.[BusinessEntityID], ...	<ShowPlanXML xmlns="http://schema...
83	471	3422	1	SELECT e.[BusinessEntityID], ...	<ShowPlanXML xmlns="http://schema...
223	0	0	1	SELECT er.session_id, er.start...	<ShowPlanXML xmlns="http://schema...

Figure 11.13: Results of the example DMV query

Each row is an in-flight request. To see a snapshot of the ongoing query execution plan, click the link in the `query_plan` column:

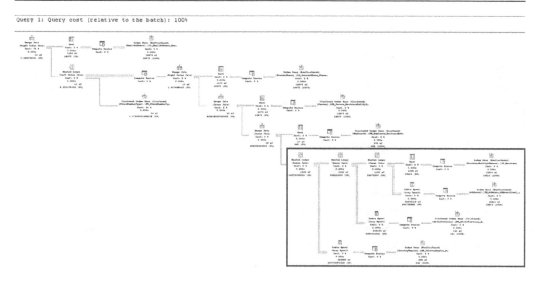

Figure 11.14: Graphical query plan as accessed through the example DMV query

If we zoom into the bottom right quadrant of the query execution plan, as shown in the following screenshot, we see some slow progress in building two Table Spools. We discussed Spools in in the *Query plan operators of interest* section of *Chapter 3, Exploring Query Execution Plans*, and the focus of analysis should be this section of the plan we made in the *Using live query statistics* section of this chapter.

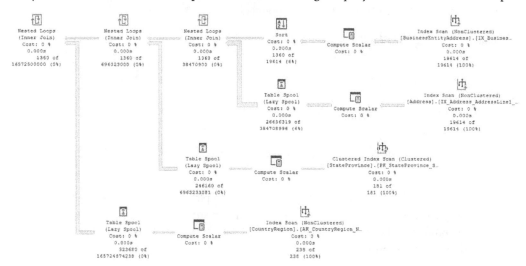

Figure 11.15: Zoomed in view of the section of the query plan highlighted in Figure 11.14

> **Tip**
> In the GitHub Tiger Toolbox (`http://aka.ms/tigertoolbox`), we can find a comprehensive script that can quickly help us diagnose performance issues with in-flight requests and blocking scenarios (`http://aka.ms/uspWhatsUp`). This script uses a combination of DMVs that includes `sys.dm_exec_query_statistics_xml`.

The sys.dm_exec_query_plan_stats DMF

SQL Server 2019 introduced a new DMF named `sys.dm_exec_query_plan_stats` that uses Lightweight Profiling by default, and like the DMF in the previous section, also works if Standard Profiling is enabled. This DMF outputs the last known equivalent of a query execution plan for any given query whose query plan can still be found in the plan cache. In other words, every data professional can now have the last actual execution plan always available for any query.

> **Note**
> This DMF only maintains a subset of what is available through XEvents using Lightweight Profiling. The available information for plans accessed through this DMF are operator-level row count, spill warnings (without I/O detail), and query-level CPU time and elapsed time. Wait statistics and operator-level I/O statistics are not included due to the potential overhead.

There are two methods to enable this DMF to be populated:

- Enable trace flag 2451 (at the session level or globally by adding the -1 parameter) using the following T-SQL command:

  ```
  DBCC TRACEON(2451, -1);
  ```

- Set the database scoped configuration `LAST_QUERY_PLAN_STATS` to `ON` using the following T-SQL command:

  ```
  ALTER DATABASE SCOPED CONFIGURATION SET LAST_QUERY_PLAN_STATS =
  ON;
  ```

The concept of always having the last known query execution plan available is a game-changer for troubleshooting just-in-time scenarios where a query's performance has suddenly regressed, and we are the database professional that gets a call informing us that the application has poor performance as a result and that we must provide root-cause analysis.

If it's a long-running query, then we can use Live Query Statistics or the DMF in the previous section. But if it's a case of a query that has been executing (to completion) repeatedly in the last few minutes, then accessing the last known actual execution plan allows us to start troubleshooting immediately, without needing to set up any kind of tracing.

> **Note**
>
> SQL Trace and SQL Server Profiler are deprecated and should not be used in modern versions of SQL Server because more complete and less intrusive XEvents are available.

If we are familiar with **Query Store (QS)**, which we discussed in *Chapter 10, Tracking Query Performance History with the Query Store*, then that may be our first go-to feature to troubleshoot our current scenario. However, QS aggregates performance data in configurable time periods, which is excellent for performance troubleshooting over time (analogous to a time series) and analyzing workload trends, but for just-in-time scenarios where the requirement is to get the query's execution plan that just executed, then this DMF is a welcome diagnostic.

> **Note**
>
> If any Query Profiling Infrastructure is enabled, the DMF captures and saves the query execution plan data for all query plans in the cache. If the query is canceled, the query execution plan will have data up to the point when the query was canceled.

Let's look at a practical example of using this new DMF. The following sample query can be executed in the scope of the `AdventureWorks` sample database:

```
SELECT TOP 1000 *
FROM [dbo].[DimProduct] AS dp
INNER JOIN [dbo].[DimProductCategory] AS dpc ON
dp.ProductSubcategoryKey = dpc.ProductCategoryKey;
```

We can then join with other DMVs, such as `sys.dm_exec_cached_plans`, `sys.dm_exec_query_stats`, `sys.dm_exec_requests`, `sys.dm_exec_procedure_stats`, and `sys.dm_exec_trigger_stats`. Next, we have examples of queries that can retrieve information on the specific query, including the last known equivalent of a query execution plan from `sys.dm_exec_query_plan_stats`.

The following query uses the `sys.dm_exec_cached_plans` DMV as a starting point, since the `sys.dm_exec_query_plan_stats` DMF can only report on query plans that are cached:

```
SELECT qps.dbid, st.text, qps.query_plan,
       cp.refcounts, cp.usecounts, cp.cacheobjtype, cp.objtype
FROM sys.dm_exec_cached_plans AS cp
CROSS APPLY sys.dm_exec_sql_text(plan_handle) AS st
CROSS APPLY sys.dm_exec_query_plan_stats(plan_handle) AS qps
WHERE st.text LIKE '%SELECT TOP 1000%';
```

This query returns the following results:

	dbid	text	query_plan	refcounts	usecounts	cacheobjtype	objtype
1	5	SELECT TOP 1000 * FR...	<ShowPlanXML xmlns="http://schemas...	2	1	Compiled Plan	Adhoc

Figure 11.16: Results of the example query

Note

If the corresponding runtime plan information is not available, the **query_plan** column shows NULL.

The following query uses the `sys.dm_exec_query_stats` DMV as a starting point in order to see performance metrics for all queries that have executed since the last SQL Server startup, where the query plan is still in the plan cache:

```
SELECT qps.dbid, st.text, qps.query_plan,
       qs.last_dop, qs.last_elapsed_time, qs.last_execution_time,
       qs.last_grant_kb, qs.last_used_grant_kb, qs.last_logical_reads,
       qs.last_logical_writes, qs.last_physical_reads,
       qs.last_rows, qs.last_spills, qs.last_worker_time
FROM sys.dm_exec_query_stats AS qs
OUTER APPLY sys.dm_exec_sql_text(plan_handle) AS st
OUTER APPLY sys.dm_exec_query_plan_stats(plan_handle) AS qps
WHERE st.text LIKE '--%';
```

This query returns the following results:

Figure 11.17: Results of the example query

Again, if the corresponding runtime plan information is not available, the `query_plan` column is NULL. On both results, click the link in the `query_plan` column to open the last known query execution plan, as shown in the following screenshot:

```
Query 1: Query cost (relative to the batch): 100%
SELECT TOP 1000 * FROM [dbo].[DimProduct] AS dp INNER JOIN [dbo].[DimProductCategory] AS dpc ON
Missing Index (Impact 90.4554): CREATE NONCLUSTERED INDEX [<Name of Missing Index, sysname,>] ON
```

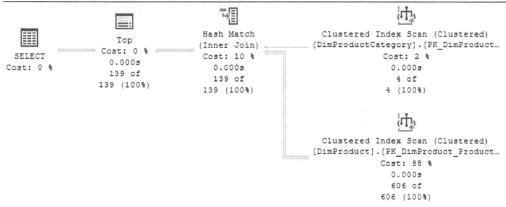

Figure 11.18: Graphical query execution plan as accessed from the link in the results shown in Figure 11.17

Tip

In the GitHub Tiger Toolbox (http://aka.ms/tigertoolbox), we can find a comprehensive script that can quickly help us diagnose performance issues with in-flight requests and blocking scenarios (http://aka.ms/uspWhatsUp). This script uses a combination of DMVs that includes sys.dm_exec_query_plan_stats.

Activity Monitor gets new life

Live Query Statistics (**LQS**) has a viable use case, as we discussed in the *Using Live Query Statistics* section of this chapter: a previously identified long-running query. But what if we haven't identified an offending query yet? What if we are the database professional that got that middle-of-the-night call asking us to solve an issue with a business-critical ETL process that runs every night, but is unusually slow today?

Note

ETL is an acronym for **Extract-Transform-Load**, which is the name given to a process that extracts data from a data source, enacts transformations in that data such as aggregations or calculations, and loads the result into a destination such as a database. A typical example of an ETL process is a SQL Server Agent job that schedules the execution of a **SQL Server Integration Services** (**SSIS**) package.

That is where **Activity Monitor** (**AM**) comes in. AM is an SSMS feature that's been there for a long time and has probably gone unnoticed by many SSMS users. AM can be enabled by right-clicking the instance name in **Object Explorer**, and then clicking on **Activity Monitor**, as shown in the following screenshot:

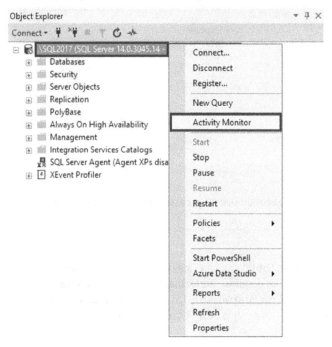

Figure 11.19: Screenshot depicting how to access Activity Monitor from the Object Explorer in SSMS

A new tab will be displayed which contains the following information sections:

- An **Overview** section showinga few key performance counters: CPU usage, number of waiting tasks, database I/O measured in MB/sec, and number of batch requests/sec. Notice the CPU is running at 80 percent now that the ETL is executing. I'm also doing six batch requests/sec, which is a very low number.

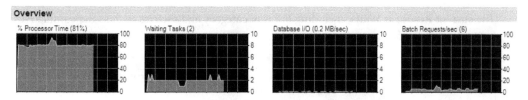

Figure 11.20: Overview section of Activity Monitor

- The current **Processes** or sessions active in SQL Server, including useful information such as the login and database that set the context for that session, the current task state (**Running**, **Runnable**, or **Suspended**) as defined in the *Query execution essentials* section of *Chapter 1, Understanding Query Processing*, wait information which shows details if the task is in the Suspended state, the calling application and host machine, and whether the current session is a head blocker of a blocking chain. All this information is coming from DMVs, which were thoroughly discussed in *Chapter 7, Building Diagnostic Queries Using DMVs and DMFs*.

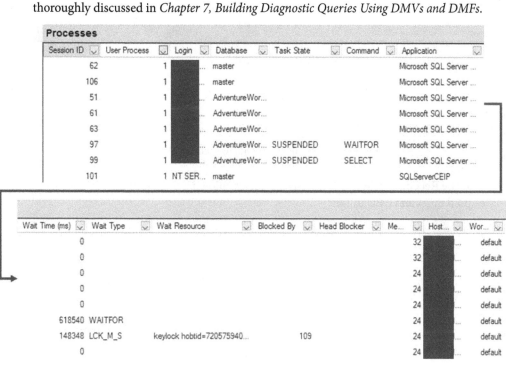

Figure 11.21: Processes section of Activity Monitor

- The current **Resource Waits**, including the wait category and metrics such as the cumulative wait time accrued for the wait type.

Resource Waits

Wait Category	Wait Time (ms/sec)	Recent Wait Time (ms/sec)	Average Waiter Count	Cumulative Wait Time (sec)
Logging	16479	20878	16.5	8259
Buffer Latch	2985	1449	3.0	479
Latch	4229	1231	4.2	308
Lock	1002	996	1.0	5798
Buffer I/O	16	1	0.0	4619
Compilation	0	0	0.0	0
Memory	0	0	0.0	0
Network I/O	0	0	0.0	1642

Figure 11.22: Resource Waits section of Activity Monitor

- The **Data File I/O** related to the read and write I/O, including access latency for each file.

Data File I/O

Database	File Name	MB/sec Read	MB/sec Written	Response Time (ms)
AdventureWorks2016CTP3	E:\Program Files\Microsoft SQL Server\MSSQL14.SQL2017\MSSQL\D...	33.4	0.0	476
AdventureWorks2008R2	E:\Program Files\Microsoft SQL Server\MSSQL14.SQL2017\MSSQL\D...	0.0	0.0	0
AdventureWorks2008R2	E:\Program Files\Microsoft SQL Server\MSSQL14.SQL2017\MSSQL\D...	0.0	0.0	0
AdventureWorks2014	E:\Program Files\Microsoft SQL Server\MSSQL14.SQL2017\MSSQL\D...	0.0	0.0	0
AdventureWorks2014	E:\Program Files\Microsoft SQL Server\MSSQL14.SQL2017\MSSQL\D...	0.0	0.0	0
AdventureWorks2016	E:\Program Files\Microsoft SQL Server\MSSQL14.SQL2017\MSSQL\D...	0.0	0.0	0

Figure 11.23: Data File I/O section of Activity Monitor

- And the **Recent** and **Active Expensive Queries**, allowing us to pinpoint queries with long elapsed times and CPU usage.

Recent Expensive Queries

Query	Executions/min	CPU (ms/sec)	Physical Reads/sec	Logical Writes/sec
SELECT e.[BusinessEntityID],	5	8631	0	18
SELECT [SalesOrderDetailID] ...	0	202	0	0
select * from [Production].[Product]	0	0	0	0

Active Expensive Queries

Query	Session...	CPU (ms/sec)	Database	Elapsed Time	Physical Reads...
SELECT e.[BusinessEntityID], ...	54	28773	AdventureW...	61917	0
SELECT [SalesOrderDetailID] ...	60	2319	AdventureW...	31437	0
SELECT e.[BusinessEntityID], ...	82	165053	AdventureW...	321641	0
SELECT e.[BusinessEntityID],	83	109021	AdventureW...	361504	0
SELECT e.[BusinessEntityID], ...	84	37779	AdventureW...	129699	0
SELECT e.[BusinessEntityID], ...	86	129078	AdventureW...	484113	0
SELECT e.[BusinessEntityID], ...	91	72192	AdventureW...	220354	0
SELECT e.[BusinessEntityID], ...	92	11600	AdventureW...	35664	0
SELECT e.[BusinessEntityID], ...	93	26028	AdventureW...	56311	0
SELECT [SalesOrderDetailID]	94	1412	AdventureW	16298	0

Logical ...	Average Duration (ms)	Plan Count	Database
222279	470060	1	AdventureWorks2016...
0	0	2	
0	0	1	

Writes	Logical Read...	Row Co...	Allocated Memory	Used Memory	Required Memory
240	771815	0	115520	7056	1024
0	10	0	136	136	136
224	4204827	0	115520	7056	1024
240	2857370	0	115520	7056	1024
232	998975	0	115520	7056	1024
240	3265784	0	115520	7056	1024
239	1799760	0	115520	7056	1024
240	327933	0	115520	7056	1024
233	701082	0	115520	7056	1024
0	10	0	136	136	136

Figure 11.24: Recent and Expensive Queries sections of Activity Monitor

Here is the interesting part about why AM should be part of our toolbox: when one of the Query Profiling Infrastructures we discussed in the previous chapter is enabled globally, the **sys.dm_exec_query_profiles** DMV is populated for every query that is executing, which means that unlike LQS, which can only show the live plan for the query running in my own session, AM can show live plans for queries in any session.

> **Tip**
>
> When the `query_post_execution_showplan` XEvent is in use, the `sys.dm_exec_query_profiles` DMV is populated for all queries using Standard Profiling. This means that using AM or directly querying the DMV has a higher impact than when LWP is used. In the previous chapter, we covered the many ways in which LWP can be enabled.

So, when I got the middle-of-the-night call, I accessed the ETL process and looked at which queries were being used. Then I used AM to easily pinpoint the query being executed by the ETL process and see its live plan. How? By using the **Active Expensive Queries** tab in AM, right-clicking a long-running query, and selecting the **Show Live Execution Plan** option, as shown in the following screenshot:

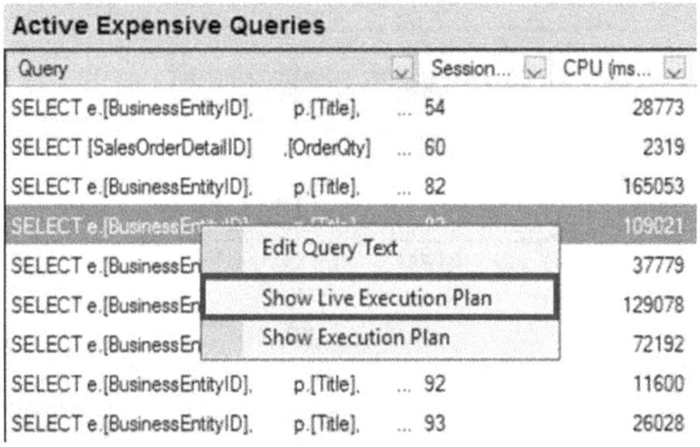

Figure 11.25: Context menu for a query in the Active Expensive Queries section of Activity Monitor showing the Show Live Execution Plan option

> **Tip**
>
> If the **Show Live Execution Plan menu option** is grayed out, this means that neither Standard Profiling nor Lightweight Profiling are enabled globally. To enable LWP globally for all queries, see the *Understanding the need for Lightweight Profiling* section.

For this query, which has been executing for over 100 seconds now, a new tab will display the live execution plan, as shown in the following screenshot:

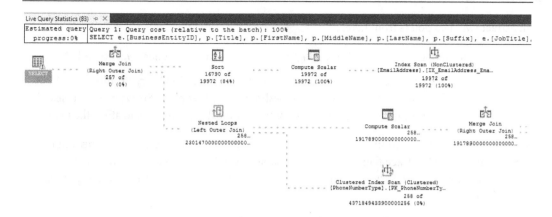

Figure 11.26: An example of Live Query Statistics for a currently running query

> **Tip**
>
> Notice that this is the same query we used in the previous section on **Live Query Statistics**
> (**LQS**), but when it's displayed in AM, the operator times are missing. Why? Remember that
> LQS leverages Standard Profiling, which tracks operator-level information such as CPU and
> elapsed time. However, in this example, we are using Lightweight Profiling, which does not
> include that per-operator information.

As the database professional who got the middle-of-the-night call, how can I analyze and possibly solve
the ongoing performance issue? Start by opening the plan properties by right-clicking the root node
and selecting **Properties** – refer to the *Plan-level properties* and *Operator-level properties* sections of
Chapter 3, Exploring Query Execution Plans for more information on the available showplan properties
that are useful for troubleshooting query performance.

It's best to first try to understand if there are any server-wide configurations that may be impacting
query execution. One good place to start is trace flags. Are there trace flags impacting this query's
execution? If I look at the trace flag information in the plan, I notice two trace flags, as shown in the
following screenshot:

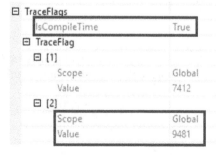

Figure 11.27: Properties window of the example query plan showing trace flag information

I can extract two data points from here:

- There were global (server-wide) trace flags present at the time this query was compiled.
- Of the two trace flags, we know now that 7412 enables **Lightweight Query Profiling (LWP)** by default, which allows me to use AM to troubleshoot in the first place. So, we need to research trace flag 9481 to see if it's impacting query optimization choices that could affect the plan.

If we look at the documentation about trace flags (`http://aka.ms/traceflags`), here is the explanation for what trace flag 9481 does: it enables us to "*set the query optimizer cardinality estimation model to the SQL Server 2012 (11.x) and earlier versions, irrespective of the compatibility level of the database*".

This is a good starting point: although this ETL is executing in a SQL Server 2017 instance and the `AdventureWorks` database is in database compatibility level 130, which maps to using CE 130, the query was optimized with CE 70 instead, as shown in the following screenshot:

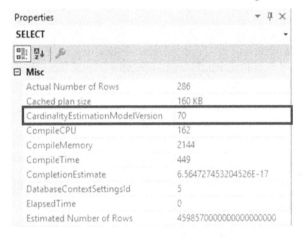

Figure 11.28: Properties window of the example query plan showing CardinalityEstimationModelVersion

So, here is a working hypothesis: using CE 130 most likely will yield a different query plan. Will it improve the query performance over the current plan?

> **Note**
>
> Refer to the *Introducing the Cardinality Estimator* section of *Chapter 3, Mechanics of the Query Optimizer*, for further context on the potentially enormous impact this CE change carries for the query optimization process.

Let's experiment with overriding the global trace flag at the query level in order to work out the effect of using the default CE model for database compatibility level 130. To do that, I will take the query from the execution plan, open a new query window in SSMS, add the OPTION (USE HINT('FORCE_DEFAULT_CARDINALITY_ESTIMATION')) hint to my query, and execute it in AdventureWorks:

```
SELECT e.[BusinessEntityID], p.[Title], p.[FirstName],
    p.[MiddleName], p.[LastName], p.[Suffix], e.[JobTitle],
    pp.[PhoneNumber], pnt.[Name] AS [PhoneNumberType],
    ea.[EmailAddress], p.[EmailPromotion], a.[AddressLine1],
    a.[AddressLine2], a.[City], sp.[Name] AS [StateProvinceName],
    a.[PostalCode], cr.[Name] AS [CountryRegionName],
p.[AdditionalContactInfo]
FROM [HumanResources].[Employee] AS e
INNER JOIN [Person].[Person] AS p
    ON RTRIM(LTRIM(p.[BusinessEntityID])) = RTRIM(LTRIM(e.
[BusinessEntityID]))
INNER JOIN [Person].[BusinessEntityAddress] AS bea
    ON RTRIM(LTRIM(bea.[BusinessEntityID])) = RTRIM(LTRIM(e.
[BusinessEntityID]))
INNER JOIN [Person].[Address] AS a
    ON RTRIM(LTRIM(a.[AddressID])) = RTRIM(LTRIM(bea.[AddressID]))
INNER JOIN [Person].[StateProvince] AS sp
    ON RTRIM(LTRIM(sp.[StateProvinceID])) = RTRIM(LTRIM(a.
[StateProvinceID]))
INNER JOIN [Person].[CountryRegion] AS cr
    ON RTRIM(LTRIM(cr.[CountryRegionCode])) = RTRIM(LTRIM(sp.
[CountryRegionCode]))
LEFT OUTER JOIN [Person].[PersonPhone] AS pp
    ON RTRIM(LTRIM(pp.BusinessEntityID)) = RTRIM(LTRIM(p.
[BusinessEntityID]))
LEFT OUTER JOIN [Person].[PhoneNumberType] AS pnt
    ON RTRIM(LTRIM(pp.[PhoneNumberTypeID])) = RTRIM(LTRIM(pnt.
[PhoneNumberTypeID]))
LEFT OUTER JOIN [Person].[EmailAddress] AS ea
    ON RTRIM(LTRIM(p.[BusinessEntityID])) = RTRIM(LTRIM(ea.
[BusinessEntityID]))
OPTION (USE HINT('FORCE_DEFAULT_CARDINALITY_ESTIMATION'));
```

This hinted query executed in 291ms, while the original query is still running at almost 3 minutes' elapsed time.

> **Note**
>
> The shape for the ETL original plan and the new plan using the hint can be seen in the *Introducing the Cardinality Estimator* section in *Chapter 3, Mechanics of the Query Optimizer*.

At this point, I have several possible actions:

- Disable the trace flag globally, unless the trace flag had been enabled as a result of workload tests that showed most queries benefit from CE 70. Even so, it's recommended to not use the trace flag, but rather the corresponding database-scoped configuration to set that behavior at the database level, using the following T-SQL command:

```
ALTER DATABASE SCOPED CONFIGURATION SET LEGACY_CARDINALITY_
ESTIMATION = ON;
```

- If the decision to disable the trace flag warrants further system-wide tests, then at least for the offending query, we know that using CE 130 yields better results. Change the ETL to add the USE HINT('FORCE_DEFAULT_CARDINALITY_ESTIMATION') hint.

- If changing the ETL code is not possible now, consider creating a plan guide that adds the required hint on the fly for any incoming execution of that query, as shown in the following example. This allows new incoming execution to use the new optimized plan, while not making any immediate changes to the ETL code:

```
EXEC sp_create_plan_guide
@name = N'Guide1',
@stmt = 'SELECT e.[BusinessEntityID], p.[Title], p.[FirstName],
    p.[MiddleName], p.[LastName], p.[Suffix], e.[JobTitle],
    pp.[PhoneNumber], pnt.[Name] AS [PhoneNumberType],
    ea.[EmailAddress], p.[EmailPromotion], a.[AddressLine1],
    a.[AddressLine2], a.[City], sp.[Name] AS
[StateProvinceName],
    a.[PostalCode], cr.[Name] AS [CountryRegionName],
p.[AdditionalContactInfo]
FROM [HumanResources].[Employee] AS e
INNER JOIN [Person].[Person] AS p
    ON RTRIM(LTRIM(p.[BusinessEntityID])) = RTRIM(LTRIM(e.
[BusinessEntityID]))
INNER JOIN [Person].[BusinessEntityAddress] AS bea
    ON RTRIM(LTRIM(bea.[BusinessEntityID])) = RTRIM(LTRIM(e.
[BusinessEntityID]))
INNER JOIN [Person].[Address] AS a
    ON RTRIM(LTRIM(a.[AddressID])) = RTRIM(LTRIM(bea.
[AddressID]))
INNER JOIN [Person].[StateProvince] AS sp
    ON RTRIM(LTRIM(sp.[StateProvinceID])) = RTRIM(LTRIM(a.
[StateProvinceID]))
```

```
INNER JOIN [Person].[CountryRegion] AS cr
    ON RTRIM(LTRIM(cr.[CountryRegionCode])) = RTRIM(LTRIM(sp.
[CountryRegionCode]))
LEFT OUTER JOIN [Person].[PersonPhone] AS pp
    ON RTRIM(LTRIM(pp.BusinessEntityID)) = RTRIM(LTRIM(p.
[BusinessEntityID]))
LEFT OUTER JOIN [Person].[PhoneNumberType] AS pnt
    ON RTRIM(LTRIM(pp.[PhoneNumberTypeID])) = RTRIM(LTRIM(pnt.
[PhoneNumberTypeID]))
LEFT OUTER JOIN [Person].[EmailAddress] AS ea
    ON RTRIM(LTRIM(p.[BusinessEntityID])) = RTRIM(LTRIM(ea.
[BusinessEntityID])));',
@type = N'SQL',
@module_or_batch = NULL,
@params = NULL,
@hints = N'OPTION (USE HINT (''FORCE_DEFAULT_CARDINALITY_
ESTIMATION''))';
```

After making this change, look at AM's **Overview** section:

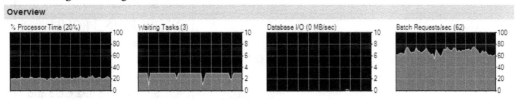

Figure 11.29: Overview section of the Activity Monitor after the plan guide has been put in place

Notice the CPU is now running at 20 percent and the ETL is still executing. I'm also doing 60 batch requests/sec, which is significantly better than my starting point of 6 batch requests/sec.

Summary

This chapter covered the important topic of tracking query progress, and how to use either Live Query Statistics to see the live progress of a single query in SSMS, or Activity Monitor to access the live progress of any running query. We also covered how these tools and underlying Database Engine features are invaluable to troubleshoot and solve query performance issues, namely for those queries that take hours to complete, or never do.

The Query Profiling Infrastructures available in SQL Server depend on the Database Engine version. The following table summarizes the options to enable either of the Query Profiling Infrastructures and the minimum required version for each option:

	Standard Profiling	Lightweight Profiling
Globally	XEvent session with `query_post_execution_showplan` XE; starting with SQL Server 2012	Trace Flag 7412; starting with SQL Server 2016 SP1
	Showplan XML trace event in SQL Trace and SQL Server Profiler; starting with SQL Server 2000	XEvent session with `query_thread_profile` XE; starting with SQL Server 2014 SP2
	–	XEvent session with `query_post_execution_plan_profile` XE; starting with SQL Server 2019
Single session	Use `SET STATISTICS XML ON`; starting with SQL Server 2000	QUERY_PLAN_PROFILE query hint + XEvent session with `query_plan_profile` XE; starting with SQL Server 2016 SP2 CU3 and 2017 CU11
	Use `SET STATISTICS PROFILE ON`; starting with SQL Server 2000	–
	Click LQS button in SSMS; starting with SQL Server 2014 SP2	–

This analysis was possible because at this point, we know how to create reasonable hypotheses about potential query performance issues by analyzing query plan properties, and what they say about the query optimization choices during compilation time.

In the next and final chapter of the book, we will investigate a tool available to us in SSMS that will help identify and remediate issues with our T-SQL query performance that arise due to changes in the Cardinality Estimator, specifically when upgrading our database compatibility level. This tool is invaluable when upgrading our database to a new version of SQL Server.

12

Managing Optimizer Changes

In this chapter, we will discuss how users can manage Query Optimizer changes throughout versions of the SQL Database Engine. We will cover a client-side feature in **SQL Server Management Studio (SSMS)** – the **Query Tuning Assistant (QTA)** – and a new feature for the SQL Server 2022 release – CE Feedback. Both features aim at addressing some of the most common causes of **cardinality estimation (CE)**-related performance regressions that may affect our T-SQL queries after an upgrade from an older version of SQL Server to a newer version, namely SQL Server 2016 and above.

At the time of writing, SQL Server 2014 is months away from completing its 10-year life cycle and reaching end of support. Also, SQL Server 2016 and SQL Server 2017 no longer have mainstream support. This can raise concerns for all those still running applications supported by these legacy SQL Server versions.

However, *modernizing* the database platform (a synonym for *upgrading* in this context) is not a risk-free proposition. The risk that, after upgrading and leaping so many years and versions, a part of an application's workload can experience performance regressions due to CE changes is very real. This is why Microsoft has invested over the years in building features that can greatly mitigate much of this regression risk Query Store, **Automatic Plan Correction (APC)**, QTA, and CE Feedback.

This chapter covers the following topics:

- Understanding where QTA and CE Feedback are needed
- Understanding QTA fundamentals
- Exploring the QTA workflow

Technical requirements

The examples used in this chapter are designed for use on SQL Server 2022 and Azure SQL Database, but they should work on any version of SQL Server, 2012 or later. The Developer edition of SQL Server is free for development environments and can be used to run all the code samples. There is also a free tier of Azure SQL Database that you can use for testing at `https://aka.ms/freedb`.

You will need the `AdventureWorks2016_EXT` (referred to as `AdventureWorks`) and `AdventureWorksDW2016_EXT` (referred to as `AdventureWorksDW`) sample databases, which can be found on GitHub at `https://github.com/Microsoft/sql-server-samples/releases/tag/adventureworks`. Code samples for this chapter can also be found on GitHub at `https://github.com/PacktPublishing/Learn-T-SQL-Querying-Second-Edition/tree/main/ch12`.

Understanding where QTA and CE Feedback are needed

The CE version that our databases use directly influences how query plans are created for queries that will be executed in those databases. And we have seen first-hand the effects of the CE every time we compared estimated number of rows with actual number of rows throughout the book – for example, in the *Query plan comparison* section of *Chapter 9, Comparative Analysis of Query Plans*, where we dealt with the **Row Goal** optimization scenario.

When upgrading from older versions of the SQL Database Engine to newer versions (for example, an older SQL Server version to Azure SQL Database or SQL Server 2022), we need to be conscious of how upgrading from an older CE version to a newer CE can affect our workloads – benefits are expected for the most part, but regressions can happen. For example, we discussed in *Chapter 6, Discovering T-SQL Anti-Patterns in Depth*, how the latest versions of the SQL Database Engine solve classic anti-patterns with little to no code changes – and these are overall welcomed changes.

Additionally, we also need to be conscious of the difference between upgrading the SQL Database Engine as **platform binaries** and upgrading the **Database Compatibility Level** setting of the user databases. For the sake of what we're discussing in this chapter, upgrading database compatibility means upgrading to a more recent CE version, and unlocking some newer engine features that we've discussed throughout this book.

> **Note**
> For example, the features **Degree of Parallelism (DOP) Feedback** and **Parameter Sensitive Plan Optimization (PSPO)** – both of which we discussed in previous chapters – require the latest 160 compatibility level to work.

The CE version doesn't change just by upgrading the SQL Database Engine version itself. In other words, upgrading the SQL Database Engine binaries doesn't necessarily mean we must upgrade the database compatibility – in fact, we shouldn't – at least not immediately after we upgrade the binaries. Decoupling the two upgrade moments – **SQL Database Engine** and the **Database Compatibility Level** – allows us to keep workloads stable after the SQL Database Engine upgrade because the Query Optimizer still works, with the rules mapping to the compatibility level. How can we do that? How do we take charge of upgrade risks?

> **Tip**
>
> We discussed how the CE version is tied to the concept of the database compatibility level, and we show their version mapping in the *Introducing the Cardinality Estimator* section of *Chapter 2, Mechanics of the Query Optimizer*.

The following diagram summarizes Microsoft's recommended steps to minimize risk with CE upgrades:

Figure 12.1: Recommended steps to minimize risk with CE upgrades

These detailed steps, which are based on the difference between upgrading the SQL Database Engine platform and upgrading a database's compatibility level, are outlined here:

1. **Upgrade SQL Server** from any older version (for example, SQL Server 2012 to SQL Server 2022), *and keep databases in the same database compatibility level as the source SQL Server version*. This step only applies to SQL Server, whether running in your own data center or in a VM hosted by a public cloud vendor. In the most common upgrade scenarios, the database compatibility level will not change on user databases after the upgrade:

   - If we do an in-place upgrade, all user databases keep the same database compatibility level as before the upgrade, 110 – this was the highest and native compatibility level in SQL Server 2012.

   - If we do a side-by-side upgrade (a migration), then all databases that are moved through attach/detach or backup/restore also keep the same database compatibility level as before the upgrade.

> **Note**
>
> If you are using Azure SQL Database, the in-place upgrade of the SQL Database Engine is a continuous, roll-forward process that is handled by Microsoft Azure. For existing user databases, much like as would happen with a SQL Server in-place upgrade, their database compatibility level is kept as-is.

2. **Enable the Query Store**, as we discussed in *Chapter 10, Tracking Performance History with the Query Store*.

3. Let Query Store *collect a baseline for the workload* that represents the typical business cycle for your applications. If we are going through this process in production, this means allowing the production workload to just execute. If we are doing this in a pre-production or **development** (**dev**) environment, then we need to ensure that whatever test workload we have is a valid representation of the production workload.

4. Once we know enough time has passed and the Query Store has accrued enough information about our workloads, *plan to change the database compatibility level to our chosen target level*; in this case, it will be 160, which is the highest compatibility level in the SQL Server 2022 release. This is a per-database operation.

   We can do this by using the ALTER DATABASE CURRENT SET COMPATIBILITY_LEVEL = 160; T-SQL command or by using the database **Options** menu in SSMS, as shown in the following screenshot:

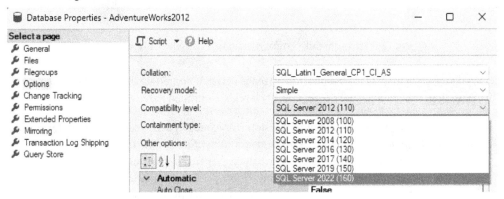

Figure 12.2: Database Properties showing the available compatibility levels

5. Monitor the **Regressed Queries** report in Query Store to *quickly find and fix regressions* with the **Force Plan** feature, as shown in the following screenshot.

Figure 12.3: The Force Plan button in the Regressed Queries Query Store report

This becomes possible precisely because a baseline collection of query plans that were produced using CE 110 – the same that drove Query Optimizer choices in SQL Server 2012 – was collected. From there, any regressions that occur due to the change in the CE version become trackable and actionable.

In our current scenario, because we have upgraded to SQL Server 2022 in this case, we can enable the **Automatic Plan Correction** (**APC**) feature, and this last step of forcing the plan becomes automated. We can enable APC using the ALTER DATABASE CURRENT SET AUTOMATIC_TUNING (FORCE_LAST_GOOD_PLAN = ON); T-SQL command.

> **Note**
>
> Automatic tuning is a database feature that was released with SQL Server 2017 and is also in Azure SQL Database. One of its functionalities is APC, which identifies query execution plan regressions based on CPU time. In the scope of CE upgrades, APC will revert to the last known good query plan, provided the recommended baseline with the source database compatibility level was collected. We discussed APC in *Chapter 10, Tracking Performance History with Query Store.*

At this point, we might ask, if the Query Store and APC can mitigate query regression problems when I upgrade the database compatibility level, why would Microsoft create the QTA tool, or invest in the newer CE Feedback feature?

The main challenge is that too many database professionals skip the recommended process and somewhat recklessly upgrade to the latest database compatibility level, immediately after the SQL Database Engine is upgraded. They become exposed to the risk of finding that a part of the database's workload has regressed, caused by not having a baseline that enables Query Store and APC to help with any plan change that resulted in performance degradation.

Therefore, **QTA** was released back in 2019 and provides a wizard-like experience to guide the user through the recommended process, from a single entry point in SSMS.

As Microsoft has continued to invest in this space, with the most recent release of the SQL Database Engine in SQL Server 2022, the CE Feedback feature has become available and largely addresses performance regression scenarios tied to CE version upgrades (changes to the CE assumptions) without the need for a previous-version baseline collection.

> **Note**
>
> We discussed CE assumption changes in *Chapter 2, Mechanics of the Query Optimizer,* and how the CE Feedback feature can detect and attempt to correct cardinality estimation inferences tied to those changes, when they prove to be detrimental to query performance. At the time of writing, CE Feedback is not yet generally available in Azure SQL Database.

While CE Feedback can automatically detect these scenarios, it will only apply feedback to queries where the skew between estimated and actual rows is orders of magnitude off, and that skew results in performance drops. This is a reasonably conservative approach, given that the feature doesn't require user input to make decisions, and therefore, it must be certain that the changes it enacts are indeed worth it.

In contrast, queries with a much lower skew between estimated and actual rows are reported by QTA because it is driven by the user, and we are in control of which queries are in scope.

Also, CE Feedback is only available if you upgrade the compatibility level to 160, and therefore, if your target version for upgrade is SQL Server 2019, only QTA is an option to manage the risk of compatibility level upgrades.

Now that we understand what QTA and CE Feedback are and why they are important, let's dive deeper into the QTA and how it works.

Understanding QTA fundamentals

While guiding us through the recommended process, QTA doesn't follow it exactly. The very last step, *step 5*, will not have the same outcome we saw in the previous section; instead of providing options to revert to a last known good plan, QTA helps to find a new state that is not the pre-CE upgrade or post-CE upgrade plan but a new plan that will hopefully outperform both of the previous plans.

The following diagram summarizes the recommended steps to minimize risk with CE upgrades using QTA, which replaces the very last step of the process described in the previous *Understanding where QTA and CE Feedback are needed* section:

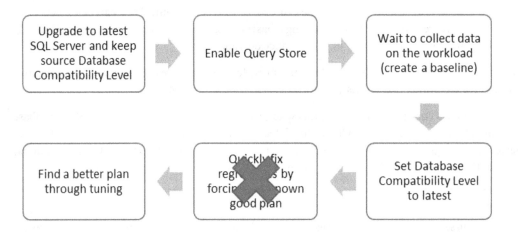

Figure 12.4: The recommended steps to minimize risk with CE upgrades using QTA

How does QTA find a better query plan for regressed queries? Starting with the same data that's available in Query Store's Regressed Queries report, QTA will look for query patterns that may be affected by changes in CE, specifically from CE 70 to CE 120 and higher.

> **Note**
>
> QTA only handles SELECT queries, both ad hoc and parameterized. For parameterized queries, QTA can only experiment on those where the compiled parameter is available in the **Parameter List** property of the query plan. We discussed this query plan property in *Chapter 3, Exploring Query Execution Plans*, in the *Query plan properties of interest* section.

QTA will then experiment with those queries, executing them with query hints that adjust several CE model choices, and those that result in alternate query plans. After the analysis is complete, who decides which plans are better and should be used? The user does. As we reach the end of the process, we will be able to see the alternatives that exist for each plan and easily pick the one that's either faster or uses less CPU, for example. We will describe the workflow in the next section, as we upgrade our `AdventureWorksDW` database to SQL Server 2022's native database compatibility level, 160.

Just like the newer CE Feedback feature, QTA can handle the following CE model changes:

- Predicate **independence** versus **correlation**. We discussed this CE assumption in the *Introducing the Cardinality Estimator* section of *Chapter 2, Mechanics of the Query Optimizer*. If the experiments indicate that using CE 70's independence assumption yields better estimations than the default correlation assumption, then the resulting query plan is added to the list of recommendations. Under the covers, QTA was able to switch the default CE assumption for the specific query being experimented on, by applying the `USE HINT ('ASSUME_MIN_ SELECTIVITY_FOR_FILTER_ESTIMATES')` query hint. This hint causes SQL Server to create a query plan that accounts for the cardinality of each column in an `AND` filter predicate, rather than the cardinality of all columns combined by the `AND` predicate.

- **Simple Join Containment** versus **Base Join Containment**: We also discussed this CE assumption in the *Introducing the Cardinality Estimator* section of *Chapter 2, Mechanics of the Query Optimizer*. Like the previous bullet regarding independence versus correlation, if the experiments indicate that using the legacy simple containment assumption yields better estimations than the default base containment assumption, the resulting query plan is added to the list of recommendations. The hint applied by QTA to include this consideration is `USE HINT ('ASSUME_JOIN_ PREDICATE_DEPENDS_ON_FILTERS')`. This hint causes the SQL Database Engine to create a query plan that assumes the estimated cardinality needs to be calculated by accounting for filter predicates applicable to tables, rather than calculating only by using the base tables (without any filter predicates). In simpler terms, first estimate the non-join filter predicates, and then the join predicates.

- **Multi-Statement Table Valued Function (MSTVF) fixed estimations**: As we discussed in the *Deconstructing table-valued functions* section of *Chapter 5, Writing Elegant T-SQL Queries*, the Query Optimizer uses a default estimation of 100 rows for MSTVFs, since the row count is not available at compile time – this is a runtime structure. This has always been the case in SQL Server, but in older versions, the default estimation was just 1 row, whereas starting from SQL Server 2014, this assumption was increased to 100 rows. It may not look like much on its own, but this estimation is used throughout the query optimization process and drives other optimizations on top of this assumption. The change back in CE 120 can be enough to impact query plans that heavily depended on the previous version's combination of optimizations based on one row. Under the covers, QTA was able to switch the default CE assumption of 100 rows back to 1 row for the specific query being experimented on, by applying the `QUERYTRACEON 9488` query hint.

> **Note**
> Performance issues tied to MSTVF-fixed estimations became obsolete with the **interleaved execution** for MSTVFs feature, introduced in SQL Server 2017. We discussed this feature in *Chapter 5, Writing Elegant T-SQL Queries*.

- If all the listed scenarios fail to improve the query plan, then, as a last resort, QTA will consider reverting to CE 70 in full, by applying the `USE HINT ('FORCE_LEGACY_CARDINALITY_ESTIMATION')` query hint. This extreme catch-all approach is not a consideration for CE Feedback. In this regard, QTA can go to the extreme of using a "hammer" approach, whereas CE Feedback always uses a very targeted "scalpel" approach.

Exploring the QTA workflow

We've briefly described what QTA does and, in greater depth, how QTA works internally. But now, it's time to actually run through the recommended database compatibility upgrade we discussed in the *Understanding QTA fundamentals* section.

QTA is a session-based tool, which means we can open and close it at will while the database compatibility upgrade process progresses. This is useful, given that the recommended database compatibility upgrade process can run for days, depending on the business cycle that our workload serves.

> **Tip**
> QTA doesn't need to run from an SSMS installed on the server. It can execute the workflow against the server from our laptop, desktop, or another designated management machine that you have available.

The way QTA stores our session's state and analysis data is by creating a few tables in the targeted user database in the `msqta` schema, as shown in the following screenshot. This schema will remain in the database, and it's not recommended to remove it.

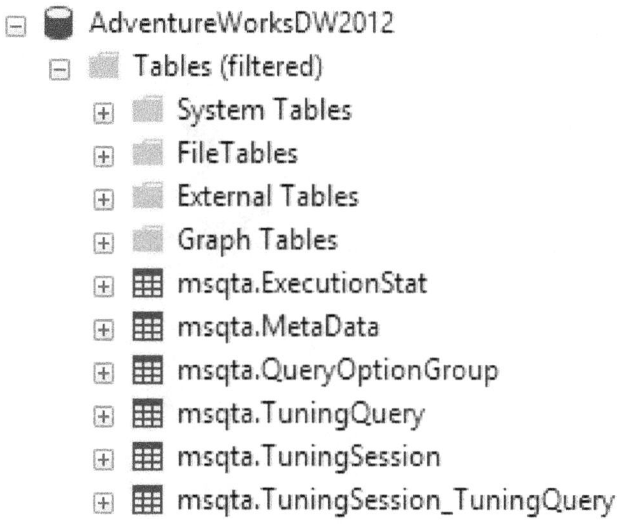

Figure 12.5: msqta schema objects in the AdventureWorksDW database

> **Tip**
>
> Multiple tuning sessions can be created on a single database over time, but only one active session can exist for any given database.

Before we start a database compatibility upgrade process, some housekeeping tasks are needed, such as configuring Query Store if it's not already running in the database. QTA can do this for us as part of the **Create Session** wizard.

For this example, we installed a SQL Server 2022 instance where we restored our database, AdventureWorksDW. Given this database was restored, it keeps the same database compatibility level, 110, that it had in the source SQL Server 2012 instance.

To start a new session, we go to **SQL Server Management Studio (SSMS)**, connect to our new SQL Server 2022, right-click the database name, select **Tasks**, select **Database Upgrade**, and click on **New Database Upgrade Session**, as shown in the following screenshot:

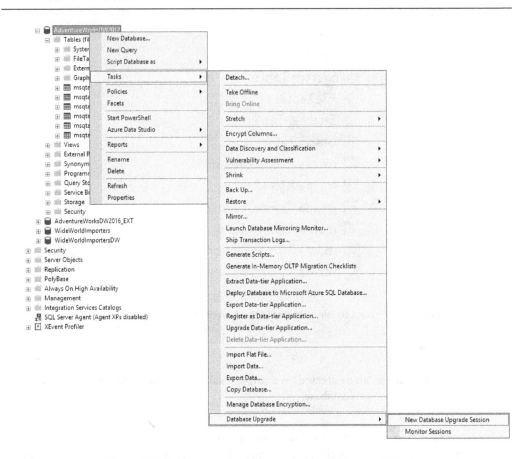

Figure 12.6: Starting the database upgrade session from SSMS

This action opens the session configuration window, where the first step is to enter some information that will drive the upgrade process:

- **The expected Workload duration (days) to capture (the minimum is 1 day), which is used to configure Query Store in the next step**: For our example, the business cycle we've identified is **5** days – meaning it can take up to five days for Query Store to capture all the application workload and some ETL processes we execute every night. We need to ensure we capture a representative baseline so that after we complete the database compatibility upgrade, any regressed queries can be found and analyzed by QTA.

- **The intended target database compatibility level that the database should be set to after the QTA workflow completes**: Given that the database is now at database compatibility level 110 and we are working in SQL Server 2022, all higher compatibility levels are available in the dropdown. For this example, we'll select **160**.

The following screenshot displays the QTA window where we configured the session:

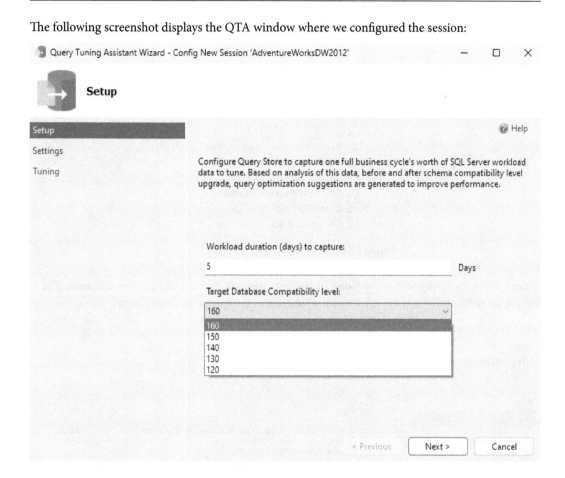

Figure 12.7: The QTA session configuration Setup screen

While QTA guides us through the recommended upgrade process, let's keep in mind that Query Store is storing all the information. This is especially relevant for the point in time after we upgrade the database compatibility. For any query that may not be eligible for QTA to deal with, we are free to use Query Store's **Regressed Queries** report to find other ways of handling regressed queries, such as forcing a previously known good plan, while we fix the query to work natively in the new CE – in this case, 160. The following screenshot shows the **Regressed Queries** report under the Query Store in SSMS:

Figure 12.8: Query Store reports in SSMS

The next step is to configure Query Store. In the **Settings** window, we can see two columns. The following screenshot displays the QTA window where we configured the Query Store:

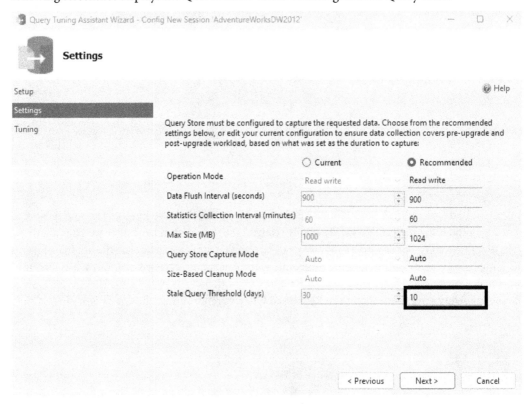

Figure 12.9: The QTA Query Store configuration setup screen

From the screenshot, we can see the following:

- In the **Current** state of the Query Store for our database, note that **Operation Mode** is set to **Off** because we have not enabled Query Store manually. If we had enabled Query Store previously, we would be able to change its settings here, editing any configuration if the **Current** radio button is selected.

- In the **Recommended** settings for Query Store, note the proposed **Stale Query Threshold (days)** setting is twice the number we entered for the workload duration on the previous screen (refer to the explanation prior to *Figure 12.7*). This is because we had selected **5** days, and Query Store needs to be able to collect our five-days baseline, plus five days' worth of workload after we change to compatibility level 160. Only then do we compare the same business cycle across CE 70 and CE 160, allowing Query Store to identify regressed queries that span the relevant time window. We can opt to accept the recommended settings by clicking on the **Recommended** radio button.

After clicking **Next**, we get a new screen with some information on how we've configured the session, instructing us to start running our workload (QTA does not generate any workload for us). If we're running QTA in a test server, then we are responsible for generating our test workload.

Alternatively, let's say I have gone through the recommended upgrade process in production manually (as we discussed in the *Understanding where QTA is needed* section). Then, we could restore the production database backup to a test server, and the Query Store for that database would allow us to jump to the analysis and experimentation step later in the QTA workflow.

In our example, we're running this process in production, which means we can just let our normal business cycle happen normally as application workloads execute. On this new screen, click **Finish** to exit the session setup – this completes *step 1* of the QTA workflow.

To start running through the upgrade process itself, we return to SSMS, right-click the database name, select **Tasks**, select **Database Upgrade**, and click on **Monitor Sessions**, as shown in the following screenshot:

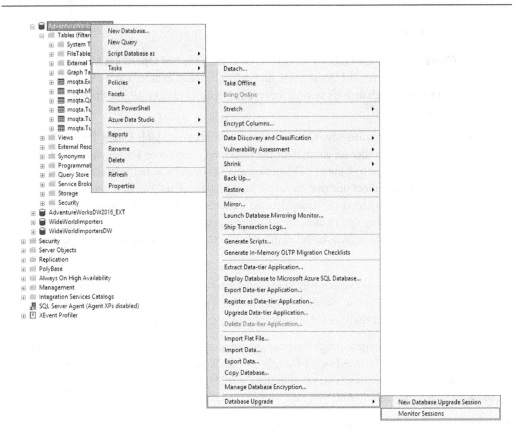

Figure 12.10: Monitoring QTA sessions in SSMS

A new window tab opens in SSMS, in the scope of QTA's session management page. In the following screenshot, we can see our current session. Click on the session name, and then click on **Details** to open it:

Figure 12.11: The QTA session currently active

Note in the previous screenshot that we are in *step 1* of five steps of the upgrade process – **Setup**. When we open the session, we enter *step 2*, **Data Collection**, in **Substep 1 of 3 - Baseline Data Collection**, as shown in the following screenshot:

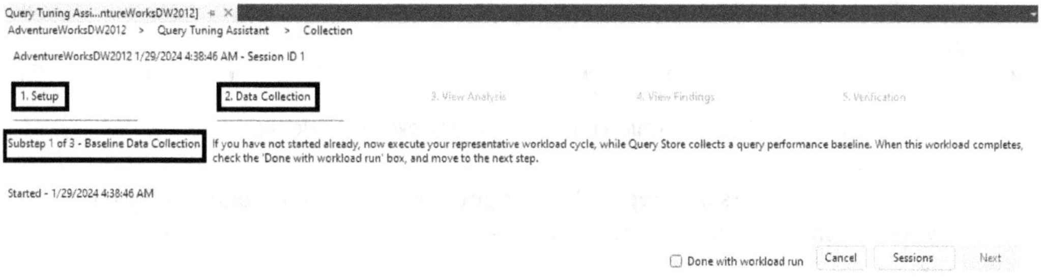

Figure 12.12: The QTA baseline data collection step

As we can see on the QTA screen, it asks us to start our workload if not already started. We're running our upgrade process in a production server, so the workload is already executing. We can close this screen and go away for five days while our baseline populates – but, for example, if we decide that after just three days we have enough data collected and don't need the full five days, we can come back to QTA via the **Monitor Sessions** task, and we'll be right where we left off.

After our baseline is complete, we return to QTA in *step 2* and check the **Done with workload run** box, as shown in the following screenshot:

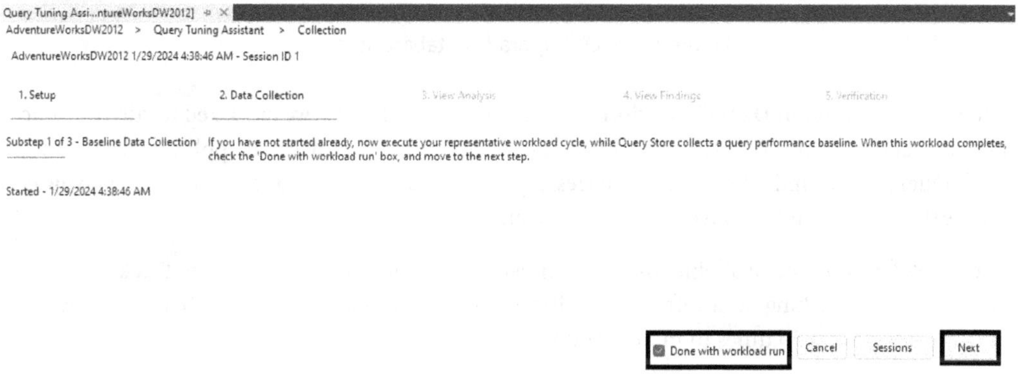

Figure 12.13: Ending the QTA baseline data collection step

This signals to QTA that it's time to move forward with the upgrade process, and when we click **Next**, the following prompt appears, asking us to upgrade the database compatibility level to our chosen target, 160:

Figure 12.14: Confirming the compatibility level upgrade step

When we click **Yes**, QTA enters **Substep 2 of 3 - Upgrade Database** and upgrades the database compatibility level, as shown in the following screenshot. Then, we click **Next** to move on to the last data collection step:

Figure 12.15: QTA upgrade database step

Substep 3 of 3 - Observed Data Collection is similar to substep 1 of 3 – we are asked to run the same workload that constitutes the baseline so that it can compare the proverbial apples to apples and, through Query Store, find all regressed queries. Again, we can close the QTA window and go away for the next five days until we have a full comparison available.

We have a **Refresh** button available, that we can use during those five days to keep track of what's been found so far. Clicking on it refreshes the list of top regressed queries – note that some queries already executed over 150 times in mere seconds.

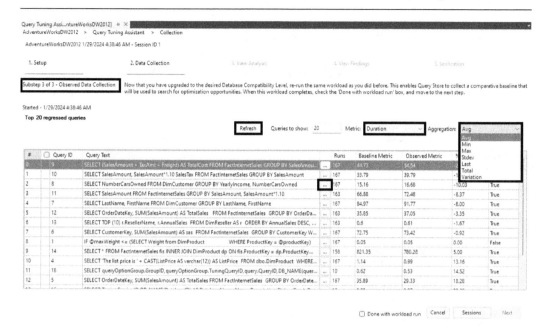

Figure 12.16: The QTA post upgrade data collection step

As we can see in the preceding screenshot, the default settings list the top 20 regressed queries, but we can change the number of queries to show – from 20 to whatever number is relevant to us. The list is built on the default metric, which is the overall query duration, but this can be changed to **CpuTime**. The default **Aggregation** setting for the chosen metric is an average (**Avg**), but others are available, as shown in the preceding screenshot. If we change any of these settings, we need to click **Refresh**.

In the query table, we can see that the query text is limited to the first 100 characters, which is still enough for us to recognize the query. If not, click the ellipsis button (**…**), and the query text will appear in a different tab, as shown in the following screenshot:

```
/*
This query text was retrieved from showplan XML, and may be truncated.
*/

SELECT NumberCarsOwned FROM DimCustomer GROUP BY YearlyIncome, NumberCarsOwned
```

Figure 12.17: The details of a captured query

We also see the number of executions, or runs, the baseline metric, and the observed metric – in this case, the duration in milliseconds for both the pre-upgrade and post-upgrade collections, as well as the % change and whether the query is tunable – meaning whether QTA can experiment on the query. Note that **Query ID** 1 is not tunable, as indicated by the **False** value in the **Tunable** column. It is a parameterized query, and the compile-time parameters are not available.

After our post-upgrade data collection is complete, we return to QTA, still on *step 2*, and check the **Done with workload run** box, as shown in the following screenshot:

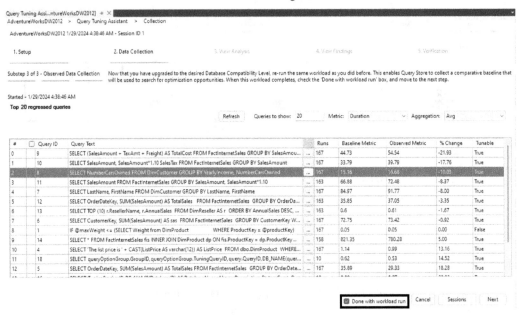

Figure 12.18: Both data collections completed in QTA

This signals QTA to move forward to the **Analysis** phase. When we click **Next**, QTA enters *step 3 – View Analysis*. Here, we look at what queries we want to submit for analysis. We look at the queries using different metrics and aggregations, and we can see a few queries that got slower or had no change after the upgrade, as shown in the following screenshot:

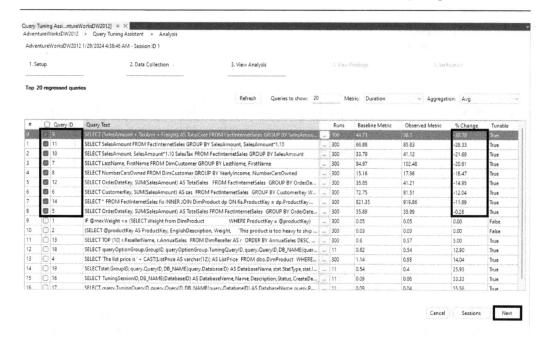

Figure 12.19: The QTA data analysis step

This is a one-time selection process, and for the sake of this exercise, I selected all queries to be analyzed. By clicking **Next**, we enter the **Analysis** process, which we must agree to, as shown in the following screenshot:

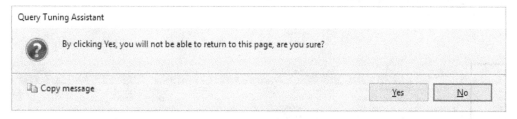

Figure 12.20: Confirmation that the QTA data analysis step can start

On the next screen, while the analysis process is ongoing, the **Status** column displays a **Initial** value for all queries. After a few minutes, the status updates to **Test complete**, which leads to *step 4* – **View Findings**, as shownn in the following screenshot, and we can see what improvements were found:

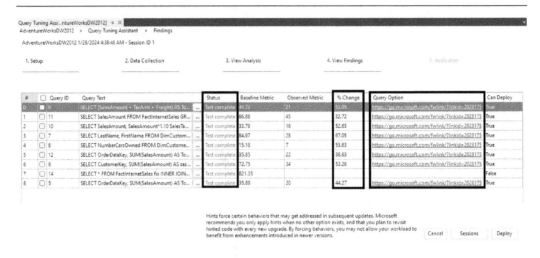

Figure 12.21: The QTA data analysis step completed

We can see the baseline metric – the workload as it executed before the database compatibility upgrade – and the new observed metric, which is the result of the analysis process. **% Change** shows us all queries, and query **7** improved by up to 67 percent. If we click on one of the links in the **Query Option** column, it will open the product documentation in the scope of the proposed hint.

After we select which queries we want to deploy the recommendations for, based on the improvement percentage (we have selected all but one), we click the **Deploy** button, as shown in the following screenshot:

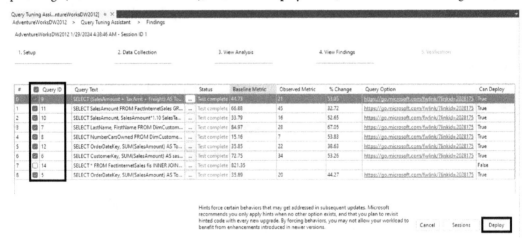

Figure 12.22: Selecting improved queries in QTA

This creates a **plan guide** with the required query hint that will improve the query performance, based on the analysis that was done, which consisted of actually executing the queries and collecting runtime metrics. After deployment of the plan guides, all queries will show a **Deployed** status, and we reach *step 5 – Verification* – as shown in the following screenshot:

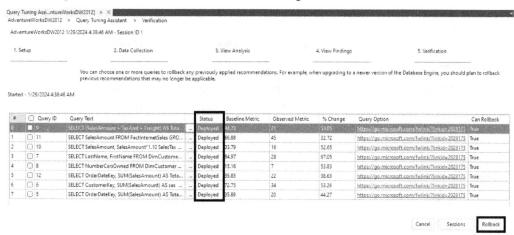

Figure 12.23: Deploying plan guides to force optimized queries

The upgrade is successfully complete, and we managed to improve the regressed queries and restore good performance to the part of our workload that had regressed after upgrading from CE70 to CE160.

> **Note**
>
> QTA uses plan guides and was not updated to use Query Store plan forcing with Query Store hints, which is a new feature in SQL Server 2022 and Azure SQL Database, as discussed in *Chapter 10, Tracking Performance History with Query Store*.

If, in the next few days, we notice that the improvement for one or more tuned queries is not as beneficial as the analysis showed, we can resume the session in the **Verification** step, select the offending query, and click the **Rollback** button to remove the respective plan guide.

Summary

From the set of regressed workloads that the SQL Database Engine team has handled over the years, the initial scenarios covered by QTA and CE Feedback are some of the most common after a database compatibility level upgrade (and, therefore, a CE upgrade), which can make users question whether to upgrade. But that is just because when upgrading from an old version, such as SQL Server 2008 or 2012, our T-SQL queries were fully tuned to the only CE model set that existed at the time. When some aspects of cardinality estimation changed, there was a possibility that some queries would have to be tuned for the new models. Fortunately, the SQL Database Engine team believes that backward compatibility is an asset in the SQL Database Engine and included these hints, which allow selective tuning opportunities for the scenarios covered by QTA and CE Feedback, as well as others less common not covered by QTA nor CE Feedback.

Whether you choose to use QTA or not, following the recommended CE upgrade process we detailed here is the *only* way we can ensure control over our workloads, as they naturally evolve and progress throughout the years of use and Database Engine versions. Even without QTA, running through the CE upgrade process by interacting directly with Query Store, APC and CE Feedback is a strong step toward ensuring our T-SQL queries remain scalable, delivering the level of performance that's expected for the applications they serve.

If you have gotten this far, congratulations – you are now an expert T-SQL developer! We hope that this book has helped unlock some of the mysteries of T-SQL query performance in the SQL Database Engine, illustrating that how a query is written can and does impact how it will perform.

In this book, we learned the following:

- How the SQL Database Engine processes queries and the various building blocks of a T-SQL query

- How the Query Optimizer estimates the cost of a query and identifies the cheapest query plan

- How plans are cached and reused to save time and resources

- How to analyze a query plan to identify areas that may cause the query to perform poorly

- Some best practices to write efficient T-SQL queries that can use indexes effectively

- Several anti-patterns that can cause the Query Optimizer to choose an inefficient query plan or make the query perform poorly

- Some of the free tools and features available from Microsoft to help you identify and troubleshoot poor-performing queries in your environment

The knowledge gained from reading this book will help identify and troubleshoot existing query performance issues, as well as avoid anti-patterns when writing T-SQL code in the future. Most importantly, you should now have the skills to write efficient and elegant T-SQL code for all your SQL Database Engine querying needs.

Index

A

ACID
  reference link 152
action 266
Activity Monitor (AM) 361, 388-397
actual execution plan 366
Actual I/O Statistics 110
Actual Number of Rows 111
Actual time statistics 111
Adaptive joins 75-78
ad-hoc plan caching 15, 16
ANSI-99 standard isolation levels
  Read Committed 153
  Read Uncommitted 153
application programming
    interface (API) 234
Automatic Plan Correction
    (APC) 355, 356, 399
Automatic Plan Regression
    Correction (APRC) 355
automatic tuning 403

B

B+ tree structure 58, 126
Base Containment 31
Base Join Containment 405
BillOfMaterials 143
blocking 247
  investigating 247-249
blocking chain 249
blocking operator 58
B-Tree data structure 58
B-Tree ID 248
build table 71

C

cached query plan issues 250
  queries, with excessive memory
    grants 253, 254
  resource-intensive queries, finding 251-253
  single-use plans (query
    fingerprints) 250, 251
cardinality 28

Cardinality Estimation (CE) 311, 399
CardinalityEstimationModelVersion 88
Cardinality Estimator
    (CE) 28, 30-35, 49, 400
  versions 32
category (keyword) 265
CE 70 30
  inclusion assumption 31
  independence assumption 30
  query plan shape 34
  simple containment 30
  uniformity assumption 30
CE 120 31
CE 140 34
  query plan shape 35
CE Feedback 32, 399, 403
channel 265
channels, SQL Database Engine
  admin 265
  analytic 265
  debug 265
  operational 265
clustered indexes, best practices 130
  order 131
  primary keys 132
  size 131
  uniqueness 130
  usability 131
  volatility 131
Clustered Index Scan operator 60
Clustered Index Seek operator 64
clustered primary key 132
  surrogate keys 132
Columnstore Index Scan 67
Columns With No Statistics* 114, 115
Common Table Expressions (CTEs) 153
  used, for storing intermediate
    results 225-228

compilation replay script (CRS) 358
compile-time 182
complex expressions 166-169
complex views
  pitfalls 213-217
composable logic 182-188
consumers 356
correlated sub-queries
  pitfalls 218, 219
correlation 31
Cost Threshold for Parallelism 39
covering indexes 141
Create Session wizard 407
cursors
  using 153

D

data
  accessing, with indexes 124
  accessing, with rowstore indexes 126, 127
data access operators 58, 59
  Clustered Index Scan 60
  Clustered Index Seek 64
  Columnstore Index Scan 67
  lookups 65
  NonClustered Index Scan 62
  NonClustered Index Seek 63
  Table Scan 59, 60
database administrators (DBAs) 49, 339
Database Compatibility Level 30, 400
Database Console (DBCC) command 94
data definition language (DDL) statement 8
data manipulation language (DML)
  statement 8, 35, 339
data warehousing (DW) workloads 31, 67
decision support systems (DSS) 31
Degree of Parallelism
  (DOP) 12, 88, 356, 368, 400

density 28
development (dev) environment 402
DMV queries
    common scenarios, troubleshooting 247
DOP Feedback 357
Dynamic Management Functions
    (DMFs) 233, 369
Dynamic Management Views
    (DMVs) 180, 233, 234, 264, 355

E

Entity Framework (EF) 190
equality column 138
estimated execution plan 366
Estimated rows 112
EstimateRowsWithoutRowGoal 113
event 264
event counter 265
event file 265
event pairing 265
Event Tracing for Windows (ETW) 265
EXECUTE
    versus sp_executesql 179-181
expensive queries
    tracking 339-348
Exploration stage, query
    optimization workflow 38
Extended Events (XEvents) 263-277, 318
Extract-Transform-Load (ETL) 387

F

filtered index 143
frequency 28
Full Optimization phase, query
    optimization workflow 39-41
FullUpdateForOnlineIndexBuild* 107
fuzzy string matching 176-178

G

globally unique identifiers (GUIDs) 131
global trace flags
    trace flag 7745 335
    trace flag 7752 336
graphical user interface (GUI) 280

H

hash aggregation 84
Hash Match operator 71-73
hash warning 72
HAVING clause 120
head blocker 249
Heap 248
hints, Query Optimizer
    FORCE ORDER 42
    MAXDOP 42
    NOEXPAND 42
    USE HINT 42
histogram 28, 265

I

implicit conversions 190-196
included column 141
index 119
index allocation map (IAM) pages 124
indexed view matching 218
indexing strategy, with rowstore index 129
    clustered indexes, best practices 130
    non-clustered indexes, best practices 132
index maintenance 146, 147
    reference link 147
inequality column 138
inequality logic 178, 179
inline TVFs 162
inner table 68

interleaved execution 164, 406
intermediate results
  storing 219
  storing, with CTEs 225-228
  storing, with table variables and
    temporary tables 220-224

J

Java Database Connectivity (JDBC) 19
JOIN clause 120
join hints
  HASH 68
  LOOP 68
  MERGE 68
  REMOTE 68
join operators 68
  Adaptive joins 75-78
  Hash Match 71-73
  Merge Join 70
  Nested Loops 68, 69

K

key lookup 127
Key Lookup operator 66
kilobytes (KB) 88
Knobs
  for query optimization 41-43

L

Large Object (LOB) 110
least recently used (LRU) algorithm 335
Legacy CE 32
Lightweight Profiling (LWP) 394
  need for 366-368

Live Query Statistics
    (LQS) 361, 367, 387, 393
  using 362-366
logical fragmentation 129
logical statement processing flow 4, 5
lookups 65
  Key Lookup 66
  RID Lookup 66

M

maximum degree of parallelism
    (MaxDOP) 12, 42, 354
megabytes (MB) 88
memory grant 12
Memory Grant* 88
MemoryGrantInfo 89
MemoryGrantWarning* 104, 105
Merge Join operator 70, 228
mining XML query plans 255
  with implicit conversions 260
  with lookups 261
  with missing indexes 255-258
  with warnings 258, 259
MissingIndexes 96-100
Multi-Statement Table Valued Functions
    (MSTVF) 33, 154, 162, 317, 405

N

Nested Loops join 68, 69
New CE 32
Node Search feature 372
No Join Predicate 116
NOLOCK
  using 152, 153
non-blocking operator 58

non-clustered indexes, best practices 132
  covering indexes 141-143
  filtered index 143-146
  foreign keys 133
  key column order 133-141
NonClustered Index Scan operator 62
NonClustered Index Seek operator 63
NULL 172-176

O

Object-Relational Mapper (ORM) 190, 354
objects
  referencing 150
online analytical processing
    (OLAP) workloads 67
online transaction processing (OLTP)
    workloads 22, 31, 67, 366
Open Database Connectivity
    (ODBC) 19, 268
operator-level properties 107, 109
  Actual I/O Statistics 110
  Actual Number of Rows 111
  Actual time statistics 111
  Estimated rows 112
  EstimateRowsWithoutRowGoal 113
  RunTimeCountersPerThread* 110
  Warnings 114
OptimizationLevel 90
Optimized Plan Forcing (OPF) 358
OptimizerHardwareDependentProperties
    90
OptimizerStatsUsage 90, 91
ORDER BY clause
  SELECT TOP query, performing
    with 202-204

orders of magnitude (OOM) 56
OR logic
  optimizing 169-172
orphaned session 249
ostress tool 285, 381, 382
outer table 68
out-of-memory (OOM) conditions 105

P

package 264
page split 128
parameterization 16
  forced parameterization 17, 18
  simple parameterization 17
Parameter List 100-102
ParameterList property 196
parameters
  caching 24
  importance 21
  Parameter Sensitive Plan
      Optimization 23, 24
  parameter sniffing 23
  performance 22, 23
  security 22
Parameter Sensitive Plan Optimization
    (PSPO) 21, 355, 400
Performance Monitor (Perfmon) 280
PlanAffectingConvert
    warnings 102, 104, 190
plan caching 14
  ad-hoc plan caching 15, 16
  methods 14
  parameterization 16
  prepared statements 19
  sp_executesql procedure 18
  stored procedures 14

Plan Comparison 350

plan-level properties 85-87

CardinalityEstimationModelVersion 88

Degree of Parallelism* 88

Memory Grant 88

MemoryGrantInfo 89

MissingIndexes 96-100

OptimizationLevel 90

OptimizerHardwareDependentProperties 90

OptimizerStatsUsage 90, 91

Parameter List 100-102

QueryHash 91

QueryPlanHash 91

QueryTimeStats 95, 96

Set Options 91-93

Statement 93

TraceFlags 93, 94

WaitStats 94, 95

Warnings 102

plan reuse

during query processing 19-21

platform binaries 400

predicate 120

functions 158-161

predicate cardinality (Pc) 28

predicate SARGability 120-123

prepared statements 19

probe table 71

producers 356

PSSDiag 280

Q

query compilation essentials 6-8

query completion 361

query execution DMVs 234

sys.dm_exec_requests 236, 237

sys.dm_exec_sessions 234-236

sys.dm_exec_sql_text 237, 238

sys.dm_os_waiting_tasks 238-240

query execution essentials 12-14

query execution plan 48, 49, 361

constraint simplification 10

eligibility, for parameter sensitivity
  optimization 10

halloween protection 10

index selection 9

join elimination 10

logical join reordering 9

parallelism 10

partitioning 10

sub-query elimination 10

views, expanding 10

query fingerprint 250

QueryHash 91

query optimization essentials 8, 9

query optimization workflow 35, 36

Exploration stage 38

Full Optimization phase 39-41

Quick Plan phase 39

Transaction Processing phase 38

Trivial Plan stage 36-38

Query Optimizer 9, 28

principles 11

query plan 48, 49, 341

accessing 49-53

comparison 294-317

navigating 54-57

query plan analyzer 317-327

query plan cache DMVs 241

sys.dm_exec_cached_plans 246

sys.dm_exec_procedure_stats 243, 244

sys.dm_exec_query_plan 244, 245

sys.dm_exec_query_stats 241, 242

QueryPlanHash 91

query plan operators 57

aggregation 81
blocking operator 58
data access operators 58, 59
hash aggregation 84
joins 68
non-blocking operator 58
Sort 81, 82
spools 78-81
stream aggregation 84
query_plan_profile XEvent 374-377
query plan properties 85
operator-level properties 107, 109
plan-level properties 85-87
query_post_execution_plan_
profile XEvent 378-380
query_post_execution_showplan
Extended Event 367
query processing
impacting plan reuse 19-21
Query Processor 6, 8
Query Profiling Infrastructure 361, 366
Query Store 330
architecture 332
Automatic Plan Correction 355, 356
configuring 332-338
degree of parallelism (DOP)
feedback 356, 357
expensive queries, tracking 339-348
features, relying on 353
for readable secondary replicas 353
hinting 354
inner workings 330, 331
optimized plan forcing 358
Parameter Sensitive Plan Optimization
(PSPO) feature 355
regressed queries, fixing 348-353

Query Store (QS) 385
query_thread_profile XEvent 369-373
QueryTimeStats 95, 96, 157, 169
Query Tuning Assistant (QTA) 399, 403
fundamentals 404-406
workflow 406-418
Quick Plan phase, query
optimization workflow 39

R

Read Committed Snapshot
Isolation (RCSI) 153
ReadTrace tool 285
rebind 69
regressed queries
fixing 348-353
Regressed Queries report 402
relational database management
systems (RDBMS) 58
remote collection
with SQL LogScout 280-284
Remote Procedure Call (RPC) 268
Replay Markup Language (RML) 263, 382
Reporter tool 285
rewind 69
RID lookup 127
RID Lookup operator 66
ring buffer 265
risk, with CE upgrades
minimizing, with Microsoft's
recommended steps 401, 402
RML Utilities
traces, analyzing with 285-291
row goal 113
Row Goal optimization scenario 400

row ID (RID) 126

rowstore 58

rowstore index

data, accessing with 126, 127

data, inserting 128

data, updating 128

page splits 128, 129

scanning 126

structure 125, 126

upside-down tree, building 128

used, for indexing strategy 129

runtime 182

RunTimeCountersPerThread* 110

S

SARGable 120

Scalar UDF inlining feature 209

seek 58

SELECT * 154-158

SELECT DISTINCT 200-202

selectivity 28

SELECT TOP 1 query

performing, with ORDER
BY clause 202-204

self-balancing 128

session 266

Set Options 91-93

Showplan XML trace event 367

Simple Containment 31

Simple Join Containment 405

Snapshot 153

sort operations 82

avoiding 196

sort warning 82

spaghetti code 182

SpatialGuess* 105

sp_executesql

versus EXECUTE 179-181

sp_executesql procedure 18

Spill To Tempdb* 115

spool operators

Eager Spool 79

Index Spool 78

Lazy Spool 79

Row Count Spool 78

Table Spool 78

spools 78-81, 228

SQL Database Engine 8, 29, 400

SQL LogScout 280

download link 280

used, for remote collection 280-284

SQL Operating System (SQLOS) 234

SQL Server 2016 Service Pack 2 (SP2) 87

SQL Server 2017 Cumulative
Update 3 (CU3) 87

SQL Server Integration Services (SSIS) 387

SQL Server Management Studio
(SSMS) 15, 49, 235, 267,
293, 361, 399, 407

Standard Profiling 366

Statement 93

statistics 28, 29

stored procedures 14

unnecessary overhead 211, 212

unnecessary overhead, avoiding
with 211, 212

stream aggregation 84

sys.dm_exec_cached_plans 246

sys.dm_exec_procedure_stats 243, 244

sys.dm_exec_query_optimizer_info 41

sys.dm_exec_query_plan 244, 245

sys.dm_exec_query_plan_stats
DMF 384, 385, 386

sys.dm_exec_query_profiles DMV 392

**sys.dm_exec_query_statistics_
    xml DMF 380-383**

sys.dm_exec_query_stats 241, 242

sys.dm_exec_requests 236, 237

sys.dm_exec_sessions 234, 236

sys.dm_exec_sql_text 237, 238

**sys.dm_exec_valid_use_hints dynamic
    management view 42**

sys.dm_os_waiting_tasks 238-240

sys.dm_os_wait_stats DMV 95

T

table cardinality (Tc) 28

Table Scan operator 59, 60

table-valued function (TVF)
    constructing 161-166
    inline TVFs 162
    multi-statement TVFs (MSTVFs) 162

table variables
    used, for storing intermediate
        results 220-224

target 265

targets, SQL Database Engine
    event counter 265
    event file 265
    event pairing 265
    Event Tracing for Windows (ETW) 265
    histogram 265
    ring buffer 265

temporary tables
    used, for storing intermediate
        results 220-224

terabytes (TB) 88

Tiger Toolbox
    URL 255

TPC-C 366
    URL 366

TraceFlags 93, 94

traces
    analyzing, with RML Utilities 285-291

**Transaction Processing phase, query
    optimization workflow 38**

Transact-SQL (T-SQL) 3
    logical statement processing flow 4

**Trivial Plan stage, query optimization
    workflow 36-38**

T-SQL querying, best practices
    cursor, using 153
    joining tables 151, 152
    NOLOCK, using 152
    objects, referencing 150

tuples 28

U

UdfElapsedTime 164

UNION
    versus UNION ALL 197-199

uniqueifier 130

UnmatchedIndexes* 105-107

unnecessary overhead
    avoiding, with stored procedures 211

**User-Defined Functions
    (UDFs) 96, 161, 205-210, 213, 317**
    pitfalls, avoiding 205-210

V

very large database (VLDB) 366

W

WaitForMemoryGrant* 104

WaitStats 94, 95

Warnings 102, 114
  Columns With No Statistics 114, 115
  FullUpdateForOnlineIndexBuild* 107
  MemoryGrantWarning* 104, 105
  No Join Predicate 116
  PlanAffectingConvert 102-104
  SpatialGuess* 105
  Spill To Tempdb* 115
  UnmatchedIndexes* 105-107
  WaitForMemoryGrant* 104

WHERE clause 120

X

XEvent Profiler
  working with 277-279

XEvents 268

XML Path Language (XPath) 255

XQueries 255

packtpub.com

Subscribe to our online digital library for full access to over 7,000 books and videos, as well as industry leading tools to help you plan your personal development and advance your career. For more information, please visit our website.

Why subscribe?

- Spend less time learning and more time coding with practical eBooks and Videos from over 4,000 industry professionals

- Improve your learning with Skill Plans built especially for you

- Get a free eBook or video every month

- Fully searchable for easy access to vital information

- Copy and paste, print, and bookmark content

Did you know that Packt offers eBook versions of every book published, with PDF and ePub files available? You can upgrade to the eBook version at packtpub.com and as a print book customer, you are entitled to a discount on the eBook copy. Get in touch with us at customercare@packtpub.com for more details.

At www.packtpub.com, you can also read a collection of free technical articles, sign up for a range of free newsletters, and receive exclusive discounts and offers on Packt books and eBooks.

Other Books You May Enjoy

If you enjoyed this book, you may be interested in these other books by Packt:

The MySQL Workshop

Thomas Pettit, Scott Cosentino

ISBN: 978-1-83921-490-5

- Understand the concepts of relational databases and document stores
- Use SQL queries, stored procedures, views, functions, and transactions
- Connect to and manipulate data using MS Access, MS Excel, and Visual Basic for Applications (VBA)
- Read and write data in the CSV or JSON format using MySQL
- Manage data while running MySQL Shell in JavaScript mode
- Use X DevAPI to access a NoSQL interface for MySQL
- Manage user roles, credentials, and privileges to keep data secure
- Perform a logical database backup with mysqldump and mysqlpump

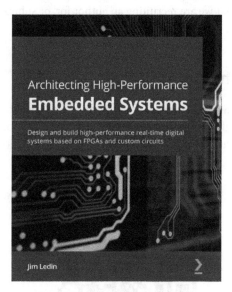

Professional Azure SQL Managed Database Administration

Ahmad Osama, Shashikant Shakya

ISBN: 978-1-80107-652-4

- Understanding Azure SQL database configuration and pricing options
- Provisioning a new SQL database or migrating an existing on-premises SQL Server database to an Azure SQL database
- Backing up and restoring an Azure SQL database
- Securing and scaling an Azure SQL database
- Monitoring and tuning an Azure SQL database
- Implementing high availability and disaster recovery with an Azure SQL database
- Managing, maintaining, and securing managed instances

Packt is searching for authors like you

If you're interested in becoming an author for Packt, please visit authors.packtpub.com and apply today. We have worked with thousands of developers and tech professionals, just like you, to help them share their insight with the global tech community. You can make a general application, apply for a specific hot topic that we are recruiting an author for, or submit your own idea.

Share Your Thoughts

Now you've finished *Learn T-SQL Querying, Second Edition*, we'd love to hear your thoughts! Scan the QR code below to go straight to the Amazon review page for this book and share your feedback or leave a review on the site that you purchased it from.

https://packt.link/r/1-837-63899-3

Your review is important to us and the tech community and will help us make sure we're delivering excellent quality content.

Download a free PDF copy of this book

Thanks for purchasing this book!

Do you like to read on the go but are unable to carry your print books everywhere?

Is your e-book purchase not compatible with the device of your choice?

Don't worry!, Now with every Packt book, you get a DRM-free PDF version of that book at no cost.

Read anywhere, any place, on any device. Search, copy, and paste code from your favorite technical books directly into your application.

The perks don't stop there, you can get exclusive access to discounts, newsletters, and great free content in your inbox daily

Follow these simple steps to get the benefits:

1. Scan the QR code or visit the following link:

    https://packt.link/free-ebook/9781837638994

2. Submit your proof of purchase.
3. That's it! We'll send your free PDF and other benefits to your email directly.